The Hardball Times Baseball Annual 2014

Featuring contributions by THT staff writers:
John Beamer • Karl de Vries • Chris Jaffe
Brad Johnson • Jeff Moore • Jon Roegele
Greg Simons • Dave Studenmund • Shane Tourtellotte
Steve Treder • Jack Weiland • Noah Woodward

Plus contributions by FanGraphs staff writers:
Dave Allen • Dave Cameron • Carson Cistulli
Blake Murphy • Mike Petriello • Mike Podhorzer
Eno Sarris • Steve Staude • Jeff Sullivan
Bradley Woodrum • Jeff Zimmerman

With additional contributions by guest writers:
Craig Calcaterra • Larry Granillo • Bill James
Alan Nathan • Rob Neyer • John Perrotto
Joe Posnanski • Kevin Tenenbaum • Craig Wright

Produced by Dave Studenmund
Edited by Joe Distelheim, Greg Simons and Paul Swydan

The Hardball Times Baseball Annual 2014

A FanGraphs production

New content daily at hardballtimes.com and fangraphs.com

Edited by Joe Distelheim, Greg Simons and Paul Swydan
Stats developed by FanGraphs
Cover design by Summer Anne Burton
Typesetting by Dave Studenmund and Paul Swydan

Copyright © 2013 The Hardball Times

Published by FanGraphs and The Hardball Times

ISBN-13: 978-1493711871
ISBN-10: 1493711873
Printed by CreateSpace

What's Inside

History

Analysis

Et Cetera

Welcome to Our Book

Long ago and far away, some of us started a website dedicated to the sport of baseball. While we were at it, we said "Hey, why not publish a book, too? It will be an annual book, something that revives the glory of the old Bill James Abstracts. It will be fantastic. People will love it so much we may publish more. Maybe even two...or three."

Welcome to the 10th *Hardball Times Annual*. The little side project that began many years ago has lasted far longer than we ever imagined it would. If you've purchased one of our previous *Annuals*, thank you for coming back. You know what to expect. If you're new to this unintended habit of ours, thanks for joining. Let me tell you what you've gotten into.

The first section of the *Annual* is a review of the 2013 season. There are seven articles: a review of the season for each of the six divisions and a postseason recap. These aren't exhaustive, detailed explanations of what happened during the year; they are designed to be illustrative and illuminating. Our hope is that you see a big picture or an insight you didn't see during the year.

Our postseason coverage is unique because we chronicle it through the lens of the ultimate "story stat." We call it Championships Added, and it's a good way to give you a somewhat different take on the vagaries of the postseason. A little later in the *Annual*, there is an article that uses Championships Added to highlight some of the biggest plays, games and series in all of postseason history. But I'm getting ahead of myself.

After the review of the 2013 season, there is a section of articles called "Commentary." It includes a wide range of things, such as Craig Calcaterra's humorous take on the season; Jeff Sullivan's overview of one of the newest trends in sabermetrics, quantifying the impact of catchers framing pitches; and Bill James discussing the differences between pitching and batting prospects.

I don't want to go into too much detail—you can find it yourself by just turning the pages—but I do want to emphasize an ongoing *THT Annual* tradition: the GM in a Box. Beginning with our second *Annual*, each year we have highlighted the career of a major league general manager by subjecting his career to a series of questions "in a box," as Bill James used to say. This year, Steve Treder gives the treatment to San Francisco's Brian Sabean.

You'll also find a couple of bonuses in the Commentary section. There are three "case studies" that examine unexpected player successes or disappointments from the 2013 season and use advanced statistics from FanGraphs to ask—and answer—the questions behind the surprises. Speaking of stats from FanGraphs, Carson Cistulli has a few unique leaderboards for your enjoyment. You can find plenty of stats on the Internet, but it's hard to find the numbers that Carson has unearthed.

After Commentary, we have four articles that look back on baseball history to reminisce or ask questions such as "Where does Roger Clemens fit on the all-time list of pitchers?" And we ask a lot of questions in our Analysis section. Did you know the strike zone is growing, or that August performances are really important in MVP balloting? We don't just ask the questions, we answer them, too.

As you read, you may come across some statistics you haven't heard of before. Acronyms such as WAR (Wins Above Replacement), FIP (Fielding-Independent Pitching) and wOBA (weighted On-Base Average) are peppered throughout the book. Our attitude is this: When simple baseball stats tell the story, we use simple baseball stats. But when there is something beyond those stats—when the basic stats simply aren't conveying the whole truth or are inadequate to the story—we use newer, more nuanced stats. The good news is that we've included a glossary of all such statistics in the back of our book, so you won't drown in a sea of obscure acronyms.

The work gets easier over 10 years, but it's still work. A lot of work, by a lot of people. Our writers obviously spent a lot of time and energy crafting their articles—I think they are all first-rate—and there are a lot of other people who have contributed to the success of The Hardball Times.

David Appelman is the top cheese at FanGraphs, our owner and partner. Tom Tango and MGL, two of the co-authors of the must-read sabermetric book (called, simply, *The Book*) have always supported us. Sean Forman at Baseball Reference has provided invaluable assistance through the years. Bill James, John Dewan and Greg Pierce of ACTA Sports have been terrific partners. Ben Jedlovec and the folks at Baseball Info Solutions. All of The Hardball Times writers, past and present. Do I have to say everyone's name?

Actually, there are a few folks who have worked diligently to create this particular THT Annual. Joe Distelheim and Greg Simons, hard-working and deeply appreciated editors of the Hardball Times website, put in many hours poring over each page you're about to read. And Paul Swydan poured a lot of his own self into editing, typesetting and producing this here book, while welcoming a new little one to his family at the same time. Without Paul, we would have stopped at eight books. MegaThanks, Paul.

Most importantly, thank you for reading what we've written. We know you're here because you love the game of baseball. You love to play it, watch it, think about it and read about it. In the end, this book is for you and maybe a little about you, too. Thank you for your passion.

May first base rise up to meet you. May the wind be always at your back at bat. May the sun shine in the eyes of that outfielder trying to catch your pop fly.

Happy Baseball,
Dave Studenmund

The 2013 Season

The American League East View

by Karl de Vries

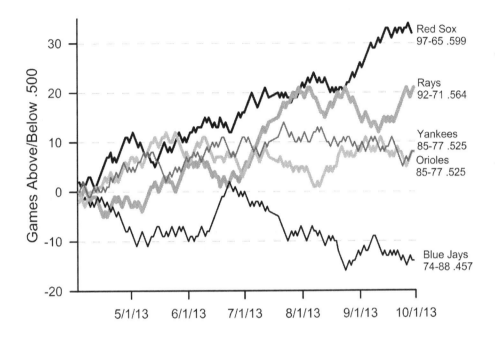

In a showdown for the American League's last playoff spot, it was the game that wouldn't end.

Oh sure, the 2013 AL Wild Card wouldn't be decided just by teams from the AL East. But it sure felt that way on the night of Sept. 20, as Tampa Bay and Baltimore traded jabs for 18 innings, a heavyweight matchup between two longtime contenders. It wasn't pretty—no fewer than 21 pitchers were used over the game's nearly seven-hour-long running time—but for two teams dogging it out to make the postseason, the game, and the 4-4 staring contest that lasted 11 innings, represented a clear line in the playoff sand.

Tampa Bay ultimately prevailed on David DeJesus' RBI single, effectively killing Baltimore's playoff chances. And in the end, it was just one game, just one playoff race. But it was a contest that encapsulated the 2013 AL East, a symbolic standoff representing a summer in which five squads combined to produce the year's best pennant hunt.

Don't believe me? Just look at the standings: No other division had four teams finish over .500. Run differential? The division combined for a +222, the majors' best. Heck, even the Blue Jays, the East's ugly duckling, provided something of a compelling storyline, the tale of a team built to win big in 2013, only to watch it crumble over the stretch of six painful months.

It was an unforgettable year for Boston

At the top of the division were the Boston Red Sox, the team with the league's best record at 97-65. Looking to rebound after 2012's disastrous 93-loss season, Beantown signed Shane Victorino, Mike Napoli, Ryan Dempster, Stephen Drew and Koji Uehara over the offseason, players who complemented a core of Dustin Pedroia, David Ortiz, Jacoby Ellsbury, Jon Lester and Clay Buchholz. But despite the acquisitions and a new manager in John Farrell, baseball pundits across the country largely doubted that the BoSox were postseason contenders, let alone a likely candidate for a division crown.

But if everything went wrong for the Red Sox in 2012, things seemed to find a way of working themselves out in 2013. When established closers Joel Hanrahan and Andrew Bailey went down with season-ending arm problems, Farrell simply tapped Uehara (21 saves, 12.2 K/9) to take over the ninth inning. He combined with Junichi Tazawa to form one of baseball's most effective late-inning tandems. Will Middlebrooks' terrible sophomore slump was hardly noticeable in the season's first half, not when Jose Iglesias was maintaining a .330 batting average through July. By the time Middlebrooks was ready to be recalled from the minors in August, general manager Ben Cherington swapped Iglesias for Jake Peavy as part of a three-team deal.

The result? Middlebrooks put together a .276/.329/.476 slash line down the stretch, while Peavy went 4-1 in his 10 starts.

The magic didn't end there for a roster stacked with aging veterans. David Ortiz (37 years old) put together his first 30-home run/100-plus RBI campaign in three years, John Lackey (34) finally turned in a good season for the Red Sox by posting a 3.52 ERA over 29 starts and Victorino (32) provided solid top-of-the-order production all season long. The Sox also received a blistering start by Buchholz (who began the season 11-1 before losing three months to shoulder bursitis), a bounceback campaign from Lester (15-8, 3.59 FIP) and key contributions from Dempster, Daniel Nava and Jonny Gomes. So the Red Sox began the season in first place and never allowed the Rays to gain an inch.

That didn't mean the season was without adversity. On April 15, New England—and the nation—was shaken by the horrific Boston Marathon bombings, which claimed three lives and injured hundreds more. Coming on Patriots' Day, the attack was personal for Boston, and for a time, fans across the country were proud to call themselves a part of Red Sox Nation.

At an emotional homecoming on April 20, the team's first Fenway Park contest following the attack, Ortiz rallied the crowd with an infamous pregame pep speech, Neil Diamond sang "Sweet Caroline" and Nava smashed one of the most emotional home runs in team history, a three-run dinger in the eighth inning off the Kansas City Royals' Kelvin Herrera that sparked a 4-3 victory. It was something of a fitting afternoon for the 2013 Red Sox, a team that provided Boston with a reprieve from April's anguish with a season-long run of superior play.

Tampa kept the young stars coming

The Tampa Bay Rays' season could be divided into two parts: BM and AM. There was Before Wil Myers, when the Rays were 36-33 and had just dropped three out of four games to the Royals. On June 17, the After Myers era began, and the Rays surged and nearly usurped the Red Sox for the throne of the AL East.

Long considered one of the majors' best hitting prospects, the 22-year-old Myers delivered 13 homers, 53 RBI and an .831 OPS in his rookie year, helping spark the team to a 56-38 record during the rest of the season. He wasn't alone, of course; his offense was joined by veterans Evan Longoria and Ben Zobrist—both of whom turned in characteristically strong seasons—by the terrific comeback campaign of James Loney (.299/.348/.430, 75 RBI) and by key contributions from Kelly Johnson, Desmond Jennings and Matt Joyce.

But if the Rays managed to field a lineup that kept them merely competitive, it was their rotation that really shined. Matt Moore emerged as the top-of-the-rotation hurler so many tagged him to be, with a sparkling 17-4 record, 8.6 K/9 and 3.29 ERA. David Price, who lost six weeks due to a tricep injury in the first half, returned to go 12-6 with a 2.53 ERA over his final 18 starts. Despite taking a line drive off the noggin in mid-June, Alex Cobb returned in August to give the Rays nine quality performances down the stretch. Chris Archer joined the cast in 2013, producing a sterling performance over 23 starts, and Jeremy Hellickson, who briefly lost his rotation spot in the second half, wasn't as bad as his 5.17 ERA might suggest, evidenced by the best strikeout and walk rates of his career.

At the end of games, Fernando Rodney might not have been able to replicate his eye-popping performance of 2012, but he still managed to save 37 games while zapping hitters at a 11.1 strikeouts-per-nine clip, Joel Peralta once again provided outstanding eighth-inning work and Jake McGee, Jamey Wright and Cesar Ramos rounded out a relief corp whose 3.36 FIP was second-best in the AL.

In the end, it almost wasn't enough; Tampa Bay had to play a 163rd game against the Texas Rangers in order to decide the league's final Wild Card spot. But Price, backed by a two-run homer from Longoria, outpitched Martin Perez in a complete-game masterpiece, 5-2, to propel Tampa Bay to the postseason for the fourth time in the past six years. For a team brimming with young talent, 2013 was a thrilling and satisfying season, though more likely a prelude to better things to come in 2014 and beyond.

Old soldiers faded away in New York

Like the Red Sox, the New York Yankees were a team of aging stars. Unlike Boston, the creaky Yankees broke down early and often. Derek Jeter and Mark Teixeira combined for just 136 plate appearances, a back injury nuked nearly all of Kevin Youkilis' season, Alex Rodriguez didn't step into a major league batter's box until August and Travis Hafner—who hit .318 in April—eventually lost time to a shoulder injury, and finished the year with a pitiful .202/.301/.378 slash line.

All told, the bats—despite finishing in the middle of baseball's pack in runs scored—produced the majors' fifth-worst wOBA (.301).

The rotation, while mostly healthy throughout the season, ultimately wasn't good enough to make up for the lack of offense. CC Sabathia, suddenly showing his age at 32, watched his strikeout prowess decline en route to a mediocre 4.10 FIP. Phil Hughes' season was every bit as dreadful as his 4-14 record would suggest and David Phelps' 4.98 ERA was not helpful, as he split time between the rotation, the bullpen and the disabled list.

Fortunately, Andy Pettitte magically made 30 starts, Hiroki Kuroda produced a 3.56 FIP over 201.1 innings and Ivan Nova, whose 9-6 record doesn't do justice to a man who played a tremendous role down the stretch, gave the Yankees quality starts on a routine basis.

Despite the setbacks, the Yankees somehow remained relevant enough to stay mathematically alive through the season's final week. For that, you can credit big years from Robinson Cano (27 homers, .899 OPS), Brett Gardner (.344 OBP, 24 steals, 81 runs) and Alfonso Soriano—acquired in arguably the majors' best trade deadline deal—who crushed 17 home runs and accumulated 50 RBI in just 243 plate appearances after coming over from the Cubs.

Standing at the summit of it all was Mariano Rivera, who fittingly finished his major league career with a terrific season. The Great Mariano, Ruler of all Relievers, breezed his way to 44 saves and a 2.11 ERA, a ridiculous six-to-one strikeout-to-walk ratio and an exemplary 86 percent save conversion rate. Because Rivera was backed by bullpen mates David Robertson (33 holds) and Boone Logan (11.5 K/9), the Yankees' late-inning corps anchored a bullpen that managed to allow the second-fewest blown saves in baseball despite a 3.91 FIP, among the worst in the game.

In some ways, 2013 was manager Joe Girardi's finest showing in his five seasons at the Yankees helm, because a -21 run differential is not supposed to result in a 85-77 record. And despite all their problems, the Yankees were 11 games over .500 on Sept. 4. But devastating three-game sweeps at the hands of the Red Sox and Rays later that month crippled the team's playoff hopes, and as the Indians surged to the finish

---

line with a 10-game winning streak to snag a Wild Card berth, the Bombers played merely .500 ball. They were close, but not close enough.

That one-run magic disappeared in Baltimore

What about the Orioles? How did a team boasting the majors' top home run hitter in Chris Davis, a squad that ranked fourth in the American League in runs scored, a club that was supposed to build off last year's 93-win Wild Card run, fail to make the playoffs? The excuse of a highly competitive division aside, a pitching staff that finished next to last in FIP in the league didn't help, especially when the mighty bullpen that helped nearly topple the mighty Yankees in the 2012 playoffs watched its save conversion rate fall by seven percentage points this season.

Jim Johnson—one of the AL's most valuable players in 2012—still managed to reach the 50-save plateau, but a higher walk rate and an increased propensity to surrender line drives helped result in nine blown saves. All told, a team that compiled an ungodly 29-9 record in one-run games in 2012 watched that mark fall to 20-31 this year.

About those bats: Davis did turn in a career year, but his hitting evaporated when the team needed it most: He compiled a .216/.304/.451 slash line in the season's final month. Ditto for Adam Jones (.233/.292/.447 in September), who otherwise emerged as a true middle-of-the-order threat in 2013.

Those two aside, Baltimore's lineup featured strong contributions from Matt Wieters (22 home runs, 79 RBI), Nate McLouth (30 steals, 76 runs) and J.J. Hardy (25 homers). Perhaps most notable was the performance of Manny Machado, who loudly established himself as one of baseball's best young players after a monstrous first half (.310 average, seven homers, six steals), all at the age of 20. He fatigued a bit in the second half before tearing a ligament in his left knee, an ugly injury that could have been much worse.

Ultimately, the Orioles' diminished pitching performance couldn't be offset by a lineup that faded in the season's second half. A 4.64 FIP among starting pitchers tied the Orioles with the Twins for the worst in the majors, and only Chris Tillman (16-7, 7.8 K/9) truly distinguished himself, and even his 4.42 FIP indicated that his 3.71 ERA wasn't all that it was cracked up to be.

In stark contrast to 2012, when the team flourished with a .760 winning percentage in the final two months, Baltimore stumbled with a 26-28 record over the same period—hardly the credentials upon which a successful postseason run is based. There are some budding and established superstars on this team, but manager Buck Showalter and crew will need to find some starters in time for 2014 if the Orioles are going to take things to the next level.

Restocked Jays saw stock drop

Meanwhile, the Toronto Blue Jays—the team picked by Vegas oddsmakers over the 2012-13 winter to win the World Series—couldn't get out of their own way.

Where to begin? The blockbuster trade that imported reigning National League Cy Young Award winner R.A. Dickey turned out to be a mere bust. Josh Johnson's injury history came with him from Miami, limiting him to just 16 mediocre starts. Brandon Morrow's year was destroyed by a forearm injury. And for good measure, J.A. Happ suffered a skull fracture after a Desmond Jennings comebacker in early May, costing him three months.

What was supposed to be a meat-grinding lineup was also ill-fated. Jose Reyes (surprise!) got hurt; a high ankle sprain limited him to just 93 games. Melky Cabrera also missed significant time with a knee injury, and his season ended early when he had a tumor removed from his spine at the end of August. Brett Lawrie turned in a second straight disappointing season, Jose Bautista lost time due to a wrist injury, J.P. Arencibia couldn't reach the Mendoza Line and Colby Rasmus still hasn't matured into the star the Cardinals once thought they had. Only Edwin Encarnacion managed to produce at a high level, popping 36 home runs and 104 RBI.

The Blue Jays had high hopes going into the season, but once the injuries struck, the team didn't have nearly enough depth to stay competitive in an ultra-competitive division. It's the sad story of just another would-be contender in the free-agent era—import the talent one year, look for ways to export it the next. Where the team goes from here is akin to a "choose your own adventure" novel, and Toronto's management will need some brighter ideas if they are to avoid 2013's pitfalls.

One thing is for sure: the AL East isn't going to be any less interesting in 2014. Whether the Red Sox can repeat, how the Rays' and Orioles' young guns will mature and whether the Yankees and Blue Jays can retool fast enough will be moving parts in the AL's most fascinating story mill. Some of these questions will begin to be answered in the coming winter months as spring, forever hinting at the promise of postseason glory, looms ahead.

The American League Central View

by Chris Jaffe

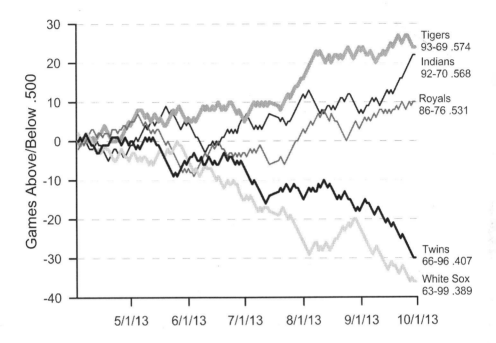

D epth. If there is one theme that describes what happened in the American League Central this year, it's depth. The squads in the AL Central showed what happens to a club that has—or lacks—roster depth.

Really, the division race itself isn't much to talk about. The defending champion Detroit Tigers were supposed to cruise to their third straight division title, and sure enough that's what they did. They led for all but two days over the last four months, and while they ultimately won the division by just a game, that's only because the second-place Indians won their last 10 games while the Tigers rested many of their stars and lost most of their final games down the stretch.

Detroit rotated ironmen

Everyone knew that the Tigers had the best star talent in the division. Miguel Cabrera won the Most Valuable Player Award in 2012 by posting baseball's first Triple Crown in over 40 years, and in 2013 he was even better. He hit exactly as many homers as in his Triple Crown season (44), drove in just two fewer runs (137 to

139), and raised his batting average 18 points (from .330 to .348). Cabrera didn't win a second Triple Crown, but he led the league in on-base percentage (.442), slugging percentage (.636), OPS (1078), and OPS+ (187).

And as great as Cabrera was, his was hardly the only Tigers bat of note. While fellow slugger Prince Fielder had a down year, Cabrera was one of five members of the Tigers starting lineup who hit over .300 on the year. Only 29 players in either league with more than 400 plate appearances hit over .300, and the Tigers had five, the most of any team. So it isn't too surprising that the team led all baseball with a .283 batting average, 27 points over the AL-wide mark. Thanks to all those hits, the Tigers were second in the league in runs scored.

But as great as the Cabrera-led offense was, the real secret to Detroit's success was its depth in starting pitching. The Tigers had the best and deepest starting rotation in baseball. All five of their main starting pitchers qualified for the ERA title by pitching 162 innings, something no other team in baseball could claim. Only three had as many as four pitchers qualify for the ERA title (Boston, Cincinnati and Washington).

And they were all good. The big news was Max Scherzer, who had a breakout season after a few nice ones over the years. Scherzer posted a gaudy 21-3 record, thanks to hot start in which he won 19 of his first 20 decisions. While run support helped make that record so impressive, Scherzer did finish fifth in the league in ERA (2.90), and second in strikeouts (240).

As great as Scherzer was, teammate Anibal Sanchez may have been even better. Was Scherzer fifth in the league in ERA? Well, Sanchez came in first with a 2.57 mark. Sanchez didn't fan as many batters as Scherzer, but that's because he didn't throw as many innings. They struck out batters at about the same rate—a hair over 10 per nine innings for Scherzer, and a hair under for Sanchez.

Then there's Justin Verlander. Remember him? He's the guy who began the season as the consensus pick as the best starting pitcher in Major League Baseball. Well, he had a bit of a down year—but we're talking a down year by Verlander's standards, not an actually bad season or anything. Verlander made 34 starts and struck out a batter per inning. Although he worked in a hitter's park, Verlander's ERA was over a half-run better than league average (3.46 versus the league ERA of 3.99).

Past the stars, even the bottom of the rotation was pretty good. Doug Fister made a full load of starts and was an above-average pitcher. Only fifth starter Rick Porcello had a below-average ERA (4.32)—but in reality he was an average pitcher. If you adjust for park and Detroit's tepid team fielding, Porcello was fine. He wasn't great, but few teams have a fifth starter who is a league average pitcher. The fifth starter is typically replacement level, nowhere near league average.

Those five started 156 of Detroit's 162 games, easily more than any other team's top five starters. And they could be counted on to keep the team in just about every game. In all, starting pitchers for Detroit had a league-best ERA of 3.44, easily outdistancing second place Oakland (3.72). The Tigers' starting staff also topped the league in innings pitched (1,023), and strikeouts (981—narrowly missing becoming the first AL team whose starting pitchers averaged a K per inning). Yet somehow they also allowed the fewest homers by any AL starting rotation (84).

The question isn't how the Tigers won, but how their eventual lead was just one game. Then again, they finished six games below their projected Pythagoras record, while the Indians did two games better than expected.

Cleveland wasn't great, but had plenty of good

The Indians had a mighty nice season for themselves, claiming the top Wild Card slot in the AL behind their 92-70 record. With a month to play they appeared to be doomed, but they had the best September in baseball, winning 21 of their last 27, including their last 10, to clinch a place in the postseason behind new manager Terry Francona.

Perhaps we shouldn't be surprised that the Indians lost the Wild Card game. Against squads with losing records, the Indians were the best team in baseball, against which they posted a 56-18 mark. But against good teams, they were a lackluster 36-52. Most importantly, the Indians dropped an amazing 16 of 19 to the division rival Tigers. Incredibly, that wasn't their most extreme record against a team; Cleveland was 17-2 against the Chicago White Sox.

Cleveland didn't have nearly as much star firepower as the Tigers did. The Indians' top two home run hitters combined hit fewer dingers than Miguel Cabrera (22 for Nick Swisher and 20 for Carlos Santana). None of their hitters batted better than .284. The ace on Cleveland's rotation would've been maybe the fourth-best starter in Detroit.

The Indians didn't have Detroit's frontline talent, but they had depth. Cleveland scored the fourth-most runs in the AL, which looks weird when you take a quick look at the roster. The starters were fine, but nothing great. The lineup had some parts that could be improved, but at least it had no huge gaping holes. That sounds like a rather backhanded compliment, but realize that most lineups—even lineups on good teams—have at least one big gap.

But to understand why Cleveland's offense was as good as it was, you need to look past the starting lineup and into the bench. That's where their depth really shines through. Backup catch Yan Gomes hit .298 with 31 extra-base hits in fewer than 300 at-bats. Utility man Ryan Rayburn was a beast, belting 18 doubles and 16 homers in 87 games.

Tally the offensive production by all non-starting position players, and according to the old Bill James stat Runs Created, they were worth 4.73 runs per 27 outs. The entire AL averaged 4.33 runs per game. As a rule of thumb, bench players are supposed to be below average. That is, after all, why they are bench players. But Cleveland's bench didn't get that memo. Oh—and the Indians' reserves did this while playing in a pitcher's park. Adjust for that, and the backups were 17 percent better than average. The Indians had the second-best batting bench in all baseball, behind only Boston.

And Cleveland's depth in quality hitting, much like Detroit's depth in starting pitchers, helped the Indians make the playoffs.

Kansas City's problems were relieved

A different kind of depth helped the Royals this year—bullpen depth. The Royals celebrated their best season in a long time in 2013. It was not only their first winning campaign in a decade, but their 86 wins is the most they've had in a season since the 1980s.

They did it despite a lousy offense. Oh, they could hit for average, but they were dead last in homers with 115, and were barely better at drawing walks. They had two good starting pitchers in James Shields and Ervin Santana, but the back of the rotation gave them problems.

But Kansas City had that glorious bullpen. Closer Greg Holland had a comically low ERA of 1.21 with 103 Ks in 67 innings, en route to 47 saves. Lead set-up man Luke Hochevar was nearly as good, with a 1.92 ERA. And it wasn't just the top guys. Every single Royals reliever had a good year. Eight men made at least 10 relief appearances, and the worst ERA of the bunch was 3.86, by Kelvin Herrera. Keep in mind, Royals Stadium is a hitter's park and the league-wide ERA was 3.99.

Upshot: The Royals posted a bullpen ERA of 2.55, the best in the AL this year. It's the best ERA by an AL bullpen so far this decade. It's the best AL ERA by an AL bullpen so far this century. To find a better one, you have to go back to 1990, when the A's bullpen had a 2.35 ERA. That team had merely the greatest bullpen in baseball history. And the Royals were the best one since that. That's how the Royals finally finished over .500.

Minnesota couldn't get started

If the good teams can explain their success by having depth, the bad teams' lack of depth can explain their failures.

The Twins trudged their way to a dismal 66-96 season, and you don't have to look long to figure out what the main problem was: a complete lack of starting pitching. They had just three pitchers start more than 20 games for them, and two of them had ERAs over 5.00. Only three teams in the AL had multiple pitchers with more than 100 innings pitched and an ERA over 5.00: Houston, Seattle and Minnesota.

Even that understates the problems the Twins starting rotation had. The entire unit had an ERA over 5.00. The team had 162 starts, with an ERA of 5.26. That was the worst starting rotation ERA in baseball, by a mile. Second-worst Toronto's starting rotation ERA was 4.81.

And when you look into the numbers, it gets even worse for Minnesota. The Twins starters threw 871 innings, fewest by any big league team. That's an average of 5.1 innings pitched per start, putting a notable workload on the bullpen. Somewhat humorously (unless you're a Twins fan), despite having the fewest innings, the Twins starters allowed the most hits: 1,072. I'm sure some other starting rotation has achieved the fewest-innings, most-hits combo, but it can't be common.

You can't blame Minnesota's defense for all of those hits, either. Twins starters fanned fewer batters than any other team: 477. And that can't be explained by a lack of innings. They averaged 4.9 strikeouts per nine innings; every other starting rotation in baseball struck out at least six per nine innings.

Only five starting units fanned fewer than 700 batters, and the Twins were under 500. It's almost impossible to strike out so few batters in this day and age. Among all AL pitchers who pitched at least 100 innings, the worst strikeout rate was by Minnesota's Scott Diamond, with 3.57. Teammate Kevin Correia had the third worst (4.90). Only four Twins threw 100 innings, and they were all among the 13 worst pitchers in the AL in strikeouts per inning.

Minnesota couldn't keep balls out of the cheap seats either. Of the 30 teams in baseball, only four starting rotations allowed more home runs per inning than the Twins did. Their starting rotation was just a complete nightmare.

The funny thing is that this terrible Twins team still resembles the glory run Twins from earlier in manager Ron Gardenhire's tenure. Back then, they didn't strike out many batters with pitchers like Brad Radke and Rick Reed, but those pitchers had great control, and the Twins had the best bullpen. But the parts of the game the Twins minimized have become huge problems, and the strengths aren't nearly as strong. Hence an annual 90-win contender has become an expected 90-loss doormat.

Chicago went from bad to worse

Things just fell apart for the last-place White Sox this year, especially at the plate. Talk about lacking depth—their entire offense was bad. All the hitters they counted on got old or just plain weren't good. They had 24 position players bat for them this year, and the highest OPS+ of the bunch was 106. In other words, the best batter was ever so barely better than league average—that was their best hitter. That's … impressive. And not in a good way. The Sox starters were bad, but at least most of them were just generically bad.

Where the Sox's offensive incompetence really showed up was on their bench. Their entire bench combined to bat .234 with a slugging percentage of .328 and an on-base percentage of .275. Sure, backups are supposed to be bad, but not that bad. In terms of Runs Created, they were worth 2.90 runs per 27 outs. Across the AL, bench players were worth 3.78 runs per 27 outs. If you adjust for park, the Sox had the worst bench in the AL. Only the Nationals in the National League were worse.

That makes sense—a team without much front line hitting shouldn't have much beyond that either. But by any standard, the Sox's lack of offensive depth in their bench was massive. The crosstown Cubs actually had even worse production from their starting position players, but possessed a far better bench than did the Sox.

In terms of roster depth, it was a year of extremes in the AL Central. On one hand, there were the deepest starting rotation, one of the best benches and the league's best bullpen. At the bottom of the pile were the worst starting rotation and the worst bench in the league. Ultimately, that explained how the division shook out.

The American League West View

by Jack Weiland

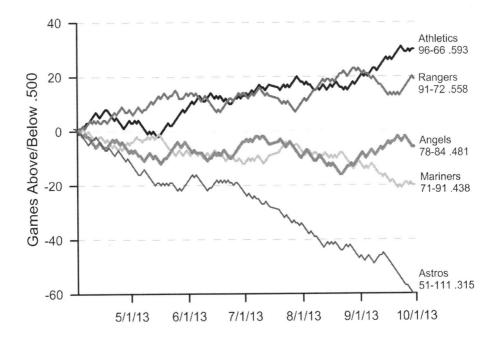

They say the baseball season is a marathon, not a sprint, but don't go telling that to the Texas Rangers.

After consecutive trips to the World Series in 2010 and 2011, and a rather epic collapse/historic run by the upstart Oakland Athletics in 2012, the Rangers were nevertheless a strong contender for the American League West title again in 2013. The Hardball Times writers picked the team to finish second only to the consensus top choice Angels (more on that disaster later).

And things were going fine, really, until September came around. As the calendar flipped August into the history books, the Rangers were in first place in the West, and had scored the biggest coup of the trade deadline, as they nabbed starting pitcher Matt Garza from the Cubs in the long-rumored, finally consummated Mike Olt swap.

On Aug. 29, Texas was three games ahead of pesky Oakland for the division lead. By Sept. 2, the teams were dead even at 79-58, and by Sept. 15, the A's had opened up a 6.5 game lead. It stretched to 8.5 by Sept. 22, and although the Rangers made a late charge at Oakland, they never got any closer than five games back.

In the relative blink of an eye, the A's had a stranglehold on the division, and the Rangers were fighting for their playoff lives. So, how did the A's do it?

The A's have it

Well, they won. A lot. Oakland swept the Tampa Bay Rays at the end of August and beginning of September, and won 20 of 26 games altogether in the season's final month, including five of six against the Rangers. The A's—who posted the AL's second-best ERA—pitched well, and were also strong at the plate, as they scored the third-most runs in the league.

Oakland had the third-most wins above replacement (WAR) among batters in the majors, and much of that credit goes to converted catcher-turned-third baseman Josh Donaldson. A relative throw-in with the package that sent Rich Harden to the Cubs in 2008, Donaldson has improbably transformed himself into one of the game's best players. His 7.7 WAR trailed only Mike Trout and Andrew McCutchen in all of baseball in 2013. He triple slashed an impressive .301/.384/.499, and combined the 14th-best weighted on-base average (or wOBA—.384 in this case) in all of baseball with plus defense at the hot corner.

The rest of Oakland's proficient lineup was a team effort; its next best player by WAR was Coco Crisp, whose 3.9 mark was 43rd in the majors. Shortstop Jed Lowrie (3.6), and outfielders Josh Reddick (2.7) and Yoenis Cespedes (2.3) also provided strong efforts in injury-shortened seasons, while journeyman Brandon Moss smacked a career-high 30 home runs.

On the pitching side of the ledger, Bartolo Colon was the closest thing the A's had to an ace. At 40, he managed to start 30 games despite his name being a constant inclusion in the Biogenesis rumors swirling throughout the season, and used pinpoint control to post a team-leading 2.65 earned run average, sixth-best in baseball.

All in all, it was another magical run for the Athletics, and another fine season for the history books—and perhaps, Hollywood.

This is not to say all was lost for the Rangers when the A's slingshot around them. Up until the season's final day (and, technically, beyond) the Rangers were in the mix for one of the two AL Wild Card spots.

Texas won its last seven games of the regular season, including four straight over the Angels, to force a tiebreaker game against Tampa Bay for the right to play in the one-game Wild Card playoff against the Indians for a spot in the Division Series.

Unfortunately for the Rangers faithful, just as was the case during the team's one-game playoff last year against the Orioles, things were not meant to be. David Price pitched a complete game and Evan Longoria thumped a home run to send Tampa Bay on to Cleveland and beyond. In another instant, an entire season was lost.

Mike Trout is bad at listening, good at baseball

They say youth is wasted on the young, but Mike Trout does not appear to have strong listening comprehension skills if that's the case. This is not an opinion piece, and so it is said here objectively that Trout is very, very good at baseball, and probably should have been the number one pick in that 2009 major league draft (yes, even ahead of Stephen Strasburg).

The Angels' season was an 84-loss pileup, but none of that can be blamed on the team's center fielder. Trout followed up his remarkable 10 WAR rookie season with an even better sophomore campaign. After his sparkling 10.4 WAR 2013, Trout has accrued more wins above replacement in his first two full seasons than Willie Mays, Ty Cobb, Honus Wagner, Barry Bonds, Ted Williams...basically name any player other than Babe Ruth, and you get the picture.

As good as Trout's near-MVP rookie season was, his 2013 was even better in certain respects. He played in 157 games for the Halos, as he did not start this season in the minor leagues as he did last spring, and increased his walk rate fifty percent. His power dropped fractionally, but his wOBA increased year-over-year, from .409 to .423.

His UZR as a center fielder did drop to just a hair above league average, after an incredible 12 in his rookie season, but it's a small quibble for a player who has carried more than his fair share of the load for the Angels over two disappointing seasons.

It's impossible to say what the future holds, but Trout's historic pace is nothing short of breathtaking, and the lone bright spot in an otherwise utterly disappointing organization.

Aces wild in the West

Trout's campaign wasn't the only impressive encore, however. Japanese imports Yu Darvish and Hisashi Iwakuma enjoyed their second seasons stateside, and both were revelatory for the Rangers and Mariners, respectively.

Darvish was certainly very good (and unlucky) in his first go with the Rangers in 2012, but he was even better in 2013. He increased his strikeouts and lowered his walks, while dropping his ERA more than a full run, from 3.90 to 2.83. His 277 strikeouts led baseball—37 ahead of Max Scherzer, and 45 ahead of Clayton Kershaw. He made his 50th career start on Aug. 1, and recorded his 407th strikeout in the process, good for second all-time for a pitcher in his first 50 starts, just 11 behind Dwight Gooden.

Since he's just entering his age-27 season next year, it seems that the Rangers have indeed been rewarded for the substantial financial investment they made in bringing Darvish over from Japan two years ago. He appears to now be firmly entrenched as one of the game's finest aces.

The same can be said for the Mariners' investment in Iwakuma. After bouncing between the bullpen and rotation in 2012, Iwakuma made 33 starts for the Mariners, and rewarded them with a paltry 2.66 ERA, and the 17th-highest WAR among major league starting pitchers.

The Mariners can keep Iwakuma in the fold through 2015 for just $13.5 million if they exercise his option after next season, and together with ace Felix Hernandez (who enjoyed another fine, Cy Young-caliber season) the team has a pair of pitchers around which they can build.

Which is good, because the rest of the Mariners' rebuild is in a muddled state.

Building blocks in Seattle and Houston

Seattle did not enter the season as a contender, per se, but it wouldn't have been the craziest thing to happen with the young talent the organization has stockpiled over the past few years. If things broke right...

Well, they didn't. Dustin Ackley, Justin Smoak and Jesus Montero did not develop as hoped; they combined for just 0.5 WAR, and it's unclear what the organization can expect from the three going forward. It may be to the point where the team just hopes to get serviceable, league-average players from one or two of those three, and it may even be fair to say that point is in the rearview mirror.

This would make things particularly ugly in Seattle if it weren't for an abundance of talent still spilling out of the farm. Catcher Mike Zunino made his major league debut in 2013, and there is still much hope for him. Pitchers Taijuan Walker and James Paxton made late-season debuts for the club as well, and neither looked out of place in their small sample of work. Things are far from perfect in Seattle, but the way out is still in viewing distance with the pieces on the major league team and in the upper minor leagues, and that's a cause for optimism.

That's not quite the case in Houston, where another rebuild is slowly taking shape. They say Rome wasn't built in a day, and it appears the same will be the case for the Astros.

At the major league level, the Astros' season was again trying. The team won just 51 games, and will have the top pick in next season's amateur draft for the third consecutive season. They were rudely introduced into life in the AL West, going just 24-51 against their new division foes, including four straight losses to start the season. In those, the 'Stros struck out a combined 56 times (13, 15, 15, and 13, respectively), in three games against the Rangers and one against Oakland.

The team had only one player earn more than 1.5 wins above replacement, and had 18 players post negative WAR, led—if you can call it that—by J.D. Martinez's -1.1, and Jimmy Paredes' -1. The lone bright spot in Houston was catcher Jason Castro, who enjoyed a breakout season. Castro posted a .361 wOBA, third best in the AL among catchers with at least 450 plate appearances, behind just Carlos Santana and Joe Mauer. He also posted a 4.3 WAR, second in the AL only to Mauer.

The Astros did continue the impressive rebuild of their farm system, however, led by the addition of first overall pick Mark Appel, the local boy and former Stanford Cardinal ace. Top prospect Carlos Correa posted a 320/.405/.467 triple slash line in his Midwest League debut, and with the top pick in next year's draft, it seems entirely likely that the club will have one of the best farm systems in baseball (that is, if it does not already). While the present may be painful at the organization's highest level, the future appears bright in Houston.

The Angels' pockets, disaster deepen

They say money can't buy you happiness, and there at least one mega-rich Mexican-American professional sports team owner is (probably) starting to agree.

Arte Moreno's Angels invested heavily again prior to the 2013 season, committing five years and $125 million to former Rangers outfielder Josh Hamilton. They were rewarded with the 32-year-old's worst professional season in almost every respect. His triple slash of .250/.307/.432 was below his career marks (by a wide margin). He walked less, struck out more, hit for less power, and played poor defense.

Albert Pujols continued his underwhelming tenure with the Angels in 2013 as well. If 2012's 3.7 WAR was considered a disappointment (and it would be fair to say it was after Pujols averaged 7.5 over 11 prime years in St. Louis), then this season was an unmitigated disaster. Like Hamilton's, Pujols' offense dropped in every respect to a very un-Pujolsian .258/.330/.437. Toss in poor defense at first, and Pujols managed just a 0.7 WAR in his age-33 season. That's 0.04 WAR per million spent, to put it another way. Not good.

The Angels have just under $320 million committed to Pujols and Hamilton over the next eight years (which does not even include the $10 million set aside for Pujols' personal services contract at the end of his playing career), and it does not appear likely that the team will reap the reward of such hefty investments.

This is, however, a division that has always defied convention. And so, whether by the blur of a weekend series in an otherwise long and winding season, or the flash of a pen, you never know what may happen next. That's the beauty of baseball, and life in the new AL West.

Maybe Hamilton and Pujols will revive their careers next year and lead the Angels to the success our collective braintrust thought they would have. Maybe the Astros' rebuild won't pan out as well as it seems to be setting up. Maybe Darvish and Iwakuma won't be the next two great aces from this pitching-rich slate of teams. Maybe Trout will not fulfill what seems to be his destiny as one of the greatest players the game has ever seen. What is and what seems to be are rarely the same thing, and the 2013 American League West race has certainly shown that even the best-laid plans can change in a moment.

The National League East View

by John Beamer

Braves
96-66 .593

Nationals
86-76 .531

Mets
74-88 .457
Phillies
73-89 .451

Marlins
62-100 .383

Imagine the scene: It is a cold March day at THT-Towers, 1 Madison Avenue, New York, and baseball's best and brightest—that is your Hardball Times staff—were in their annual prognostication meeting, using the latest statistical wizardry to estimate who would win the various divisions, and ultimately the World Series.

Do you know what they said about the National League East? Out of the 21 staff writers, 19 had the Washington Nationals down to claim the East. Moreover, 13 had the Nationals down to play in the World Series.

The thesis was built on the belief that with Stephen Strasburg, Gio Gonzalez and Jordan Zimmermann, the Nationals had the best 1-2-3 pitching punch in the game. In addition, a couple of bold offseason moves had seen Denard Span's bat added to the lineup (along with his glove in center field) and Rafael Soriano scoop up the closer role. That, on the back of a 98-win campaign in 2012, is what led many to believe that the Nationals would burst through the 100-win barrier.

In some ways the narrative of the NL East played out as our writers predicted—the division was sewn up shortly after the All-Star break by the team with the best pitching staff in baseball. However, the rather large, genetically modified, fly in the proverbial ointment was that it was those pesky Atlanta Braves who took the spoils, rather than the Nationals of Washington. It was Atlanta's first triumph since 2005, the year it recorded its then-14th-consecutive division title.

And if you were expecting a heavyweight ding-dong, forget about it...it wasn't even close. In fact, the NL East in 2013 produced one of the most boring division races in recent memory.

Atlanta made it look easy

The short version of this review is: The Braves moved into a tie for first on April 5 and did not spend a subsequent day in second place. To make matters worse (in the snooze stakes), the Nationals—who eventually claimed second place with an 86-76 record—never seriously threatened even for the Wild Card, having been a .500 team entering September before finishing 18-9 over the closing stretch.

The cynic's view is that the Braves were a mediocre team that played decidedly average ball sandwiched between two lengthy win streaks. After opening the season 2-1, they went on a 10-game burn, largely helped by Justin Upton's bat. Upton the Younger clubbed 12 home runs and posted a 1.100 OPS for the month of April. By this point the Braves had built a 4.5 game lead in the division.

Over the next 90 games the Braves went 45-45 (this stretch included another eight-game winning run). Somehow, the Tomahawks stretched their lead to eight games in that period!

Shortly after this stretch, immediately after the All-Star break, the Braves stitched together their second double-digit win streak of the year, winning 14 games on the bounce. That included sweeps of division rivals Washington and Philadelphia, effectively punting both teams out of the division race. At that point, the Braves had a 15.5-game lead and the best record in the bigs.

Nary a Braves fan would have dreamed about such an outcome back on April 1, when Tim Hudson took the mound against Cole Hamels for the opener. The Braves' offseason was largely about revamping their offense, trying to inject more power into the lineup. To that end, they snapped up B.J. Upton on a five-year, $75 million deal—about the largest free-agent acquisition the Braves have ever made. Then, in January, Atlanta made its second hot-stove splash by trading Martin Prado, Randall Delgado and change to Arizona for Justin Upton and Chris Johnson.

With the Upton brothers reunited, there was a lot of excitement that a lineup previously bereft of bite would generate awesome spark. Predictably, there was spec ulation that by being on the same team, the brothers would inspire each other to play better. After Justin's monster April, this speculation seemed to have turned into concrete fact.

Unfortunately, time was unkind to this particular narrative. Justin Upton barely doubled his long ball tally for the remaining five months of the season, and he ended the season with the rather uninspiring slash line of .256/.343/.409. Moreover, B.J. was simply terrible, managing to deliver -0.6 WAR (yes, that's a negative number) and sinking below the Mendoza line with a batting average of .184.

After a while, the press ignored the Super Upton Bros. story until, again predictably, they appeared on the front cover of Sports Illustrated with namesake Kate Upton (no relation, I'm told) to burnish the Braves' playoff credentials. The SI curse guaranteed elimination by the Dodgers in the NLDS.

It wasn't only the Uptons who were misfiring. Dan Uggla—coincidentally the last big Braves free agent signing before B.J. Upton—was equally bad, with a slash line of .179/.309/.362. Jason Heyward—one of the best hitting prospects in baseball at one point—wasn't much better at making contact but did display decent power, clubbing .254/.349/.427, still someway short of his undoubted potential.

All in all, the Braves were 13th in the league in runs scored and 20th in the league in batting average (yet fifth in home runs). As a sabermetrically inclined publication, we shouldn't focus so much on batting average, but that inability to make more frequent contact meant that when the Braves did stack the bases, they'd more often than not come away empty-handed.

The pitching story was altogether different. Behind a rotation of Tim Hudson, Mike Minor, Kris Medlen, Paul Maholm and Julio Teheran the Braves, on paper, had as good a starting set as any in baseball. Add to that Brandon Beachy coming off Tommy John surgery and there was some depth as well. The starters duly performed, and the Braves became the stingiest team in the bigs, as they yielded just 512 runs.

Teheran was particularly impressive. He had a slow start, giving up 13 runs in his first three games for a 7.31 ERA. However, from that point onward he pitched like an ace, and finished with a creditable 3.20 mark. There is tremendous upside as well: he has three plus pitches: a four-seam fastball, a two-seamer sinking fastball and a change-up, and mixes those with a curve and slider.

Also let's not forget Craig Kimbrel. After a monster 2012—1.01 ERA, 0.78 FIP, 3.3 WAR— some regression was expected, but he still posted a 1.21 ERA, 1.93 FIP, 2.3 WAR season this time around. It is hard to overstate how good the kid is. He has just three years of major league service, so the Braves still have a good couple of years to decide whether to tie him to a (doubtlessly expensive) longer-term contract.

The trouble with Washington

As good as the Braves' rotation was, many expected it to play second fiddle to Strasburg and company up at Nationals Park. Strasburg put up decent (but not stratospheric) numbers—3.20 FIP/3.2 WAR, for the record—but what killed him was a lack of run support, especially before the All-Star break.

The game against the Brewers on July 2 is a microcosm of the problems. Strasburg pitched as well as he had all season—he was clean through seven innings, notching eight strikeouts, including a comedic moment when Aramis Ramirez lost his helmet flailing at a nasty curveball. In the eighth, the Brewers took a 4-0 lead, partly due to a fumble by Bryce Harper in the outfield. Milwaukee closed out what became Washington's ninth shutout of the season.

Up to the Milwaukee game, Strasburg's run support was as follows: 2-3-1-1-2-2-5-2-6-2-6-3-0-2-2-0.

In the same period Strasburg yielded: 0-6-0-2-3-2-4-0-1-1-1-1-1-1-2-0.

Enough said. As a result, Washington won fewer than half the games the ace started.

Elsewhere in the rotation, Zimmermann and Gonzalez pitched well. However, Dan Haren, who had a $13 million, one-year contract, was a firm bust. Having come off his worst ERA in 10 years (4.33 with the Angels) he figured to have some decent upside. After giving up six runs in four innings in his debut against the Reds, upside became downside and by August he'd cleared waivers. But no one bit.

Another much heralded offseason acquisition was center fielder Span, acquired from the Twins for hot prospect Alex Meyer. Three months into his tenure as a member of the Nationals, Span was declared a bust. Through June his OPS hovered around the .660 mark, 80 points below his career average. However, he recovered nicely to end the season near his career OPS mark on the back of 29-game hitting streak.

The other big bat expected to come through was Bryce Harper, the 2011 first overall draft pick. For a 20-year-old, Harper had an incredible season, belting 20 home runs and recording an .854 OPS. At one point it looked like it would be a lot more—the defining point was on May 13, against the Dodgers when Harper, chasing down a fly ball by A.J. Ellis, smashed face first into a concrete (unpadded) wall. At this point his OPS was a lofty 1.020, and he was tracking for one of the best age-20 seasons of all time.

In truth the Nationals never felt like contenders. The closest they got to the Braves was a half-game back in mid-May—and the Nationals had only a 22-19 record at this point.

In Philadelphia, dreaming produced a nightmare season

Although the Braves and Nationals were bona fide championship contenders, things were a little different in New York and Philadelphia. Actually, the Phillies still clung to the hope of October ball, but an aging squad was always pointing to a struggle.

With Cliff Lee, Cole Hamels and Roy Halladay fronting the rotation and Ryan Howard, Chase Utley and Jimmy Rollins in the heart of the lineup, general manager Ruben Amaro was obviously hoping it was 2010 again. It wasn't, and when the wins and losses were counted, the Phillies finished fourth with a 73-89 record.

One of the big questions entering the season was how Halladay's health would hold up. After he dominated for so long, his 2012 was a significant down year—his ERA jumped to 4.50. The root cause was injury, which resulted in decreased velocity on his heater. There were big questions afoot as to whether 2012 was a blip or a trend.

In his first game against the Braves on April 4, he notched nine strikeouts but gave up five runs—over just 3.1 innings! Historically, he has had strong command, but on this day he threw just 55 of his 95 pitches for strikes. His next outing was worse, as he yielded seven runs in four innings against the Mets. By early May, Halladay hit the disabled list with shoulder trouble.

Lee and Hamels pitched as well as ever, but it wasn't enough to compensate for Halladay's ills and the cadre of other replacement pitchers who started games for the Phillies.

The hitting side of the ledger wasn't much better, with only Utley and Dominic Brown delivering decent production. Brown was the only Phillies hitter to clear 20 home runs on the year on a team that played half its games in a bandbox. Howard was more or less a bust, playing in only 80 games. He hit decently, but his value was nowhere near the $20 million he was being paid—and certainly not the $25 million he will receive each of the next three years.

Perhaps the biggest story in Philadelphia was the firing of Charlie Manuel in mid-August. Manuel is definitely an old-school manager—a "people manager" in the vernacular—and it wasn't really a surprise that he took the fall for the Phillies' struggles rather than Amaro, who should have.

Exhibit 1: Delmon Young as an offseason acquisition to bolster the lineup! Everyone in the bigs knew that despite a .907 OPS in the 2012 postseason Young had next-to-no offensive value, and that is before taking into account his glove, which is among the worst in baseball. He had been replacement level in 2011, and worth negative WAR in 2012. He was as awful as predicted, with another negative WAR season.

Exhibit 2: Trade deadline stasis! Coming to the trade deadline the Phillies were eight games below .500 and 13 behind the Braves—in short, a long way from contention. Instead of trading Michael Young, Lee and Jonathan Papelbon for prospects, Amaro stuck to the strange belief the team might become good. It didn't work. It can't be too long before there is change at the top.

Mets' Harvey was great, but now he's out

While the Phillies fans (and front office) were hopeful, if not expectant, of challenging for the Wild Card, even before the first pitch was thrown most Mets fans knew the 2013 campaign was a write-off.

With Johan Santana sidelined for the year and Lucas Duda, Mike Baxter, Juan Lagares and Kirk Nieuwenhuis all genuine contenders for outfield spots, the vision was always out of reach. At least the club had the decency to dump Jason Bay, who took his impotent bat to the Mariners.

On the hitting side of the equation, only Marlon Byrd and David Wright showed much pop, and with the Mets 15 games off the pace approaching the trade deadline, it was little surprise that Byrd was traded to the Pirates, who were contending in the NL Central for the first time in a generation. There was minor speculation about trading Wright, but the Mets were never going to release their franchise player.

Pitching was a more positive story, with Matt Harvey and Dillon Gee having strong years, and with Jon Niese and Zack Wheeler eating innings for decent return. Gee's rise as a top-of-the-rotation starter was particularly fascinating. He struggled for the first two months of the campaign, posting a dismal 2-6 record and a 6.34 ERA. At one point there were calls to stick him in long relief. Gee turned the corner after a May 30 outing against the Yankees in which he fanned 12 to secure a 3-1 victory. Over the remainder of the season Gee was positively ace-like, notching a 2.71 ERA and winning 10 games for the Mets.

While there are questions about Gee's ability to carry this form into 2014, there were no such doubts about Harvey, who has the potential to be one of the best pitchers in the game for the next decade. A number of times in 2013 he pushed greatness.

On April 13, he took a no-hit bid into the seventh inning against the Twins. On May 7, he was perfect through 20 batters against the White Sox. He finished it for his first complete game, a one-hit shutout with a career-best 12 strikeouts. And on June 18, Harvey took another no-hitter into the seventh inning against the Braves.

Unfortunately for the Mets, Harvey was diagnosed with a ulnar collateral ligament tear in his right elbow in late August and before the end of October he elected for Tommy John surgery. It will likely be 2015 before we see his talent grace the NL again.

Miami lost 100 games. That was a victory.

And that brings us to the Miami Marlins. They weren't historically bad, but as of May 30 they were on pace to lose 123 games (only the 1899 Cleveland Spiders have lost more). They recovered, if you can call it that, and ended up losing 100. At one point it looked like it would be more, but they managed to sweep playoff-bound Detroit in three one-run games to close out the season. Only the Houston Astros finished the year with a worse record.

The one bright spot was the advent of 20-year-old Jose Fernandez, whom the Marlins drafted No. 14 overall in 2011. Initially he was pegged to start at Double-A Jacksonville, but was promoted to the bigs after injuries to Henderson Alvarez and Nathan Eovaldi. He was brilliant all year, as he struck out more than a batter per inning and finished his season with a 2.19 ERA (2.73 FIP). It was the best age-20 pitching effort in the game since Doc Gooden, who threw 16 complete games behind a 1.53 ERA in 1985.

However, unearthing another gem is unlikely to do the Marlins much good in the long run. After briefly splurging on free-agent talent in 2012, they reverted to form with a $39 million payroll that is unlikely to get more generous any time soon.

And with that we close the narrative of the 2013 NL East. If we are honest with ourselves, it was all a bit soporific. With luck, everyone will be well rested to make 2014 more of a contest. The Phillies and Mets both need significant reconstruction. Without that, it will be the Braves' and Nationals' show again—and here's hoping Strasburg, Harper and company put on more of a show.

The National League Central View

by Greg Simons

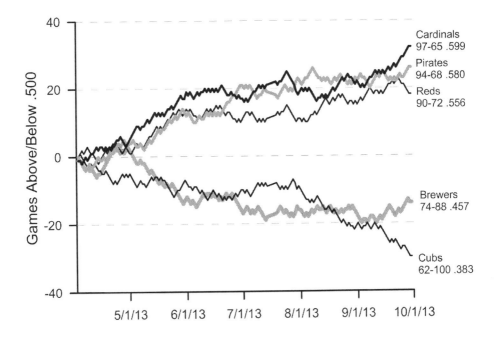

No division ever plays out exactly as it's expected to. That's just baseball. While the National League Central didn't have a last-to-first team like the Boston Red Sox, a wire-to-wire dominating squad like the Atlanta Braves, or an insane midseason turnaround like the Los Angeles Dodgers, the senior circuit's Midwest representatives did make some history all their own.

St. Louis has the formula

The Cardinals have one of the most impressive histories in baseball. St. Louis' 11 World Series championships are the most among NL teams, (a distant) second only to the New York Yankees' 27 titles. The Redbirds' 2013 division title was their first NL Central crown since 2009, and it earned the team its 10th postseason appearance in the last 14 seasons and 26th overall.

The Cardinals have developed a long-term blueprint that has allowed them to continue fielding highly competitive teams season after season on a mid-level budget, while building a farm system that is the envy of most other franchises. This work began under the direction of former general manager Walt Jocketty, now with the Cincinnati Reds, but the efforts of the last several years have been led by John Mozeliak, the team's one-time scouting director who was promoted when Jocketty left.

Not only has St. Louis' plan soldiered on despite the departure of its top front-office man, it has continued to be effective after the resignation of Tony La Russa, who stepped down from his managerial role following the Redbirds' improbable 2011 championship run. Mike Matheny has continued to oversee the Cardinals' day-to-day on-field success as skipper since the start of 2012.

The 2013 campaign challenged St. Louis management even before the season began, with starting pitcher Chris Carpenter, shortstop Rafael Furcal and closer Jason Motte all lost for the year prior to Opening Day. They soon were joined by hurler Jaime Garcia, who succumbed to shoulder surgery after making only nine starts. However, one aspect of the St. Louis plan was the creation of depth to cover for the inevitable injuries and sub-par performances every team encounters.

In the rotation, Shelby Miller had been groomed for greatness ever since he was chosen in the first round of the 2009 draft. And Miller impressed everyone in his first full big-league season, going 15-9 with a 3.06 ERA and 169 strikeouts in 173.1 innings. Joining Miller in providing rotation assistance were Joe Kelly and Michael Wacha. Kelly was selected the same year as Miller, though with less hype as a third-round selection. Wacha was the Cardinals' first-round choice in 2012, and he rocketed through the minor leagues and made his major league debut less than a year after signing. Lance Lynn—taken as the 39th pick in the 2008 draft—is one of the rotation's stalwarts, but he's been in the role for only two seasons.

Those four starting pitchers—along with a bunch of young bullpen arms, including Trevor Rosenthal (21st round, 2009), Kevin Siegrist (41st round, 2008, a round that no longer exists), Seth Maness (11th round, 2011), and Carlos Martinez (amateur free agent, 2010)—demonstrate the successful strategy St. Louis has employed when selecting pitchers. The team loves high-velocity arms, and it had several options to choose from in every situation this season.

It's not just the pitcher's mound that has benefited from the Redbirds' excellent drafting, but the whole diamond. Slugger Matt Adams (a 23rd-round pick in that gluttonous 2009 draft) and shortstop Pete Kozma (first round, 2007) were the rookies who demonstrated their skills most often for the Busch Stadium faithful in 2013, but many other in-house position players are helping St. Louis to succeed.

Matt Carpenter (13th round, 2009 again) broke out big-time this past season, as he led the NL in runs scored and batted .318 with a .392 on-base percentage. Carpenter was joined in the starting lineup most days by center fielder Jon Jay (second round, 2006) and long-time star catcher Yadier Molina (fourth round, way back in 2000). David Freese (ninth round, 2006, taken by San Diego) wasn't a Cardinals draftee, but he was acquired when he was still in the minors, and his St. Louis roots make Freese feel like a home-grown guy.

Meshing all these in-house-developed players with a few carefully selected free agents and trade acquisitions has allowed St. Louis to stay competitive while staying within a reasonable budget, typically around $100 million over the last several seasons. And with outfielder Oscar Taveras (amateur free agent, 2008) primed for big-league duty and another strong draft class this past summer, the Cardinals are likely to be in the fight for the division title for years to come.

Pittsburgh finally sniffs success

The wait, the drought, the misery of the long-suffering fans has ended. After 20 seasons of sub-.500 ball—a North American record for major team sports futility—it is over! For the first time since the 1992 campaign that featured the MVP-winning exploits of Barry Bonds, the Pirates not only finished the year with a winning record, they made the playoffs, capturing the top Wild Card slot on the final weekend of the regular season.

It's a massive understatement to say it's been a difficult two decades for baseball in the Steel City. But a home-grown-based approach with a unique recipe all its own—and several external acquisitions thrown into the mix—finally allowed Pittsburgh to escape its doldrums.

Following failed runs by general managers Cam Bonifay and David Littlefield, primarily under the ownership of Kevin McClatchy, Robert Nutting took over control of the franchise in 2007 and soon installed Neal Huntington as the new GM. Facing the reality that a total rebuild was necessary, Huntington emptied the roster of players who didn't appear destined to help the team long-term, dealing for a number of prospects with whom to rebuild the farm system. Interestingly, few of these prospects have worked out thus far.

Where Pittsburgh has seen the greatest success is in nabbing down-on-their luck veterans in trade and signing low-cost free agents to team-friendly deals. A.J. Burnett was picked up from the Yankees after washing out in the Bronx, while the suddenly cost-conscious Bombers let Russell Martin go to the Pirates via free agency. Francisco Liriano, Marlon Byrd, Justin Morneau, Wandy Rodriguez, Gaby Sanchez, Clint Barmes, Travis Snider, Jose Tabata and Mark Melancon all were added to the roster as small-dollar free agents or by trading with teams looking to shed payroll. Yes, the Pirates were taking on salaries while teams in larger markets were unloading them!

These savvy pickups were combined with the homegrown core of Andrew McCutchen (first round, 2005), Pedro Alvarez (first round, 2008), Neil Walker (first round, 2004), Starling Marte (international free agent), and Gerrit Cole (first round, 2011) to create a winning formula. Notice all those first-round successes? That reflects a complete turnaround of fortune for a franchise that excelled at selecting first-round busts year after year throughout the 1990s. While Littlefield must be given credit for drafting McCutchen and Walker, it has been Huntington who has melded all of these players into a unit strong enough to compete with the best teams in baseball.

The 2014 season will be full of question marks for the Pirates. Was this a one-year fluke akin to the 2003 Kansas City Royals, who popped up above .500 before sinking own again for another decade? Will Pittsburgh be able to continue drafting well with later picks while mixing in thrifty free agent and trade targets?

It's never easy to be a top team, because everyone else wants what you have, so there's always a target on the leaders' backs. And when a team makes the journey from oblivion to relevance in one year, there are those who question the sustainability of that success. But in 2013, Pittsburgh showed that it knows how to draft, develop, trade and sign the right players to create a winner. And the Pirates' smart front office is a good bet to return a winning baseball tradition to the Steel City.

Cincinnati has an effective blend

The Reds had a couple of big holes to fill most of the 2013 season, with ace Johnny Cueto and left fielder Ryan Ludwick missing large chunks of the season. They plugged those gaps well enough to make it to the postseason for a second consecutive year and the third time in four seasons. While the minor league system hasn't produced a true star in a while, the studs Cincinnati has developed in the last few years are now mature veterans waiting for the next wave of youngsters to join them on the major league roster.

Joey Votto (second round, 2002) and Jay Bruce (first round, 2005) were a tremendous home-grown combo last season, combining for 54 home runs, 182 RBI and 190 runs scored. Votto clearly was the better player, with a .305/.435/.491 triple-slash line, numbers that are becoming wonderfully monotonous for Reds fans. Bruce may not have the same batting eye as his teammate, but he has excellent thump, reaching 30 long balls for the third straight season.

The next tier of players from the Cincinnati developmental system provided adequate support to the lineup, though several players are new enough to the bigs that they still have time to grow. Devin Mesoraco (first round, 2007) was about average for a catcher, but players at that position often take time to reach their potential. The same opportunity for improvement applies to shortstop Zack Cozart (second round, 2007), Todd Frazier (first round, 2007) and Chris Heisey (17th round, 2006). That 2007 draft sure did a lot to populate the 2013 roster.

On the mound, Homer Bailey (first round, 2004), Mike Leake (first round, 2009) and Tony Cingrani (third round, 2011) combined to go 32-23 with a 3.33 ERA and 441 strikeouts in 506 innings. Putting them in the rotation with trade acquisitions Mat Latos and Bronson Arroyo covered quite nicely for Cueto's absence, though he was around long enough in short bursts to make 11 productive starts.

The decision to leave Aroldis Chapman—a Cuban free-agent signing in 2010— in the bullpen again may have sealed his fate as a life-long reliever after the Reds spent the last few winters toying with the idea of having him start. His triple-digit velocity works so well in the pen—as evidenced by this year's 112 punchouts in 63.2 innings—that ninth-inning duties appear to be in his foreseeable future.

Reds fans got a taste of another part of that future at the end of the season with the promotion of Billy Hamilton (second round, 2009), widely regarded as the fastest player in the game. After swiping a professional-record 155 bases in 2012, Hamilton stole "only" 75 bags in 2013. More advanced competition, both at and behind the plate, certainly played a part in keeping his batting and running numbers well below his previous year's phenomenal output, but Hamilton certainly fits the phenom label once he reaches first base. He nabbed the first 13 bases he attempted to pilfer in the majors before being gunned down by the unforgettable Juan Centeno (Centeno may be the answer to a trivia question some day, so sock that name away in your mental vault for future reference).

With on-base (and, not coincidentally, hit-by-pitch) master Shin-Soo Choo eligible for free agency this winter, Hamilton may have a starting spot available to him next season. Of course, with all the money pouring into the game, it's possible the Reds will keep both Choo and Hamilton, giving them an excellent table-setter with pop and an absolute burner on the basepaths. If Cincinnati could combine those attributes, they'd have Rickey Henderson, but for now they'll have to decide if, and how, to use the two halves of that Hall of Famer.

Milwaukee's brew has grown stale

Clearly, the downward spiral is accelerating for the Brew Crew. Two years after losing a six-game NL Championship Series, Milwaukee saw its win total plummet for a second consecutive season, with a 12-6 finish propping their victory total up to 74.

The biggest story of the Brewers' season was Ryan Braun's 65-game, PED-related suspension. The 2005 first-rounder is signed through at least 2020, so the club has to hope Braun comes back to produce something close to his typical numbers. If not, it would be another step down for a team that's likely to be looking up at the division leaders for a while. It's not that Milwaukee is an awful team; it has a number of solid players contributing on both sides of the ball. It's just that the overall package is struggling to keep up with the competition.

The outfield is composed of Braun (first-round draft pick, 2005), all-around impressive center fielder Carlos Gomez (2002 amateur free-agent signee acquired from the Twins in 2009), and slap-and-dasher Norichika Aoki (picked up in 2012 via Nippon Professional Baseball's posting system). That's an outfield a team can win with, and its composition shows a creative talent-acquisition approach.

In the infield, Jonathan Lucroy (third round, 2007) is a strong-hitting catcher, third baseman Aramis Ramirez (free agent) was his usual self when healthy, and shortstop Jean Segura (snagged in the Zack Greinke trade) was among the league's stolen base leaders. But the right side of the infield is where the problems are. Rickie Weeks (first round, 2003) and his disappearing bat are a drain on the team's offense and pocketbook. And first base, a typical thumper's position, was manned by the anemic combination of Yuniesky Betancourt, Alex Gonzalez and Juan Francisco, though the expected return of Corey Hart (11th round, 2000) should improve things.

On the mound, starting pitchers Yovani Gallardo (second round, 2004), Kyle Lohse (free agent), Wily Peralta (amateur free agent, 2005) and Marco Estrada (sixth round, 2005) were adequate, but nothing more. The bullpen featured the jettisoned John Axford and Francisco Rodriguez closing at times, though Jim Henderson grabbed control of the role as the year progressed.

Notice how long ago all of those Milwaukee-developed players were chosen. This is not a young, up-and-coming roster. It's populated with a few peak talents, some past-their-prime veterans, an up-and-coming star shortstop, and a whole lot of mediocrity, with a future that appears rather dim. The minor league system doesn't seem likely to fill many big holes, so the Brewers either can plug the gaps with eight-figure annual outlays for known quantities such as Lohse, take their chances with bargain-bin signings, or let the kids undergo trials by fire.

There was a version of that approach this year, and the results weren't good. For Milwaukee to become relevant again, the front office needs to develop a cohesive plan and diligently stick to it. Finding early-round success stories in the draft again would help, too. In the meantime, Brewers fans will need to be very patient.

Chicago: Wait 'til year after next

Batting average is far from an ideal way to judge a player, or an entire team, but the best average by a Cubs regular in 2013 was Welington Castillo's .274, with the worst being Darwin Barney's .208. On-base percentages ranged from Castillo's solid .349 down to Barney's atrocious .266. Two of the four starters to slug over .400—Alfonso Soriano and David DeJesus—were traded during the season. While a few new faces were given chances late in the year, Junior Lake, 23, was the only truly young hitter to receive playing time come August and September.

The two 23-year-old infielders who had starting jobs all season long didn't live up to expectations. Starlin Castro's bat all but disappeared, as he hit .245/.287/.347, and his defensive work—when he is actually paying attention—never has earned quality reviews. Following a solid 2012 campaign, Anthony Rizzo's bat also fizzled, his 23 homers barely masking a .233/.323/.419 line that was well short of what's expected from a first baseman. With both players locked up for several more seasons via pre-arbitration deals, the team has to hope both can get back to the top of their game.

On the mound, Travis Wood was a revelation, Jeff Samardzija was middling, Edwin Jackson was worse and Matt Garza was traded. Chicago didn't deal closer Kevin Gregg, though he should have been gone for the best offer, while somehow the Cubs did find a taker for one-time closer and full-time wildman Carlos Marmol.

The result of this transitional season was a last-place finish that provides Chicago with a top-five pick in next summer's draft. And that pick needs to be a good one, because the future of the Cubs lies in their minor league system. The top signings of the last few years—first-rounders Javier Baez (2011), Albert Almora (2012), Kris Bryant (2013) and 2012 Cuban free agent signee Jorge Soler—hold the keys to the Cubs' future. How these youngsters perform as they move up the minor-league ladder and (fans hope) to the bigs will determine Chicago's ability to compete.

"Wait 'til next year" has been the theme of Chicago's North Siders for 105 seasons now. The past is not necessarily prologue, but while 2014 is likely to produce that same mantra, the 2015 season could be the time to start taking the Cubs seriously.

The National League West View

by Mike Petriello

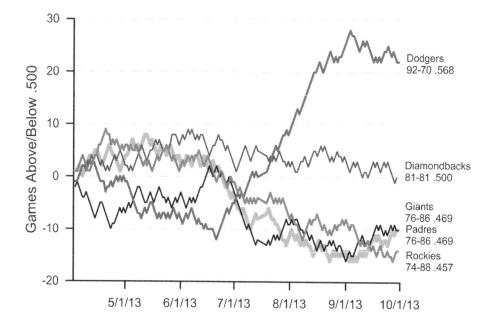

H eading into the 2013 season, there wasn't a whole lot of uncertainty regarding what the National League West was going to be about.

The San Francisco Giants would attempt to repeat their 2012 championship magic by returning most of the roster that won the title, and the Arizona Diamondbacks would try to prove that trading Justin Upton wasn't a mistake, that "the right kind of player" would keep them in the race. In Colorado and San Diego, the Rockies and Padres hoped to reverse two years of losing while trying to build a future. Looming over them all was the specter of the *nouveau riche* Los Angeles Dodgers, fresh off an unprecedented spending spree, and poised to crush all comers with a talent-laden roster.

The Dodgers did end up winning the West by a comfortable margin of 11 games over second-place Arizona. But it's how they got there that's interesting, because it didn't at all happen in the way anyone expected, and along the way, new foes were created while past champions stumbled.

The Birth of a Rivalry

For months, the Diamondbacks were endlessly panned for their offseason moves—particularly the trade of Upton to Atlanta, just a year removed from an MVP-quality season—as general manager Kevin Towers attempted to rebuild his roster in the image of manager Kirk Gibson.

For many of those same months, the Diamondbacks did their best to shut everyone else up. Arizona held first place for 81 days of the season, while Upton's red-hot April in Atlanta deteriorated into an up-and-down remainder of the year. Led by Paul Goldschmidt, who drove in 77 runs before the All-Star Game, and breakout starting pitcher Pat Corbin, who saw his team win 18 of his first 20 starts, the Diamondbacks led the division for most of the first half.

There were holes, to be sure. Starters Trevor Cahill, Wade Miley and Ian Kennedy were all unable to recapture past success. Young outfielder Adam Eaton and closer J.J. Putz missed chunks of time with elbow injuries. Veteran hitters Jason Kubel and Miguel Montero got off to terrible starts. But as Corbin and Goldschmidt starred and the rest of the division trod water or worse, Towers' plan looked sound.

Meanwhile in Los Angeles, the first half could not have gone more terribly considering the high expectations of new ownership. Expensive free-agent acquisition Zack Greinke had his collarbone broken by Carlos Quentin in an April brawl with the Padres, while fellow starter Chad Billingsley's attempt to pitch through a partially torn elbow ligament lasted all of 12 innings. Matt Kemp was constantly injured and unproductive when he was on the field. And the team that had so much starting pitching in March that veteran Aaron Harang was pawned off for lack of room had to use nine starters in April alone, including minor leaguers Stephen Fife and Matt Magill.

At times, it seemed like a cruel joke. Shortstop Hanley Ramirez, who had hurt his thumb during the final game of the World Baseball Classic, returned in late April, but lasted for only four games before seriously injuring his hamstring—injuries that doomed the Dodgers to months of awful play from replacements Dee Gordon and Justin Sellers. Adrian Gonzalez missed time due to a sore neck incurred when he ran into an umpire; Ted Lilly's injury-plagued season ended due to a neck problem of his own suffered when he was accidentally run over on the basepaths by San Diego's massive Kyle Blanks.

By May, after the team's second losing streak of at least six games, the calls for manager Don Mattingly's head were deafening; it seemed he was retaining his job on a game-by-game basis. By June, the most expensive team in the game was on pace for its worst season since the Dodgers moved west in 1958.

But while it didn't seem like Arizona and Los Angeles would be contending with each other for anything this year, multiple incidents kept them on one another's radar. During the first matchup of the year in April in Arizona, Diamondbacks owner Ken

Kendrick demanded that Dodgers fans behind home plate—and, of course, visible on television—change out of their Dodgers blue gear. That made national headlines.

In June, the Diamondbacks' visit to Dodger Stadium produced a vicious brawl after Kennedy hit Dodgers rookie sensation Yasiel Puig with a pitch and Greinke retaliated in kind. Eight participants were suspended and a dozen were fined, with bad feelings left on both sides. A few weeks later, in Arizona, the Dodgers found themselves in the middle of another firestorm: An Arizona radio host reported that Puig had "snubbed" Diamondbacks legend—and fellow Cuban—Luis Gonzalez prior to a game. That added to a growing national blowback against Puig, the rookie who had taken the sport by storm.

Still, the fireworks were mainly restricted to off the field, because the Dodgers kept losing too much to make it a race. On June 21, a week after the brawl, they lost the second game of a series in San Diego and fell a season-worst 9.5 games behind Arizona. They appeared to be dead in the water. But the Dodgers won the next day, and the next, and the next, and ran off streaks like baseball has never seen before—10 of 11, 14 of 15, 23 of 29 in August alone, 42-8 over 50 games.

They had nine streaks of four or more consecutive wins. They won 15 in a row on the road, the fourth-longest run in baseball history. Between June 22 and Sept. 3, they won 52 of 66 games, moving from last place to a shocking 13.5 game lead over Arizona.

Other than adding Miami starter Ricky Nolasco for depth in early July, the Dodgers hadn't made any major moves to fuel the run. They simply got healthy. Greinke posted a 1.85 second-half ERA. The wonderful Clayton Kershaw's 1.83 ERA made him just the third pitcher in history to lead the bigs in ERA for three straight years. There was the sensational debut of Puig (.319/.391/.534), the rebirth of Ramirez (.345/.402/.638 around his many injuries) and the shocking rebound of third baseman Juan Uribe (worth five wins after being a bust his first two years in town). All that allowed the Dodgers to gloss over the fact that Kemp's continuing health problems made him a non-factor.

As the Dodgers inevitably slowed and they ran into a September slump, the Diamondbacks gamely tried to keep pace, preventing the Dodgers from clinching until Sept. 19. When they finally did, it came with even more controversy. After winning 7-6 in Arizona in the season's final meeting between the two teams, several Dodgers ran out to the pool in Chase Field's outfield to celebrate, raising the ire of not only the Diamondbacks organization, but national figures like Arizona Sen. John McCain as well. Threats of on-field retribution abounded, along with charges of lack of "respect" and "class."

What's next for these two after all this bad blood? Well, how about an international incident? The Dodgers and Diamondbacks are slated to kick off the 2014 season against one another in March in Major League Baseball's first trip to Australia. It might be worth staying up until the wee hours of the night for that.

The End of an Era?

While Arizona and Los Angeles stole the headlines, it was easy to forget that the San Francisco Giants came into the season with two championship rings over the last three seasons—or as many as the rest of the division has won, combined, in the last quarter-century.

With that as a backdrop, general manager Brian Sabean was content to roll out nearly the exact roster as the one that had won the World Series, making only a few peripheral changes. As late as September, some lineups had the same names as the ones that manager Bruce Bochy had used in the 2012 World Series.

For a while, that seemed to work; the team held a share of first place in late May. But while the 2012 Giants were fueled by inexplicable magic—remember Marco Scutaro outproducing fellow midseason trade acquisition Hanley Ramirez, or the team playing better after outfielder Melky Cabrera was suspended, or Barry Zito, playoff hero?—the 2013 edition merely looked like an older and inferior version of the same product.

Nowhere was that more obvious than in the rotation, where the San Francisco starters topped only the aging Phillies and mile-high Rockies in run prevention, allowing a 4.37 ERA. While 23-year-old lefty Madison Bumgarner transitioned from "good starter" to "ace" in collecting 199 strikeouts over 201.1 innings of 2.77-ERA ball, there was decline from almost every other member of what is usually among the most stable rotations.

Zito, mercifully in the final year of his albatross contract, went from "acceptably mediocre" to "unspeakably awful," allowing a 5.74 ERA and losing his job before the end of the year. Reclamation project Ryan Vogelsong, who had matched Bumgarner's 3.37 ERA in 2012, was injured for much of the year and put up numbers similar to Zito's when he could pitch. Tim Lincecum was somewhat better than 2012's disaster, but still nowhere near the Cy Young Award winner he'd once been. Most concerning of all, the always-reliable Matt Cain had his worst year since he was a 21-year-old rookie in 2006.

As the rotation problems mounted, the farm system offered little help, and so the Giants were forced to patch with journeymen Chad Gaudin and Yusmeiro Petit. Because of the trade that sent Zack Wheeler to New York for rental Carlos Beltran in 2011, along with the declining prospect status of Gary Brown, the Giants may not see an impact prospect make it to the bigs until highly regarded pitcher Kyle Crick. He's expected to need at least another full year in the minors.

Any team that has perennial MVP candidate Buster Posey still has hope, of course, and Posey was actually outperformed by a breakout season from young first baseman Brandon Belt (.289/.360/.481). But while the team got generally solid production from nearly every position, even Posey was unable to keep up the pace. His .821 OPS was down more than 150 points from 2012, and his second half was a mess; he hit only .244/.333/.310 with two homers.

While the rotation is likely to see some turnover, Giants fans may need to get used to the same faces in the lineup—at the end of the year, Hunter Pence signed an extension, so seven of the eight Opening Day starters remain under team control.

Struggling for Relevance

Every year, the Rockies and Padres try to show that they're building teams that are worthy of the wonderful cities and parks in which they play. And nearly every year, save for some occasional high points like the unexpected Colorado run to the 2007 World Series, their seasons end with little more than "wait until next year."

Colorado, however, failed its way to a last-place finish in a slightly different way than usual, because the Rockies actually spent some time in first place and managed to come up with some decent pitching for once. They quickly abandoned their short-lived 2012 four-man rotation plan, and the Rockies' team FIP (Fielding Independent Pitching) started with a three for just the fourth team in team history.

Jhoulys Chacin and Jorge De La Rosa combined for 365 innings of 3.48 ERA ball at the front of the rotation; by the second half, they'd been joined by 23-year-old former Angels prospect Tyler Chatwood, who pitched in with 20 solid starts. While Juan Nicasio struggled to keep pace and the veteran trio of Jon Garland, Jeff Francis and Roy Oswalt was a black hole of terrible at the back end, the Rockies managed to put together three reasonably productive starters. In Coors Field, that's no small achievement.

First-year manager Walt Weiss was able to take advantage of that pitching and help the Rockies get off to a good start, ending April in first place and maintaining a share of it as late as May 25. But that nice first impression quickly evaporated, because after going 16-11 in April, Colorado lost either 15 or 16 games in every succeeding month of the season.

The pitching began to crumble; the team's ERA went from 4.19 to 4.80 after the All-Star break. Underrated closer Rafael Betancourt pitched only three second-half innings due to a potentially career-ending elbow injury, and while Rex Brothers proved an able replacement, the collection of pitchers forced to move up to fill his setup innings were a never-ending—and only rarely competent, with Adam Ottavino being one exception—source of trouble.

Though Michael Cuddyer ended up being one of the more surprising batting champions in years, taking the crown with a .331 mark, the offense wasn't able to provide enough action to make up for the declining pitching. As expected, shortstop Troy Tulowitzki (.931 OPS) and outfielder Carlos Gonzalez (.958) put up elite offensive numbers; also as expected, they missed time due to injury, sitting out 88 games between them. Josh Rutledge had excited many filling in for Tulowitzki at shortstop in 2012, but flopped (.630 OPS) in an audition as the starting second baseman, and DJ LeMahieu (.673) didn't do much better as his replacement.

While there was some pitching hope and the welcome debut of 22-year-old rookie third baseman Nolan Arenado, who flashed an outstanding glove and looks like he may be a keeper, the story of this season in Colorado is that of an organization that doesn't seem to know in which direction it's headed. Team icon Todd Helton's farewell song at first base ended with the worst season of his arguably Hall of Fame career, and his departure should have been the catalyst for the team to move into the future.

Instead, the Rockies are stuck with one of the most awkward front-office structures in baseball. Longtime general manager Dan O'Dowd ceded some of his responsibilities prior to the season to assistant Bill Geivett, who maintained an office in the clubhouse in a flagrant breach of baseball etiquette. Despite grumblings that the situation is untenable, it's expected to continue. There's no indication that it's providing any tangible dividends.

The team also never replaced team president Keli McGregor, who passed away in 2010. Team chairman Dick Montfort attempted to fill the role, although his expertise is in business, not baseball. Montfort wrote a letter to fans after the season, trumpeting the few 2013 bright spots and insisting that he does not believe "we are a middle of the pack team." While you wouldn't expect a team's chief executive to admit otherwise, you wonder what is going to make the 2014 Rockies any different from the last few editions.

Down in San Diego, the Padres had entered the season with some hope, due to the fact that they'd ended 2012 by winning 42 of their final 70 games. But instead of contending, they slipped into a bizarro-world mirror image of the Rockies. While Colorado managed to scrounge up some decent pitching, San Diego had arguably the worst pitching staff in baseball despite its pitcher-friendly home at Petco, finishing ahead of only the moribund Houston Astros in terms of WAR.

With previously useful starters Tim Stauffer (limited to relief) and Cory Luebke (out for the year) not available in the rotation due to injury, the Padres were forced to scrape the bottom of the barrel. Ageless Jason Marquis was given 20 starts—and somehow won nine games—despite a 5.65 FIP before mercifully going down to injury. Clayton Richard was mostly injured and always ineffective, and Edinson Volquez managed to start 27 games (with a 6.01 ERA!) before he was finally cut loose in August.

While the team found some utility in journeyman Eric Stults (3.53 FIP in 203.2 innings) and talented young Andrew Cashner (3.35 FIP in 175 innings), never-ending health problems left the Padres scrambling to fill staff spots at times. That concern carried over to the rest of the roster, torpedoing any chances they might have had. Not that they ever made any noise; the high point of the season for the Padres was a mere two games over .500.

Truly, it was absence that shaped the entire season. Shortstop Everth Cabrera, the Padres' nearly unquestioned MVP of the first half, played just 95 games due to a suspension for performance-enhancing drug usage. Catcher Yasmani Grandal missed most of the first two months to a suspension of his own, then collected only 108 plate appearances (and a single homer) before blowing out his knee in a collision at the plate, an injury that could affect his 2014 season as well.

It never seemed to end. Center fielder Cameron Maybin made it into just 14 games because of injuries to his right wrist and left knee; left fielder Carlos Quentin played in only 82 games due to knee trouble and a suspension for injuring Greinke. Third baseman Chase Headley, the breakout star of the 2012 season, missed the first two weeks with an injured thumb, then massively underperformed (putting up an OPS approximately 130 points lower than 2012's); it was revealed after the season that he'd been playing on a sore left knee all year, which required October surgery.

There were bright spots, to be sure. Outfielder Will Venable put up 22 homers and steals apiece in his first year with more than 500 plate appearances, while fellow outfielder Chris Denorfia stepped into the everyday lineup for the first time and was worth nearly four wins. Rookie infielder Jedd Gyorko hit 23 homers while proving that he could handle the defensive demands of second base, and might have made noise in a Rookie of the Year class that didn't include Jose Fernandez, Puig, Shelby Miller, and many others.

Yet again, the Padres ended strong, winning 16 games in September, the third-most in the league, and yet again, they'll enter 2014 hoping they can ride that momentum to a successful year. But without some answers to that rotation, they may be looking ahead to another year of mediocre baseball in a gorgeous setting.

The One About the 2013 Postseason

by Brad Johnson

It was an interesting postseason to say the least: a World Series matchup of relatively new managers who produced a wide array of comical circumstances and novice mistakes. In this modern age of analytical front offices, the on-field staffs still seem unable to adapt.

As in any other postseason, there were heroes. There were villains. There were victims. In the end, the Red Sox were left standing as the World Series champions while the other nine playoff teams were left to wonder, "what if…"

Over the past few years, we at The Hardball Times have taken to viewing the postseason through the lens of a specially designed statistic called Championships Added (ChampAdded). It has two components.

The first is Win Probability Added (WPA). Every play in every game moves that game forward and increases a team's chances of winning (or losing) the game. This is measured by WPA, which takes into account the score, inning, base situation and number of outs.

The second component is the Championship Value of each postseason game. Just as a play moves a game forward, each game moves the postseason forward and increases a team's chances of winning (or losing) the championship.

For example, Game Seven of the World Series is worth one full championship, since the winner takes home the trophy and the loser doesn't. In ChampAdded parlance, that's a value of 1.000. All other games are worth a fraction of a championship.

Had Detroit forced a Game Seven in the American League Championship Series, for instance, that game would have been worth .500 ChampAdded because the winner would have then had a 50 percent chance to win the World Series. Below is a chart that notes the ChampAdded for each game.

Championship Value of Playoff Games										
	0-0	1-0	1-1	2-0	2-1	2-2	3-0	3-1	3-2	3-3
Wild Card Game	0.125	X	X	X	X	X	X	X	X	X
Division Series	0.094	0.094	0.125	0.063	0.125	0.250	X	X	X	X
Championship Series	0.156	0.156	0.188	0.125	0.188	0.250	0.063	0.125	0.250	0.500
World Series	0.313	0.313	0.375	0.250	0.375	0.500	0.125	0.250	0.500	1.000

Once we know the value of each game, we can convert each play into a share of a championship by multiplying the WPA times the game's championship value. The stat is expressed as a decimal, similar to many familiar baseball stats like batting average. For example, a hitter may contribute .050 ChampAdded, which can also be read as "five percent of a championship."

Starting with the Division Series round, each of the eight teams had a 12.5 percent chance of winning the World Series. Through the remainder of the playoffs, players on the World Series champion Red Sox contributed a total of .875 ChampAdded (1.000 minus .125 equals .875). All other teams have a total ChampAdded of -.125. It is a zero sum game.

Each series will be recapped below using ChampAdded to identify a series MVP, a series goat, and the biggest play of the series. The MVP will have made the greatest contribution to his team's championship hopes. The goat is the player who hurt his team the most. The play with the highest ChampAdded is considered the biggest play of the series.

NL Wild Card Game: Cincinnati Reds vs. Pittsburgh Pirates

In his only appearance of the 2012 postseason, Reds starter Johnny Cueto lasted just one-third of an inning before an oblique strain forced him to leave the ballgame. This time around, Cueto was recently recovered from a lat strain and looking for redemption.

Instead, the Pirates put pressure on Cueto early and the fans jumped on board with monotone chants of CUE~TO. Marlon Byrd kicked off the scoring in the second inning with a solo home run. Two batters later, with Russell Martin at the plate, Cueto dropped the ball while preparing to take the rubber. The apparent show of nerves caused the Pittsburgh faithful to redouble their jeering and the very next pitch went for a second solo home run.

Cueto lasted just 3.1 innings while allowing four runs. It was more than the Pirates would need en route to a 6-2 victory. Pittsburgh starter Francisco Liriano was nasty from the first pitch and allowed only five baserunners over seven innings.

Game MVP: The Pirates acquired Byrd on Aug. 27 to patch a hole in the outfield with an adequate player. They probably weren't counting on him to play hero in the first playoff game of his career. He takes home MVP honors with a .022 ChampAdded. In other words, Byrd helped the Pirates to 2.2 percent of a championship.

Game Goat: Who but Cueto? He pitched to a -.029 ChampAdded and also recorded the old-fashioned loss. Getting flustered in the second inning certainly didn't help his cause, although it made for great television. Pirates fans will remember that dropped-baseball-to-home-run sequence for a long time. You can bet that those in attendance will still be talking about the game 30 years from now.

Big Play: The first run of 2013 postseason was also the biggest play of the game. Byrd's second inning, leadoff home run tallied .015 ChampAdded for the Pirates. It's not the play that everybody will remember, but that's when the Pirates took control.

AL Wild Card Game: Tampa Bay Rays vs. Cleveland Indians

This one featured a marquee match-up between two of the game's best young pitchers. Alex Cobb put together an excellent season by combining a good strikeout rate, low walk rate, and heavy ground ball rate on his way to a 2.76 ERA. He missed time midseason after being struck on the head by a batted ball, but he picked up where he left off after a two-month recovery.

Cobb was opposed by Danny Salazar who—like Teddy Roosevelt—spoke softly and carried a big 96 mph fastball. He earned the postseason nod with an impressive 3.12 ERA in 10 late-season starts. Salazar struck out nearly 31 percent of batters faced while walking only seven percent. To put that in perspective, Detroit's Max Scherzer, who fanned 240 over the season while winning 21 games, struck out almost 29 percent of hitters while walking about seven percent.

With both youngsters featuring advanced command and control, the game was supposed to be a pitchers' duel. Instead, Delmon Young and the Rays struck first with a solo home run in the third inning and chased Salazar after plating two more in the fourth inning. The Indians threatened in the fourth and fifth innings, but never got a runner past third base.

Game MVP: Cobb takes home top honors with .039 ChampAdded. By keeping the Indians off the board over the first 6.2 innings of the game, he gave the Rays the opportunity to build a commanding three-run lead.

Cobb was fortunate to escape some tight spots, especially in the fourth and fifth innings. When he was relieved in the seventh inning, he had allowed eight hits, one walk, and struck out five. It wasn't the most dominant outing of the postseason, but it got the job done.

Game Goat: Asdrubal Cabrera had a rough game, going 0-for-4 and tallying -.030 ChampAdded. He made some critical outs, including an inning-ending fly out in the second with a runner in scoring position. But most of the damage was done when he came to the plate in the fourth inning. The bases were loaded with one out, and Cabrera grounded into an inning-ending double play.

Big Play: Desmond Jennings delivered a two-out, two-RBI double in the top of the fourth inning that drove in James Loney and Evan Longoria. The play went for .023 ChampAdded.

NL Division Series: Los Angeles Dodgers vs. Atlanta Braves

The Atlanta Braves led the National League in wins for nearly the entire season. The St. Louis Cardinals overtook them late in the season, forcing the Braves to face a juggernaut Dodgers roster in the Division Series.

The Dodgers took Game One amidst a trouncing of Kris Medlen. Clayton Kershaw completely stymied the Braves offense by allowing only three hits and three walks over seven innings while striking out 12 batters.

A strong start by Mike Minor allowed the Braves to even the series at one game apiece, but the wheels fell off from there. The two clubs exchanged blows early and often in Game Three. The Dodgers broke things open in the fourth inning and rode a comfortable lead to a 13-6 victory.

Things got interesting in the final game of the series. Rather than use Ricky Nolasco in Game Four and reserve Kershaw for Game Five, the Dodgers opted to bring back their ace on short rest. Meanwhile, the Braves were forced to rest their postseason hopes on an unlikely candidate—late-season acquisition Freddy Garcia.

Garcia kept the Braves in the game, allowing two runs over six innings of work. Kershaw also allowed two runs over six innings, but his were unearned. The Braves held a narrow 3-2 lead after seven innings, but the bullpen fumbled the lead in the eighth inning. Dodgers closer Kenley Jansen slammed the door by striking out the side in the ninth.

Series MVP: Juan Uribe quietly posted a strong 2013 season, just in time for his latest foray into free agency. He was especially slick with the leather in the regular season, but it was his bat that helped the Dodgers advance to the NLCS. His 6-for-16 performance included two home runs, four runs scored, and four RBI. It all adds up to .062 ChampAdded, although most of it came on one big play.

Series Goat: David Carpenter draws the ignominious honor with his -.083 ChampAdded. Carpenter was one of the Braves' relief aces in 2013, but his short postseason was not his best work. He appeared in three games and allowed four runs over 2.2 innings.

Big Play: The big play of the series pits our MVP against the goat. The Braves had a narrow 3-2 lead in Game Four after seven innings. Yasiel Puig led off the eighth with a double against Carpenter. Uribe followed with a two-run home run that put the Dodgers ahead for good—all with Atlanta relief ace Craig Kimbrel watching, unused, from the bullpen. The play went for .055 ChampAdded.

NL Division Series: Pittsburgh Pirates vs. St. Louis Cardinals

The Division Series featured a NL Central intra-division rivalry between the Pirates and Cardinals. The two teams each spent time leading the division in 2013, with the Cardinals ultimately earning the division crown.

In their first return to the postseason—and first winning season—since 1992, the Pirates fought well but were ultimately defeated by St. Louis.

Game One wasn't much of a contest. Adam Wainwright dominated the Pirates lineup while the St. Louis offense scored seven early runs off A.J. Burnett.

Game Two was a reversal of the first, as the Pirates plated five runs off Cardinals starter Lance Lynn en route to a 7-1 victory. Rookie Gerrit Cole shined over six innings, as he allowed just two hits and one walk and struck out five.

The third game was more closely fought. The Pirates busted a 3-3 game open in the eighth on RBI singles from Pedro Alvarez and Russell Martin to win, 5-3.

Unfortunately for Pirates fans, that marked the high point of the season. Cardinals rookie and postseason hero Michael Wacha nearly silenced the Pirates bats altogether as part of a 2-1 Cardinals victory in Game Four. Wainwright returned for Game Five and continued the abuse of Pirates hitters with a complete-game victory.

Series MVP: Wainwright stole the show for St. Louis with .106 ChampAdded. He was dominant in Game One, but it was his complete game in the series clincher that sealed his role as the MVP. The Cardinals lineup was nice enough to spot Wainwright with a comfortable lead in both games.

Series Goat: Starling Marte was the Pirates' breakout star in 2013, but the postseason did not go his way. He went just 3-for-24 with one walk. He did manage to hit a home run, but it came in a game that the Pirates were already winning 6-1, so it didn't help his personal cause. His ChampAdded totaled -.072.

Big Play: Through most of the 2013 postseason, David Freese seemed nothing like the guy who practically won the 2011 World Series single-handedly. However, he did contribute the biggest play of the division series. The two-run home run Freese delivered in the second inning of the series finale netted .053 ChampAdded.

AL Division Series: Tampa Bay Rays vs. Boston Red Sox

The Rays took the long road to the ALDS, first defeating the Texas Rangers in Game 163 and then the Indians in the AL Wild Card game. Having burned through David Price and Cobb to reach the division series, the Rays turned to Matt Moore to start Game One. The Sox spanked both him and reliever Jamie Wright as part of a 12-2 victory. They continued the assault in Game Two by plating seven runs against Price.

An exciting Game Three went the Rays' way. Evan Longoria tied the game in the fifth with a three-run home run. With two outs and the score tied 4-4 in the bottom of the ninth, backup catcher Jose Lobaton played the unlikely hero with a walkoff home run.

The Rays went all-hands-on-deck for Game Four, calling on nine pitchers total. The plan worked in the early innings, with the Rays carrying a narrow 1-0 lead into the seventh, but Rays reliever Jake McGee was charged with two runs. The Red Sox later tacked on one more against Fernando Rodney and that was all she wrote for the Rays.

Series MVP: Shane Victorino managed to hit just .216/.333/.314 over the course of the postseason, yet he played hero for the Red Sox on multiple occasions.

He was busiest in the Division Series. He stroked six hits in 14 plate appearances while compiling a .041 ChampAdded. Hitting early and often in a series that featured three close ballgames is a good way to earn the MVP honors.

Series Goat: In an unusual twist, the series goat is Joel Peralta with -.036 ChampAdded. The twist is that Peralta technically allowed zero runs in 2.1 innings.

Here's how it happened. In Game Four, the Rays headed into the seventh with a 1-0 lead. McGee began the inning and recorded the first two outs. He also allowed two base runners, so manager Joe Maddon turned to Peralta to finish the inning.

A wild pitch to Victorino allowed Xander Bogaerts to score from third base. Victorino later singled to drive home Jacoby Ellsbury. And that's how Peralta blew the lead without being charged with the runs.

Big Play: The Rays squandered one of the top feel-good moments of the postseason. Lobaton's walkoff home run in Game Three was all kinds of unlikely. Without Wil Myers' injury, Lobaton would not have been batting in that spot. Frankly, it was an example of extremely suboptimal management by Maddon that happened to work out in the Rays' favor. The play itself was worth .030 ChampAdded.

AL Division Series: Detroit Tigers vs. Oakland Athletics

In recent history, the Athletics have had a hard time advancing past the Division Series and the Tigers in particular. Since 2000, they have appeared in seven postseasons. In one, they reached the ALCS, but they were swept by the Tigers that year. The A's were knocked out in the Division Series the other six times, all by a 3-2 game margin.

2013 was one of those years. The series featured some great pitching performances. Scherzer dazzled in Game One, but Justin Verlander and Sonny Gray stole the show in Game Two with an excellent pitching duel. The game ended when A's catcher Stephen Vogt hit a bases-loaded, walk-off single in the ninth.

The two teams split the third and fourth games, bringing about a rematch between Verlander and Gray. This time, the Tigers chased Gray after five-plus innings, while Verlander twirled an eight-inning gem. The A's managed just two hits and a walk and struck out 10 times. Miguel Cabrera's two-run home run in the fourth was more than enough to propel the Tigers to a 3-0 victory and the ALCS.

Series MVP: Verlander had the spottiest season of his impressive career, but his postseason run was excellent. He was the top hero of the Division Series round with .140 ChampAdded. While the A's did manage to win their first game against him, he shut them down in the decisive Game 5.

Series Goat: Anibal Sanchez started Game Three in the Division Series and it did not go his way. He allowed six runs in 4.1 innings. Meanwhile, the Tigers offense actually kept the game close until the fifth inning. Sanchez blew a tied ballgame twice, which allowed him to rack up -.057 ChampAdded.

Big Play: Miguel Cabrera spent much of the 2013 season reigning over the Tigers lineup like Zeus, but he was noticeably mortal in the postseason. Injuries held Cabrera to a meager .262/.311/.405 line, but he did manage to deliver a very timely blast in Game Five that was worth .057 ChampAdded. With Verlander dealing, the two-run home run was all the Tigers would need.

NL Championship Series: Los Angeles Dodgers vs. St. Louis Cardinals

The Legend of Carlos Beltran grew a little taller in Game One of the NLCS when he smacked a walk-off hit in the bottom of the 13th inning. Hanley Ramirez—who helped carry the Dodgers offense in the Division Series—was hit by a pitch and suffered a broken rib early in the game. He played through the injury, but was a non-factor in the series.

A pair of pitching duels followed, as Wacha outlasted Kershaw in Game Two and Hyun-Jin Ryu outperformed Wainwright in Game Three.

The next two games were split. Matt Holliday played hero in Game Four for the Cardinals, and Adrian Gonzalez carried the Dodgers in Game Five with a pair of home runs.

With the series 3-2 Cardinals and headed back to St. Louis, the Dodgers put Kershaw back on the hill in a rematch against Wacha. The Cardinals' rookie ace threw another gem, but Kershaw allowed 10 hits, two walks, and seven runs over just four innings. The Cardinals coasted to a 9-0 victory.

Series MVP: Beltran winning a series MVP is not a surprise. He does this year after year (at least when his team reaches the postseason). His .286/.423/.476 line over 26 plate appearances was good, but hardly mind-blowing. However, he provided some timely hitting. His two runs scored and six RBI accounted for eight of the 21 runs scored by the Cardinals in the series and .111 ChampAdded.

An honorable mention goes to Wacha. If we consider just his pitching numbers, his .114 ChampAdded beats Beltran. Unfortunately, Wacha gave away -.015 ChampAdded as a hitter.

Series Goat: You wouldn't expect a batter with only seven plate appearances to be the series goat, but that's exactly what Michael Young accomplished. He totaled -.098 ChampAdded, as he made big outs in big spots, including the big play of the series.

Big Play: In the 10th inning of Game 1, Young came to the plate with runners on first and third and one out. He flied out to right field. A.J. Ellis—the runner on third—was caught at home when he tried to tag. That failed sac fly amounted to -.050 ChampAdded.

AL Championship Series: Detroit Tigers vs. Boston Red Sox

The Tigers opened the series with an interesting victory. Anibal Sanchez no-hit the Red Sox through six innings, but he did walk six batters. The pen provided some tidier work, with just one hit allowed over the final three frames.

Detroit looked to have an easy win in Game Two until David Ortiz erased a 5-1 deficit in the eighth with a grand slam. Jarrod Saltalamachia completed the come-from-behind victory in the ninth.

The Red Sox built a 3-2 series lead heading into Game Six. The Tigers failed to sustain a rally in the sixth inning, which included a bad baserunning gaffe by Prince Fielder. In the Red Sox half of the seventh, a questionable non-strike call and a costly error by Tigers shortstop Jose Iglesias set the stage for a Victorino grand slam that capped the game.

Series MVP: Koji Uehara was leaned upon heavily in the ALCS. He provided six innings of scoreless baseball and struck out nine. Most of those outings were in high leverage situations, which is why he racked up .176 ChampAdded. He recorded three saves and also finished the final game.

Series Goat: Even though the Red Sox won the series, it was Stephen Drew who played goat. That's what happens when you contribute a painful 1-for-20 performance with one walk and 10 strikeouts. Some of those 19 outs came in important situations, which led to his -.102 ChampAdded. His inability to provide any offense also indirectly resulted in a crazy walk-off win during the World Series.

Big Play: Victorino shows up once again despite his tepid postseason numbers. His grand slam in the seventh inning of Game Six was one of the biggest individual plays of the postseason by any measure. It allowed the Red Sox to overcome a 2-1 deficit and clinch the series. The play totaled .093 ChampAdded, or close to 10 percent of a World Series championship.

World Series: St. Louis Cardinals vs. Boston Red Sox

The postseason held its fair share of questionable managerial decisions and poor on-field play, but baseball saved some of its worst for the final six games.

The first two games resulted in a fairly tame 1-1 series split. That's where things picked up.

Game Three featured a plethora of managerial gaffes, which ranged from poor reliever usage to Boston manager John Farrell's mismanagement of a double-switch. That mistake resulted in reliever Brandon Workman batting in the ninth inning of a tied ballgame. Of course, that was all just foreshadowing for the biggest mind-trip ending in World Series history—a broken play that resulted in a walk-off obstruction call and a Cardinals win.

The mistakes continued in Game Four, in which Cardinals manager Mike Matheny attempted to ride starter Lance Lynn an inning too long. It set up a three-run home run by Jonny Gomes against Cardinals reliever Seth Maness. The Sox probably had a win in the bag with a 4-2 lead in the ninth. Cardinals rookie Kolten Wong had entered as a pinch runner on first base, and with two outs, Carlos Beltran was at the plate. But instead of giving Beltran the chance to play hero yet again, Wong was picked off to end the game.

Games Five and Six were anticlimactic by comparison. The Sox won both games, including an easy 6-1 win in the series clincher.

Series MVP: The Red Sox lineup generally struggled throughout the World Series, with the exception of one hitter. Ortiz dominated the Cardinals with an unholy .688/.760/1.188 line. That breaks down as an 11-for-16 performance with eight walks, four intentional walks, seven runs scored, and six RBI. His dominance was worth 34 percent of a championship, or .340 ChampAdded.

Series Goat: Cardinals fans would have you believe that Matheny was the series goat. After all, he was responsible for quite a few mistakes with the pitching staff. Fans and analysts alike wondered where Shelby Miller and Edward Mujica were and why they were clogging the roster if they weren't going to play. There's also the whole matter of the 12 walks to Ortiz, most of which were intentional to some degree. Unfortunately, ChampAdded doesn't measure managerial influence, so we don't know concretely if Matheny was the goat.

As in the ALCS, the actual goat was a member of the Red Sox. Craig Breslow appeared in three games, but retired only one batter, and was charged with two runs. All three outings went poorly for him, but the first included a double error by Saltalamacchia and Breslow that propelled the Cardinals to victory. His combined ChampAdded was -.222. Stated differently, he "contributed" 22 percent of a championship to the Cardinals.

Big Play: Many an analyst speculated that Gomes shouldn't have been in the starting lineup against St. Louis' phalanx of right-handed starting pitchers. In retrospect, Red Sox fans should be very happy that he did. His home run in the sixth inning of Game Four earned the Red Sox the lead and eventually the game. The play went for .139 ChampAdded. Hidden in the box score is one of those pesky unintentional, intentional walks to Ortiz.

Victorino very nearly returned for another cameo. His three-run double in Game 6 broke open the scoring, but the .127 ChampAdded narrowly trailed Gomes' homer.

Playoff MVP: With some help from the opposing manager, Ortiz really turned it on when it mattered most. Nearly all of his ChampAdded came in the World Series, which was precisely when the Red Sox needed it.

His World Series performance was historic and includes the second-highest batting average and on-base percentage behind Billy Hatcher in the 1990 World Series. Ortiz also ranks seventh in OPS and is tied for eighth in slugging percentage. His ChampAdded total was the second-greatest performance by any batter in a series that didn't go seven games, bested only by Willie Mays Aikens of Kansas City in the 1980 World Series (you can read more on historic postseasons in Dave Studenmund's article elsewhere in this *Annual*).

As an interesting aside, Lester's pitching totaled .287 ChampAdded, but negative hitting outcomes dropped him to fifth on this list.

Player	Team	ChampAdded
David Ortiz	BOS	.352
John Lackey	BOS	.244
Carlos Beltran	STL	.238
Shane Victorino	BOS	.223
Jon Lester	BOS	.206
Justin Verlander	DET	.195
Trevor Rosenthal	STL	.148
Xander Bogaerts	BOS	.139
Koji Uehara	BOS	.137
Jonny Gomes	BOS	.111

The Chief of the Goats was Drew, whose futility also led to a substitution in Game Three of the World Series that hurt the Red Sox even more. Overall, he went 6-for-54 with two walks and 19 strikeouts.

Player	Team	ChampAdded
Stephen Drew	BOS	-.226
Matt Adams	STL	-.197
Craig Breslow	BOS	-.143
Jarrod Saltalamacchia	BOS	-.131
David Freese	STL	-.123
Omar Infante	DET	-.120
Pete Kozma	STL	-.107
Seth Maness	STL	-.107
Michael Young	LAD	-.100
Daniel Descalso	STL	-.085

Saltalamacchia probably deserves a goatier stew than we observe here. His mistakes featured prominently in both World Series losses for the Red Sox, yet neither play was charged against his ChampAdded. Farrell picked up on this though, and left him on the bench for the final two games of the Fall Classic.

References

- Dave Studenmund, "The One About Win Probability," The Hardball Times, *hardballtimes.com/main/article/the-one-about-win-probability*

Commentary

The Year in Frivolity

by Craig Calcaterra

This book is chock full of information about the 2013 baseball season. If you read even a portion of it and don't know who won, who lost, and why this past year, there's no helping you.

But you can be forgiven if you forgot the year's ephemeral, trivial, embarrassing and pathetic events. That stuff doesn't stick in a fan's mind like who won the Most Valuable Player Award. That's why I'm here. So, without further ado, I give you an overview of all things funny, sad, stupid and ignominious of the 2013 baseball season!

Off-season and Spring Training

Spring training opens with the specter of performance-enhancing drugs looming. In late January, it is reported by the Miami New-Times that several players— including Ryan Braun and Alex Rodriguez—patronized an anti-aging clinic in Miami called Biogenesis, and received banned PEDs from its crooked owner. This offends the sensibilities of baseball officials, who are hellbent on retaining the monopoly on crooked owners for themselves.

A week after the Biogenesis report comes out, Curt Schilling reveals that as a player the Boston Red Sox encouraged him to use performance-enhancing drugs in an effort to get back on the field following an injury. This is shocking news to all who hear it, as the one-week delay marks the longest time Schilling has waited to insert himself into a public controversy that has nothing to do with him whatsoever.

Rockies first baseman Todd Helton is arrested for drunk driving in Colorado. It is revealed that Helton—who has made over $150 million playing baseball—had been at home, but left to go to a nearby gas station to purchase lottery tickets after drinking several red Solo cups full of wine. All agree that for all of his fame and riches, it is admirable that Helton has not outgrown his eastern Tennessee roots.

The Giants' Brandon Belt is quoted disparaging the Los Angeles Dodgers and their big-spending ways, claiming that "you can't buy good chemistry." Meanwhile, in Miami, Marlins hitting coach Tino Martinez compares the 2013 Marlins to his 1996 Yankees in terms of character and esprit de corps. The Giants finish in fourth place, the Marlins lose 100 games and Martinez is fired in midseason after a shouting match and physical confrontations with his own players. Experts disagree on when, exactly, the Giants and Marlins ceased to have good chemistry, but are unanimous in holding that chemistry is not a retrospective characterization applied to winning teams as opposed to an actual thing that is totally not baloney.

In mid-February Miguel Montero is quoted blasting former teammate Trevor Bauer for his immaturity and for failing to take instruction from coaches and veteran players. This is not the first time Montero has publicly criticized a former teammate, so many take his words with a grain of salt. Later that month, however, Bauer releases a rap song in which he "disses haters." Upon hearing the song, the public lines up to apologize to Montero for ever doubting his judgment.

April

Despite previously saying that he would be ready for Opening Day, Yankees shortstop Derek Jeter is placed on the disabled list to start the season due to a small fracture in the leg he broke in last year's American League Championship Series. The Yankees' captain, however, assures fans that he will be back and ready to play soon.

Yankees second baseman Robinson Cano, who will be a free agent following the 2013 season, fires agent Scott Boras and hires rapper Jay-Z to represent him. When asked why he made the move, Cano referred to the free-agency portfolios Boras had previously compiled for his clients, such as the one in which Oliver Perez was compared to a young Sandy Koufax. "I'm a humble person," Cano says, "and frankly, I prefer the more reasonable claims of superiority and self-worth one can find in the rap industry to the over-the-top braggadocio typical of my previous agent."

Josh Hamilton, now a member of the Angels, returns to Texas for the first time since leaving the Rangers via free agency. Rangers fans have more ire for Hamilton than one usually sees for a player who left via free agency due to comments Hamilton made in the offseason about Dallas not being "a baseball town." All 11 of the people in the stands at the Ballpark at Arlington boo Hamilton. The other 40,000 who would normally be in attendance couldn't make it because Dallas Cowboys coach Jason Garrett was going to be on local news that night talking about what he might do during offensive drills at an upcoming Cowboys minicamp.

In other Angels news, Albert Pujols, who posted his worst season in 2012 and who has started off slowly once again, says that he will walk away from his 10-year, $240 million contract if he is not able to perform up to his usual standards. When he is shut down for the season at the end of July, his performance still not having rebounded, Pujols says, "Well, I started walking away from the contract. I really did. But then my foot started hurting really bad and I just couldn't do it."

One year after they opened a publicly-funded ballpark and signed multiple high-priced free agents, the Marlins gut their roster and put a team on the field consisting of unproven youngsters and nearly anonymous veterans. With fan morale at an all-time low, a handful of fans show up to an early April Marlins game wearing t-shirts and carrying signs critical of team owner Jeff Loria. Loria, never one to take criticism well, has the protesting fans ejected from the ballpark. Loria's impetuous decision immediately reduces Marlins season-long attendance by 47 percent.

Reports swirl that representatives of Alex Rodriguez attempted to purchase the records of the Biogenesis clinic, which Major League Baseball is actively pursuing and which purport to establish Rodriguez's use of performance-enhancing drugs. A-Rod assures MLB, however, that he is merely attempting to make sure nothing happens to the documents and that he will be sure to place them in his personal safe just as soon as he gets back from the bonfire being held by some of his good friends who happen to own a paper shredding business.

Adam Dunn, who at the time is hitting a cool .108, tells reporters that "if people didn't post people's batting averages on the scoreboard or in the media, people would be batting .400. I'm serious. I believe that." Surprisingly, most experts agree with Dunn that people would be batting .400 if less attention were paid. That is, other people. Dunn himself, it is believed, would still likely be hitting around .217.

San Diego Padres CEO Tom Garfinkel is secretly recorded referring to Dodgers pitcher Zack Greinke's social anxiety disorder via reference to the movie in which Dustin Hoffman provided an over-the-top and often inaccurate portrayal of a person with exaggerated, challenging and often maddening personality traits and quirks. "Garfinkel's comments were way out of line," one noted mental health activist says in a prepared statement. "There is absolutely no comparison between the behaviors of those with social anxiety disorder and that awful schtick Hoffman performed in Meet the Fockers."

May

Yankees shortstop Derek Jeter, who has been rehabbing his broken leg, suffers a setback when he runs too hard during his rehab, leading to stiffness and soreness which will require more recovery time. The Yankees captain, however, assures fans that he will be back and ready to play soon.

Researchers at the University of Electro-Communications in Tokyo and the Okinawa Institute of Science and Technology announce that they have created a robot that can play baseball. Its sophisticated brain crunches pitch trajectory data so that it can determine exactly when the robot should swing. If the scientists change the pitch speed, the robot will relearn the task all over again. Scientific opinion as to the robot's utility is mixed. On the one hand, it seems superfluous in a world containing Mike Trout. On the other hand it seems like a major breakthrough in a world containing Delmon Young.

New York authorities make multiple arrests in connection with a Russian high-stakes poker ring which, at one time, counted Alex Rodriguez as one of its most prominent players. Many speculate as to whether A-Rod is still involved in the poker games. He assures Major League Baseball, however, that if he says his days of engaging in illicit activity are behind him, you can take him at his word on that.

Blue Jays analysts Dirk Hayhurst and Jack Morris accuse Red Sox pitcher Clay Buchholz of doctoring the baseball during a start against the Jays. The suspected foreign substance: sunscreen, which Hayhurst and Morris believe Buchholz has slathered on his forearm. Buchholz denies the allegations, saying that if he had sunscreen on his arm it was only because he's very careful about avoiding excessive exposure to the sun, because everyone knows that's bad for you. When it's pointed out that the game was being played in Rogers Centre under a retractable roof, Buchholz points behind reporters, says "what's that?" and runs in the other direction.

Adam Rosales of the Oakland A's hits what appears to be a game-tying home run against the Cleveland Indians, but it is erroneously ruled a double by umpire Angel Hernandez and the Indians go on to win the game. There is considerable talk afterwards of MLB overturning the call and forcing the teams to replay the end of the game, but the idea is rejected due to lack of precedent. Not precedent prohibiting the replay of games—that has happened before—but lack of precedent in which MLB has acknowledged that Hernandez is an awful, awful umpire.

After a series of transactions, Yankees outfielder Ben Francisco still manages to stay on the big league roster roster despite the fact that he's hitting a mere .114 in 21 games. When asked why Francisco wasn't demoted or released, Yankees general manager Brian Cashman says that he's "holding on to him to piss everyone off." Fans report back: "it's working."

After years of resisting the public's calls for expanded instant replay, commissioner Bud Selig—who once said that he has never heard fan complaints on the matter because he does not have access to email—says his position on the matter has "evolved" and that baseball will soon expand replay. Sources close to Selig suggest that this evolution is the result of the commissioner receiving a promotional CD-ROM for dial-up service from America Online, after which a man's voice told him "[he's] got mail," whereupon he found several million complaints dating back to 1994. Selig subsequently announces that all replay reviews will be conducted via state-of-the-art digital video, which will be transmitted to MLB headquarters via lightning-quick 56K baud connections. The only downside: Game times are expected to increase by several hours due to buffering.

June

Yankees shortstop Derek Jeter, still rehabbing his broken leg, has his recovery timetable altered once again. This time there is nothing wrong with the leg. Rather he is the victim of a freak accident in which he fell down the empty elevator shaft of his Midtown Manhattan condominium, suffering multiple injuries. The Yankees captain, however, assures fans that he will be back and ready to play soon.

With their offense stalling and the development of their young hitters going poorly, the Kansas City Royals call on Hall of Famer George Brett to become their new hitting coach. Brett holds the position for just under two months before returning to his front office job. During Brett's tenure the Royals go 22-26 and see their team batting average dip from .261 to .248, on-base percentage drop from .314 to .309

and runs per game decline from 3.98 to 3.81. During his farewell press conference the Royals hang a "Mission Accomplished" banner and GM Dayton Moore presents Brett with a Medal of Freedom.

The Dodgers' awful start continues and they fall to 9.5 games back of first place as speculation swirls about not if manager Don Mattingly will be fired, but when. As things hit rock bottom, general manager Ned Colletti calls up prospect Yasiel Puig from Double-A Chattanooga. As if some Double-A rookie who is overly-aggressive on the basepaths and has holes in his swing can ignite a season turnaround. I mean, c'mon.

Shin-Soo Choo is hit by a pitch for the 12th time so far this season, putting him on pace to challenge Hughie Jennings for the all-time major league HBP record. Asked for comment, Choo said "Ow."

It is reported that Major League Baseball's investigation into the Biogenesis matter will ultimately result in mass suspensions, with Alex Rodriguez and Ryan Braun chief among the suspects in the league's crosshairs. Braun, who has long maintained his innocence, releases a statement in which he says "the truth has not changed." Which, for as much flak as Braun has taken over all of this, is a technically true statement if you think about it.

Indians closer Chris Perez and his wife are arrested for drug possession after a package containing marijuana is delivered to their Cleveland-area home. The package is actually addressed to the Perez's dog. The Cleveland Indians issue a statement commending the Perez family for taking responsibility and hoping that the Perez's dog can get the help it needs to break its awful drug addiction.

Cubs third baseman Ian Stewart, frustrated that he's playing in Triple-A Iowa rather than in the big leagues, writes a series of tweets lamenting his lot with the organization and voicing his belief that the Cubs were content to let him rot in the minors and then non-tender him after the season. Cubs GM Jed Hoyer shows, however, that nothing could be further from the truth: He lets Stewart rot in the minors for only a couple more weeks and then releases him.

Following a Mariners-A's game, raw sewage floods the visitors clubhouse in the Oakland Coliseum, forcing the Mariners to share shower facilities with the A's. Major League Baseball, already four years into one study about the increasing untenability of the Oakland A's stadium situation, vows to launch Study Number Two.

July

Yankees shortstop Derek Jeter finally recovers from his multiple injuries and returns to the field. He plays four games in the space of 20 days, after which he is diagnosed with dropsy, rickets, beri-beri and a strain of swamp fever experts had previously thought was eradicated. The Yankees captain, however, assures fans that he will be back and ready to play soon.

Bill Madden of the New York Daily News compares Alex Rodriguez to gangster Whitey Bulger. Back in May, another New York columnist, Bob Klapisch, compares A-Rod to Freddy Krueger. On the surface, these comparisons seem preposterously overheated. After all, Bulger stands accused of killing at least 18 people and Krueger murdered hundreds across nine movies. Madden and Klapisch acknowledge that but remind us that at least Bulger and Krueger did it the right way, without resorting to a syringe for their accomplishments. Well, Krueger probably did at some point—he got pretty creative in the latter movies. But seriously: A-Rod is the worst.

Orioles first baseman Chris Davis continues his torrid home run pace en route to a breakout, 53-home run season. Speculation is rampant, however, that Davis must be using performance-enhancing drugs, with columnists such as Rick Teland- er of the Chicago Sun-Times essentially leveling accusations. He and others make comparisons to another Orioles hitter who had a breakout home run season: Brady Anderson, who hit 50 in 1996. If Davis is using PEDs, one hopes that he obtained better drugs than Anderson did, as Anderson's worked only for a single year and then, somehow, became totally ineffective the following season.

On the heels of another patriotism-packed Fourth of July around the majors, ESPN columnist Howard Bryant observes that conspicuous displays of patriotism at ballparks since Sept. 11, 2001, have become mechanical, rote and obligatory and that, perhaps, this has caused them to become empty in important ways. Many commend the column as "gutsy," but find his concern misguided and, in some cases, threat- ening. No one, however, seems to acknowledge that calling a critique of how one exercises or declines to exercise political expression "gutsy" sort of makes Bryant's point for him.

The All-Star Game takes place at Citi Field in New York. The American League beats the National League, 3-0, but the highlight of the game is Mariano Rivera's final appearance in the Midsummer Classic. He is awarded the game's Most Valuable Player Award despite pitching in the eighth inning rather than the ninth and despite the fact that Joe Nathan, not Rivera, got the save. It almost, but not quite, causes people to wonder whether (a) pitching in the ninth inning truly is a bigger deal than other innings; and (b) the All-Star Game truly counts as Bud Selig and Major League Baseball so desperately tell us it does or if, rather, it's a meaningless exhibi- tion. Bryant considers writing a column to that effect, but even he isn't gutsy enough to challenge such ingrained orthodoxy.

Mets starter Matt Harvey turns heads when he poses nude in ESPN The Maga- zine's "Body Issue," which features provocative photos of the day's most notable athletes. The issue sets sales records over previous years' versions containing New York Mets players such as the 2002 "Body Issue" featuring Mo Vaughn and the 1997 issue featuring Rick Reed.

Reds second baseman Brandon Phillips gives a magazine interview in which he voices his displeasure with Reds ownership giving Joey Votto a $200 million contract extension while giving Phillips only a $75 million deal, which he calls a "slap in my face." One gets the impression that Phillips has never truly been slapped in the face. Because, really, it's way less enjoyable than getting $75 million is.

Major League Baseball suspends Brewers outfielder Ryan Braun for 65 games for his involvement with the Biogenesis clinic and his use of performance-enhancing drugs. Notably, 65 games just happens to be the number of games the Brewers have remaining in the season at the time the suspension is announced. Major League Baseball issues a statement defending the length of the suspension and maintaining that it was based on Braun's level of culpability compared to others in the Biogenesis matter, not a mere desire to see him suspended for the remainder of the season. "Ryan Braun would have been more culpable if our investigation had been wrapped up a couple of games earlier, less culpable if it had taken a couple of games more," a MLB spokesman does not add.

August

Yankees shortstop Derek Jeter plays a game on Aug. 2, but then misses the next 24 days of the season following a horrific zeppelin accident in which 30 souls were lost, 40 more injured and three went missing. The Yankees captain, however, assures fans that he will be back and ready to play soon.

Major League Baseball announces discipline in connection with the Biogenesis scandal for 12 players, all of whom have agreed to 50-game suspensions and have agreed not to appeal. Among those disciplined are New York Yankees catcher Francisco Cervelli, New York Mets outfielder Jordany Valdespin, minor-league players Fernando Martinez, Cesar Puello and Sergio Escalona and free agents Jordan Norberto and Fautino de los Santos. In an official statement, Bud Selig says that "these suspensions will send a message to others that Ds are not acceptable in today's game." When asked if the statement contained a typographical error and should have read "PEDs are not acceptable..." Selig said "have you seen the stat lines on these guys? There was no 'PE' about it."

After being unable to reach a settlement, MLB announces that it has suspended Alex Rodriguez for 211 games as a result of the Biogenesis scandal. In light of this unprecedented discipline which could feasibly end A-Rod's career, baseball observers begin to speculate whether his legacy will be tainted by his suspension. This is only a passing concern, however, as most eventually recall that A-Rod's legacy had been systematically tarnished, multiple times a year, through his own acts and omissions and through the criticism of others—fair or otherwise—dating back at least 12 years and maybe longer. Indeed, it comes as more of a surprise that there are still any scraps of his legacy over which to fight.

Following an A's-Rangers game in which Matt Garza engages in a shouting match with A's infielder Eric Sogard on the field, Sogard's wife offers a couple of relatively harmless jokes about it on Twitter. Garza then takes to Twitter and says of Sogard, "certain people can't shut there [sic] women up!" He adds that where he comes from "women don't speak up" for their husbands and that Sogard's wife should "give [her] husband his balls back." Observers believe that where Garza, who is married and is a father of two daughters, will soon "come from" is a somewhat dreary apartment complex a short drive from his former family's home in which he will be granted visitation rights every two weeks and from where he will write substantial alimony checks for the foreseeable future.

Former Cardinals first baseman-turned-radio-host Jack Clark takes to the airwaves to accuse fellow former Cardinals first baseman Albert Pujols of using PEDs. Pujols issues a quick denial, Clark is fired and, later, Pujols sues Clark for defamation. On the undercard, Bob Horner fights Pedro Guerrero, Andres Galarraga fights Keith Hernandez and a tag team match pitting Mark McGwire and Craig Paquette against John Mabry and Tino Martinez are featured. Orlando Cepeda is the honorary referee.

Major League Baseball announces that, starting in 2014, instant replay will be substantially expanded. The kicker: A challenge system will be introduced in which managers have a certain number of opportunities to challenge questionable calls during the course of the game. A process in which the mistakes of umpires suddenly become the responsibility of managers puts to rest any dispute regarding whose union is the strongest in the world.

Kansas City Royals infielder Miguel Tejada is suspended 105 games for testing positive for amphetamines. In other news, Miguel Tejada is still playing baseball? Really? I'll be damned.

The Los Angeles Dodgers complete a run in which they have won 42 of 50 games to catapult themselves into first place in the National League West. The Dodgers, composed of high-priced free agents, castoffs from losing teams and alleged head cases of various stripes, force baseball writers everywhere to reassess their beliefs about home-grown players, character and team chemistry being the key to winning. Hahaha, just kidding. It really causes them to make up silly stories about how these players have "changed their attitude" and "learned to play as a team," despite there being no discernible change on the part of anyone on the roster apart from their health and batting average on balls in play.

September

Yankees shortstop Derek Jeter returns to action on Sept. 1 and plays for seven straight days without injury or incident. The Yankees shut him down for the season on the seventh, however, after the Acme Anvil & Giant Rocket Corporation opens up directly across from Yankee Stadium. The Yankees captain says "man, forget this. I'm too rich and too pretty to keep doing this to myself."

After a series of incidents in which Yasiel Puig misses cutoff men, runs the bases recklessly and, on one occasion, arrives at the ballpark late, Dodgers manager Don Mattingly benches Puig. The benching lasts only a few innings, however, as Mattingly calls on Puig to pinch hit, whereupon he hits a game-winning home run. Columnist Bill Plaschke laments the fact that Mattingly didn't bench Puig for the whole game, writing "Mattingly showed that he's unwilling to possibly sacrifice a victory to finish the lecture...With one swing Puig won a game, but, in playing him, the Dodgers risked losing much more." After he files his column, the *Los Angeles Times* suspends Plaschke from the Dodgers beat and requires him to attend remedial baseball training classes so he may learn what, exactly, the bleedin' point of the game he purports to cover truly is.

Ryan Braun, in an effort to atone for his use of performance-enhancing drugs and overall deceit, personally calls Milwaukee Brewers season ticket holders to apologize for his transgressions. Ten percent of the call recipients were not home, 35 percent never answered because they had caller I.D. and thought it was a 2014 season ticket sales pitch and 55 percent thought it was their brother-in-law, Marty, pulling a prank. Marty is notorious for that in Wisconsin.

Alex Rodriguez, having made his return to the Yankees lineup in August, has put together a few weeks of decent performance and, with it, the Yankees are unexpectedly challenging for the American League Wild Card. This produces many hand-wrings over the prospect of baseball's Public Enemy No. 1 appearing in the playoffs. Bud Selig would not comment on the matter, but all of his public relations staffers are too busy writing glowing press releases about high playoff television ratings to be bothered to return calls from the media.

The Pirates win their 82nd game and, with it, break a 20-year streak of losing seasons in Pittsburgh. Derek Bell awakes on his houseboat, looks at the standings in a newspaper and decides that now is the time to end Operation Shutdown. Neal Huntington inexplicably does not return his calls.

Bobby Valentine gives an interview in which he complains about how, 12 years prior, the Yankees were nowhere near as active in the community following the Sept. 11 attacks as were the Mets. People are not shocked that Valentine would use 9/11 as a means of self-promotion and the settling of personal scores. They're mostly shocked that he waited 12 years to do it.

Barry Bonds loses the appeal of his 2011 conviction for obstruction of justice in connection with the BALCO investigation. He will soon be forced to serve his sentence of 30 days of home confinement. Bonds, for what it's worth, resides in a six-bedroom, 10-bathroom Beverly Hills estate that he purchased in 2002 for $8.7 million. Yet people still insist on claiming that he lost his criminal trial.

Rockies first baseman Todd Helton announces his retirement. In his public statement Helton says that he feels he can still be a productive major league ballplayer but that since he won the $10,000 in the "Bucks-a-Palooza" scratch-off game, he finally feels he can afford to retire. Later that month in an emotional ceremony, the Colorado Rockies bid Helton farewell in his final home game. Among the tributes and gifts given to Helton is a $45,000 horse who will live on his 4,000-acre ranch.

The Rockies thoughtfully equip the horse with two Solo cup holders and install a hitching post for it outside the convenience store closest to his ranch.

The Red Sox, fresh off an epic collapse in 2011 and a nightmare year in 2012, clinch the AL East title and the AL's best record as well. Most observers credit team chemistry and cite the departure of players and coaches who were on the scene for the bad old days of the previous two years. These same people fail to acknowledge, somehow, that the Dodgers—who feature Adrian Gonzalez and Carl Crawford on their roster—and the Indians—who are now managed by Terry Francona—are also playoff-bound. That's because most observers tend to be slaves to their preferred narratives.

October

The playoffs. All of the fans pray for an A's-Pirates World Series. All of the people at the Fox Network and Major League Baseball headquarters pray for the Dodgers to play the Red Sox. Judge for yourself whose prayers are more important in the grand scheme of things.

Six Years to Glory: The Pirates Return to October

by John Perrotto

Neal Huntington admits he doesn't take time to enjoy certain moments as much as he should.

The Pittsburgh Pirates general manager spent six years working non-stop to turn one of the worst franchises in professional sports into one that qualified for the postseason for the first time in 21 years in 2013. Huntington is equally driven to try to keep the Pirates competitive for a number of years to come, dispelling notions that his organization is a one-year wonder and understanding the constraints of running a team in one of the major leagues' smaller markets.

Yet in the hours leading up to Game One of the National League Division Series at Busch Stadium in St. Louis, Huntington allowed himself a chance to bask in the moment. Two nights earlier, the Pirates had dispatched the Cincinnati Reds 6-2 in the NL Wild Card Game before a raucous home crowd at PNC Park and now they were getting ready to take on the Cardinals.

"This is really special," Huntington said as he stood in front of the visitor's dugout watching his team take batting practice. "This is what you hope for while you're putting in all those hours, making all those calls and watching all those games. It's pretty neat."

The Pirates were certainly one of the neater stories in baseball in 2013. They not only got to the postseason but ended a streak of 20 consecutive losing seasons. It was the longest stretch of sub-.500 finishes in the history of major North American professional sports.

Yet to tell the story of the 2013 Pirates and how the franchise broke through the two-decade malaise of losing, it is instructive to go back to when Huntington was hired on Sept. 25, 2007.

The Pirates were in disarray.

Dave Littlefield made an overwhelming number of bad moves during his seven years as GM, but the topper came two months earlier when he traded with the San Francisco Giants for broken-down pitcher Matt Morris and took on the remaining $14 million on his contract. The Pirates were stumbling to a 68-94 finish under manager Jim Tracy, who had become disconnected from his players, and there was little help coming from one of the most fallow farm systems in the game.

Into the breach stepped Huntington, then a fresh-faced 38-year-old who had worked his way up to farm director and then special assistant to the general manager with the Cleveland Indians, but had never interviewed for a GM position. Huntington won over Pirates owner Bob Nutting and club president Frank Coonelly with a comprehensive plan to turn the franchise around, including large helpings of scouting and sabermetrics.

"I think there is a tremendous opportunity here with the Pittsburgh Pirates," Huntington said on the day he was hired. "We're going to change the culture. We're going to change how we do things. Every one of our decisions will be a progressive process in bringing a winner back to Pittsburgh."

At the time Huntington was hired, the Pirates did not have any full-time statistical analysts and their scouting staff was one of the smallest in the major leagues. Huntington convinced Nutting that the best way for a small-market team to win was to scout and sign players who could form the backbone of the major league club and use sabermetrics to help identify players who could be obtained at a reasonable cost in trades or free agency.

Six years later, there is a totally different culture, and it goes beyond the Pirates finishing with a 94-68 record.

Nutting committed to spending more in the draft and on the international free agent market, while also upgrading player development facilities at the Pirates' spring training base in Bradenton, Fla., and in the Dominican Republic. Now, the Pirates have a deep farm system, particularly from a pitching standpoint. They also have a five-person army of numbers crunchers and are one of the most sabermetric-savvy major league organizations.

It wasn't easy. Huntington faced conflict almost the minute he was hired. Tracy had a year left on his contract and Huntington wanted him to make changes to the coaching staff. When Tracy balked, Huntington fired him and brought in John Russell, then the manager of the Philadelphia Phillies' Triple-A Ottawa farm club.

The quiet Russell was the quintessential "bridge" manager, someone to oversee the team until it reached the point where the Pirates could get serious about winning. After Huntington gutted the major league roster with a series of trades in 2009, the Pirates went into a 57-105 freefall in 2010.

However, Huntington had put together the organization he had envisioned. In addition to purging the roster, he had turned over almost the entire front office and the player development and scouting departments. Huntington felt it was time for the Pirates to have a new face as manager, and they hired Clint Hurdle in November, 2010.

The choice seemed curious on the surface. Hurdle had compiled a 534-625 record in eight seasons with the Colorado Rockies and had won more than 76 games in a season only once—in 2007, when they captured the NL pennant before getting swept in the World Series by the Boston Red Sox.

What Hurdle brought was a change from Russell—a booming voice filled with optimism and the presence to command the attention of any room. The players bought into Hurdle's enthusiasm and his talk of completing the triangle by having the Pirates be equals with Pittsburgh's other two wildly popular professional sports franchises, the National Football League's Steelers and the National Hockey League's Penguins.

The Pirates improved by 15 wins to 72-90 in 2011, and by seven wins to 79-83 in 2012. The only negative is that both teams fell apart in the final two months of the season, going a combined 37-78 from Aug. 1 on.

However, Hurdle kept preaching that the Pirates were on the right path, and that the late-season woes were nothing more than a young team hitting a pothole on the way to eventual success.

"People talk about three-year plans or five-year plans," Hurdle said. "I didn't have a plan coming in. I had a contract, and you'd better get something good done before that thing expires or you won't get another one.

"After my second year, I felt really positive about what was going on. Even as bad as the year finished on the field, the challenges that came with it and the adjustments we made through the winter, I felt really good going into spring training this year. I felt maybe we were ahead of schedule a little bit."

Following the collapse, some fans and media members called for Huntington to be fired—though, curiously, Hurdle seemed to be absolved of most blame. However, Nutting and Coonelly stood behind Huntington, who had two years remaining on his contract, and the Pirates broke through in 2013.

"The support I've received from Bob Nutting from day one has always been great, both from a resources standpoint and an encouragement standpoint," Huntington said.

While Huntington slowly rebuilt the infrastructure in his first five years, he used the 2012-13 offseason to upgrade the roster into one that could be a contender with a series of good moves.

Huntington struck quickly in the free-agent market by signing catcher Russell Martin to a two-year, $17-million contract after the New York Yankees made no effort to re-sign him. The Pirates had the good fortunate of Martin entering free agency during an offseason in which the Yankees were closely watching their spending in hopes of getting their payroll under the $189 million luxury tax threshold for the 2014 season.

"We identified catcher as our No. 1 need in end-of-season meetings, and it became our top priority," Huntington said.

The Pirates' primary catcher in 2012 had been Rod Barajas, who hit .206 with 11 home runs in 104 games and threw out just six percent of runners attempting to steal. Martin's offensive numbers weren't much better, as he posted a .226 batting average and 15 homers in 127 games, but he threw out 40 percent of runners who tried to steal.

"As a small market team, any time those type of dollars are to be committed, there is some hesitation, as our margin for error is much smaller than that of the large markets," Huntington said. "That said, we felt catcher was the spot we could make the biggest impact on our club. We aggressively targeted Russ because of his defensive package, his attitude and energy, and we believed he would have a better offensive season as well.

"We believed Russ could have the largest impact on the Pirates of any realistically attainable player on the free-agent market."

Even in the lean years, Huntington had been able to build good bullpens without spending large sums. He followed that formula again when he re-signed set-up man Jason Grilli to a two-year, $6.75-million contract as a free agent. Then, as part of a six-player deal, he traded arbitration-eligible closer Joel Hanrahan, who had a combined 76 saves in the 2011-12 seasons and was slated to make $7 million in salary arbitration, to the Red Sox for right-handed reliever Mark Melancon.

The Pirates promoted Grilli to closer and installed Melancon as set-up man. They proved to be an outstanding late-inning duo.

Grilli converted 33 of 34 save opportunities with a 2.70 ERA in 54 games, despite missing six weeks during the second half with a strained forearm. Melancon pitched to a 1.39 ERA in 72 games and converted 16 of 20 save chances, a year after posting a 6.20 ERA in 41 games with Boston.

Hanrahan, meanwhile, needed season-ending Tommy John surgery after pitching in just nine games for his new team.

"We were prepared to have both Hanrahan and Grilli at the back end of our bullpen after we re-signed Jason," Huntington said. "We also recognized that we may be able to trade Joel for a package of players that could impact the organization at both the major league and minor league levels.

"We particularly liked Melancon. We had liked him since his days with the Yankees when he was breaking into the big leagues, and felt like he was a quality bounce-back candidate. When we had a chance to get Melancon, it allowed us to relocate the dollars that were available by trading Hanrahan."

That is where the Pirates' final major acquisition came into play: They signed left-handed starter Francisco Liriano, though the courtship and negotiations took some odd turns before the sides signed off on a deal Feb. 8.

The Pirates and Liriano agreed to a two-year, $12.75 million contract, in mid-December pending a physical examination. Liriano was due to come to Pittsburgh on Dec. 26 for the physical, but suffered a broken right arm on Christmas Day when, he said, he playfully slammed a door with two hands at his home in the Dominican Republic in an attempt to startle his children.

A one-year contract with a vesting option was worked out a few days before spring training, guaranteeing Liriano only $1 million.

He earned an additional $2.875 million in bonuses for being on the active roster for 142 days, which also triggered the option that guarantees him an $8 million salary next season, with the opportunity to earn an additional $150,000 in performance bonuses if he pitches as many as 200 innings.

Liriano proved to be a bargain with a breakthrough season at age 29, going 16-8 with a 3.02 ERA in 26 starts, then dominating the Reds for seven innings in the Wild Card game. Liriano's season was fairly shocking considering that a year earlier he had gone a combined 6-12 with a 5.34 ERA in 34 games with the Minnesota Twins and Chicago White Sox.

Liriano became the Pirates' second successful reclamation project from the American League in as many seasons. Just before spring training in 2012, they had acquired right-hander A.J. Burnett from the Yankees for a pair of marginal prospects.

Burnett had posted 5-plus earned run averages in his final two season with the Yankees. With the Pirates, he was 10-11 with a 3.30 ERA this past season after going 16-10 with a 3.51 ERA in 2012.

Both pitchers' strikeout rates told Huntington that they still had good stuff. Burnett averaged 8.2 strikeouts per nine innings in 2011—and led the NL with a 9.8 mark this season—while Liriano struck out nine-plus batters per nine innings in 2013, just as he had the year before.

"Our scouts saw a plus pitch package in both of them," Huntington said. "Metrically, there were positive indicators for both. Anecdotally, we felt there were some factors that would also lead to improved production in Pittsburgh. Overall we liked the upside of both pitchers if all things came together, and still felt the risk of the downside was worth the investment."

Martin, Melancon and Liriano were the final pieces of the puzzle that Huntington had been painstakingly trying to fit together since he took the job.

While Littlefield's trade record as a GM was abysmal, he left the organization with four players who were key to the Pirates making the playoffs in 2013. Second baseman Neil Walker was the Pirates' first-round pick in 2004 and star center fielder Andrew McCutchen was taken in the first round the following year. Left fielder and leadoff hitter Starling Marte was signed as an international amateur free agent from the Dominican Republic in 2007, and left-handed reliever Tony Watson was the Pirates' ninth-round draft pick that summer.

McCutchen was the Pirates' team MVP in 2013, hitting .317 with 21 home runs, 84 RBIs and 27 stolen bases in 157 games. Walker batted .251 with 16 homers in 133 games. Marte had a .286 batting average, 26 doubles, 10 triples, 12 home runs and 41 stolen bases in 135 games. Watson's ERA was 2.39 in 67 games.

Huntington landed two-fifths of his 2013 starting rotation, left-hander Jeff Locke and right-hander Charlie Morton, from the Atlanta Braves in a 2009 trade for center fielder Nate McLouth that was wildly unpopular with Pittsburgh fans at the time. McLouth had won a Gold Glove and appeared in an All-Star Game in 2008, but the Pirates got two live arms and opened the center field job for McCutchen, who was called up from Indianapolis.

Though he faded badly in the second half, Locke finished 10-7 with a 3.52 ERA in 30 starts. Morton missed the first 10 weeks of the season while recovering from Tommy John surgery, then went 7-4 with a 3.26 ERA in 20 starts.

Nine years after whiffing on the first pick of the amateur draft when they chose right-hander Bryan Bullington from Ball State in 2002—he never won a game in a Pittsburgh uniform—the Pirates got it right in 2011 by selecting big right-hander Gerrit Cole from UCLA.

The Pirates were criticized in some corners because Cole's teammate, right-hander Trevor Bauer, had better statistics for the Bruins. However, Huntington decided to rely on his scouts' opinions and took the projectable Cole. It may turn out to be Huntington's signature move.

Cole made his major-league debut on June 11, and went 10-7 with a 3.22 ERA in 19 starts. Unlike most 23-year-old pitchers, Cole got stronger as the year went on, finishing the regular season with a string of seven consecutive quality starts. He then beat the Cardinals—the highest-scoring team in the NL—in Game Two of the NLDS by holding them to one run and two hits in six innings.

Bauer was taken third overall by the Arizona Diamondbacks, but has already been traded to the Cleveland Indians and is 2-4 with a 5.67 ERA in eight career starts.

The Pirates' strength in 2013 was undoubtedly run prevention: They allowed just 3.56 runs a game, second best in the majors to the Atlanta Braves' 3.38. Much of that came on the strength of a stable of good pitchers, but the Pirates were also third in the NL and fifth in the majors with a .715 team defensive efficiency.

The Pirates have installed an organization-wide philosophy on run prevention that relies heavily on infield shifts and their pitchers throwing sinkers to induce large numbers of ground balls. They used the fourth-most shifts in the major leagues, and led the majors by inducing ground balls on 52.5 percent of balls in play, easily outdistancing the second-place Cardinals at 48.5 percent.

Hired by the Pirates in 2008, former Hardball Times writer Dan Fox had spent many hours charting each batted ball in the major leagues and came up with a comprehensive plan that would radically change how the team played defense.

"We've played infield positions conventionally for years, but if you look at hundreds of thousands of balls put in play, data shows that we're actually off a little bit," Huntington said.

Huntington and Hurdle met at Hurdle's suburban Pittsburgh home a week after the 2012 season, and Huntington laid out the plan.

"It's the conversation where we decided to push all the chips in," Hurdle said. "It's the most aggressive presentation and defensive program I've ever been around."

The Pirates wound up using four times as many shifts as they did the previous season.

Huntington and Hurdle knew it wouldn't be an easy sell to ask the players to change the way they have played the game their whole lives. Thus, on the first day the full squad reported in spring training, there was a long team meeting in Bradenton about shifting.

"We had a buy-in that we were going to do it starting in spring training," Hurdle said. "We brought Dan, and I brought in all my coaching staff. I know this game is built upon tradition, and players are territorial. They have comfort zones in the infield. You lay out the factual information. With facts, there is no argument."

The players, for the most part, have adapted, though there was some resistance. When a ball got past shortstop Clint Barmes for a two-run single in a game against the Texas Rangers, Burnett threw his hands up in disgust, giving the impression he was showing up his teammates. However, that wasn't the case.

"I don't have a problem with Clint Barmes," Burnett said angrily when asked about the incident. "I love Clint Barmes. I hate [bleeping] shifts."

Walker, too, was hesitant at first about the full-scale shifting strategy.

"I think there was almost a trial period through [2012] and kind of half of the year before that in 2011 that we kind of threw some things against the wall and the organization threw some things against the wall, and a lot of them stuck and some of them didn't stick," Walker said. "But I think, over most of last year and this year, we've all kind of given into it.

"To be honest with you, there are certain times you feel like you're in no man's land as a middle infielder. You're playing far in that four hole or the shortstop's playing way in the six hole, or he's playing over the top of the bag, and you're in certain spots that when you catch the ball you kind of feel like you don't know where you're at, and that's kind of a strange feeling. But giving in to it has been, in my opinion, pretty successful."

In the long run, it reinforced the age-old adage that pitching and defense win. It was just that the Pirates pitched and defended in a different way.

And while new-age thinking helped the Pirates break on through to the winning side of things, Hurdle said old-fashioned determination of his players also enacted change.

"It's similar to the city of Pittsburgh. It's a blue collar mentality," Hurdle said late in the season. "We're going to persevere. We're not perfect. We're going to get knocked down. We're going to get up. We'll get knocked down again, we'll get up again.

"We're relentless in our pursuit of what we want to do and what we believe in. We're much more in tune to the fact it's going to take all of us, it's going to take everything we've got from all of us, all the time, to get something done. There's not one guy that has to be the focal point, because every guy in there has been picked up by a teammate and an opportunity, whether it be a starter or a bullpen guy sometime along the time, whether it's been lack of performance or injury. We've had that 'next man up' mentality throughout the season.

"And I think our guys have just gotten real good with good old-fashioned effort and grit," Hurdle added. "That's been a formula that's played well for us."

The Pirates have become a forward-thinking organization during Huntington's era, and they get excited when they look ahead to some of the prospects who should be joining the major league club in the future.

FanGraphs had four players in the Pirates farm system among its Top 50 midseason prospects—right-hander Jameson Taillon at No. 7, outfielder Gregory Polanco No. 19, second baseman Alen Hanson No. 27 and right-hander Tyler Glasnow No. 42.

Taillon and Polanco both ended the season at Indianapolis, while Hanson finished at Double-A Altoona. Glasnow could wind up having the best career of all; he showed flashes of brilliance at Low-A West Virginia, where he went 9-3 with a 2.18 ERA in 24 starts and struck out 164 in 111 1/3 innings.

The Pirates also had the top prospect in two short-season leagues, according to Baseball America's rankings. Center fielder Harold Ramirez topped the New York-Penn League chart, and center fielder Austin Meadows—the Pirates' first-round draft pick in 2013—was picked as the best in the Gulf Coast League.

"We feel like we've positioned ourselves to be competitive for a number of years, but it's always going to be a challenge in [our] market," Huntington said. "We're never going to have some of the advantages of the bigger-market clubs, and that's something we're going to have to deal with. We've finally had a taste of success, but we don't want it to be a one-time thing. The key is sustaining it, and it won't be easy."

Huntington then smiled.

"Fasten your seat belts," he said.

The Science of the Art of Receiving a Pitch

by Jeff Sullivan

In mid-February 2010, Jose Molina signed a free-agent contract with the Toronto Blue Jays. Molina, at that point, was 34 years old, and he was being brought in to compete with backup alternative Raul Chavez. Molina's contract was non-guaranteed, containing a roster bonus in the event he broke camp. There was a chance the Blue Jays would just take a quick look and then dump him. Said the team's general manager to MLB.com's Jordan Bastian:

> *"Raul Chavez did a great job for us last year, too," [Alex] Anthopoulos said. "So it'll be an interesting competition in camp."*

In late November 2011, Jose Molina signed a free-agent contract with the Tampa Bay Rays. Molina, at that point, was 36 years old, but he was being brought in as a regular. Though his deal wasn't big, it was bigger than the previous one, and it was guaranteed. It came, additionally, with a club option for 2013—an option the Rays would ultimately exercise without giving it a second thought.

What happened between February 2010 and November 2011? Well, Molina hit a little. One can't completely ignore his .263 average and .720 OPS. He also threw out 39 percent of would-be base-stealers. But more importantly, research had been done, and published, on the subject of pitch framing, or pitch receiving. Contributions were made by individuals like Dan Turkenkopf, Max Marchi, Matthew Carruth and Bill Letson, and then the home run was hit by Mike Fast. Fast played around with strike zones and PITCHf/x data, and the long and short of it is that he found that Jose Molina caught a lot of extra called strikes.

Said Anthopoulos upon signing Molina in Toronto:

> *"We got rave reviews from a lot of players who have thrown to him. What he does for a clubhouse, what he does to help young guys along, those are things that don't necessarily show up in a box score or on a stat sheet."*

Fast found a way to put it in a stat sheet. People around the game have long understood that there's a right way to catch the ball, and a wrong way to catch the ball. People have long had a sense of who were the best and worst handlers of pitching staffs, and the best receivers of their pitches. From his beginning, Molina had a particularly strong and positive defensive reputation. Fast put numbers to his value. The numbers, for Molina and for some other catchers, were eye-popping.

Ironically, even though this research is still so new, most of you probably have a good grasp of it. Framing is everywhere in today's analytical baseball writing, and now Molina's practically a household name, at least among certain sorts of households. It's an exciting field that deals with an ability that can make a whale of a difference, and framing has been discussed on ESPN.com, MLB.com, Grantland and many other places. It's extended beyond the Internet, showing up on ESPN and the MLB Network. In no time at all, the fascination spread, presumably because it captures a skill people have known about for decades. It's applying stats to scouting, as it were.

Here's a quick summary of what this is. Through the magic of PITCHf/x, we have a record of almost every pitch that gets thrown, with the data including the pitch's location. By examining both the locations and the outcomes, it's possible to calculate a called-strike probability.

Let's say, for example, there's a pitch that goes for a strike 60 percent of the time. Let's say a catcher catches such a pitch, and it's called a strike. That catcher can be credited with +0.4 strikes above average. By repeating this for every pitch for every catcher, we can get an idea of pitch-receiving value.

Sometimes, of course, it's a fluke, or sometimes it doesn't have anything to do with the catcher. But what we see over big samples is that patterns emerge, and certain guys stand out as good or bad receivers. There are techniques to catching pitches near the borders of the zone, and some techniques make the pitches look better, while others drag the pitch further away. There's real skill here, and so this is something absolutely worth measuring.

The last step is going from strikes to runs, because runs are the currency of the sport. You might hear that a catcher is 50 strikes above average over a season, but it's not immediately apparent how valuable that really is. But we know that different counts have different expected run values, and the way a pitch gets called changes the count. It's possible to figure out the difference between a ball and a strike—roughly 0.13 runs, overall—and then it's a matter of simple multiplication. The end result: Player value, from the act of catching pitches. Good receivers effectively expand the strike zone, while worse ones make everything more tricky.

At this point we can abandon the introduction and get to the meat, where the meat is the statistics. By now, you should have a fine enough understanding of what this is, and once you understand a stat, it's only natural to wonder who're the best and who're the worst. All of the numbers below come from research done by Matthew Carruth and published on StatCorner.com. Carruth figures out the average umpire strike zone as it's actually called, and then he figures out strikes or runs above or below average for each catcher, adjusting for count. The first table features 2013's 10 best receivers, by total value and by strikes per game (which is more of a rate stat). I set a minimum of 1,000 called pitches received. RAA refers to Runs Above Average. SPG refers to strikes above or below average, per game.

Best Pitch Receivers, 2013			
Catcher	RAA	Catcher	SPG
Jonathan Lucroy	31.1	Rene Rivera	3.25
Chris Stewart	22.7	Yasmani Grandal	3.03
Yadier Molina	19.8	Hank Conger	2.13
Jose Molina	19.3	Jonathan Lucroy	1.93
Hank Conger	18.1	Martin Maldonado	1.90
Russell Martin	17.9	David Ross	1.85
J.P. Arencibia	15.8	Jose Molina	1.79
Yan Gomes	15.4	Chris Stewart	1.78
Buster Posey	11.4	Francisco Cervelli	1.78
Martin Maldonado	10.4	Yan Gomes	1.50

By runs above average, it's Jonathan Lucroy for 2013, and it's not even particularly close. If you stick with the popular estimate of 10 runs or so being equivalent to a win, then Lucroy's receiving was worth more than three wins to the Brewers, and he was about a win more valuable than second place. You'll notice, additionally, at the bottom of the table, that his teammate Martin Maldonado sneaks in, too. This past season, the Brewers didn't do that many things right, but this they did better than anyone.

As expected, Molina was great once more. As expected, his brother Yadier was also outstanding, and the Yankees got quality work from Chris Stewart. What the Yankees lost in Russell Martin, they replaced with Stewart, at least in this one department.

Move over to the per-game column and you find a couple of Padres blowing away everyone else. You might not have ever heard of Rene Rivera. Even if you had, you might not have realized he was playing in the majors in 2013. But not only did he play a little—he allowed his pitchers to pitch to the biggest strike zone in the league. Teammate Yasmani Grandal was basically just as good, and then you end up with the Lucroys and Molinas and so on. Hank Conger looks surprisingly good, given his reputation of being an offense-first backstop of whom Mike Scioscia isn't the biggest fan.

No one did a better job than Rivera of getting should-be strikes called strikes. Just 8.1 percent of pitches in the average called zone were called balls with Rivera behind the plate, so you can think of this not as stealing strikes, but as preserving them. But then, Rivera was also second-best at stealing strikes, getting 10.3-percent strikes on pitches out of the average called zone. The only catcher better: Grandal, at 11.3 percent. Padres.

The second table features 2013's 10 worst receivers, by total value and by strikes per game. The same definitions and minimum apply.

Worst Pitch Receivers, 2013			
Catcher	RAA	Catcher	SPG
John Buck	-21.2	Koyie Hill	-4.35
Wilin Rosario	-19.3	Ryan Doumit	-2.77
Welington Castillo	-16.7	Jesus Montero	-2.15
Ryan Doumit	-15.9	Gerald Laird	-2.01
Chris Iannetta	-15.1	Kelly Shoppach	-1.88
A.J. Pierzynski	-11.4	Josmil Pinto	-1.75
Koyie Hill	-9.4	John Buck	-1.65
Rob Brantly	-9.3	George Kottaras	-1.56
Kurt Suzuki	-9.1	Chris Herrmann	-1.49
Matt Wieters	-9.1	Anthony Recker	-1.48

By runs above average, no one ran away with it, or should I say, no one sank away with it. John Buck's at the top, about two wins worse than average, then you've got a youngster in Colorado with a pretty lousy defensive reputation that it sure seems like he's earned. Welington Castillo was also fairly inexperienced in the major leagues, and after him one finds Ryan Doumit. Just as all the research has highlighted Jose Molina's hidden value, it's dragged Doumit over a bed of nails. Doumit, consistently, comes away looking like one of baseball's worst receivers, giving away a lot of the value he gains from catching. He might give away all of it. Where video evidence shows that Molina keeps his body quiet, and anticipates a pitch's movement, Doumit has more movement in his catching, and his glove can exaggerate a pitch's tail or sink.

The per-game column is telling. Koyie Hill looks absolutely godawful, having quietly caught several innings for the Marlins. Behind him, it's no surprise to find Doumit, and behind him, it's no surprise to find Jesus Montero. Montero is no longer even a catcher, after the Mariners grew tired of his inadequacy across the board. He doesn't move well, he doesn't throw well, and he doesn't catch well, so now the hope is that he'll hit well. Two spots down, there's another Mariners receiver. One more spot down, there's another Twin. Three more spots down, there's a third Twin. It's also a list with two Mets.

No one did a worse job than Hill of getting strikes called strikes. Nearly a quarter of pitches in the zone were called balls with Hill behind the plate, and then behind him there's Doumit, at one-fifth. Neither of these catchers excelled at making it look like the pitcher hit his spot. Going outside of the zone, Hill was also the worst, getting strikes on just 3.9 percent of would-be balls. Cody Clark was second-worst, followed by Recker and Doumit.

How can we know that we're really capturing anything with these data? After all, if you take any distribution of numbers, there are going to be minimums and maximums. What we need to consider is sustainability, because if these numbers hold up year after year, what that implies is that we're measuring a skill, and not random noise. With that in mind, here's a simple graph. There were 57 catchers who caught at least 1,000 called pitches in both 2012 and 2013. On the x-axis here, 2012 SPG. On the y-axis, 2013 SPG.

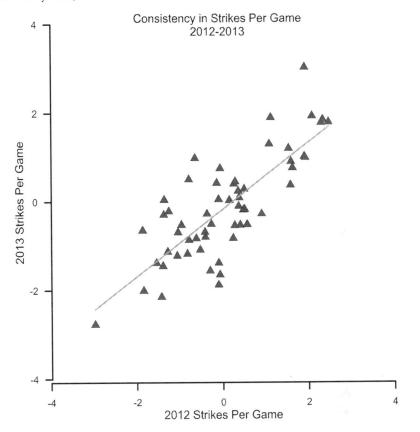

This could be examined more rigorously, by taking into consideration more than one group covering two years, but that's actually already been done, by Fast himself. Fast demonstrated that this ability tends to hold up year after year, strongly suggesting that what we're getting is a measurement of catcher skill. The correlation, obviously, isn't perfect, but it's strong, and it measures up with a lot of the strongest correlations we see in the game with other statistics.

So if we figure that pitch receiving is a real skill, and if we figure that it's generally pretty stable each season, there's reason to be interested in the players who show the biggest changes between seasons. Below, you'll see 10 catchers: the five catchers whose SPG increased the most, and the five catchers whose SPG decreased the most, from 2012 to 2013. Again, the minimum is 1,000 called pitches.

Biggest Changes in Performance, SPG, 2012-2013							
Catcher	2012	2013	Diff	Catcher	2012	2013	Diff
J.P. Arencibia	-0.64	0.98	1.62	Kelly Shoppach	-0.10	-1.88	-1.78
Taylor Teagarden	-1.36	0.04	1.40	John Buck	-0.06	-1.65	-1.59
Hector Sanchez	-0.78	0.50	1.28	Henry Blanco	-0.09	-1.38	-1.29
Carlos Santana	-1.86	-0.65	1.21	George Kottaras	-0.29	-1.56	-1.27
Yasmani Grandal	1.92	3.03	1.11	Carlos Corporan	1.59	0.37	-1.22

No catcher took a bigger step forward than J.P. Arencibia, who really needed to take some big steps forward somewhere. And for him, this isn't necessarily a one-year thing. Going back to 2010, when Arencibia debuted:

- **2010:** -1.42 SPG
- **2011:** -1.26
- **2012:** -0.64
- **2013:** 0.98

It was said during the season that Arencibia worked hard on improving his defense with Sal Fasano, and at least here, the numbers show that he made some real gains. As recently as 2011, Arencibia was a problem receiver, but now it looks like more of a strength than a weakness, which is one of few Arencibia bright spots.

The most interesting among the other big improvements is Carlos Santana, and we'll touch on the Indians a little later. Looking at the catchers who slid the most, there are two guys who joined the Mariners, which might or might not be a coincidence. Blanco was acquired for his experience and defensive excellence, but in this department he came up short. Buck dropped from being average to being one of the league's worst. Neither George Kottaras nor Carlos Corporan is going to be a long-term starter.

It's not obvious quite what to make of big changes. It stands to reason players might deliberately try to improve their receiving skills, and those gains should be fairly permanent. Arencibia, for example, might well be a good framer, now. But, anecdotally, there's curious evidence. In 2012, the 10 catchers who made the biggest positive gains averaged a 0.67 SPG. In 2011, they averaged -0.21. In 2013, they averaged -0.13, giving back almost everything. Meanwhile, in 2012, the 10 catchers who had the biggest negative drops averaged a -0.51 SLG. In 2011, they averaged 0.61. In 2013, they averaged -0.54, not re-gaining any ground. This is something that could be explored in greater depth.

Having looked at individual players, we'll turn now to the teams. The following table details all 30 teams, sorted by total framing runs above average.

Team Runs Above Average, 2013			
Team	RAA	Team	RAA
Brewers	41.4	White Sox	-1.1
Yankees	32.3	Phillies	-2.2
Rays	19.7	D-backs	-2.6
Padres	18.4	Nationals	-4.0
Cardinals	18.2	Orioles	-4.8
Pirates	14.7	Astros	-6.0
Blue Jays	13.2	Rangers	-10.7
Giants	11.2	Dodgers	-13.5
Braves	7.9	Royals	-13.6
Indians	7.3	Mariners	-20.7
Tigers	5.3	Cubs	-20.8
Reds	4.6	Marlins	-21.8
Red Sox	3.9	Twins	-25.7
Angels	2.9	Mets	-27.5
Athletics	0.8	Rockies	-27.6

As noted earlier, the Brewers dominated this category, besting second place by more than nine runs. The Yankees then beat *third* place by more than a dozen runs, so there was considerable separation at the top. The Rays, in third, were helped in large part by Molina, while the Padres, in fourth, were pushed by Grandal and Rivera. The Cardinals rode their own Molina into fifth, easily clear of sixth.

At the other end, it was almost a dead heat between the Rockies and the Mets. The Rockies, though, were already using their potential catcher of the future, while the Mets folded theirs in later, in the person of Travis d'Arnaud. Though we still have a limited sample, it looks like d'Arnaud is at least an average framer, and he could be better than that. The Twins' best receiver sustained a season-ending concussion. The Marlins were pushed down by Hill and Rob Brantly, while the Cubs were sunk by Castillo. The Mariners suffered through a host of inadequates, but there's reason for optimism with Mike Zunino.

What about team-level changes in performance between 2012 and 2013?

| Changes in Performance, RAA, 2012-2013 | | | | | | | |
Team	2012	2013	Diff	Team	2012	2013	Diff
Indians	-36.8	7.3	44.1	Rockies	-27.3	-27.6	-0.3
Pirates	-26.4	14.7	41.1	Cardinals	19.2	18.2	-1.0
Blue Jays	-6.2	13.2	19.4	Red Sox	5.7	3.9	-1.8
Padres	3.3	18.4	15.1	Nationals	-1.3	-4.0	-2.7
Tigers	-6.6	5.3	11.9	Yankees	37.6	32.3	-5.3
Athletics	-9.8	0.8	10.6	Rays	26.6	19.7	-6.9
Dodgers	-22.5	-13.5	9.0	Giants	18.7	11.2	-7.5
Royals	-20.0	-13.6	6.4	D-backs	7.0	-2.6	-9.6
Orioles	-11.0	-4.8	6.2	Marlins	-9.3	-21.8	-12.5
Rangers	-16.8	-10.7	6.1	Astros	9.0	-6.0	-15.0
Brewers	35.6	41.4	5.8	Cubs	-5.5	-20.8	-15.3
Angels	0.3	2.9	2.6	Phillies	17.2	-2.2	-19.4
White Sox	-3.3	-1.1	2.2	Reds	30.4	4.6	-25.8
Twins	-26.5	-25.7	0.8	Braves	37.0	7.9	-29.1
Mariners	-21.2	-20.7	0.5	Mets	3.4	-27.5	-30.9

With individual catchers, I looked at performance changes by tracking SPG, because of the varying sample sizes. With teams, the sample sizes are all pretty similar, so I'm comfortable looking at total runs above or below average. And over the last two years, there were some incredibly large differences, both at the top and at the bottom.

The Indians and Pirates improved by leaps and bounds more than other teams, and perhaps not coincidentally, both of those teams advanced past the regular season. The Indians replaced Lou Marson with Gomes, and not only did Gomes receive well, Santana made himself better. As for the Pirates, they dropped Rod Barajas, they reduced the playing time of Michael McKenry, and they leaned heavily on free-agent acquisition Russell Martin. Martin was excellent across the board, standing as perhaps last offseason's most underrated pick-up. Both of these teams turned a weakness into a strength.

Down below, the Mets missed Josh Thole, as we've already seen Buck and Anthony Recker's names. Quietly, the Braves got a lot worse, for a few reasons. David Ross was an excellent receiver, and he left. Gerald Laird is a poor receiver, and he came aboard. Finally, Brian McCann started the year on the disabled list. The Braves were overall positive, but this wasn't a strength of theirs.

For the Reds, it was as simple as neither Ryan Hanigan nor Devin Mesoraco doing as well. The Reds, like the Braves, remained above average, but they gave back more than a couple wins from the season previous. More than half the teams in baseball changed by fewer than 10 runs in either direction.

So, what now? That's the big question. We've managed to quantify something few ever thought realistically possible, and what we're measuring seems to be a skill. We have a great idea, now, that guys like Jose Molina and Lucroy are really good. We have a great idea that Doumit is really bad. What's left is mostly the boring stuff: Making improvements, incremental as they'll probably be.

As one example, future framing calculations could take into consideration pitch type or pitch movement, beyond just the umpire and the count and the batter's handedness. Not all pitches get seen and caught the same way, so this could make a difference. It's unlikely it would change much about the order of things, but better accuracy's better accuracy.

There is the matter of trying to better separate the catcher influence from the pitcher influence. It's been demonstrated that some catching techniques increase the likelihood of getting a strike call, but no catcher is going to get many strikes when a pitcher badly misses his spot, even if the resulting pitch is still around the zone. There's a relationship between command and framing numbers, and unfortunately we still don't have a great grasp on command as a statistic. Why did Blanco and Kelly Shoppach get so much worse with the Mariners? Why did Buck get so much worse with the Mets? Did the catchers themselves decline, or were the pitching staffs prone to missing locations? This isn't all about the catchers. We just don't know how to divide the responsibility.

Anecdotally, there's also something hard to ignore, shown in 2013 by the Brewers and Padres having good framing numbers and bad pitching numbers. It's possible that pitchers pitch differently with good receivers, taking more chances out of the zone, thereby throwing more balls. In that way, the advantage could be virtually negated. More generally, what isn't yet understood is the effect having a good receiver has on a pitching staff. We also don't understand very much about game calling, which is a separate skill, but that's a whole other article or three. Don't believe for a second that we've figured out catcher value. We haven't. We're just getting closer.

Finally, there's the elephant in the room: is pitch framing, or pitch receiving, even a good thing? Is this something we want, or is this a stain on the game? The argument against framing is that the rule book defines a certain strike zone, and every team ought to work with the same rules. Why should it be allowed for one pitching staff to have a bigger strike zone than the next? We've seen on so many occasions the last few years a catcher steal strike three out of the zone, with batters like Cody Ross and Brett Lawrie responding poorly. Oftentimes, those called strikes aren't strikes. Why celebrate bad calls?

It wouldn't be possible to instruct umpires to simply not pay attention. It's not realistic to expect a human umpire to observe the baseball until it crosses the plate, and then ignore everything after. How the catcher catches the ball is within an umpire's field of vision, and it happens immediately after the baseball crosses the front plane, and that visual has an effect. No umpire would admit as much, but it's both subtle and real. How the pitch is caught can alter the perception of the pitch up to that point, and that's a limitation of the human brain. As long as there are human umpires, they're going to be subject to getting fooled. Part of being human.

If there's good news, it's that umpires do seem to be getting better. Elsewhere in the *Annual*, Jon Roegele talks about the expanding strike zone. I'm going to take a different angle here. The table below lays out the percentage of pitches that have been called incorrectly, by type, according to the PITCHf/x data.

MLB Average Umpire Performance, 2008-2013		
Year	% in zone called balls	% out of zone called strikes
2008	19.5%	7.9%
2009	17.6%	7.7%
2010	15.5%	7.8%
2011	15.5%	7.2%
2012	14.7%	7.1%
2013	14.1%	6.9%

Now, the strike zone here is the zone that umpires actually called, and PITCHf/x has improved over the years, so we can't conclusively say this table shows anything, but it does make suggestions. Relative to a few years ago, fewer pitches in the zone are getting called balls. Relative to a few years ago, fewer pitches out of the zone are getting called strikes. Umpires still get calls wrong, but they've become more accurate and more consistent, which is certainly progress. Maybe they're better about dealing with framing. Maybe they're learning more, given the availability of PITCHf/x data. Maybe they're being graded harder, with greater threats of discipline.

Across the major leagues, umpires seem to have improved, which is better than not improving. Because they're human, however, only so much improvement is possible, and there will always be errors, especially around the borders. This is why so many people are in favor of an automated strike zone. Humans can get to be only so good, and the umpires in the major leagues are already almost there. We can't help but make mistakes, because our eyes and our brains lie to us. A robot strike zone? Maybe there would be the occasional glitch, but those glitches would be far fewer in number than the glitches we deal with today.

Yet the reality is that we're not close to having an automated strike zone. They've discussed it, but the technology isn't in place, the reliability isn't there. At the moment, it's simply not feasible. We've got human umpires for the foreseeable future, and human umpires can be fooled by good and bad catchers.

The way I see it, fans don't like it when a game is put in the hands of the umpires. They don't like it when the umpires make a meaningful difference. At least with pitch framing, we can pin it on the players. A baseball game is a game between two teams with two sets of ability. Pitch framing, based on all the evidence, is an ability, where a player can be either good or bad. If an umpire blows a call at second, that's on the umpire. If he calls a ball a strike or a strike a ball at home? The catcher might've had something to do with that.

And at least then the game's still being determined by the players. Nobody likes bad or inconsistent umpiring, but at least when it comes to catching pitches, players are taking it under their own control. I can imagine a worse reality.

Resources and References

Key research mentioned in this article includes that by:

- Dan Turkenkopf, "Framing the Debate," Beyond The Box Score, *beyondtheboxscore.com/2008/4/5/389840/framing-the-debate*
- Matthew Carruth, "Framing the Framing Debate," Lookout Landing, *lookoutlanding.com/2010/2/1/1285412/framing-the-framing-debate*
- Bill Letson, "A First Pass at a Catcher Framing Metric," Beyond The Box Score, *beyondtheboxscore.com/2010/3/26/1360581/a-first-pass-at-a-catcher-framing*
- Max Marchi, "Evaluating catchers: Framing pitches, part 2," The Hardball Times, *hardballtimes.com/main/article/evaluating-catchers-framing-pitches-part-2*
- Mike Fast, "Spinning Yarn: Removing the Mask Encore Presentation," Baseball Prospectus, *baseballprospectus.com/article.php?articleid=15093*

Stats provided by:

- StatCorner, *http://statcorner.com/CatcherReport.php*

Expunging Frank: The Dodgers' Remarkable Turnaround

by Mike Petriello

If it's difficult to pinpoint the actual "lowest point" of the period when Frank McCourt's ownership of the Los Angeles Dodgers began to crumble after he and wife Jamie separated, that's only because there are so many contenders for the title.

For pure bad timing, it had to have been announcing the separation hours before the first game of the 2009 National League Championship Series was set to kick off at Dodger Stadium. If it's slack-jawed disbelief that gets your attention, then perhaps it's paying an elderly Russian self-proclaimed "healer" six figures to send his positive "V energy" from thousands of miles away. Maybe it was when Major League Baseball commissioner Bud Selig moved to appoint MLB oversight of the club, or when the team actually had to file for Chapter 11 bankruptcy, or when manager Joe Torre had to clarify to the media that no, working for the team wasn't really "a living hell."

And on a human level, nothing could have had more of a lasting real-world impact than the tragic 2011 beating of Giants fan Bryan Stow in the Dodger Stadium parking lot, after which it was revealed that the team hadn't had a permanent security chief in place for months.

All worthy choices, yet all only a few among dozens of other incidents. It's possible that deciding when things actually hit rock bottom is a very personal decision, at least for those who lived through it daily. But from this point of view, nothing showed just how far a once-great franchise had fallen than early in the 2011 season, when success for the Dodgers wasn't measured in "runs" or "wins." It was measured in "was payroll met?" as in, "could an increasingly desperate McCourt keep finding ways to raise cash—including taking out personal loans and accepting long-term discounts on sponsorship deals for immediate upfront payments—in order to not default every two weeks?"

That's the kind of thing that's more appropriately seen in the gossip mags or the Wall Street Journal than in the sports pages, and that's exactly where stories about the McCourts could be found. That was when the Dodgers ceased to be a baseball team in the traditional sense and became a larger story about American greed, debt and undercapitalization.

Just over two years later, the Dodgers aren't in bankruptcy. They're not in the tabloids, and they're not embarrassing themselves and their fans at every turn. They're among the richest franchises in sports, with an on-field product that has returned to the playoffs, and they're back atop the major leagues in attendance. It's a lightning-quick turnaround that's enough to make your head spin, because it's one thing to come in with big ideas and the endless money to back them up, as new ownership surely did. But it's quite another to take an organization in such disrepair, one that had fallen into the toilet after having been a jewel of the sport for decades, and whip it into shape in such a short time.

The process of winning back the respect of fans and players started almost without delay, long before any tangible changes were made on the field. At the first press conference introducing the new Guggenheim ownership group, most visibly led by former Atlanta Braves and Washington Nationals president Stan Kasten and basketball legend Magic Johnson, they went for the low-hanging fruit: They announced that parking prices would immediately be cut by a third, reversing an increase McCourt had implemented in 2007. The team soon left on a road trip, and when it returned, found that the wives and family room had already been renovated, which Cindy Ellis (wife of catcher A.J.) referred to as "a breath of fresh air."

But that was mere table-setting, some quick fixes designed to gain early support. Among the many broken promises of the McCourt era had been a stadium upgrade plan, unveiled in early 2008 to improve the charming, yet aging Dodger Stadium. Originally expected to be complete by Opening Day 2012, the project had never gotten off the ground, thanks to McCourt's continued financial difficulties. New ownership eyed an opportunity, and hired stadium superstar Janet Marie Smith—well-known for her contributions to Camden Yards in Baltimore and the upgrades to Fenway Park in Boston—as a senior vice president to lead the initiative.

That was in August of 2012, and by the time fans walked into Dodger Stadium on Opening Day 2013, over $100 million worth of upgrades was not only well underway but nearly complete. In addition to two massive high-definition video screens in left and right field, concessions and restrooms were upgraded around the park and picnic areas added in some sections. At the top of the park, a new concourse was built, complete with retired number monuments, additional concessions and views of downtown.

Even the Cool-A-Coo, a frozen dessert treat that had long been a fan favorite but which hadn't been offered at the park since the late 1990s, made a triumphant return. Behind the scenes, electrical and plumbing systems were improved, the training facilities were expanded, and the Dodgers clubhouse—long-reviled for its small size, as well as the requirement for visiting players to pass through in order to reach the batting cages—was doubled in size.

If the goal was to quickly regain fan confidence, it worked: More than 3.7 million flocked to Dodger Stadium in 2013. That figure was not only the most in the big leagues, it came just two seasons after the team failed to break the three million mark for the first time in over a decade. That was in the midst of active "Boycott McCourt!" movements from angry fans who didn't want their dollars to be used to pay McCourt's divorce lawyers. In addition, the season ticket base has doubled in less than a year, if one recent ESPN.com report is to be believed.

But it's long been proven that the most effective way to draw fans to the park is to give them the best possible product on the field, and in that, the Guggenheim group had much work to do.

Though the new owners famously spent wildly on the big-league product—and we'll get to that—the resurrection of the Dodgers required far more than throwing dollars at veteran free agents. A return to success required attention at every level of the organization, because McCourt's failings had impacted the team at the lowest levels.

Take, for example, international scouting. For decades, the Dodgers had been at the forefront of the global talent game, winning legions of fans with successful foreign players like Mexico's Fernando Valenzuela, Japan's Hideo Nomo, and Korea's Chan Ho Park, and signing legendary greats Roberto Clemente from Puerto Rico and Pedro Martinez out of the Dominican Republic, though they made their names with other clubs. The pipeline had once been so flush with talent that in 1996, Nomo and Park teamed with Mexican Ismael Valdez and Dominicans Ramon Martinez and Pedro Astacio to make 135 of the team's 162 starts.

As McCourt tightened the belt on the team while allegations that he and his family had taken millions for personal use surfaced, the scouting department was one of the hardest-hit areas. International scouting all but disappeared, with the financial outlay on global prospects coming in last among all teams in 2010-2011. The number of paid scouts shrank as well. Partially as a result, the 2012 Dodgers had 100 percent of their games started by American-born pitchers for the first time since 1980. At one point, just seven members of the 40-man roster were from outside North America, and other than ace reliever Kenley Jansen and veteran third baseman Juan Uribe, they were backups or low-impact players.

The Guggenheim group responded as it has with every other crisis so far: Quickly, and loudly. Since the sale, the team has hired more than a dozen new scouts and added well-respected baseball lifers like Bob Engle, Gerry Hunsicker and Pat Corrales to the front office, all while allocating dollars to identify talent and bring it into the system.

The effects were immediate. In June of 2012, days before the new collective bargaining agreement would place limits on such spending, the Dodgers guaranteed $42 million to virtually unknown Cuban outfielder Yasiel Puig. While the move raised eyebrows across the sport, Puig was a sensation in his first season in the bigs in 2013—he hit .319/.391/.534 with 19 homers in just 104 games and caused waves both with his all-out style of play and his sometimes rough acclimation to American life. Over the winter, they won a posting fee of $25.7 million for the right to negotiate with Korean left-hander Hyun-jin Ryu; after signing him to a six-year deal worth a guaranteed $36 million, they pushed him straight to the big leagues and watched him blossom with 30 starts and an even 3.00 ERA.

The Dodgers, who were never able to be seriously in the market for Japanese star Yu Darvish when he came to America following 2011, have now signed the two most impactful foreign players of the last year, with more than a dozen younger low-level players signed as well. (One to watch: Mexican lefty Julio Urias, who more than held his own while playing most of the 2013 season at age 16 for Class-A Great Lakes, making him likely the youngest player in Midwest League history.)

As Kasten would perhaps be the first to tell you, developing your own players is the only way to stay successful over a long period of time, thanks to the current compensation system that has young star players being nearly criminally underpaid before they reach free agency. But—Puig and Ryu aside—between the time needed and the usual attrition rate for teenage prospects, that process can take years. To get the big league team up to par, and quickly, ownership unshackled general manager Ned Colletti and told him to do what he needed to bring in talent.

That, more than anything, is probably what the Dodgers are known for these days: The unprecedented spending spree that bought them the roster that put them back into the playoffs.

In 2003, the final season before McCourt had purchased the team, the Opening Day payroll was approximately $105 million. On his final Opening Day, in 2012, the payroll was...still approximately $105 million, and it had dipped below that more than a few years in between. By the time 2013 kicked off, an orgy of spending had more than doubled it, to well north of $200 million.

The fun started in June of 2012, barely more than a month after the ownership transition had been finalized, when long-time outfielder Andre Ethier received a five-year extension worth a guaranteed $85 million. (In the interest of fairness, fellow outfielder Matt Kemp's eight-year, $160 million extension had happened the previous winter, when McCourt was still in charge, though by that point it was all but certain he was on his way out and wouldn't have to pay for it.)

The Puig signing happened weeks after Ethier's, and it took only a few weeks after that for the next move: In July, the Dodgers acquired talented-yet-troubled shortstop Hanley Ramirez (and all of the approximately $36 million still due him) and veteran reliever Randy Choate from the Miami Marlins in exchange for a good-but-not-elite prospect in starter Nathan Eovaldi and a minor league reliever.

Even that was merely a prelude to the August shocker of a deal with the Boston Red Sox in which the Dodgers agreed to take on approximately $262 million in contract commitments, including the injured-and-ineffective Carl Crawford and the past-his-prime Josh Beckett, in order to bring star first baseman Adrian Gonzalez on board. The sheer size of the move signaled that it was more than just a trade, it was a statement. Along with smaller deals for veterans Joe Blanton, Brandon League and

Shane Victorino, it said that new ownership wanted to win, and win now, and had the means to back it up.

Though it was too late to save 2012—the Dodgers finished two games out of the wild card, largely because Kemp had injured his shoulder and was ineffective while trying to play through the pain, while starters Clayton Kershaw and Chad Billingsley missed time due to injury—that didn't stop the team from spending even more to reload for 2013. In addition to Ryu, the Dodgers guaranteed $147 million to free-agent starting pitcher Zack Greinke, at the time the largest contract ever given to a right-handed starter.

They also gave League a guaranteed $22.5 million to return. That was a move seen by many as foolish at the time and even more so when he quickly fell apart, but it is mentioned here simply because his failure was merely a mild speed bump, not the fatal blow it might have been for other teams.

For a good portion of the season, it seemed like the spending may have been wasted, as the team—slowed by injuries to Kemp, Greinke, Crawford, Ramirez and others—sank to last place in June, amid near-constant reports that manager Don Mattingly would be fired. But as the injured finally got healthy, and the arrival of Puig and the performance of Ramirez helped to light a fire behind the consistently elite pitching of Kershaw and Jansen, the Dodgers ran off a historic streak of 42 wins in 50 games and easily made it to October. When reinforcements were needed, Colletti again turned to Miami, picking up useful starter Ricky Nolasco in July for an underwhelming return. Once again, as he had with Ramirez, he covered for the lack of top-end prospects in the system by agreeing to pay every dollar of Nolasco's contract.

While it's unfair to suggest that the 2013 success is entirely due to payroll—homegrown, pre-free agency players like Kershaw, Jansen, Ellis and others certainly played a part—it's also naive to think that the Dodgers get to October without the Guggenheim money. When Greinke returned from an April broken collarbone, he and Kershaw made for perhaps the most dominant one-two duo of starters in baseball. Despite a prolonged midseason slump and missed time due to injury, Crawford was among the team's most dangerous hitters both in April and October.

Gonzalez, if not quite the superstar he once was, provided a large upgrade on years of underwhelming first base play from James Loney, and was one of the few Dodgers to remain healthy and in the lineup all season long. Since Kemp was constantly hurt and a non-factor for most of the year, the controversial signing of Puig proved to be an invaluable boost. That also doesn't mean all the spending was wise, because many didn't like the Ethier deal and more than a few suggested that there were better ways to spend $262 million than on the Boston players, but it's hard to argue with the results.

As Kasten has publicly stated, the long-term goal is not always to have a payroll that's multiple times the size of other teams'. The hope is that that a revamped scouting organization can improve the quality of young, cost-controlled players coming up from the minors, so the short-term spending was needed to quickly improve the major league team. But lest you think the spending is over, well, know that the 25-year-old Kershaw is on a Hall of Fame trajectory and (at press time) hadn't yet signed a deal that would prevent him from reaching free agency after 2014. When he does, it's expected to be for at least $200 million (and might be for as much as $300 million), and the Dodgers have already made another international splash by guaranteeing $28 million over four years to Cuban infielder Alexander Guerrero, who will likely be their starting second baseman in 2014.

All this work culminates in the 2014 launch of SportsNet Los Angeles (SNLA), the new Dodger television network that was behind both the purchase of the team and McCourt's efforts to keep it.

McCourt knew that when the existing television deal with Fox expired at the end of 2013, a new deal—either to keep the Dodgers on Fox or move them elsewhere— would be worth billions, enough to pay his debts should he be able to keep the team afloat that long. He wasn't, and now it's the Guggenheim group that will reap the benefits of what was reported to be a deal in the $6-$7 billion (!) range with Time Warner to get SNLA off the ground. (McCourt, it should be noted, to the consternation of many still retains a part ownership of the parking lots around the stadium, but is said to have no role in their game day operation.)

In that light, the $2.15 billion the group paid for the team seems slightly less shocking than it did at the time, as does the hundreds of millions it has put into roster and stadium upgrades. By reinvigorating the fan base and reviving the team, new ownership has turned around the Dodgers brand. That's going to be important when it comes to ratings and advertising on the new network, which is really the lifeblood of all this.

Considering how low things were just two seasons ago, it's an incredible turnaround, and one that ought to keep the rest of the NL worried for years to come.

Everything But the Game: The 2013 Astros

by Larry Granillo

The idea was floated in the final week of the season by none other than New York Yankees manager Joe Girardi. Mariano Rivera, the greatest relief pitcher of all-time, the last man to wear number 42 in the big leagues and the owner of the all-time saves record at 652, would spend his final appearance in the major leagues playing center field against the Houston Astros in a meaningless game. Rivera, who has always enjoyed shagging flies in batting practice—his 2012 injury came while doing just that in Kansas City—would get his one chance to enjoy the experience in a real game as a gesture of friendship from his manager.

Imagine that scene. Number 42 standing alone in the outfield grass, thousands and thousands of fans, some wearing Yankees gear, others wearing Astros gear, cheering his every move, flashbulbs going off the second any pitch is batted into the air. Meanwhile, an anonymous crew of young, underpaid Astros players stand on the sidelines, background performers for a stirring moment in the history of another franchise.

It never happened. Though it was his own manager who brought up the possibility, Rivera declined any opportunity to take the field in Houston, recognizing how perfect his sendoff was in his final game at Yankee Stadium. Instead, the discussion that final weekend was focused on two things, the imminent retirement of Andy Pettitte and Rivera's missed opportunity, with writers around the country endlessly debating what our "final image" of the celebrated closer should have been. One thing the discussion was most certainly not about was the young club in Houston.

It was a fitting final scene for the Astros' season, as 2013 will be remembered more for the impact the Houston franchise had on the rest of the league than for anything the club did itself.

Resetting the Schedule

It all started in November 2011, when the Office of the Commissioner announced that the sale of the Astros was complete. New owner Jim Crane, who purchased the team from owner Drayton McLane for more than $600 million, had been awarded the franchise after agreeing to Major League Baseball's final caveat—the Astros would move from the National League Central division to the American League West in 2013.

Big league baseball came to Houston in the spring of 1962, when the Houston Colt .45s joined the league as part of the expansion promised in the wake of the Dodgers' and Giants' escape to the west five years earlier. Though they were technically the first expansion club to play in the National League (beating the New York Mets by a day), it didn't take long for the Colt .45s to abandon their Wild West identity and instead embrace the space race that was overtaking 1960s Houston. In 1965, the club moved from hot, sticky, and wholly uninviting Colt Stadium into the space-age Astrodome, complete with glass roof and all-season air conditioning, taking on the "Astros" name in the process.

Fifty years later, the NL's first expansion club moved to the American League with the stroke of a pen. Like the Brewers switching leagues in 1998, the shift was made as an effort by the commissioner's office to balance out the leagues. For years, teams in the NL Central were forced to compete in a six-team division while their NL opponents had to deal only with five-team divisions, making it that much harder for any single Central club to make the postseason. In the AL, the West's four-team division looked like a cakewalk compared to the other divisions in the junior circuit. But now, with the Astros joining their in-state rivals in the AL West, those unbalanced division issues were gone.

Of course, the new divisional structure brought about another problem. The uneven number of teams in each league meant that the standard MLB schedule, which kept the annual interleague games in a separate block on the calendar, was no longer feasible. Thanks to the Astros, from 2013 and on, there would be at least one interleague game on any given game day. The experiment that had begun in 1997 as a way to boost attendance and fan involvement would now be a permanent fixture in the game.

But, unlike the case in other professional sports leagues, this change was more than a just superficial reshuffling of the schedule. The differences between the American and National Leagues, most notably the designated hitter rule, are just too drastic for it to be such a simple matter. As long as the DH remains in only the AL, the schism between the two leagues will always cause interleague play to be controversial—and for good reason.

By playing under different rules depending on the affiliation of the home team, the visiting team in any interleague game is at a disadvantage. If it's a NL club playing in an AL park, the visitors are making do without a permanent DH. Any substitute placed in the lineup as the night's DH will be, almost necessarily, worse than the club's normal starters.

For the opposite situation, with an AL club in a NL park, the drawbacks are even more pronounced. In that case, the visitor is forced to decide between playing its regular DH in the field (where he almost certainly doesn't belong) or just keeping him on the bench for the night. Either way, the visiting team has the weaker hand.

All of this is magnified when the interleague portion of the schedule goes year-round. Now, instead of having to deal with a non-ideal roster for a few games at a time, some clubs are forced to deal with those deficiencies for a week or more straight, while others are spared the worry entirely.

Take the Red Sox. In 2012, Boston played 15 of its 18 interleague games in one two-week stretch, the same as everyone else in baseball. In 2013 though, those games were spread around the schedule, beginning in May and ending in September. In August, the Red Sox played six straight interleague games against the Giants and Dodgers in California. In that stretch, regular designated hitter David Ortiz, who was hitting .327/.408/.588, was forced to sit out three of the games thanks to the lack of a DH in the NL parks. Before that, Ortiz's off days had come once every two weeks or so, and never in such a clump. It was not an issue of rest, but one of inequality between the two leagues. Luckily for the Red Sox, they ended the season with the best record in baseball. The extended disadvantage that they were saddled with during interleague play did not affect their shot at the postseason.

For the Tampa Bay Rays, who beat the Texas Rangers in a Game 163 play-in game to decide the final Wild Card participant, things could have been very different. From Aug. 6 through Aug. 11, the Rays played five straight interleague games on the road. In those five games, regular designated hitter Luke Scott totaled four at-bats, each coming in pinch-hit appearances for the pitcher. The Rays lost all five games.

On the NL side, the Cincinnati Reds played five consecutive road interleague games in late June. Rather than mess with his everyday lineup, manager Dusty Baker filled in the DH spot with bench guys Chris Heisey and Xavier Paul, two players who had a combined .309 on-base percentage over 2013. In the case of Heisey, the choice came at the expense of some defensive maneuverability. The Reds went 1-4 on that swing.

In fact, for all 13 teams that had five-plus consecutive interleague games on the road in 2013 (including playoff hopefuls the New York Yankees, Baltimore Orioles and Arizona Diamondbacks), the record in such games was 32-44—and that includes the Pirates' 5-0 swing through the West Coast! The combined .421 winning percentage in those 76 games is nearly 100 points worse than the .508 winning percentage the 13 teams earned over the full season.

But things could have been worse. Before the Astros moved to the AL, the unbalanced divisions meant that two teams within a division could have completely different interleague opponents. This was especially true for the teams facing the AL West or NL Central. With the Astros switching leagues, those problems were mostly fixed. In 2013, every team within a division played the same opponents as their divisional foes save for their "natural rivals." It didn't fix the interleague issues completely, but it was one small benefit created by the Astros move.

Poor Play and the Postseason

Houston's switch to the AL had a wide-ranging effect on the league as a whole, but the more drastic effect the Astros had on their opponents came not from the desks of the schedule makers, but from their play on the field. Because, let's face it, the 2013 Astros were not a good ballclub.

Not that this was unexpected in any way. The main order of business over the first year of Crane's stewardship has been to reset the franchise into something better matching his vision. This meant hiring new front office staff, including manager Bo Porter, general manager Jeff Luhnow, and ex-Baseball Prospectus writer Kevin Goldstein as pro scouting coordinator. It also meant getting rid of old, expensive contracts. Carlos Lee, Brandon Lyon, J.A. Happ and Brett Myers were all traded from the Astros in the first year of Crane's ownership in order to save money and focus on the future.

Coming into the 2013 season, the Astros' projected payroll was only $25 million—or less than what the Yankees were paying for Alex Rodriguez's age-37 season. The most expensive player on the Astros' Opening Day roster was pitcher Bud Norris, who was traded to the Orioles in July. By the end of the season, there wasn't a single player on Houston's payroll earning more than $1.2 million, roughly one-third the average major league salary. It's little wonder that the Astros ended with the worst record in the major leagues.

The 15-game losing streak to end the season didn't help, either. At 51-111, it was the Astros' third straight season with 106 or more losses after having never lost more than 97 in any year prior to 2011. As bad as a 111-loss season can be, Houston's campaign was actually worse thanks to the change in leagues.

When the Astros lost 107 games in 2012, they did it as part of the six-team NL Central. They played 79 games versus their division-mates that year, and won 29 of them. That sounds bad, but the resulting .367 winning percentage was actually better than their season-long .340 average. Furthermore, thanks to the larger division, those 50 losses were spread out among more teams. The most losses the 2012 Astros had against any one team was 12.

In 2013, now playing in a five-team division, Houston's 51 AL West losses were spread among only four clubs. Therefore, Houston's ineptitude had a greater impact on the playoff race in the AL than it ever did in the NL, without any change on Houston's part. In 38 games versus the top two teams in the West, Houston squeaked out only six victories. The Rangers took 17 of the 19 games, while the A's took 15 of 19. That's 32 losses to playoff teams just within the division. In 2012, the Astros didn't even play 32 games against the Central's two playoff teams!

It wasn't just their fellow AL West clubs whose record the 2013 Astros helped pad. Each of the AL's playoff teams did well against Houston. In seven games versus the Rays, the newest junior circuit squad won two and lost five. It was, sadly, the most wins Houston managed versus the non-Western playoff teams. Boston, Detroit and Cleveland all faced the Astros seven times throughout the season, and they all walked away with 6-1 records. The combined .212 winning percentage Houston managed against these four teams was 100 points worse than their season average.

This abysmal performance came into even sharper focus in the closing weeks of the season. Houston was mathematically eliminated from the postseason in late August, but still had to play the games. Beginning on Sept. 19, the Astros began a seven-game road trip to Cleveland and Texas. In four games against the Indians, Houston was outscored 17-5 en route to a sweep. The Rangers series went even worse, with Houston losing all three games by a combined score of 22-5.

Meanwhile, the Rays were busy closing out their season with 11 of 14 games against teams with winning records. The difference in strength of schedule was not missed by sports writers. In an ironic twist, Houston's poor performance against these teams was the best possible outcome from a postseason perspective. Because the Astros lost to each team equally, it meant that the final playoff teams were decided by their performance against the rest of the league and not just against the league's designated doormat.

Houston's postseason impact didn't end on the scoreboard. With one move nearly a year before, the new-look Astros were even able to dramatically impact a playoff team's season despite only three head-to-head matchups.

As part of the Astros' effort to rid the team of any contracts worth more than a cell phone bill, Luhnow traded Wandy Rodriguez, the last member of the 2005 World Series club, to Pittsburgh for a handful of minor leaguers at the July 2012 trading deadline. It was Houston's fourth big trade in less than a week. Rodriguez performed well enough for the Pirates, finishing his season with the Bucs with a league-average ERA. As the team began the 2013 season, the southpaw was slated as Pittsburgh's number-two starter. He lasted only 12 starts. In June, Rodriguez was placed on the 60-day disabled list with a forearm strain. To replace him on the roster, Pirates general manager Neal Huntington called up top prospect Gerrit Cole, a 22-year-old flamethrower from southern California.

Cole was a hit from the start. In his major league debut, the 6-foot-4 right-hander faced off against the defending World Series champion San Francisco Giants and two-time Cy Young Award winner Tim Lincecum. Cole took a shutout into the seventh inning against the Giants and even helped himself with a two-run single in his first major league at-bat. In 19 starts for the Wild Card-winning Pirates, Cole posted a 3.22 ERA while striking out 100 batters in 117 innings. For a franchise that has gone through so much turmoil over the last two decades, including an impressive collapse at the end of 2012, the injury to Rodriguez could easily have been a sign of another forgotten season. Instead, it led directly to the debut of Rookie of the Year-candidate Cole—and all of it can be traced back to the Astros. It's almost uncanny.

A Mess on Television

Though the Astros' effect on the rest of the league was their biggest story of the season, there were still plenty of interesting stories swirling around the club itself throughout 2013. The biggest of these stories came on the media side.

On Sept. 16, it was announced that the Astros' weekend game against the Angels—a game that saw Houston earn its 97th loss of the season—had only 1,000 viewers in the Houston market, one of the largest in the country. The reports came from the Nielsen Media Research company. It was a particularly troubling report, especially when placed alongside the ratings for the National Football League's Houston Texans game the next day. Played not even 24 hours later, the football game had nearly 2.5 million Houston-area households tune in.

Things got even worse a week later when Nielsen reported a 0.0 television share for a weekend Astros/Indians game. That's just what it sounds like. According to the Nielsen market research, the Saturday, Sept. 21 game in Cleveland, which was the Astros' eighth straight loss and dropped the team to 51-104, was seen by literally no one in the Houston area. Did this signal a remarkable lack of interest in Crane's club? Was it poor market research? And what did these reports bode for Luhnow's and Crane's dream of packing Minute Maid Park with fans in upcoming years?

The answers to these questions are more complicated than they seem, touching on issues far beyond a simple television experience. In August, Forbes.com made waves by claiming that the Astros, through all of their spendthrift ways, were the "most profitable team" in major league history. The article, written by Dan Alexander, said that Crane and his team were set to see $99 million in operating income after the 2013 season, with $80 million of it coming from the club's partial ownership of regional sports network CSN Houston. League and club officials quickly denied Alexander's findings, contending that Alexander had many of his facts wrong.

The crux of the controversy rested on the report's information about CSN Houston, the cable network showing Astros games—which, according to Nielsen, no one was watching. The reason for those low viewership totals was that CSN Houston is available to only about 40 percent of households in Houston. The network, which started in late 2012, has been having trouble signing deals with cable providers to be part of their channel lineups. The lack of carriership agreements meant a lack of viewers, which, in turn meant a lack of revenue for the company and a lack of money for the Astros. In late September, CSN Houston filed for Chapter 11 bankruptcy protection. As part of this filing, it was revealed that the station had not paid its rights fees to the Astros for three months while the club continued to pay the station's operating costs.

In short, Houston's television deal was costing the team both money and viewers, all the while causing controversy across the country. It's not exactly an ideal situation. As management works to complete its plan to bring the club back into contention in future years, this will be a serious obstacle.

Lasting Impression

When doing a season-in-review for any sports club, it's always best if one can focus on the action on the field. The wins and losses. The amazing plays that got fans out of their seats. The prospects breaking through and the superstars earning their keep. The drama as the season winds down. And, sure, the 2013 Astros had some moments that would qualify. Jose Altuve was signed to a club-friendly contract. Brandon Barnes hit for the cycle. Jarred Cosart nearly no-hit the Rays in his major league debut. And the club does have one of the best farm systems in baseball, with affiliates at every minor league level reaching the playoffs. There are reasons to watch Astros baseball.

But the most fascinating stories about this year's Astros team were away from Minute Maid Park. Their move to the AL and the subsequent schedule changes. New ownership continuing to leave its mark. Terrible play. Cheap pay. A controversial media setup. Mariano Rivera *almost* playing center field. These are the stories we'll be taking away from this Houston club for years to come. They may have had a tough year in the standings, but one thing is for sure: as long as you weren't watching their play on the field, the 2013 Astros season was quite exciting.

Case Studies: Breaking Out and Breaking Bad

Every season, a bevy of players capture our attention in ways that they had not previously. We tend to gravitate towards the positive (or at least, we'd like to hope that we do), but unfortunately it doesn't always work out that way. What's more, each player is unique in the way in which he progresses or regresses. As such, we thought it would be instructive to take a look at the journey of four different players throughout the 2013 season.

After doing his best Babe Ruth impression for most of the summer, Chris Davis was an obvious choice to examine. Also on the docket are two young pitchers in Jose Fernández and Shelby Miller—both of whom were relatively anonymous before the start of the season, but are certainly now well on their way to establishing themselves as household names. Finally, Josh Hamilton already *is* a household name, but if his 2013 season is any indication, his success story may draw to a close sooner than expected.

Chris Davis
by Blake Murphy

Perhaps Chris Davis knew what was to come.

In March, for a vignette with MLB Network, Davis explained the changes he had begun implementing, foreshadowing a major change in his approach for the 2013 season.

"When I'm going my best, I'm going to left-center," said Davis.

However, to that point in his career, his weighted on-base average (wOBA) was higher on balls that were pulled or hit to center than on balls hit to left field.

In 2012, that began to shift a bit, and it's at least in part due to the work Davis was putting in. (A lot started to change for Davis late in 2012, in fact, and his hitting saw a major surge in September of that year. His 10 home runs and .440 wOBA that month should have been a warning.)

As he explained it, he used a batting tee to work on his swings in six specific zones: thigh-high and away (tee placed on the back outside part of the plate); waist-high and away (same); thigh-high and at the front of the plate; waist-high and front; and then middle-in (front corner of the plate on the inside) and waist-in.

Now, these changes to batting workouts aren't simply taking the same swing and putting it on new ball placements.

As Orioles hitting coach Jim Presley told Jonah Keri of Grantland in June, another problem was that, "he was so pull-conscious." Davis had pulled 42 percent of his balls in play through 2012 and he had hit home runs on just 13 opposite-field balls compared to 38 pulled balls and 26 to center.

So, he was a pull-hitter who hit for power only to his pull side.

What the exercises worked to do was level his swing plane, forcing him to keep his hands back and fluid through the zone. Rather than selling out for inside pitches and flailing if an adjustment was needed, the tee work and new commitment to driving the ball away helped him cover far more of the plate.

Gone was the uppercut swing of the past meant to crush everything it could touch. In its place was a more level swing that used Davis' considerable size and strength to send the ball great distances instead.

And, of course, it worked.

Davis led the major leagues with 53 home runs this year, nine more than the next best hitter. He had 96 extra-base hits, 21 more than the next best hitter. His isolated slugging percentage was .060 higher than the next best hitter.

All things considered, Davis was perhaps the most dangerous hitter in baseball, rivaled only by Miguel Cabrera and Mike Trout.

And it's hardly fluky when you consider how the changes he made to his swing and to his approach manifested themselves in his statistics.

This wasn't a hitter suddenly showing a surge in power; the power had always been there. That's why Davis was a touted prospect and was given several opportunities to prove he wasn't a Quad-A player. Instead, this was a power behemoth figuring out how to use his considerable power without looking like Potato facing Henry Rowengartner's floater pitch on anything not in his wheelhouse.

Consider his slugging percentage on the outside portions of the plate and how they changed starting in September of 2012 (per Brooks Baseball).

Location	Pre-SLG	Post-SLG
Middle outside corner	0.742	1.392
Low outside corner	0.509	0.759
Middle away	0.253	0.442
Low away	0.490	0.730
Low middle	0.243	0.535

Davis' whiff rates didn't noticeably improve in these areas—he was still susceptible to swings and misses—but the balls he connected on did significantly more damage.

This makes sense, since his strikeout rate remained at its previous levels (29.6 percent). This isn't a player whose change in approach entailed becoming less aggressive. Rather, he applied a better bat path to those aggressive choices, keeping his hands back and driving the ball the other way when presented with the opportunity.

What resulted was a jump in fly ball rate to 45.7 percent, almost entirely at the cost of ground balls. Rather than rolling over a pitch with an uppercut swing, the even bat plane allowed him lift and drive. His fly ball rate in the eight low, away and low-and-away zones jumped from 29.3 percent to 36.4, with his slugging percentage jumping from .438 to .671 (per Brooks Baseball).

He also managed to take 14 balls the opposite way for home runs, compared to 18 to center and 21 on pulled balls, a significant change. What didn't change, however, was his pull percentage, which actually climbed from 42 percent to 46.5 percent. Davis didn't abandon his pull-hitting nature at all; he simply became a better hitter on the rest of his swings.

Area	08-12 BIP%	13 BIP%	08-12 wOBA	13 wOBA
Pull	46.5%	42.0%	.485	.553
Center	30.7%	30.6%	.474	.586
Opposite	27.3%	22.9%	.413	.648

Of course, there's the matter of his improvement in the other zones, too, which are present but less extreme.

Most people immediately point to Davis' plate discipline because his walk rate spiked to a career-best 10.7 percent this year. Part of that is due to an improved approach and part of it is simply a better understanding of what pitchers were trying to do against him; Davis saw fewer than 40 percent of pitches in the zone and his outside swing percentage took a significant drop for the second straight season.

Overall, Davis still swung at more pitches than most players and made contact on fewer pitches than most. He made improvements, sure, but his success isn't solely attributable to being a little more selective.

Instead, it's possible, perhaps even likely, that an improved swing plane and success in new areas of the strike zone allowed Davis to be more comfortable waiting for a pitch he liked. His first-pitch swinging percentage dropped from 41 percent to 37 percent, resulting in Davis seeing far more hitter's counts, as his rate of plate appearances ending in a hitter's count rose from 28.5 percent to 35.2 percent (per Baseball-Reference).

Back in March, Davis knew what he was doing. The changes he had begun to make to his hitting approach in September of 2012, from tee-work out, had started to produce results. Davis was confident enough to give away his "secret" on MLB Network, because he already knew what was to come.

You can still strike Chris Davis out, sure. But you damn well better.

José Fernández and Shelby Miller
by Mike Podhorzer

There is a particular cliché in baseball. It even has an acronym (doesn't everything in baseball?). You may have heard of TINSTAAPP. It stands for There Is No Such Thing As A Pitching Prospect. But in recent years, the mantra has been laughed at and stomped on by a plethora of young pitchers who dominated immediately upon their promotion to the big leagues.

This season was no exception. A pair of rookie right-handers, Jose Fernández and Shelby Miller, turned the concept of TINSTAAPP upside down and succeeded from the get-go. But the question of what the future holds looms large.

Jose Fernández

It wasn't supposed to happen this way.

It wasn't supposed to happen so quickly.

It wasn't supposed to be this easy.

Ranked as the fifth-best prospect in baseball during the preseason by Baseball America and the eighth-best by FanGraphs, the then 20-year-old Jose Fernández figured to open the 2013 season perfecting his craft in the minor leagues. After all, he had yet to throw a pitch above the High-A level. As a result, no one questioned the Miami Marlins when Fernández was reassigned to minor league camp in mid-March. This was expected and the assumption was that Fernández would return to the big league club later in the season, depending on how he handled his first taste of Double-A competition.

Several weeks later, the baseball world was stunned when the organization purchased the contract of this same Fernández. Soon after, it was announced that Fernández had made the Opening Day roster as a member of the team's starting rotation and would be limited to 150-170 innings.

While he had just 138.1 professional innings under his belt, which all came at the lower levels of the minor leagues, Fernández's rookie performance could be described as nothing short of spectacular. He tallied a smidge more innings than the upper limit prescribed for him and posted a 2.19 ERA (3.22 SIERA), which ranked as the second best in baseball among qualified starting pitchers. He even struck out more than a batter per inning and posted a strikeout percentage that ranked fourth in baseball. Remember, this is a kid who wasn't even legally allowed to drink alcohol when he made his major league debut.

Although Fernández features serious gas, having averaged 94.9 mph with his fastball (this ranked as the third-highest velocity among qualified starters), he is far from a one-trick pony. His pitch repertoire also includes a curveball and change-up. Some, including Fernández himself, call his curveball a "slurve," which is in between a true curve and a slider. Given the pitch's horizontal and vertical movement, that is probably the more appropriate description.

That slurve was an absolutely dominant pitch for Fernández during his rookie season. It induced a swinging strike more than 16 percent of the time, compared to a league average for the pitch of about 13 percent. When the batter did manage to put the pitch into play, it usually resulted in either a ground ball or a harmless pop-up.

Perhaps most impressive, though, was that Fernández handled left-handed batters nearly as well as right-handed opponents, holding the former to a .252 wOBA (compared to a .218 mark against righties). The change-up is often the weapon of choice to neutralize opposite-handed hitters and Fernández's pitch selection exemplifies this preference. Against righties, Fernández is essentially a two-pitch pitcher, throwing his fastball-slurve combination 99 percent of the time. Versus lefties, he introduced the change-up, having thrown it 15 percent of the time, and used his fastball and slurve less frequently.

The change-up generated a slightly better-than-league-average swinging strike percentage, but induced a ton of ground balls. Typically, a pitcher will use his change-up as a swing-and-miss strikeout pitch or to get the hitter out in front and to roll over on the ball, leading to a weak grounder. The Fernández change-up was able to do both, but he did struggle with the long ball, presumably when he left the pitch up in the zone. The pitch had by far the highest home run rate allowed of any he threw to batters from either side of the plate.

So after one of the best rookie starting pitcher performances in years, what does Fernández do for an encore? It may sound silly to suggest that he could still improve as a pitcher after recording a 2.19 ERA, but this is indeed the case. While on the whole, Fernández didn't find left-handed hitters too troublesome, his walk rate actually doubled against them compared to right-handers. The problems stemmed from his inability to throw his fastball for strikes as often, which led to fewer swings and fewer misses. Most starting pitchers perform worse against opposite-handed hitters, so this is certainly no cause for alarm. But it does show us a path for possible improvement: Sharpening his control against lefties could truly push him into the elite.

He's just 21, and the future looks extremely bright for Fernández. If he can avoid the injury nexus, he has a strong chance of becoming one of the best starting pitchers in the game.

Shelby Miller

It was an impressive rookie campaign for Shelby Miller: He posted a 3.06 ERA over 173.1 innings, while punching out nearly a batter per inning. But Miller almost missed out on the opportunity to put his impressive skills on display in St. Louis.

Let's rewind to spring training, a time in which Miller was engaged in a battle with fellow hurlers Joe Kelly and Trevor Rosenthal to earn the fifth spot in the

Cardinals rotation. Rosenthal lasted a couple of weeks in competition before being moved to the bullpen and went on to become an absolutely dominant force. Soon after, Miller bested Kelly and was named as the team's fifth starter.

It was not all smooth sailing, however. In actuality, it was a tale of two halves, though you wouldn't necessarily come to this conclusion by just looking at his ERA. After all, his 3.28 second-half ERA was not far off from his 2.92 first-half mark. But looking under the hood, SIERA (an advanced pitching stat that includes batted ball information) tells a different narrative of a pitcher whose skills deteriorated after an impressive first three months. Before delving further into his peripherals decline, let's start from the beginning and learn how Miller's 2013 story unfolded.

Over the first half of the season, Miller was outstanding, posting a 2.92 ERA and a 112/29 K/BB ratio in 104.2 innings. That's more than a strikeout per inning for a starting pitcher who threw his fastball more than 70 percent of the time. Typically, we'll see that many fastballs from a sinkerballer, one who generally pitches to contact and induces myriad ground balls. Miller is no such pitcher. All his fastballs were of the four-seam variety and he threw them up in the zone. That's a strikeout/fly ball fastball and one we rarely see thrown as frequently as Miller did. In fact, Miller's full-season fastball rate of 71 percent ranked fourth among all qualified starters and 15th over the last five years.

His fastball-heavy approach worked wonders in the first half. He did complement the heater with a curveball and change-up, but he was essentially a two-pitch pitcher, throwing his fastball seven out of 10 times and dropping in a curve on two of those occasions. The curve wasn't particularly effective, though, as it induced a below-average rate of both swinging strikes and ground balls.

So why did Miller throw his fastball so frequently when the pitch typically has the lowest rate of swings and misses and is more often used as a setup pitch than an out pitch? Because his fastball is darn good. It averaged close to 94 mph and generated a whiff rate of nearly 12 percent compared to a league average of about seven percent. With a fastball that strong, it begins to make sense that he would fall in love with it.

In the second half, Miller tried to become a more complete pitcher. He introduced a cut fastball, upping his usage of the pitch from just five thrown during the first half to 117 (10 percent rate) thrown, while mixing in his change-up more often. The increased use of these two pitches came primarily at the expense of his curveball, and it reduced his fastball rate a smidge as well. The cutter yielded good results, inducing a multitude of ground balls.

Unfortunately, he struggled to control the more frequently thrown change-up, and threw his curveball for a strike less often as well. Both his first-pitch strike and zone percentages fell as a result. Those control issues triggered a spike in his walk percentage from 6.8 percent to 9.4 percent from the first to the second half of the season. His strikeout percentage also dropped precipitously, from a first half 26.4 percent to 19.1 percent in that second half. However, his swinging strike and opposition contact rates remained essentially the same, so the missing strikeouts could be due to a decline in his called or foul strike rates, both, or poor sequencing. Whatever the explanation, the flat swinging strike rate suggests that the overall strikeout rate decline isn't as alarming as one might suspect on first glance.

Throwing the fastball so frequently, even when the pitch is as strong as Miller's, is a risky proposition. Of every pitch type, the fastball results in a foul most often. Of course, a foul ball isn't bad in and of itself, as it counts as a strike and that's a good thing. But a foul ball on a two-strike count drives up a pitcher's pitch count and leads to an earlier exit from the game than hoped for.

Miller's rate of foul strikes ranked fourth highest in baseball among qualified starters, which likely led to his high pitches per plate appearance—second in the majors—and his low 5.6 innings pitched per start. That innings pitched per start mark was by far the lowest of any pitcher within .30 runs of his ERA and it hampered his ability to reach the 200-inning plateau, while heavily taxing the Cardinals bullpen during his starts.

When we evaluate the prospects of young starting pitchers, we generally like to see at least a three-pitch mix. It is certainly possible for a starting pitcher to survive, and even thrive, using just two pitches and there are many examples, both past and present, of those who have. Miller already has a head start in that his fastball is electric. But he will have to improve on his secondary offerings and mix them in more frequently to keep hitters guessing and prevent them from sitting on that fastball. If he does that, then he promises to be one of the best young starting pitchers in baseball.

With 95+ mph heat and above average control, it is clear that both Fernández and Miller are set to become stars. When you compare their repertoires, you come away thinking that these two pitchers aren't so different. Aside from the hard fastball, each leans on some sort of curveball as his primary secondary pitch and throws the change-up less than 10 percent of the time. Fernández's curveball has more horizontal movement that gives it slider-like qualities and the pitch is much more devastating than Miller's curve.

And therein lies the difference between the two. Both are essentially two-pitch pitchers, especially against right-handed batters. But, Fernández's slurve is much more advanced than any of Miller's breaking and off-speed stuff. Furthermore, Fernández relies significantly less often on his fastball, as overpowering as it is, which makes it more difficult for hitters to predict what's coming next.

It is also worthwhile to consider how the two ended their respective seasons. Both pitchers recorded about the same number of innings, but Fernández was shut down a couple of weeks before the regular season ended as he reached his innings cap. He glided toward that finish line, flashing even better second-half skills than the impressive peripherals he had during the season's first three months. On the other hand, Miller limped through September, posting a weak 15/13 K/BB ratio in 29.1 innings, which resulted in a 5.43 SIERA. His 2.76 ERA over the month was deceiving, but it didn't fool the Cardinals; the team decided to leave Miller out of its postseason rotation, choosing fellow rookie Michael Wacha to start instead.

The skills deterioration Miller experienced at the end of the season raises questions about his stamina, while there is currently no such concern with Fernández. Moreover, despite being a year and nine months younger, Fernández appears further along the growth curve and has less to improve upon. Miller will likely have to back off on his fastball usage, especially as he begins to lose velocity as he ages, and improve his other pitches to sustain a high level of success. Miller's outlook is strong, but the future of the more polished Fernández looks even brighter.

Josh Hamilton
by Carson Cistulli

After having recorded his second four-win season in a row in 2012—and having produced 16-plus wins total over the previous *three* seasons—outfielder Josh Hamilton signed with the Angels last offseason a deal for five years and $125 million.

If there was some concern about the contract among Angels fans, it wasn't unfounded. For one thing, the club had made a large commitment to a *different* 32-year-old, Albert Pujols, just the year before. Pujols started miserably with his new team, as he had finished April as one of baseball's worst hitters—and, although he rebounded excellently, the final product was something less than Vintage Pujols.

There were also red flags regarding Hamilton himself. For the first two months of the 2012 season, he'd been nearly invincible; after that impressive interval, however, he became something a lot closer to vincible. Jeff Sullivan noted the change last December at FanGraphs, shortly after Hamilton had signed with the Anaheimers:

> *Through the end of last May, Josh Hamilton had a 1.184 OPS. He struck out in 19% of his plate appearances. Over the remainder of the season, Hamilton posted an .809 OPS, and he struck out in 29% of his plate appearances. Hamilton started off as the greatest player in the world, and he finished getting booed by his own hometown fans as the Rangers somehow missed the playoffs.*

To grossly oversimplify the situation, what made Hamilton excellent for those first two months of 2012 was his capacity for hitting the ball hard almost regardless of where it was pitched. When that proclivity for swinging persisted but the frequency of hard contact *didn't*, Hamilton's offensive production declined.

Indeed, it appears as though the concerns mentioned above were realized. In his first season as an Angel, Hamilton was basically an average major-leaguer—

not a disaster in itself, but certainly a disappointment for the Angels relative to the resources they'd invested in their new outfielder.

In the end, Hamilton recorded a 1.9 WAR—this, after producing a 4.2 WAR in 2012. "Where did those two-plus wins go?" is a question the reader might ask him- or herself. "Allow me to tell you," the present author has been paid to say, it appears.

Ultimately, any player has control over six component parts of the game that directly inform WAR: walk rate, strikeout rate, home-run rate on contact, batting average on balls in play (BABIP), baserunning and defensive value (itself a combination of position and runs saved at that position).

What I've endeavored to do below is account for the degree to which Hamilton's performance in the six relevant categories either did or didn't influence his poor 2013 season. All numbers are per 636 plate appearances—or, the total (conveniently) recorded by Hamilton both in 2012 and 2013.

Baserunning and Defense

In attempting to deconstruct a player's WAR into the aforementioned component parts, it's easiest to begin with baserunning and defense, as those numbers are already expressed in runs—about 10 of which together are worth a win.

In point of fact, Hamilton's performance by these two measures, when considered together, actually *improved* in 2013 relative to 2012.

By way of illustration, regard this table, which contains three lines. Act is his actual 2013 season. Hyp is a hypothetical 2013 season that he may have produced had he stayed in Texas, which was computed with the aid of a WAR calculator. And then Diff is the difference between the two. On the top, BsR stands for total runs from baserunning; Pos, for positional adjustment; and Fld, for runs saved defensively, per UZR:

Line	PA	BsR	Pos	Fld	Tot	WAR
Act	636	2.9	-8.4	-0.6	-6.1	1.9
Hyp	636	4.0	-2.4	-12.5	-10.9	1.4
Diff	---	-1.1	-6.0	11.9	4.8	0.5

Because he played much less center field in Anaheim than he had previously in Arlington, Hamilton's penalty for position was greater with the Angels, but UZR reckons that he more than compensated for it in terms of saving runs defensively.

Despite never stealing even 10 bases in any one season, Hamilton has always been a net-plus as a baserunner. This past year was no exception. Hamilton lost a run relative to 2012, but more or less approximated his established levels in that regard. Moreover, Hamilton's defensive figures—the invocation of which ought to be accompanied by all the caveats one makes when discussing defensive figures—were better than in 2012.

Again, there are caveats to be made, but so far as WAR is concerned, it's neither Hamilton's baserunning nor defense that harmed his overall production.

Value Lost: None. In fact, 0.5 WAR *gained*.

Walk and Strikeout Rates

As noted above, Hamilton's 2012 season was marked by a decay in plate discipline. However, despite posting career highs both in O-Swing rate (43.6 percent) and strikeout rate (25.5 percent), the outfielder still managed to produce slightly more than four wins.

Was the drop in Hamilton's value this past season due, perhaps, to a *further* decay in plate discipline?

The answer: if so, not in any way that's tied directly to walk or strikeout rate. Consider, by way of example, the following table:

Line	PA	BB%	K%	wOBA	Off	WAR
Act	636	7.4%	24.8%	.319	6	1.9
Hyp	636	9.4%	25.5%	.322	8	2.1
Diff	---	-2.0%	-0.7%	-.004	-2	-0.2

Again, the second line features a hypothetical 2013 season (estimated roughly by means of a WAR calculator) had Hamilton replicated *exactly* his walk and strikeout rates from 2012. The difference, one finds, is limited.

Value Lost: Not much. About 0.2 WAR, probably.

Home Run Rate on Contact (HRC%) and BABIP

Park effects play only a small role, if at all, in the four categories considered above. Home run rate on contact and BABIP, however, are much more prone to environmental factors. Rangers Ballpark in Arlington is notably hitter-friendly; Angel Stadium of Anaheim, largely the opposite.

It stands to reason, then, that Hamilton wouldn't have to produce the same raw home-run rate on contact or BABIP to record the same value overall as he had in 2012 as a member of the Rangers.

To get a sense of the differences, consider this table:

Line	PA	HRCon%	BABIP	wOBA	HR	Off	WAR
Act	636	10.4%	.320	.387	43	34	4.2
Hyp 1	636	7.9%	.320	.367	33	34	4.2
Hyp 2	636	10.4%	.278	.367	43	34	4.2
Hyp 3	636	8.5%	.310	.367	35	34	4.2

The first line of numbers is Hamilton's actual line from 2012, as produced while playing roughly half his games at Rangers Ballpark. The three lines after that each depict hypothetical changes in HRC% or BABIP for Hamilton's 2013 that would have allowed him, all things being equal, to have once again produced a four-win season—in this case, while playing roughly half his games at Angel Stadium.

Were Hamilton to have preserved a .320 BABIP on the Angels, for example, he could have hit approximately 10 fewer home runs and still managed to post a 4.2 WAR in 2013. Likewise, were he to have maintained the same home-run rate on contact, somehow, as an Angel, he could have recorded a BABIP over 40 points lower and still maintained a 4.2 WAR in 2013.

The third hypothetical line is slightly different. Here I've attempted, using park factors, to translate Hamilton's HRC% and BABIP from 2012 to 2013. Hamilton's 10.4 percent HRC with Texas is roughly equivalent to an 8.5 percent figure with Anaheim; his .320 BABIP with Texas, a .310 mark in Anaheim. This line also produces a 4.2 WAR.

The value of this translated value, however rough, is that it provides a baseline to assess Hamilton's 2013 relative to his 2012. This first table does that for his BABIP:

Type	PA	BABIP	wOBA	Off	WAR
Act	636	.303	.363	31	3.9
Hyp	636	.310	.367	34	4.2
Diff	---	-.007	-.004	-3	-0.3

If one is to say that a .310 BABIP for an Angels hitter is roughly equivalent to a .320 BABIP for a Rangers hitter, then Hamilton's .303 BABIP from 2013 represents a loss of about three runs over his 636 plate appearances.

Value Lost (BABIP): Not much. About 0.3 WAR.

This second table concerns Hamilton's home-run rates on contact in 2012 versus 2013.

Type	PA	HRCon%	HR	wOBA	Off	WAR
Act	636	4.9%	20	.327	11	1.8
Hyp	636	8.5%	35	.367	34	4.2
Diff	---	-3.6%	-15	-.040	-23	-2.4

The line on top is Hamilton's actual 2013 season with the Angels; the one on bottom, his actual 2013 season, except with the "translated" home-run rate on contact from 2012.

The difference, one finds, is significant. Hamilton loses 15 "true talent" home runs, as it were; about 40 points of wOBA; and 23 runs offensively, overall.

Value Lost (HRC%): Quite a lot. About 2.4 WAR.

Summary and Totals

As stated above, the objective here has been to understand more clearly in what ways the 2013 version of Josh Hamilton underperformed the 2012 version and how that performance might be understood, on a slightly more granular level, in terms of WAR. What's clear is that Hamilton was worse in 2013. What, perhaps, has been less clear is the precise way in which he was worse—that is, within the context of the six categories that inform WAR.

The short answer is "Hamilton's power numbers were to blame." Below is a table, however, that summarizes the raw difference in 2013's performance (relative to Hamilton's 2012 season, that is) and also the estimated value of that difference in terms of WAR.

Cat	Diff	WAR
BB%	-2.0%	-0.3
K%	-0.7%	0.2
HRC%	-3.6%	-2.4
BABIP	-.007	-0.3
BsR	-1.1	-0.1
Def	4.8	0.5
Total	---	-2.4

How Six Teams Are Rebuilding (Or Not)

by Jeff Moore

Rebuilding. The word itself suggests failure, at least in the world of sports, because no one rebuilds without having first failed at building. The term is over-used, as are most idioms at this point in our saturated world of sports coverage, but it's over-used to the extent of losing its effect.

To a fan base, rebuilding means lean years ahead, with a stress on the plural. The road through the rebuilding process is not a quick one, taking an organization slightly out of its path the way a beltway around a major city serves as only a slight detour. If done right, the rebuilding process is arduous. If done improperly, it can turn into an unfortunate way of life, ruining generations of childhoods for entire cities of baseball fans who instead turn to the likes of football, lacrosse or NASCAR.

There are phases to a rebuilding effort, and much like the steps toward recovering from alcoholism, admitting there is a problem is the first and most crucial. The inverse is also important, however, as the need to completely rebuild is often overblown by petulant fans or media members looking for an angle.

Assessment of the situation is key. For most franchises, being competitive in major league baseball is about windows of opportunity. Sure, the Yankees of the 2000s and the Dodgers of today, with their willingness to blow the luxury tax threshold out of the water, are able to outspend their mistakes and the inflated salaries of aging veterans. But most major league organizations, even those that are well-run, will deal with the ebbs and flows of good years and bad.

Deciding when to gut what's there and rebuild or stay the course and re-tool is based on the assessment of this window of opportunity, as is recognizing when to end the rebuilding process and rejoin the world of competitive teams. In any given season, a number of teams are going through the various stages of rebuilding, from ignorance to recognition to overhauling to competition. These are some of those teams.

Ignorance: Philadelphia Phillies

The opposite of the overuse of the rebuilding phrase is what's taking place in Philadelphia these days. Do the Phillies need a complete overhaul? Probably not, but they are significantly further from being a competitive team than they are from being sold for parts.

The plan, or lack thereof, that general manager Ruben Amaro undertook last offseason combined a dangerous mixture of poor evaluation of talent and poor evaluation of where the team stood in the league. Most teams with a payroll of close to $160 million have plenty of talent, but they don't all have four players each making over $20 million per year, two of whom (Roy Halladay and Ryan Howard) were significant question marks entering the 2013 season. And the Phillies had three more salaries on the books that were eight digits long, two of which were going to aging former starts (Jimmy Rollins and Chase Utley) and the other to a closer (Jonathan Papelbon). With around $125 million locked up on these seven players, Amaro had little payroll for the other 20-25 guys necessary to form a competitive team.

That the Expensive Seven didn't end up being the core of a competitive playoff team came as a shock to no one, other than perhaps members of the Phillies front office. Halladay was coming off his worst season in almost a decade and his first extensive time on the disabled list. At 36 and with the mileage of a man 10 years older, it was possible that Halladay would not return to any kind of effective state and virtually impossible that he would return to being a Cy Young Award candidate.

It was even more of a long shot that Howard would return to his former MVP-candidate self in 2013, given that he hasn't been anything close to that since 2010, around the time Amaro gave him an extension two years before it was necessary. Howard was coming off of an injury-riddled 2012 campaign and there was no reason other than blind faith to believe that Howard would be anything more than a league average hitter who still can't hit lefties. That he got hurt again just added fuel to the fire.

The point with the 2013 Phillies is this: It was an incredible long shot that Halladay and Howard were going to return to their previous superstar forms, yet the Phillies approached the offseason as though it was a likely scenario. In reality, even if they had returned to form, the team probably wouldn't have been good enough to overtake the Atlanta Braves and Washington Nationals.

But it wasn't just self-evaluation that was bad. The Phillies' outside assessment of possible help was equally misguided. The two biggest additions to the roster before the 2013 season were the Youngs, Michael and Delmon, each of whom was flawed.

The Rangers, a contending team in their own right, were willing to pay $10 million of the $16 million owed to Michael Young in the final year of his contract. That negotiation made him significantly cheaper for the Phillies, but the $6 million they took on for him still was too much of the roughly $35 million they had left to fill out their roster after paying the big boys. What the Phillies got for that money was a league-average offensive player, a terrible defensive player, and exactly zero wins (0.0 WAR).

The Phillies would have killed for that kind of production from Delmon Young, whom they inexplicably thought could play the outfield. Not surprisingly, he couldn't, nor did he hit well for them. He ended up costing the Phillies a win during his time with the team (-1.0 WAR) before being released.

What does all of this have to do with rebuilding?

In the 2012-13 offseason, the Phillies looked at themselves, their competition and their options and determined that they were Michael and Delmon Young away from competing for a playoff spot. That was a terrible assessment.

Should they have blown things up and started over? Not necessarily, but they had the parts to do it. You can make the case that they should have flipped some combination of Rollins, Cliff Lee, Papelbon, Utley and others to infuse an aging team with new young talent, or at least to open up room on the payroll.

Compare the Phillies' situation to that of the Red Sox after the 2012 season. Boston was coming off a disastrous 93-loss season that came with a bad managerial situation and a fractured clubhouse—a significantly worse situation than the Phillies'. With a core of Jacoby Ellsbury, Dustin Pedroia, David Ortiz and a few others, the Red Sox weren't lacking talent, but they had issues, the biggest of which was an inflated payroll.

Their 2012 midseason jettisoning of Adrian Gonzalez, Carl Crawford and Josh Beckett for a relatively small return set them up to be players in the offseason free agent market. Their newfound payroll freedom allowed them to sign Mike Napoli, Shane Victorino, Stephen Drew, Jonny Gomes and Ryan Dempster. What that group lacked in star power and name recognition compared to the three players sent to the Dodgers, it more than made up for in depth and production.

The 2013 Phillies had more holes than their inflexible payroll could afford to fix, and their 2014 version is at risk of falling into the same category if they approach the offseason the same way. Any roster led by a pitching staff containing Lee and Cole Hamels has a chance to be a .500 team, but as the Phillies stand right now, they're heading for a third straight season in baseball purgatory—not quite bad enough to blow the thing up, but not close enough to compete. This is where organizations like the Brewers and Mariners live. Teams that spend like the Phillies shouldn't be subletting an apartment there.

The concern is whether they realize where they stand. As the July trade deadline loomed, the Phillies demonstrated how far away from contending they were. During the All-Star break, Amaro said that the next week would determine whether his team would be buyers or sellers at the trade deadline. They then lost nine of 11 games from that point to the trade deadline, falling to seven games under .500, 12.5 games out of the division lead and 7.5 games out of the Wild Card race. It was a blatant smack in the face that this was not a competitive Phillies team.

Yet Amaro stood still. He waited another month to move Michael Young, who no longer had any reason to take up a roster spot on a team playing for the following season. He stood pat on Papelbon, who would have been a solid addition to any number of playoff teams. If there is one thing a non-competitive team with a strapped payroll can't afford to do, it's overpay a closer, yet Amaro continued to insist on Papelbon's presence on the team.

The Phillies have another chance to move Papelbon this offseason and open up his $13 million for other things. Much like the Red Sox did last season, the Phillies have a chance to trade quality for quantity, in a sense. If they save Halladay's $20 million and $13 million for Papelbon, the Phillies can take on four or five quality players in the $5-8 million range and help fill holes in the outfield, starting rotation and bullpen.

The question remains however, whether they will. Amaro has not shied away from making big moves as Phillies GM, but has resisted admitting when things are heading in the wrong direction. The Phillies' next step toward rebuilding, whether with a complete overhaul or a slight re-adjustment, will hinge on their ability to properly evaluate where they stand in the context of their competition. They did a poor job of this before the 2013 season. They have a similar opportunity in 2014, if they want to take it.

Recognition: New York Mets

Where the Phillies have failed in recent years to properly evaluate themselves, the Mets have succeeded. It should serve as no surprise then that the team trying to load up for a playoff run with an aging core finished a game behind a Mets team that made no bones about not contending this year and building toward the future.

Frightened Phillies fans need look no further than the Mets to see what happens when management misevaluates its own chances to contend. After a successful run from 2006-08, the previous Mets management led by general manager Omar Minaya spent the 2009 and 2010 seasons trying to hang on to that success through over-priced free agents like Jason Bay and generally poor talent evaluation, like the year-plus of playing time given to Jeff Francoeur.

New GM Sandy Alderson has not had the same pitfalls, despite the pressures of succeeding in New York.

Alderson accurately assessed that the 2012 Cy Young campaign by R.A. Dickey would be a career year for the 37-year-old knuckleballer and traded him when his value was at its highest. The return helped invigorate the franchise with young talent, such as 2014's likely starting catcher Travis d'Arnaud (who would have been in the majors more in 2013 had it not been for injury) and Noah Syndergaard, who is one of the best pitching prospects in the minors. Dickey was not going to be around to be a part of the Mets next competitive team, but d'Arnaud and Syndergaard can be.

On a smaller scale, Alderson did the same with Marlon Byrd this season. After claiming Byrd off the free agent scrap heap for virtually nothing this winter, Alderson flipped Byrd's breakout production in 2013 to the contending Pirates for Dilson Herrera, a young infielder with some real potential, and Vic Black, a power-armed reliever. Properly assessing that Byrd's career year at age 35 was unlikely to be repeated, Alderson turned nothing into something for the organization's future.

Alderson's ability to recognize that the Mets' window for competition is coming, but most importantly that it is not yet here, has allowed the Mets and their fans to see brighter days ahead. Matt Harvey's Tommy John surgery, which will cause him to miss the 2014 season, has changed when that window will open in Queens, but with a nucleus based on young pitchers like him and Zack Wheeler, we can feel the Mets trending in the right direction. The time is coming soon for them to get back to spending and bringing in free agent talent, but Alderson has, to this point, properly assessed that the time has not been right.

Recognizing an organization's place in the ebb and flow of the baseball world is a key step in returning to the competitive side of the coin, and after a few years of Minaya's miscalculations, Alderson has this team headed in the right direction.

Overhauling: Houston Astros

The aforementioned baseball purgatory plagued the Astros for roughly a half decade before they decided to tear down and rebuild. And, oh my, did they tear down.

Rarely have we seen a team strip and sell itself for parts the way the Astros did for the sake of actually fielding a competitive team. We've seen a baseball luminary like Connie Mack sell players because he was broke, and recent owners like Jeffrey Loria of the Marlins sell because he's Jeffrey Loria, but it's not often we've seen the kind of massive overhaul the Astros are undertaking that is actually lauded by the baseball community. Over the past two years, the Astros have traded away virtually every player on their major league roster with any value, dealing with the gusto of a chop shop that just got its hands on a stolen car.

Why? They had spent four straight seasons fluctuating between third and fifth place in the NL Central, and during that time were victims of the same issues that plagued the Mets' old and Phillies' current regimes—poor evaluation of their own talent.

As the careers of two of the best players in franchise history—Jeff Bagwell and Craig Biggio—came to an end, the franchise tried to reload through free agency, giving big contracts to players like Carlos Lee and acquiring aging veterans like Miguel Tejada and Ivan Rodriguez. That formula, and the addition of some young talent like Michael Bourn and Hunter Pence, led to teams that weren't good enough to contend but weren't bad enough to have no hope.

The GM during that time was Ed Wade, who had overseen a similar time in Philadelphia just before the Phillies' years of contention. His ability to run an organization has been questioned on more than one occasion, and he was relieved of his duties in 2011 when the Astros were sold to new owner Jim Crane.

Crane brought in Jeff Luhnow in December of 2011 and gave him permission to completely dismantle the organization and begin anew. The only asset with any value that remains from that time two years ago is second baseman Jose Altuve. Every other player who had any value to any other franchise was traded for anything the team could get in return.

The result has been two more 100-loss seasons (and three in a row since 2011), but also a complete rebuilding of a farm system that had been considered the worst in baseball and one of the worst in decades. It is now considered among the best. The combination of acquiring talent such as Jonathan Singleton and Domingo Santana in trades and drafting the likes of Carlos Correa, Mark Appel and George Springer in the first round in recent years has given the fans in Houston some excitement.

The Astros' thought process was simple—what is the value of trying to win 75 games? The team wasn't selling out its home games and wasn't close to being competitive, so why not dismantle completely and rebuild the right way?

It's a decision that sounds good on paper, but is difficult to execute in real life because it requires some lean years and the patience to see the light at the end of what can be a very long tunnel. The Astros haven't fielded anything remotely close to a competitive team in three years, and probably won't in 2014 either.

Their futility has led to a third straight top overall pick in the amateur draft, but that doesn't excite a fan base the way it does in football, where draft picks are brought to the forefront immediately. Staying the course of a long-term rebuilding plan takes great confidence, from the top of an organization to the bottom. Once the plan was set in place, there was no way to stop it from continuing to roll. Once the Astros began trading away pieces, they set their course down the long road they are still on.

But that road is heading in the right direction. Springer will be in the majors in 2014, and Appel and Correa appear to be good uses of the top pick. They will be a part of the Astros' next competitive team.

Some lean years remain, but the talent is beginning to reach the majors. The 111-loss 2013 season should be the nadir for this franchise, and the higher end talent within the organization, such as Springer, will make an impact soon.

The key to their rebuilding process was the recognition that it could not be done halfway. Without having committed to the process, the Astros wouldn't have been able to acquire the organizational depth they now have or land Appel and Correa, those top overall picks. Without having committed to the process, they would have been stuck in the same perpetual cycle of mediocrity that plagued them before Lunhow took over. Because of their willingness to be bad first, they have a chance to be very good later.

Perpetuation: Miami Marlins

Fans in Miami, assuming there still are any, are familiar with the rebuilding process. After titles in 1997 and 2003, the organization shipped off the very players who had helped them hoist a trophy and fill their stadium the year before. Such was the life of a Marlins fan, as long as they played in a decrepit old stadium, at least so said owner Jeffrey Loria. He contended that it didn't generate enough revenue to pay for better players and threatened to leave town if he didn't get a new stadium.

The stadium was an excuse for having a pathetically low payroll for years, until the new palace in south Florida was built before the 2012 season. Loria responded with an offseason spending spree that would make a teenager with his or her first credit card jealous. Less than a year later, those big acquisitions—Jose Reyes, Mark Buehrle and Heath Bell—were all elsewhere and the team was once again rebuilding, this time in a much newer yet still empty stadium.

It's difficult to label where the Marlins stand on the rebuilding timeline because of the way they do business. They appear to be heading in the right direction behind a young nucleus of Giancarlo Stanton, Jose Fernandez and Christian Yelich, but with Loria at the helm, that trajectory could change at any point. The market has been clamoring for Stanton since the Marlins decided to rebuild again last winter, and it's not going to be getting any quieter anytime soon. He's young, still inexpensive and a centerpiece type player, but he could be gone at any minute.

What the Marlins have done, at the very least, is flood the organization with good young talent. They hit on first-round picks in Fernandez and Yelich, and acquired some top talent when they traded away their veterans. The organization has shown an ability to rebuild in the past, and the Marlins appear to be on the right path again, assuming they stay on course.

But with Loria at the helm, anything is possible. Reports toward the end of the 2013 season said that Loria, the owner, was acting as the de facto general manager, making personnel decisions a la George Steinbrenner or Jerry Jones. The history of professional sports doesn't bode well for Loria in that regard, and even with new president Michael Hill and new GM Dan Jennings in place for the 2014 season, we known Loria's influence will be felt, even if it is behind the scenes.

The young talent to build a winning team is in place, but the question, as always in Miami, is for how long?

Deviation: Kansas City Royals

The Royals have had a plan for a long time. Their run of futility has been impressively bad, and Royals fans have had to deal with the rebuilding phrase being tossed around by management for almost a decade.

After a few failed attempts, the Royals' new plan looked like it couldn't fail. As recently as a few years back, the Royals had what was considered the deepest farm system in the game, one of the deepest in recent memory. A prospect core that centered on hitters Eric Hosmer, Mike Moustakas, Salvador Perez and Wil Myers looked to join established major leaguers like Billy Butler and Alex Gordon to form a formidable lineup. On the mound, depth in the form of Mike Montgomery, John Lamb, Danny Duffy, Tim Melville and others seemed likely to give the Royals at least a few quality home-grown starters.

A few years later, things got derailed, as happens so often in the developing-from-within process. Hosmer took longer than expected to develop as a hitter, with serious questions about his future before the 2013 season. Moustakas has yet to show any flashes of the power production that made him a highly regarded prospect. Perez had trouble staying on the field before 2013.

But the troubles weren't nearly as bad at the plate as they were on the mound. Despite an enviable amount of organizational pitching depth, the Royals ended the 2012 season having failed to develop a reliable starter since Zack Grienke.

Their latest rebuilding plan called for the 2012 season to be the year when the youngsters were ready to help the team compete. The failure to develop any starting pitching was a major reason why they again failed to field a .500 team.

Before the 2013 season, GM Dayton Moore deviated from his plan. With one big trade chip still in the minors—outfielder Wil Myers—Moore veered his team off the path that had seen the Royals build almost exclusively from within and used Myers to shop for pitching help. He landed a big fish in proven borderline ace James Shields from the cost-conscious Rays, who were happy to take six cheap years of Myers in the middle of their lineup in exchange. It was a move that likely cost the Royals the best hitter of their previously imagined core, but it accomplished what the farm system had been unable to do—give them a reliable rotation horse on whom the team could depend.

There is no doubting that this move was made with the 2013 season in mind, even if it meant sacrificing at least a portion of the future. I won't say it was a bad move; Shields' brilliance helped lead to the best season in recent Royals history and competitive games in late September, but it did signal a change from long-term building to a win-now attitude. You can argue that the move wasn't enough to "go for it," an argument that was made repeatedly when the trade was made and turned out to be prophetic, but it did make the Royals better in 2013.

Most importantly, however, it changed the Royals' trajectory. An argument can be made whether it was changed for better or worse for 2014-2016, but for 2013, the trade made the team better than it would have been with a half-year of Myers. It will remain to be seen whether that was worth the price the Royals paid—I would argue that it was certainly not—but it does demonstrate what a team can do when it feels it's gone as far as it can in a rebuilding process. The reconstruction doesn't have to be done completely from within.

The Royals built the majority of their first competitive team in a decade from within, but the front office added the missing pieces from elsewhere in a fashion that left less up to chance. It didn't prove to be enough to win, but it was the execution of the plan that was the problem, not the philosophy itself. It's important to remember that, if you're going to make a short-term move in a rebuilding process, it had better work.

Competition: Pittsburgh Pirates

To say that the Pirates are the organization that these franchises should look toward for rebuilding inspiration would be to ignore two decades of futility. But if we focus in on their recent progress, it shows how to get out of the doldrums of the bottom of the standings and all the way into the playoffs.

At the core, the Pirates have shown the importance of hitting on first-round picks, especially those near the beginning of the draft. The biggest reason for 20 straight losing seasons in the Steel City isn't bad contracts or a low payroll (although those didn't help), but the team's inability to draft well and develop young, cheap talent.

In a stretch lasting from 1993 until 2003, the Pirates selected 11 players in the first round of the draft, with an average draft position of 10.09. Just two of them—Kris Benson and Paul Maholm—earned more than 10 career WAR. Of the other nine, four never reached the majors, and the other five—including number-one overall pick Bryan Bullington—totaled -3.6 career WAR.

It's no coincidence that the Pirates' first competitive team in 20 years was centered on first-round picks who worked out. Andrew McCutchen (2005), Pedro Alvarez (2008), Neil Walker (2004) and Gerrit Cole (2011) all played major roles on this year's playoff team, and there is more talent on the way in what has become one of the deeper farm systems in the league.

Unlike misguided predecessors, the Pirates' current GM Neal Huntington did not fall victim to the pressures of the losing streak and hand out ill-advised contracts to less-than-worthy players. The payroll, though still among the lowest in the league, has risen steadily since 2010. It went up $15 million for the 2013 season because of offseason acquisitions like Russell Martin and Francisco Liriano, both of whom worked out even better than Huntington could have envisioned.

Huntington must be praised for avoiding the temptation of making a big splash before the team was ready for such a move, and for spreading his limited wealth around to fill a number of holes. It's the opposite of the approach that led to a 89-loss season in Philadelphia.

The Pirates, with their nucleus intact for the foreseeable future, are now in a position where they can spend effectively, if they continue to do so wisely. With the trend of locking up young players, the free agent markets have looked worse each year. That may prevent the Pirates from shooting themselves in the foot. Still, there are pieces to be had and the Pirates' recent run of success could allow them to continue to expand the payroll.

The Pirates will never spend with the big boys in the league, but with their ability to develop young talent, they don't have to. What has allowed them to take the next step from up-and-comer to playoff team is their ability to assess where they stand. After late-season collapses in 2011 and 2012, Huntington accurately assessed that this was a team that was a few players away. He may have been a little lucky in acquiring two of those in one offseason as his own young talent developed, but when you make smart decisions, you tend to make your own luck. Huntington's ability to properly gauge his own organization and where it stood in the context of the rest of the National League is what made the Pirates' next step possible.

No matter at which step along the path from rebuilding to competitiveness a franchise stands, the most important characteristic is the ability to figure our where that step is. What gets an organization in trouble more often than not is an improper evaluation of where it stands.

The ability to self-assess leads to the best decision making.

On the Difference Between Pitching and Hitting Prospects

by Bill James

The following is a reprint of an article that first appeared at Bill James Online (billjamesonline. com) on Dec. 12, 2012. You can subscribe to Bill James Online for $3 a month. His latest book, Fools Rush In, *will be available at actasports.com in February.*

In regard to the Wil Myers trade, a local sports columnist wrote these words:

> In time, Wil Myers might develop into one of the top power hitters in the game. At 21, he hit .314 with 37 home runs and 109 RBIs in 134 games of a season split between Double A (35) and Triple A (99). His pitch recognition might develop to the point he can strike out at a less disturbing rate than 140 times in 522 at bats. He's an excellent prospect, all right.

The word "might" and "prospect" need not enter discussions about James Shields, the main player acquired by the Royals in the deal with the Tampa Bay Rays.

Oh, I can give you a long list of *mights* that enter into the James Shields evaluation, but let's fast forward. In time, Wil Myers might be something; he isn't anything yet, but later on, down the road, he might become something. Not trying to parody the sportswriter's words or to state them unfairly; I think that's an accurate summation of his point; Wil Myers isn't anything yet, but later on he might be something.

Most of us guys, I suspect, see the situation a little differently: that Wil Myers *is* a very good baseball player, right now. He was a very good baseball player in 2012; there is every reason to believe that he will be the same player in 2013, although his statistics will not be the same because the players he will be playing against are better. Later on, he may develop to an even higher level, true, but he is the same thing now that he will be in a year, and therefore the distinction between "prospect" and "player" is, on some level, a silly distinction. It relies on doubt that exists only because of ignorance, and thus exists only for the ignorant.

We cannot make absolutely accurate projections as to what any player will hit next season, whether he is a rookie or whether he has been in the league for 10 years. But we can project what Wil Myers will hit in 2012 as accurately as we could project the same if he had been in the league for 10 years, and this is a fairly high level of accuracy. The sportswriter thinks of Wil Myers as he does because he fails to understand this. He believes that there is an element of doubt in the equation that is not really there, or does not need to be there. Thus, he is basing his analysis of the trade on a categorization of the players, and basing the categorization of the players on his own ignorance, his own lack of sophistication. It's an analysis that is based, at the deepest level, on the ignorance of the writer.

But wait a minute; I'm not here to castigate the sportswriter in question; rather, I wanted to point out that I do the same thing. Within the last two months, a trade was offered to the Red Sox that would have involved our trading a major league pitcher—let's call him Camilo Pascual—for three excellent pitching prospects. A group of us were discussing the trade, and in that context I said "Most pitching prospects are going to fail, 60 percent of them are. If we trade Camilo Pascual for three pitching prospects, two of them will fail, we'll wind up trading Camilo Pascual for somebody who will be Camilo Pascual in three years. I don't see the point in it." In other words, I was analyzing that trade exactly the same way the local guy was analyzing the Myers trade: A pitcher is one thing; a prospect is something else, a different animal.

Now, it may be that I am just wrong, and it may be that I am operating out of my own ignorance. What people often don't understand, when I "accuse" them of ignorance, is that in my view, we're *all* ignorant. None of us really understand the world or the game of baseball. We're all just projecting outward from small islands of understanding into a limitless ocean of ignorance, like a tiny island nation claiming the sea as its lawful territory. The question I am trying to get to is, why is there this distinction? Why is it that minor league *hitters* can be projected into the major leagues accurately and reliably, but minor league pitchers cannot? I am trying to (a) think that question through, and (b) outline some research that could help us understand it better.

We could, as a starting point, determine whether it is actually true that 60 percent of pitching prospects fail. I *believe* this to be true; it has been my experience that this is true. If you go back to, let us say, 2008, you can see that the baseball world was very excited about Joba Chamberlain, and Phil Coke, and Zack Kroenke, and Michael Bowden, and Hunter Jones, and Craig Hanson, and Francisco Liriano, and Kevin Slowey, and David Purcey, and David Huff, and Aaron Laffey, and Zach Jackson, and 40 or 50 other guys who didn't turn out to be anything special, either...and no, I'm not exaggerating when I say "40 or 50"; there actually are 40 or 50 other guys who were top-of-the-line pitching prospects four years ago who are middle relievers and ex-major league players now; don't make me name them, because I will.

But it could be that this is a fault of my perception, in that—in my ignorance—I failed to distinguish between those who were *legitimate* top-of-the-line pitching prospects, and those who merely seemed to be that to those of us who don't know any better. It would be a worthwhile project, as a starting point, to pull out an old John Sickels prospect book or Baseball America prospect book, using that as a fixed frame of reference to determine who was a legitimate project and who was a pretender, and then figure out what percentage of pitching prospects from five years ago have since failed. But not having done that, I'm saying it is 60 percent, or higher—if by "failed" you include those who are still in the majors but in a very limited role, like Aaron Laffey, and those who pitched brilliantly in the major leagues for three months and then disintegrated, like Dallas Braden, Matt Palmer, Brett Cecil and Jeremy Sowers. And also, some guys who were not prized prospects then are good pitchers now, but that's not relevant to this discussion, because what we're talking about here is failure rates among prized prospects.

OK, since we haven't done that, let's assume for the sake of argument that it is true that most pitching prospects are going to fail, whereas virtually 100 percent of position prospects who are of the stature of Wil Myers are going to succeed. The question is, then, why? What are the differences between pitching prospects and positional prospects which make it so much more difficult to identify the pitchers who will succeed?

Theorizing:

Pitchers get hurt more, particularly at those moments when they are first exposed to heavier workloads than they have experienced in the past.

I think this is true, and I think it is a very important part of why pitchers are so hard to figure. I would also point out that there is a non-obvious "workload" problem here, which is that making 20 starts and pitching 140 innings in the major leagues is vastly more difficult than making 20 starts and pitching 140 innings in the minors. If you pitch 140 innings in the minors—let us say that you face 600 batters—you might face really tough hitters, guys like Wil Myers, in 20 of those confrontations. In the majors, you're going to face high-quality hitters in 150 or 200 of those plate appearances, guys like Ryan Howard and Mark Teixeira and Jason Heyward. The major league pitcher is under vastly more pressure to make good pitches, thus is working much harder, even if his innings pitched are the same.

But while I do think the injury risk is an important part of this dichotomy, I don't by any means think this is the whole enchilada. There is something else going on here.

Despite the gains we have made in better understanding pitchers' records, it is still true to some extent that pitchers' records reflect and embody the performance of the team, thus are not true indicators of a pitcher's ability.

In 2010 Mike Pelfrey went 15-9 with a 3.66 ERA for the Mets. If he had done that in 1975, it would have been universally assumed and accepted that Pelfrey had turned the corner. In the modern world, most of us kind of understood right away that that was more mirrors than smoke, and we weren't really that surprised when his career went south in 2011, because his strikeout/walk ratio wasn't all that impressive to begin with.

But while we have made progress in this area, it is still somewhat difficult to distinguish between what is done by a pitcher and what has been done by his teammates and stored in the pitcher's record. If a pitcher goes 11-3 with a 2.06 ERA in Double-A, we tend to assume that he pitched really well. Sometimes he didn't actually pitch all that well; he was just pitching for a good team in a pitcher's park. We are still misled by pitching records to a certain extent.

A pitcher faces batters in clusters. A batter faces pitchers in discrete events, separated from one another in time and place. This also causes the pitcher's record to be misleading.

Because the pitcher faces batters in clusters, small advantages can multiply and give the impression that they are much greater than they are. If a pitcher has a 5 percent advantage over the level of the competition, let us say, that becomes 5 percent times 5 percent times 5 percent in each inning, because the events are interacting with one another—and there can be nine innings a start (more likely seven). A small advantage compounds rapidly. If you're 5 percent better than the league, you might have a .700 winning percentage and a tremendous ERA, particularly in a run of 12 or 15 starts. A pitcher who is in fact 5 percent better than the league can easily appear to be dominating the competition—whereas a batter who is 5 percent better than the league, because his at-bats do not interact with one another, merely appears to be 5 per cent better than the league.

What I am really talking about here is precise calibration of a player's skills. Wil Myers, you can argue about whether he is 30 percent better than the league or 40 percent, but it's not 5 percent. But with pitchers, the "clustering" effect makes pitchers who are 5 percent better-than-league *look* very much the same as pitchers who are 20 percent or 25 percent better than the league. It's difficult to say *exactly* how good a pitcher has been, if he is good enough to win 70 percent of his decisions. This makes pitchers more difficult to evaluate.

There is a second and perhaps more important effect from this clusters/isolated events distinction. The pitcher, in coming to the major leagues, has to make adjustments many times more rapidly than a hitter.

A hitter might get 25 at-bats a week. He has time, between games and on days that he isn't playing, to work on his adjustments. Wil Myers, I will let you know, has a lot of trouble with a pitch away from him, particularly a slider going away from him or a hard fastball low and outside. That's why he struck out 140 times; it's that pitch.

In the majors, that's going to cause him more trouble than it has in the minors, because in the majors everybody will know that, and the ability of the pitchers to hit that spot will be significantly greater. But Myers will adjust. He'll figure it out. He'll watch video before every game—and I absolutely guarantee you that he will, whether he likes to watch video or not. A veteran hitter can say, "I don't need to watch video; I know how this guy pitches me." A veteran hitter can make that call. A rookie, no way; he's watching video before every game.

For a pitcher, those adjustments have to take place within the game, within the inning. Wil Myers' 25th at-bat will be a week into the season. Tyler Skaggs' 25th batter will be in the sixth inning—if he's lucky.

Further, again because of the clustering of his plate appearances, *the short-term tolerance for failure in a pitcher is much less.* The Red Sox have this shortstop prospect, Jose Iglesias. We don't know whether he is going to be our shortstop in 2013 or not. But we all understand that, if he is our shortstop, he's probably not going to hit .280—and we're fine with that, even if he's 30 or 40 or 50 percent less-than-league as a hitter.

A pitcher who is 30 percent worse-than-league…there is no way in hell. Because the at-bats form clusters, you can't live with a pitcher who is 10 percent worse than the league, much less 30 percent worse. If he's 5 percent better-than-league, a pitcher might go 10-2 in a stretch of 15 starts—which means that if he is 5 percent worse-than-league, he might go 2-10. A small disadvantage catches up with the pitcher much more rapidly.

And, for that reason (primarily) **the pitcher must make adjustments at a dramatically higher rate of speed.** A batter who has five straight bad games… that's nothing. Ted Williams had five straight bad games at least a few times. A rookie pitcher who has five straight bad games is out of the league. The team simply can't live with a pitcher who gets beat up while he is trying to figure it out.

Players fail in the major leagues essentially for two reasons:

1. They fail to make adjustments, and
2. They make bad adjustments.

I would argue that it is 90 percent the latter. The *real* risk isn't that Wil Myers will fail to adjust to pitchers pounding the outside corner; the real risk is that he'll over-react and over-adjust, and fall into a frustration cycle in which he is lunging at outside pitches and getting beat inside, or vice versa. Other people don't necessarily agree with me here. Other people, and people whose opinions I respect, will say that players fail because they fail to make adjustments.

But either way, whether players fail because they don't adjust or because they make bad adjustments, the adjustment cycle is much more difficult for a pitcher than it is for a position player—and this causes pitchers to fail when they try to make the minors-to-majors transition.

The constant demand for pitching in the major leagues, combined with the somewhat indiscriminate nature of the pitching position, tends to cause

pitchers to vault to the major leagues as soon as they are perceived as ready to play—whereas position players normally have to wait their turn.

I did a study in the 1970s, again in the 1980s, again in the 1990s, comparing the average number of minor league games and at-bats for position players over time... that is, if you look at the players of the 1930s, look at the position players of the 1940s, etc., you will find that the number of games they have played in the minor leagues has not changed essentially at all over time. Those studies are a little out of date, and I should re-run them, but I would bet that that is still true. Position players, on average, play about 450, 470 games in the minor leagues before they come to the majors. This number dropped slightly after each expansion, but then quickly returned to its historic norm—and the shocking thing is that the historic norm hasn't moved at all, over many decades.

For position players. But for pitchers, I would bet that it *has* moved, and I would bet that it has moved dramatically, particularly in terms of innings pitched. I am not suggesting that you should take my word for it; I am suggesting this as an area of study. There are a lot of guys who come to the majors now who haven't pitched 250 innings in the minor leagues. I don't think that was true, in 1955, or even so much in 1975.

Minor league systems are a lot more fluid now than they were years ago. In 1955 if you were assigned to Danville, you were going to play for Danville. If you hit 51 homers and drove in 166 runs for Danville, you were still going to finish the season at Danville.

Now, if a player hits 20 homers the first two months, he moves up a level. The systems are more fluid.

However, the fluidity doesn't substantially impact the length of the training period for a position player, because the player still has to wait his turn. Will Middlebrooks is an exciting young player, but he put in his 416 games in the minor leagues anyway, because that was how long it took until (a) his position opened up, and (b) he was the top dog in the organization at that position. When Kevin Youkilis got hurt, Middlebrooks got his shot—but not before then. If Youkilis didn't get hurt, Middlebrooks would have put in a full season at Pawtucket.

But with pitchers...well, everybody always needs pitching. *Some* pitcher will get hurt, sometime during the season. If you're the top dog in the organization, your time is going to come very quickly.

Some of you who are older will remember that in the 1980s, when you went to the airport, there would be four ticket counters with four separate lines. If you got into line behind some guy who was going to Kuala Lumpur, you would stand in line for 20 minutes waiting for a ticket agent. At some point it occurred to everybody that this would work better if you had *one* line feeding all four agents; that way the line would keep moving. In the space of a year, everybody switched to the system in which all the lines fed one agent.

There is the same distinction between pitchers and hitters. Hitters very often find themselves in a line that isn't moving—whereas the line for pitchers almost always moves. This distinction has greased the rails for pitchers—plus, many pitchers now are relievers in the minor leagues. They might face 180 batters a season. In 1952 Larry Jackson was 28-4 at Fresno. He probably faced 1,300 batters that season. A whole lot of pitchers come to the majors now having faced less than a thousand batters in the minor leagues. Craig Kimbrel faced 627. Aaron Crow faced 791. Aaron Loup de Loup faced 864.

Pitchers have to make adjustments many times faster when they get to the majors—*and, as a group, they have much less experience to fall back on in making those adjustments.*

Plus, to be honest, we're all afraid of leaving a guy's best years in the minor leagues. Larry Jackson went 28-4 at Fresno in 1952—yet he pitched 14 years in the majors, pitched 244 innings at the age of 37 and retired. In the modern world we don't have the stones to let that happen. A guy goes 7-1 at Fresno, we don't want him leaving his career year in Fresno. We rush pitchers to the majors before they get hurt—and sometimes before they are ready—because we're afraid they will get hurt before we get major league value from them.

This is my thinking about this issue; not absolutely claiming that any of this is correct, but this is what I think.

Five Fateful Offseason Decisions

by Rob Neyer

In the long term, many decisions are fateful. When the Royals drafted George Brett instead of Mike Schmidt—who went to the Phillies with the very next pick—they altered the course of the franchise's history for at least the next couple of decades. When you consider that Brett might have "fixed" Eric Hosmer last June, we might believe the Royals are still feeling the effects of that draft pick, more than four decades along.

In the short term, though, most single decisions are not fateful. Very few decisions make the difference between making the playoffs and not making the playoffs, and it's making the playoffs that is almost every team's goal on Opening Day. It's not that great players can't make that sort of difference; it's that finding great players, whether via trade or free agency, is exceptionally difficult. One might also find a fateful player in the farm system, but teams usually give such players a chance in the majors only when a) it's obvious that he deserves that chance, or b) they're forced into that decision by a major leaguer's injury or ineffectiveness. And sometimes even that's not enough (see the Cardinals' shortstops in 2012).

So what follows is a list of five immediately fateful decisions from the 2012-2013 offseason, and within you won't find (for example) the Royals trading Wil Myers and Jake Odorizzi to the Rays for James Shields and Wade Davis. Because I suspect that, while that deal will have weighty ramifications for years to come, it didn't change anything truly important in 2013 (unless you think the Royals' television ratings were important).

Nov. 30, 2012: Pirates sign free agent Russell Martin ...

... for two years and $17 million. Without checking (because I don't know where to check; if only someone would invent a searchable storehouse of knowledge, accessible to anyone with electricity), I'm going to guess that $17 million is the most money the Pirates had ever committed to a free agent. And they committed it to a player who hadn't been even an average major-league hitter since 2008.

But in 2013, Martin was a perfectly average National League hitter, which would have made him an outstanding player all by itself, considering that he's also a catcher. His Baseball-Reference.com Wins Above Replacement was slightly north of 4.0 ... but that doesn't account for his pitch-framing, which, as we've learned, is both real and occasionally fantastic, with Martin usually showing up as a master of the art.

The Pirates aced out the Reds for home field in the Wild Card game by four games, and I don't believe that happens without Russell Martin.

Dec. 6, 2012: Rays sign free agent James Loney ...

... for one year and $2 million, guaranteed; he might have earned another million dollars in performance bonuses.

In 2012, the Rays won 90 games but finished three games short in the Wild Card standings. In related news, their first basemen—mostly Carlos Peña—finished 12th in the American League with a .683 OPS, and 13th with 66 runs batted in. For that production, they paid Peña $7.25 million.

Also in 2012, Dodgers first baseman James Loney struggled. Again. Not bringing back Peña in 2013 must have been an easy decision for the Rays. Handing his job to Loney must not have been. But they spent the $2 million—not a lot, but apparently more than anyone else was willing to spend—and in return they got a fine season from Loney, and the Rays' first basemen as a group improved to seventh in the league in OPS.

Loney wasn't great. But considering the price, he was exactly what the Rays, in retrospect, needed.

Dec. 11, 2012: Reds trade for Shin-Soo Choo ...

... in a complicated, three-team, nine-player deal. Of significance so far, though, Choo went to Cincinnati, Drew Stubbs went to Cleveland, and Didi Gregorius went to Arizona. Gregorius showed some good things as the Diamondbacks' regular shortstop, and the Indians wound up in the playoffs despite the loss of Choo (and the presence of Stubbs).

But the only real difference-maker—again, so far—in the entire deal was Choo. Taking over from Stubbs in both center field and the leadoff spot in the lineup, Choo served as the perfect table-setter for Joey Votto, Jay Bruce and Brandon Phillips (who drove in 103 runs despite his sub-.400 slugging percentage).

In 2012, Reds leadoff hitters finished last in the majors with a .254 on-base percentage.

Take a moment to roll that .254 figure around in your skull, while I mention that no other team's leadoff hitters were lower than .281.

The Reds' single biggest need in 2013 was a good leadoff man. They traded for Choo, and their leadoff hitters finished first in the majors, with a .415 OBP. The Reds finished four games ahead of the Nationals in the Wild Card standings, and it's not a terrible stretch to suggest that with Stubbs in center field, the Reds would have been in a big fight for their lives down the stretch.

Dec. 21, 2012: Indians sign free agent Scott Kazmir ...

... for one year and one million dollars, guaranteed (with modest performance bonuses). The Indians made a big and unexpected splash last winter when they signed free agents Nick Swisher and Michael Bourn, two of the more attractive hitters on the market. Both players were reasonably good, although their four-year deals might not look so good in 2016.

Scott Kazmir, though? Kazmir was barely an afterthought, given just a decent chance of winning a spot in the Indians' rotation. He was insurance, signed just in case the younger, more promising pitchers didn't answer the bell. After all, the one-time strikeout king hadn't won a game in the majors since 2010, hadn't pitched well in the majors since 2008, and had spent most of 2012 racking up a 5.34 ERA with the Sugar Land Skeeters in the independent Atlantic League.

Hardly the stuff of which postseason dreams are made.

But Kazmir did some good things in spring training. Enough to hang around, anyway, even while filling the No. 7 slot on the rotation depth chart. But when Trevor Bauer and Brett Myers couldn't handle the No. 5 slot, Kazmir got his chance. And while he finished with the worst ERA (4.04) among Cleveland's top five starters, he also posted the best strikeout-to-walk ratio of his career while going 10-9 in 29 starts.

And considering the Indians went 15-14 in his starts and needed all 15 of those wins just to avoid a three-team tie in the Wild Card standings, I'm happy to say that Scott Kazmir was the difference between a great season and a good one for the Tribe.

Feb. 8, 2013: Pirates sign free agent Francisco Liriano ...

... for one year and one million dollars. Guaranteed, that is. Liriano wound up earning a few more million, because he spent most of the season off the disabled list. For the same reason, he's locked into a 2014 contract that will pay him well, if still below market value for a pitcher with his 2013 numbers.

In 2011 and '12, pitching for the Twins and (briefly) the White Sox, Liriano went 15-22 with a 5.23 ERA. His strikeout rate was fine, but his walk rate—five per nine innings—was not. Still, the Pirates saw something in Liriano; so much, in fact, that in December of 2012 they'd essentially agreed to pay him nearly $13 million over the next two seasons ... only to rescind the offer when he broke his right (non-pitching) arm while horsing around with his kids at Christmas time.

Liriano didn't join the Pirates' rotation until the 11th of May, but still wound up going 16-8 with a superior ERA, then dazzled the Reds in the National League Wild Card game. It's easy to say the Pirates really weren't taking any sort of risk, considering the guaranteed money ... but then again, they apparently were willing to take a bigger risk than anyone else was willing to take. And for that, they deserve more than a dollop of credit.

Blowing Up the Spot: Why Third Basemen Stand How They Do

by Eno Sarris

As the pitcher gears up his motion, the third baseman settles into his crouch. It's a ritual that's performed thousands of times a day across baseball, and it looks like second nature. No big thing. The ready position.

Except, at that moment, the player is actually performing rather intricate calculations, and his entire ready stance is the result of that problem solving. As Eric Chavez put it when I asked him about that moment, "there's velocity, there's action on the pitch, there's the hitter, the hitter's speed, and this all gets calculated fairly quickly—it all gets processed almost immediately."

So whether the third baseman crouches low or stands tall, whether he hugs the line or ranges left, all of this is a product of a long process, some of which was determined years before the moment. The player has all the things he's learned from his coaches along the way. His current infield coach has numbers, and advice, and helps the third baseman think about the hitters before the game starts. And then, once the game starts, there's more information: how the pitcher's arsenal looks that day, the evolving game plan for each hitter, the swings from each hitter, each hitter's batted ball tendencies and speed. And so the third baseman continues to process each of these pieces before he puts himself in that ready position.

Over this past year, I talked to prominent third basemen about this process. Set against charts and tables from Baseball Info Solutions that chart their range, we might learn how each hitter's personal tendencies affect their defensive outcomes. It turns out, it's probably all one big game of give and take. You might be surprised at some of the reasoning that goes into a simple crouch.

The Coaches

Every team's coaching staff puts together a scouting report for the fielders. Not every third baseman puts the same stock in those numbers. Josh Donaldson likes the reports, and thinks "you have to stay with them." Evan Longoria? "To be honest with you, I don't really look at the stats that we have," said the Rays third baseman; he would rather "read and react."

For the most part, though, the players seem appreciative of the reports, even if they tend to improvise beyond the script once the game gets going. "You play the numbers," David Wright felt, but added: "There's no exact science." Chavez may best sum up the players' philosophy about reading the scouting reports: "It's just the smart thing to do, to take in as much information. But when you're out there, you have to go with what you feel."

The most remarkable thing about this approach might be that the coaches agree with the players. Orioles third base coach Bobby Dickerson says that the Orioles "set most of the alignments for the players." And they'll be proactive, especially with a talent like Manny Machado, whom they almost consider a "roving infielder," since they can shift his position anywhere from right field to the third-base line. According to BIS, the Orioles shifted their third baseman to right field more than anyone in baseball (and almost twice as often as the second team on the list). They shifted their third baseman sixth-most in general.

But Dickerson agrees that members of the coaching staff "don't take away their instincts." If they see something happening, they're free to move. He admitted that the veterans have a little more freedom, perhaps because they know what to look for. Matt Williams, former third baseman and most recently coach with the Diamondbacks, went even further in that direction: "There are certainly scouting reports that say, 'Hey this guy doesn't hit the ball here or there,' but the game changes with every pitch sometimes—I think the feel for the game in the player is probably more important, so the player is most responsible because they feel the game."

That's a coach, saying the player's instincts are more important than the numbers the coaches provide.

The Line

For third basemen, positioning yourself with respect to the line is a question that persists from hitter to hitter. Ask any hot corner defender about the foul line, and he knows whether he generally plays close to it.

Among the third basemen I talked to, most play close to the line. But they have different reasons for that choice. Longoria said he plays close to the line because he feels he can go to his left better. Maybe he's gone too far, since BIS has him just below zero to his left and almost 10 runs saved to his right. Chavez made the same decision, but feels it's because the opposing offense would "get something going with a double as opposed to a single." Williams feels it might be related to whether you used to be a shortstop—if you weren't a former shortstop like he was, you might stick closer to the line because you weren't used to ranging to your right.

But protect the line to save doubles, and you open the hole to your left. Wright, on the subject: "I just feel like there are more balls hit to my left then there are to my right, and I know that if a ball is hit to my right, it's probably a double." And it's not just his own limitations that he's talking about. Listen to Matt Dominguez, one of the best defensive third basemen in the majors, and he says something similar. "I take away more hits in the hole." Then again, BIS has Dominguez saving more than

20 runs up the middle and to his left, but costing his team double-digit runs to his right. Maybe he could move closer to the line.

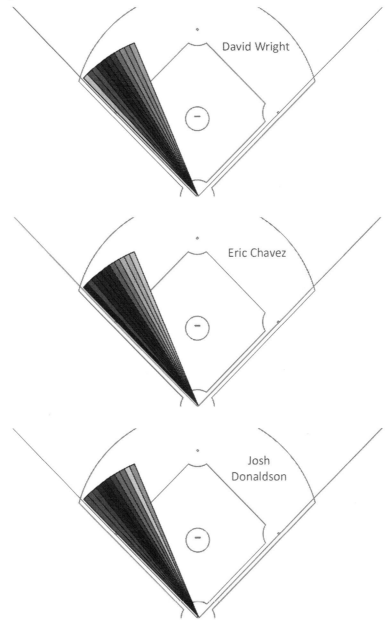

There's a give and take here. Look at Wright's defensive spray chart. The darker the band, the more likely he tracks the ball down. See how he ranges perhaps too far into the hole—the bands start to get lighter right at the foul line. On the other hand, Chavez plays closer to the line, and there's no daylight up the line. He might move to his left to broaden his range toward the hole at the cost of a hit or two down the line. Right down the middle of the two, you'll find Josh Donaldson, who sticks to the scouting reports, pushes toward the hole, but doesn't have any light-gray bands near the line. That seems ideal, especially since he had one of the more balanced left/middle/right splits among the top 10 defensive third basemen this year.

The following data, courtesy of BIS, shows the same information statistically. For each third baseman, you can see the number of runs saved (RS—the number of runs saved above or below average by making plays in a specific area) to his left (in the hole), right (third base line) and middle (in between).

Player	Innings	LeftRS	MiddleRS	RightRS	BuntRS	Total
Manny Machado	1,390	10.6	11.4	8.4	0	30.4
Nolan Arenado	1,110	3.8	16.0	4.6	2	26.4
Juan Uribe	900	1.5	7.6	8.4	0	17.5
Jeff Bianchi	263	2.3	6.1	3.8	-1	11.2
Matt Dominguez	1,312	12.2	9.9	-12.9	1	10.2
Josh Donaldson	1,373	0.8	1.5	6.8	1	10.1
Evan Longoria	1,289	-0.8	-0.8	9.9	1	9.3
David Wright	1,003	4.6	7.6	-4.6	1	8.6
Luis Cruz	276	0.8	3.8	0.8	0	5.4
Luis Valbuena	761	0.8	0.8	1.5	2	5.1

The Crouch

Every defender has to get in the ready position. And so, if you ask some third basemen about how low they crouch, you'll get a quizzical look in return. "I don't think about it, I just get ready," said Dominguez. "I'm just trying to get in a comfortable, athletic position," said Donaldson. "You have to have a pre-pitch preparation, whatever it is, to get yourself in position to make an athletic move, one way or the other," said Longoria.

Then again, there's no denying that some third basemen crouch lower than others. And, if you put yourself in a deep squat, you have to admit that it's easier to go in some directions than others.

For Wright, it's "easier to come up than to go down." Since his first step is so important, he feels he should be closer to the ground, especially on hard-hit balls that will require him to go down there. Conversely, Dominguez—even though he doesn't think about it much—feels that he's quicker when he's taller, so he might stand a little more upright when he thinks a bunt is coming. Two different approaches from two very different defenders, but there's Dominguez, third in the majors at saving runs on balls right at him, and Wright, fourth. And both have saved a run on bunts.

If there is a consensus on the crouch, it seems to be that lower is better for going forward. Donaldson said the further back he plays, the taller he'll stand, and the closer he comes in, looking for a bunt or a ground ball, the more important it is for him to be closer to the ground. Red Sox third baseman Will Middlebrooks echoed Wright. "If you're up high, your first movement has to be to go down," Middlebrooks said. "That's obviously where the ball is most of the time." Orioles coach Dickerson was the most direct about it. "The closer you are to the ball, the lower you need to be in your stance," he said. "If the third baseman is playing in, he needs to be in a lower position. If he's playing further away, he can be more upright to make his moves. Distance determines your stance." His point is exemplified pristinely in the below photo of Wright, playing in on the lip of the grass.

David Wright at Dodger Stadium, 2012 (Image credit: Wikimedia Commons user Cbl62)

The Spot

The final spot the fielder settles into is a result of all of these different calculations. But there's more to it than even the scouting reports and your personal philosophy on how low you should crouch and how close to the line you should play. In-game adjustments are huge.

Some adjustments relate to how the hitter looks at the plate. Though numbers may tell Longoria that left-handed hitter Brandon Moss hits the ball on the ground the other way 80 percent of the time against a lefty like David Price, "I don't know if I'm going to believe those numbers," said the Rays third baseman. "I'm going to see what his swings look like, and I'm going to judge where I'm positioned based on how Price looks that day and how Moss looks that day."

Chavez tries to stay on top of what's happening at the plate, too, but it can be tough on a third baseman. He can't see the spin on the ball, or the catcher's signs. But he wants to "know what the ball is doing." So Chavez will ask the shortstop what the pitch was, so he knows how the hitter is reacting to that pitch. And if the shortstop doesn't know, he'll ask the pitcher in the dugout. He just wants to know more. Middlebrooks has a similar mindset, and tries to anticipate pitches. "When I see a catcher set up in on a righty, I'll often take a step toward the line, Middlebrooks said. "Or I'll know, 'Here comes a cutter,' or 'Here comes off-speed in,' and that impacts whether I might move in either direction from the line."

Wright says his final position comes from a combination of factors, including "working off the shortstop." Because the hole between third and short is so critical, Wright wants to make sure it doesn't get too large. The shortstop has a better view of what's going on at the plate, so some deference to his positioning is important (for what it's worth, both Wright and Brett Lawrie had their worst defensive years with Jose Reyes up the middle next to them). Middlebrooks agreed, adding that the shortstop will "sometimes help me as well—he'll give me a little noise to let me know off-speed is coming, and I can play to pull a little more."

Defensive positioning is a font of current innovation. The Pirates led the league in shifts and ground balls, and rode that to their first postseason in years. The Rays are known for their shifts as well. Coaches are preparing more and more detailed scouting reports for their players, and strategies are becoming more complex.

But sometimes it ends up being a feeling, as Williams puts it. Sometimes, after you've decided where to stand, you see a peek over in your direction from the batter and think a bunt is coming, so you crouch a little lower and take a step towards home plate. Or you notice that the catcher is setting up inside on a righty, so you take a step toward the line. Or your shortstop makes a noise.

Whatever it is, baseball is a game of both adjustments and inches, and watching the third baseman anticipate, even on the last pitch of a lazy August laugher, contains multitudes worth unraveling.

Thank yous

Special thanks to David Laurila for gathering quotes from Bobby Dickerson and Will Middlebrooks.

GM In A Box: Brian Sabean

by Steve Treder

Record and Background

Age: 57

Previous organizations: The New York Yankees. In 1985, 28-year-old Brian Sabean entered professional baseball as a scout for George Steinbrenner's Yankees. Just two years later he was promoted to director of scouting, a position he held through 1990. In 1991, he was promoted again, to vice president, player development and scouting.

Years of service with the Giants: Twenty-one. Under new ownership in the 1992-1993 offseason, the San Francisco Giants re-staffed the front office. Their new general manager was Bob Quinn, who'd overseen Sabean in the Yankees front office from 1987-89. Quinn recruited Sabean away from New York to become assistant to the GM and vice president of scouting and player personnel.

Sabean held that role through 1995. In 1996, he was promoted to senior vice president, player personnel, and then succeeded the retiring Quinn as general manager in September of that year, at the age of 40.

Now completing 17 consecutive years in charge of the Giants, Sabean is not only the longest-serving GM in the majors today (a year-and-a-half longer than the Yankees' Brian Cashman), his tenure is one of the longest in history.

Cumulative record: 1,468-1,284, .533 winning percentage in the regular season. Their cumulative postseason record is 34-25 (.576), and it includes one Wild Card (and lost another in a one-game playoff), five division titles, three pennants, and two World Series.

Playing career: Sabean played baseball in high school (Concord High, Concord, N.H.) and college (Eckerd College, St. Petersburg, Fla.). He then coached baseball at the University of Tampa, as an assistant from 1980-82, and head coach from 1983-84.

Personnel and Philosophy

Notable changes from the previous regime?

Sabean has been in place for so long that this question doesn't apply. Indeed Sabean's tenure has been so long that it can be sensibly divided into four distinct phases:

- 1996-1999, when he rebuilt the ball club around centerpiece superstar Barry Bonds (and negotiated a new long-term contract with Bonds)

- 2000-2004, the peak run of success with Bonds (reaching the postseason three times in five years and never winning fewer than 90 games)
- 2005-2008, as Bonds' career found its noisy end, a sequence of losing seasons and more rebuilding
- 2009-present, a run of success (two World Series championships) with the ballclub now constructed around organizationally developed young stars Tim Lincecum, Matt Cain, Pablo Sandoval, Buster Posey and Madison Bumgarner

Whether the team's bad year in 2013 signals the end of the current era, or just a momentary stumble, remains to be seen.

What characterizes his relationship with ownership?

The fact that Sabean has kept his job through not one but two changes in ownership indicates that he "manages upward" quite well. Working within not-always-lavish payroll budgets imposed from above, he's delivered highly competitive teams in 12 out of 17 seasons, and steadily grown in corporate stature to become one of the franchise's most valued assets.

What type of people does he hire?

Sabean's manner is disciplined and methodical. He's rarely outspoken in the media, and strives to avoid drama and controversy. His front office staff reflects his steady, workmanlike style.

Sabean is highly loyal to his employees, and they are loyal in return. Upon assuming the Giants' general manager role, Sabean promoted Ned Colletti from director of major league administration to assistant GM. Colletti remained Sabean's right-hand man for nine years, until leaving (on good terms) to become GM of the Los Angeles Dodgers. Sabean then promoted Dick Tidrow, who'd been working in various capacities in the Giants' front office since 1996, to replace Colletti, and Tidrow has remained in place ever since.

In both high school and college, Sabean was a teammate of future major leaguer Joe Lefebvre. In 1991, Sabean hired Lefebvre to replace himself as the Yankees' scouting director, and in 1996 Sabean brought Lefebvre into the Giants' organization, where he has remained ever since in a variety of roles.

Others who have worked for Sabean through his entire 17-year San Francisco term are vice president Bobby Evans and scouting/minor league specialist Matt Nerland.

Has he ever been outspoken in the media?

The only time Sabean made a controversial public statement was in June 2011, immediately following the serious ankle injury suffered by superstar catcher Buster Posey while attempting a tag at home plate. In rude and blustery terms, Sabean as much as accused the baserunner, Scott Cousins, of intentionally hurting Posey.

Sabean obviously was reacting emotionally and not sensibly, was roundly criticized, and promptly apologized. It was entirely out of public character for Sabean, whose statements to the media are normally as blandly innocuous as any skilled politician.

Is he more collaborative or authoritative?

He is extremely collaborative. Sabean openly describes himself as being less expert at any particular facet of the operation than the specialists who work for him, and that his job is to keep his eye on the big picture and let his people do their work. The loyalty of so many members of his staff is evidence that Sabean genuinely listens to his employees and treats them with respect.

What kinds of managers does he hire?

He's hired only two, as they are also given long tenure. Sabean inherited Dusty Baker and kept him through 2002, at which point Baker wasn't fired, but was allowed to leave for Chicago when they couldn't agree on San Francisco contract terms.

Sabean then hired proven veteran manager Felipe Alou. After four years, the septuagenarian Alou retired to serve as Sabean's special assistant, and Sabean hired proven veteran manager Bruce Bochy, who remains in place today.

Alou and Bochy share characteristics: they're big, strong, physically impressive men, calm and dignified in demeanor, patient and cerebral. They command respect without being demonstrative. Both clearly fit within Sabean's "no drama" approach.

How closely does he work with them?

In keeping with avoidance of micro-managing the front office, Sabean accepts on-field decisions without interference. He also welcomes his field manager's input on roster-management choices.

Player Development

How does he approach the amateur draft?

It was the young Sabean's success in the Yankees organization scouting and recommending the drafting/signing of players such as Derek Jeter, Andy Pettitte, Jorge Posada, Mariano Rivera and J.T. Snow that made his reputation and got him on the executive fast track. The amateur draft would seem to be Sabean's sweet spot.

Yet for nearly the first decade of his tenure as GM with the Giants, the drafts overseen by Sabean yielded meager results. They produced some useful major league pitchers, but no stars until Matt Cain (drafted in 2002), and virtually no quality position-player talent at all.

Since the mid-2000s, the Giants' drafts have been much more successful. Between 2005 and 2009 the team drafted Brandon Belt, Madison Bumgarner, Brandon Crawford, Tim Lincecum, Buster Posey and Sergio Romo.

Does he prefer major league-ready players or projects?

Not necessarily major-league ready, but Sabean prefers more polished prospects. One aspect the Giants explicitly acknowledge that they prioritize is a prospect's mental/emotional "makeup," including demonstrated work ethic and commitment.

Tools or performance?

Perhaps unsurprisingly for a GM who began his career as a scout, under Sabean the Giants were late adopters of modern cutting-edge performance metrics. But in 2010, Sabean created a director of quantitative analysis position on his staff to augment the traditional scouting reports.

High school or college?

The vast majority of Sabean's early-round draft picks have been college players. Yet it isn't an absolute rule, as both Cain and Bumgarner were drafted out of high school.

Pitchers or hitters?

Sabean has had far more success identifying young pitching talent than hitting. However, the development in recent years of Belt, Crawford, Posey and Sandoval—as well as 23-year-old switch-hitting catcher Hector Sanchez, who might become a serious hitter—suggests that perhaps Sabean and his staff have learned something.

Does he rush players to the majors or is he patient?

Belt, Lincecum and Posey flashed through the minors, but generally Sabean requires even his top prospects to climb the ladder gradually.

Roster Construction

Is he especially fond of certain types of players?

Sabean loves to provide opportunities to fringe prospects who've knocked around other organizations without breaking through.

Does he like proven players or youngsters?

In the early-to-mid 2000s, with the Bonds career window narrowing year by year, Sabean collected a supporting cast of extraordinarily elder—as in exceptionally elder, on an historical scale—veterans. But he hadn't done so before that period, and he hasn't done so since; it's apparent now that it was a strategy adopted (if ardently) for that particular circumstance.

Offensive players or glove men?

The Giants' rosters have often featured speedy defenders covering the outfield corners, but that appears to be more a reckoning of the spacious outfield at AT&T Park than any particular preference of Sabean's. They always had multiple power bats in the lineup surrounding Bonds, and the 2010 champion team's offense was structured around home runs.

Power pitchers or finesse guys?

No particular preference. Cain and Lincecum both made their names as power pitchers, but Bumgarner has never been a really hard thrower, and Romo is a finesse guy being deployed as the closer. And one of Sabean's very favorite pitchers for a long time was Kirk Rueter, as soft a tosser as can be.

Does he allocate resources primarily on impact players or role players?

Despite the cascading torrents of revenue the Giants' franchise generates, particularly since moving to the beautiful downtown ballpark in 2000, Sabean has never been authorized by ownership to rack up a league-leading payroll. Yet through 2007, a major chunk of Sabean's budget was committed to Bonds, and since then to Barry Zito (whom we'll get to later) and others. It's apparent that Sabean's first priority is to secure his core of impact players.

How does he flesh out his bullpen and bench?

Perhaps because he's had to do it on the cheap, the back end of Sabean's roster has always been patched together with bargain-bin pickups, retreads, and Quad-A marginalities. And it is the case that Sabean has displayed a knack for getting positive mileage out of these misfit toys, especially in the bullpen.

Does he often work the waiver wire, sign minor-league free agents, or make Rule 5 picks?

He doesn't use Rule 5 a lot, but Sabean has always tirelessly scoured the waiver wire and the minor league free agent market. He's endlessly tinkering, and the shuttle between San Francisco and Triple-A Fresno is chronically busy.

When will he release players?

Several times, Sabean has cut loose a prominent player in whom he lost confidence. He flat-out released 28-year-old first string catcher A.J. Pierzynski in December 2004, evidently in response to Pierzynski's extreme unpopularity with his teammates. In midseason 2004 he released veteran Neifi Perez, and in midseason 2011 he released veterans Aaron Rowand and Miguel Tejada, when they weren't cutting the mustard. He's unafraid to acknowledge a mistake.

On whom has he given up?

In midsummer 2001, Sabean dumped 26-year-old catcher Bobby Estalella in a deal that appeared to have more to do with some sort of clubhouse issue than an on-field purpose. He cut loose high-ceiling 23-year-old pitcher Jerome Williams in May 2005 when the Giants were dissatisfied with Williams' conditioning.

To whom has he given a shot?

The list of knockabout journeyman castaways finding refuge in Sabean's bullpen or on his bench is far too long to fully present. Among his successful reclamation projects have been pitchers Santiago Casilla, Jeff Fassero, Chad Gaudin, Dustin Hermanson, John Johnstone, Jean Machi, Brad Penny, Felix Rodriguez, Ryan Vogelsong, Tyler Walker, Keiichi Yabu and Chad Zerbe, catchers Eliezer Alfonzo, Damon Berryhill and Todd Greene, infielders Joaquin Arias, Felipe Crespo, Deivi Cruz, and Eugenio Velez, and outfielders Gregor Blanco and Andres Torres.

Moreover, multiple times Sabean has been willing to salvage high-profile "has-been" veteran bats off the midseason scrap heap, such as Pat Burrell, Joe Carter, Jeff Francoeur, Andres Galarraga, Jose Guillen, Jeffrey Hammonds and Xavier Nady. Sometimes he's caught lightning in a bottle.

Does he cut bait early or late?

Early. Sabean is acutely sensitive to the concept of freely available replacements.

Is he passive or active?

Active. Sabean clearly prefers to face the risk of action than to miss an opportunity.

An optimist or a problem solver?

A problem-solver.

Does he want to win now or wait out the success cycle?

Throughout the Bonds era, Sabean was entirely focused on the now. But since then he's much more readily stocked the roster with homegrown young talent. It will be quite interesting to see how he responds to the team's poor 2013 showing. Ownership, not wanting to risk killing the golden goose of AT&T Park sellouts, would likely have little patience for a long-scale rebuilding project.

Trades and Free Agents

Does he favor players acquired via trade, development, or free agency?

Earlier in his career, Sabean was more dependent upon trades and free agency than he has been in recent years. He's willing to make use of every available channel.

Is he an active trader?

Very much so, and this has been true from the get-go. Sabean launched his GM career in the autumn of 1996 by immediately pulling the trigger on the massive blockbuster deal that surrendered beloved star Matt Williams and netted, among others, Jeff Kent.

Sabean's very busy trading record hasn't been perfect. He's committed a couple of giveaways, most notably Russ Ortiz-for-Damian Moss, and Joe Nathan-and-Francisco Liriano-for-Pierzynski, and while Carlos Beltran was good for the Giants, Zack Wheeler may end up a prominent member of the New York Mets for some time. But he's had many big wins, including the Kent deal, as well as the acquisitions of Melky Cabrera, Livan Hernandez, Robb Nen, Angel Pagan, Hunter Pence, Jason Schmidt, Marco Scutaro, Snow and Randy Winn.

Does he tend to move talent or hoard it?

He moves it. It's plain that Sabean highly values his system-developed young pitching as trading capital at least as much as for its capacity to stock his own staff. The most common type of trade Sabean has made has sent away one or more (often highly touted) pitching prospects to fill a specific short-term need.

And Sabean's record in deciding which ones to keep and which to deal has been remarkably good. Liriano and Keith Foulke have been the only two Giants prospects who've really blossomed elsewhere (though Wheeler might be joining them), and the list of coveted Giants pitchers who've failed to develop after being traded includes David Aardsma, Kurt Ainsworth, Tim Alderson, Nate Bump, Jesse Foppert, Jason Grilli, Vogelsong and Jerome Williams. Meanwhile, San Francisco has hung on to Bumgarner, Cain, Lincecum and Romo.

With whom does he trade and when?

Sabean doesn't trade a whole lot within his division, but he's ready and willing to deal with anyone else.

Will he make deals with other teams during the season?

Will he ever! Sabean has executed at least one midsummer trade in every single one of his 17 seasons, and usually more than one. He's equally willing to be a buyer (in years the Giants are contending) or seller (the less frequent years when they aren't). It's obvious that Sabean loves trade-deadline dealing, and is confident in his ability.

How does he approach the trade deadline?

With eagerness and relish.

Are there teams or general managers with whom he trades frequently?

Sabean has never made a trade with the arch-rival Dodgers, but otherwise he plays no favorites.

Under what circumstances will he sign free agents?

As the height of the win-now-with-Bonds period mounted, Sabean committed to many large-scale free agent contracts, including Edgardo Alfonzo, Moises Alou, Armando Benitez, Ray Durham, Mike Matheny, Bengie Molina, Matt Morris and Omar Vizquel, and finally the biggest of all, the seven-year, $126-million investment in Barry Zito. He followed that up a year later with a four-year deal with Aaron Rowand.

The record there would kindly be described as "mixed," and in the years following, with the Zito fiasco looming over the budget, Sabean has become far more restrained. The free-agent contracts since 2007 have been either short-term veteran deals or re-signings.

Has he ever gone to any extremes with his free-agent signings?

In 2003 and again in 2004, Sabean deployed a peculiar and unique free-agent-signing strategy. Aaron Gleeman described it this way on The Hardball Times website in November 2004:

> Last offseason [the Giants] signed free agent Michael Tucker before the deadline for teams to offer players arbitration, thus handing over the 29th overall pick to Tucker's old team, the Royals, and now they've done the exact same thing with [Omar] Vizquel and the Indians. While I can't say that I agree with the strategy, it certainly is an interesting one. In fact, it is in direct contrast to Oakland's plan each year, which is to basically hoard as many draft picks as they can for losing free agents and then use them to restock their organization.
>
> Last offseason I wondered why the Giants didn't just wait a little while on Tucker so they could sign him and keep the draft pick (since I didn't expect the Royals to offer him arbitration), but now I realize San Francisco GM Brian Sabean sees the loss of a pick as a bonus that comes along with signing their first free agent of the offseason. In other words, if you don't believe paying a first-round pick the sort of money it takes to get them to sign is a smart investment, then certainly losing the pick for signing someone a couple weeks too soon is of no concern.
>
> Of course, one could say that the Giants' undervaluing and now completely discarding their draft picks might be what has led to them filling major holes with players like Vizquel and Tucker when they've got one of the clearest windows of opportunity for winning in baseball history.

While the wisdom of Sabean's effectively "trading" the first-round pick for the free agent was assuredly dubious, it was boldly original as well. In any case, he didn't persist in the practice in the years to follow.

Contracts

Does he prefer long-term deals or short?

He's always liked short-term veteran deals, but wisely or not he's also demonstrated the willingness to go long-term with younger players.

Does he often backload his contracts?

Every time he can. Most of San Francisco's long-term contracts, whether bringing free agents into the organization or re-signing current players, have been backloaded.

Does he lock up his players early in their careers or is he more likely to practice brinksmanship?

For a long time, Sabean didn't have many young players worthy of being locked up. But in recent years long-term commitments were made to Bumgarner, Cain and Posey well before they could test the market. Reportedly the Giants were also willing to sign Lincecum to a long-term deal, but he turned them down.

Does he like to avoid arbitration?

Yes. Sabean strongly prefers forging a mutual agreement to engaging in an adversarial posture with his players.

Anything unique about his negotiating tactics?

It isn't unique to Sabean, but he's firmly within the school that handles contract negotiations behind closed doors in a discreet and professional fashion.

Is he vocal? Does he prefer to work behind the scenes or through the media?

He is not at all vocal, and absolutely prefers to work behind the scenes.

Bonus

What is his strongest point as GM?

His political acumen and people-management skill.

What would he be doing if he weren't in baseball?

He would be the chief of police in a large Northeastern city.

White Bred: Major League Baseball's Intern Issue

by Dave Cameron

"What should I do if I want to work in baseball?"

This is probably the most common question that I get asked when having conversations with people at various conferences and events around the country, even though I do not actually work in baseball. There are seemingly endless numbers of intelligent high school and college students whose dream job is running a major league front office. Despite possessing minds and degrees that could land them comfortable white collar jobs upon graduation, they're all eager to find out how they can get selected for one of the scarce, low-pay, long-hour, entry-level jobs that will get their foot into the baseball operations door.

This is the market that results when supply and demand are hopelessly lopsided. There are 30 major league teams—or maybe 29, depending on your feelings about the Marlins—and most have small intern programs, bringing in a couple of interns for the entire season, and occasionally one or two more during the summer. While no exact count exists publicly, there are likely fewer than 100 interns working in baseball ops departments at any given time.

And, being internships, these positions are designed to be temporary. Some last just a few months, with the lucky recipients committing vast quantities of their time to an organization for a short window, only to find themselves sending 29 other franchises an updated résumé when their internship ends. At times, internships do lead to full-time positions, but most do not, and it is often expected that a potential long-term employee should first go through multiple internships, often with different organizations, before he is offered a position in the front office.

While it may seem glamorous to work in an office where decisions about the major league roster are being made, the lifestyle that accompanies such a position is often extremely taxing. In most organizations, the hours required are extremely intense, as most (or all) baseball operations staffers are expected to put in a full day's work during regular business hours and then attend every inning of every home game, often manning the video or pitch tracking systems installed in the ballparks and syncing that information to the team's larger database for daily reporting needs.

That kind of schedule means that, for extended home stands, members of the baseball operations staff could be in the office for 12-16 hours per day, every day, for 10 to 14 consecutive days. And it's not like they get comp days when the team goes on the road, as there is always video to be captured, information to be analyzed, and various work to be aggregated.

Even with the understanding that the position comes with absurdly long hours, however, every team gets hundreds of applications for each internship it posts, and the demand for these positions allows the teams to offer minimal financial compensation.

In 2013, the official poverty threshold—as set by the United States Census Bureau—for a single person household in the contiguous 48 states was $11,490 in annual income, or $960 per month. While obtaining exact pay figures for every major league team that runs an internship program was not possible, I conducted a survey from a cross-section of team employees and found that the average wage reported for a baseball operations intern in 2013 was around $850 per month. In other words, entry-level positions in a major league front office pay somewhere in the neighborhood of the poverty threshold.

These figures are a sample, which may or may not be representative of all 30 teams, and shouldn't be taken as the official word on major league internship pay, but I'm comfortable that the number is at least in the ballpark of the actual figure.

And that average wage doesn't account for the geographic requirements that these jobs demand. Major league teams are, for obvious reasons, located in the population centers of the United States, and these positions predominantly require the prospective employee to relocate to a major metropolitan area where the cost of living is far above the national average.

For context, here is the cost of living index from the U.S. Census Bureau's 2012 Statistical Abstract for 29 of the major league cities—Toronto is not included—with a mark of 100 being exactly equal to the average cost of living across the 320 metro areas being measured:

- New York (Manhattan): 217
- San Francisco: 164
- New York (Queens): 159
- Washington, D.C.: 140
- Oakland: 139
- Los Angeles: 136
- Boston: 133
- San Diego: 132
- Philadelphia: 127
- Seattle: 121
- Baltimore: 119
- Chicago: 117
- Minneapolis: 111

- Miami: 106
- Denver: 103
- Milwaukee: 102
- Cleveland: 101
- Phoenix: 101
- Detroit: 99
- Kansas City: 98
- Atlanta: 96
- Cincinnati: 94
- Tampa: 92
- Dallas: 92
- Pittsburgh: 92
- Houston: 92
- St. Louis: 90

So, 20 of the 29 U.S. teams play in markets where the cost of living index is over 100, and Toronto is an expensive place to live as well, so we're really talking about 21 of the 30 major league teams. And we're not just talking about slightly above average in most cases. New York, the Bay Area, D.C./Maryland, Los Angeles, Boston and San Diego combine to house 10 of the 30 major league teams, and they all have a cost of living index over 130. Toss in Toronto and Philadelphia, and 12 of the 30 major league teams play in essentially the most expensive places to live in North America.

In most industries, wages vary significantly depending on the geographic location of the employer and the cost of living in that area, but because there is national demand for scarce positions from candidates who are willing to live and work in any of the cities that have a major league team, it is not necessary for major league teams to inflate their entry-level salaries to keep up with the cost of living in that area. The increased supply of talent by essentially turning each of these jobs into a national search suppresses wages to the point where a team can use its internship programs to solicit nearly free labor from a group of highly-educated candidates.

Now, my point here is not to debate the ethics of internship programs, and there certainly are non-monetary rewards for working in a major league front office. These entry-level positions are not permanent employment positions, so they can be seen as an investment in future earnings in a candidate's desired field. If these internship programs weren't effective in helping a significant number of candidates end up with high-level front office positions, there wouldn't be such a strong demand to fill them. People take these jobs because of where they may lead, so the value of the position cannot be measured simply by wages.

However, this system has had an unintended consequence on major league front offices: homogeneity.

Because of the selection process and the requirements that allow an individual to be able to pursue and thrive in these conditions, the primary variable in getting your foot into the baseball operations door may be your family's net worth. As a result, baseball front offices are starting to not only look very similar—they have always been very white and very male, so that isn't a new trend—but are being repopulated with people who often have similar backgrounds and life experiences. And those life experiences often include access to significant amounts of money.

During this past year, I was included as a recipient on a résumé drop for a recent baseball analytics conference, so I was able to peruse a brief list of qualifications for nearly 100 individuals who were interested in pursuing a career in baseball operations. The stack of résumés reads like a list of the best—and most expensive—universities in America. Harvard, Yale, M.I.T., Columbia, Cornell, Northwestern and the University of Chicago were all represented, often on more than one résumé, and occasionally on the same résumé.

While these universities do offer significant financial aid, the fact remains that attendees to such prestigious universities often come from upper-class families. Those who do not will likely graduate with a significant amount of student loan debt, which can be a primary motivator to pursue a high-paying career in a less desirable field. However, a candidate pursuing a position with a major league team is almost certainly looking at early career earnings that wouldn't make a dent on a student loan principal, and that's before accounting for minor necessities like food and shelter.

Unlike the universities, major league teams do not offer financial aid packages. The candidates who were already at a disadvantage from having a state school or lower profile university on their résumés must also now overcome a second major financial hurdle if they want to pursue a job in a major league front office: How to not only pay down their student loans, but how to live in an expensive metropolis on something that would resemble minimum wage if they didn't work so many hours.

And this is not a short-term commitment. Upon graduation, many eventual full-time employees will go through two or three full-season internships, potentially spending some time in the commissioner's office as well. The path from graduation to full-time employment is usually measured in years, not months. And these are the success stories; I have a number of friends who spent years bouncing from internship to internship and have still not parlayed their experience into a permanent position with an organization.

I also have friends who have made it, and who hold positions of some note in a baseball operations staff. By and large, the ones who have yet to reach managerial positions make less than I did during my first year working for Hanes as a low-level cost accountant back in 2005; that job, by the way, was located in a metro area that shares a cost of living index with Lufkin, Texas and Rockford, Ill.

Those success stories, the ones who land several internships, cultivate experience, and are offered a full-time position in the baseball operations department are often still not earning enough to do more than pay the most basic bills, especially in a major city with very high rents. And if they've accumulated any debt during their years of working for almost nothing, that's added to the pile of student loan debt that has likely been sitting in deferment, waiting for them to start earning an income capable of paying back those loans.

I know I'm painting a fairly bleak picture here, but the picture is fairly bleak for people wishing to pursue a job in a baseball operations department who do not have access to a significant stockpile of cash to burn through. And that means that most major league teams are primarily hiring analysts from the same pool of candidates: Children of the well-off.

Certainly, having financially successful parents is a significant advantage in other aspects of life as well, and baseball is not alone in having employment structures that favor the upper class. However, because of the barriers to entry and the limited number of jobs that are available to begin with, the primary flow of analysts into major league front offices are 18-25-year-old affluent single white males who are strong at mathematics and programming. And while it makes perfectly rational sense for each major league team to hire the best database architect or mobile programmer it can find, the sport as a whole will suffer if the next generation of decision makers all are cut from the same cloth.

Similar backgrounds breed similar perspectives. Similar educations breed similar lines of thought. And homogeneity across front offices may eventually stifle creativity. Diversity isn't good just because it's equitable, but because it forces perspectives to be defended regularly and protects against the echo chamber effect. Even within a single organization, it is valuable to have people pushing back against the accepted ideas so that traditions don't become entrenched simply because it is the cultural norm for the majority of the employees.

It doesn't have to be this way. Major League Baseball is figuratively swimming in money, with ever-escalating television contracts providing record wealth for nearly every franchise in the sport. The game is as prosperous as it has ever been, and the sport has the financial capability to change the playing field to ensure that the intellectual talent flowing into front offices can come from a more diverse and varied background than is the case today.

A simple first step would be to establish a minimum monthly pay for interns working for a major league team, and to set that minimum at a wage that allows those without access to family wealth to be able to meet the expenses that go along with living in a major city. The overall increase in expenses would still be a relative drop in the bucket of the increased revenues the league is currently experiencing, and would simply be an investment in the sport's human capital. The long-term payoff from growing the talent pool would outstrip the marginal costs that went along with increasing wages for the chronically underpaid.

For those reading this who dream of working in a front office someday, I do not wish to dissuade you from that goal. I would, however, make one suggestion: Learn how to code. If there's a loophole around the current system, it is a loophole that leans heavily in favor of those who can write programs and develop systems, especially on mobile products.

The advancing technologies being used by major league front offices have been mostly restricted to the physical office, but there is a push coming to integrate these systems onto mobile devices, allowing access from anywhere an employee can find a reliable Internet connection. If you can show teams that you can write programs or help them develop software that will push their information out from the office to their employees around the world, then you may be valuable enough to skip over large parts of the intern circle. Coding is currently the great equalizer. If you can build a useful system, where you went to college becomes of minimal importance, and doors open that would be otherwise closed.

Otherwise, perhaps consider finding a wealthy family that might want to adopt you. That would also be very helpful.

Finding the Translation: Quantifying Asian Players

by Bradley Woodrum

On a sunny, yet brisk Tuesday afternoon at Candlestick Park, Hideo Nomo took the mound against the San Francisco Giants. It was his rookie debut in what Japan still called the "major leagues," despite the fact Nomo had been a professional baseball player in Japan's top league for five full seasons before signing with the Dodgers. Nomo and his distinct windup—a long, slow stretch above his head, a long, patient twist behind his back leg—was a new experience for the Giants lineup, which featured Barry Bonds, Matt Williams and Glenallen Hill. And against this solid lineup, Japan's biggest sports story lasted five innings with four walks and seven strikeouts.

Major League Baseball noticed.

East Asian players have started appearing in the majors in yearly waves since Hideo Nomo's debut. Does that mean the talent levels of Japan, South Korea and Taiwan are on the rise? Not necessarily, but major league teams are paying closer attention to east Asia now more than ever.

From the beginning of major league history in 1876 until Nomo debuted in 1995, four players born in Japan had played in the United States. Three of those players—Bobby Fenwick (debuted 1972), Steve Chitren (1990) and Jim Bowie (1994)—were born to American parents and raised in American schools. The first Japanese player, Masanori Murakami, played only a season and change out of the 1964 and 1965 Giants bullpen. But a contract row between Murakami's original Japanese team and the Giants escalated to the point where Major League Baseball and Japan's league office, Nippon Professional Baseball, quit communicating.

During that same span, from 1876 to 1995, only one Korean player, Chan Ho Park (debut 1994), and zero Taiwanese players reached the majors. Over the following 19 seasons (1995 through 2013), Japan produced 55 major league players, Korea 13 players and Taiwan 10 players.

Suffice it to say: East Asian baseball has transitioned from a curiosity to a talent mill. In the 2013 season alone:

- Hyun-Jin Ryu challenged for the NL Rookie of the Year with 192 innings pitched and a 3.00 ERA.

- Yu Darvish—with 209.2 innings pitched and a 2.83 ERA–earned Cy Young Award consideration.

- At age 32, Hisashi Iwakuma gave the Mariners a legitimate second starter (219.2 innings, 2.66 ERA).
- Hiroki Kuroda continued his late-career dominance (201.1 innings at age 38).
- The Koji Uehara-Junichi Tazawa duo developed into a shutdown one-two relief punch for the American League champion Red Sox.

Along the fringes, Norichika Aoki posted another solid season as a full-time outfielder, Munenori Kawasaki overcame his rookie struggles and became a useful utility infielder for the Blue Jays, Chia-Jen Lo and C.C. Lee (Chen Lee) made their relief debuts, and veteran Kyuji Fujikawa posted some impressive strikeout and walk rates before succumbing to Tommy John surgery early in the season.

East Asia has also recently lured away better major league talent than in years past:

- Andruw Jones signed with the powerhouse Rakuten Golden Eagles and hit a strong .243/.391/.454 with 26 homers.
- Casey McGehee manned third base for the Rakuten Golden Eagles and hit an impressive .292/.376/.515 with 28 homers.
- Bryan LaHair, Nyjer Morgan and Kila Ka'aihue all crossed the ocean as well, with varied results.
- Buoyed by a new league-standard ball (which returned the league's offensive levels to earlier seasons) and a considerable development in his power, former Reds first baseman Wladimir Balentien broke and set Japan's home run record at 60 (not to mention his pigpen-filthy slash line of .330/.455/.779).

Even Manny Ramirez spent several months in Taiwan's Chinese Professional Baseball League (CPBL) before signing a minor league deal with the Texas Rangers and then fizzling off into oblivion. And the Korean Baseball Organization (KBO) gathered its annual collection of former major leaguers, though these players—such as Jo-Jo Reyes, Dana Eveland and Garrett Olson—were not drawing major-league interest before crossing the ocean.

Having former and recent major league players go to east Asia does not imply that the talent level of Asia is on the rise, but it at least indicates that the level of competition is. In other words: If, say, Japan has a Triple-A talent level among its native players, adding a quad-A or major league player to the league can only help improve that first player. It also means that a player of lower talent level has been crowded out, so to speak. This increases the average talent level in the league and can help push the remaining native players to become major league-level talents.

I'm going to talk about some of the top talents, such as Japanese pitcher Masahiro Tanaka, who may be making their way to the United States soon. I also plan to review the talent level of the other east Asia leagues, and the possibility that some former major leaguers now experiencing success abroad (Balentien, for instance) may return to the majors.

But first, I'd like to discuss why comparing players and statistics between these two sides of the world is difficult.

Some Confounding Factors

One of the trickiest facets of Nippon Professional Baseball (NPB) is its recent changes in the league-wide ball. From the earliest days of the league until 2011, the NPB teams used their own individualized baseballs when playing at home. In other words, while home games for the Yakult Swallows used a baseball designed by the Yakult Swallows; Hanshin Tigers games used a special Tigers baseball.

In 2011, the NPB adopted a new, league-wide baseball that more closely mimicks the major league-style baseball. As a result, offense across both the Pacific and Central leagues depressed almost a full run per game. Two years later, in 2013, the league's front office unilaterally changed the league baseball, this time adding more pop—and runs per game rebounded close to their previous levels. In other words, raw statistics over the past few years must be adjusted for the league run environment, because the environment has been changing dramatically.

Further confounding our ability to analyze players in Japan is the different style with which the game is played. Beyond significant differences in the mechanics of the game, such as pitcher windups and hitter swing motions and follow-throughs, game managers often call on their players to drop bunts in almost any medium-to-high leverage situation.

As a result, Japan executes more successful bunts than the major leagues. Far more. In the American League, one in about 167 plate appearances ends with a sacrifice hit. In Japan's Pacific League, which also has a designated hitter, sacrifice hits occur once in every 43 plate appearances.

Japan and Korea love bunting. The average Japanese player drops far more bunts than any AL or NL manager would prefer, and this no doubt affects the statistics of both hitters and pitchers. Widening the focus, this means there is an even greater emphasis on situational hitting.

It is hard to say, without a play-by-play database or a complex PITCHf/x data analysis, how much this affects a player's total statistics. Does the average NPB player hit for greater contact and less power with a runner on base? Does plate discipline change dramatically with runners in scoring position? Do the third and fourth hitters have considerably altered statistics because they bat with more runners on base? We cannot say.

Moreover, major league teams issue almost twice as many intentional walks as Japanese teams. In the National League, this results in a modest OBP boost for No. 8 hitters, but in Japan, these intentional walks are being replaced with sacrifice hits. This cements the necessity for scouting, for eyes on a player's performance, when predicting a player's major league ability. The numbers in Japan—and for that matter, Korea and Taiwan—come from a wholly unique baseball context.

Seeing the baseball performance that precipitates the statistics isn't just useful, it is required.

How Predictable Have Recent Transitions Been?

The following visualization represents the success levels of pitchers transitioning into the major leagues from Japan. I'm going to refer to FIP- here (that's FIP, followed by a minus sign) because FIP speaks directly to the true talent of the pitcher. FIP- is engineered so that the league average is around 100. Anything lower than 100 is better than average. Each pitcher's major league FIP- is on the left-hand axis; his NPB FIP- is on the bottom axis. The best performers will be in the lower left-hand quadrant (note: The following NPB FIP- and NPB wOBA+ statistics are not park-adjusted).

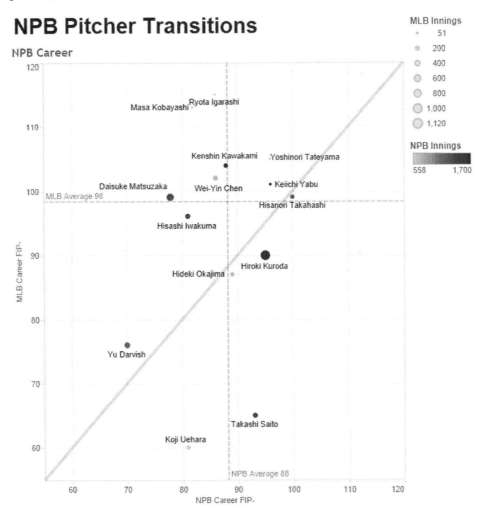

The main point here is that there is only a rough relationship between performance in the NPB and in the major leagues. The absurd success of Koji Uehara and Takashi Saito (both of whom were starters in Japan) and the flagrant disappointments of Kei Igawa (too far north to appear in the graphic) and, relatively speaking, Daisuke Matsuzaka, throw the system askew.

The solid gray line marks a 45-degree angle. Any player underneath the line performed better in the majors than in Japan. Players above the line had a better FIP- in Japan. Most players, understandably, are above the line. The most notable exception, Takashi Saito, spent most of his NPB career as a starter, but was exclusively a reliever in North America.

We must remember these are career numbers, and careers do not follow linear paths. Darvish and Matsuzaka arrived in America at or near what we usually consider the physical peak (age 27), but others—Kuroda (33), Iwakuma (31), and Saito (36)—arrived well after their peaks. So the data here represent moving targets.

That said, a 10-point difference in FIP-, which is the average difference in FIP- in the NPB and major leagues among these pitchers, does not seem far off base, especially after we factor in the selection bias (only the best Japanese pitchers have reached the major leagues and only those pitchers preemptively deemed by scouts as capable of succeeding in the majors).

The One Sure Thing?

With a 10-point average penalty applied to Japan's top pitchers, one might suspect there is a cavalcade of Japanese pitchers poised for major league success. But the league is more top-heavy than that. Consider this list of the best pitchers in the NPB since 2005:

Player	IP	FIP-
Kyuji Fujikawa	539	45
Daisuke Matsuzaka	401	64
Yu Darvish	1,267	69
Tetsuya Yamaguchi	436	70
Masahiro Tanaka	1,283	70
Mamoru Kishida	604	73
Toshiya Sugiuchi	1,571	75
Kazumi Saito	430	75
Tadashi Settsu	676	78

The first three pitchers on this list are already in the majors. Tamaguchi, Kishida and Settsu are relievers, and Saito is retired. That leaves only two players, Masahiro Tanaka (a 25-year-old righty) and Toshiya Sugiuchi (a 33-year-old, 5-foot-9 lefty), who both start and have performed well enough in the NPB to possibly succeed in the major leagues.

Though the success of 5-foot-10 Kris Medlen should damper our pitcher height bias, it is hard not to think that Japan's only impact pitcher at this time is Masahiro Tanaka. Tanaka appears poised for an immediate or near-immediate transition to the majors. And more than just being a likely candidate to come to the major leagues, Tanaka has a chance to replicate the success of Kuroda, Iwakuma or even Darvish.

Entire books could be published on why Matsuzaka did not succeed in the major leagues the way he succeeded in Japan, but one popular belief was that the number of innings in his pre-major league career doomed him to injury and velocity issues in the major leagues. Like Daisuke, Tanaka has pitched in the NPB since his 18-year-old season. Like Daisuke, though perhaps to a lesser extent, Tanaka had some over-usage heroics in his appearances during Japan's premiere high school tournament, the Spring Kōshien tournament.

But injuries are hard to project. So the best we can do is analyze his pitching technique, his ability and his statistics. According to Brian Cartwright's Oliver projection system, Tanaka's statistics are pretty. The righty's NPB numbers portend an impressive 2.92 ERA with a 23 percent strikeout rate and a four percent walk rate in the majors. Connor Jennings' NOM Projections forecast a 3.41 ERA. The next-best starter, according to NOM, is Seth Greisinger (3.98 FIP), and Greisinger already has a 113 FIP- through 220+ innings pitched in the majors. The lefty Sugiuchi comes in third with a 4.07 FIP.

Clint Hulsey of the blog I R Fast reports that Tanaka throws—like many Japanese pitchers—an absurd total of seven pitch types. Of those, his top selections are his four-seam, two-seam, slider and splitter/forkball. His four-seam fastball (38 percent usage) is in the low-90s and his slider (29 percent usage) travels in the mid-to-high 80s. But Hulsey rates Tanaka's splitter as his best pitch.

The movement is both arm side and down, more aggressive than a traditional change-up, but not the straight down movement of a true forkball. Some of the worst swings I have ever seen in high level professional baseball have come off Tanaka's splitter.

Jennings suggests that Tanaka struggles to pitch out of the stretch and his stuff more directly compares to Daisuke Matsuzaka than Yu Darvish. That said, the walk rates of these pitchers differed considerably: Of Matsuzaka (8.7 percent), Darvish (6.7 percent) and Tanaka (5.2 percent), Tanaka has separated himself in the walk-rate category. This may portend well since both Daisuke (10.9 percent) and Darvish (10.2 percent) increased their walk rates upon reaching the majors.

What About the Hitters?

Historically, major league teams have been less eager to try NPB position players, and less patient when they do. The success of Ichiro Suzuki and Hideki Matsui represents a stark contrast against the more common experiences of Tsuyoshi Nishioka, Hiroyuki Nakajima and Kosuke Fukudome.

This graph is similar to the pitcher graph, except that I'll be using wRC+ and wOBA+ to rank the hitters. Like FIP- and ERA-, these are rate stats for which 100 is average. The difference is that it's better to be higher than average, so the best performers will appear in the upper right-hand quadrant.

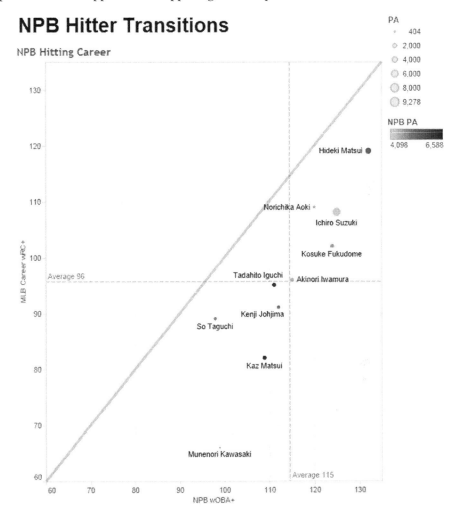

In this graphic, players above the solid-gray 45-degree line hit better in the majors than in Japan. Unfortunately, there are no players above the line. Unlike the selection of pitchers who crossed the ocean, these hitters without exception did worse in the U.S. than they had in Japan. Also unlike the selection of pitchers, the lower volatility here has resulted in a much more clear and linear relationship between career NPB numbers and career major league performance. In general, we can simply subtract about 20 points of wOBA+ to get a projected wRC+ in the U.S. For instance, Kosuke Fukudome's career 124 wOBA+ in the NPB is almost exactly 20 points above his 102 wRC+ in the majors.

Using Japanese-based linear weights could significantly improve the predictability of hitter (and pitcher) transfers, but until a public, unified and reliable database of NPB play-by-play statistics appears, we are left to a 10- and 20-point rule (a 10-point FIP- addition for pitchers with little reliability and a 20-point wOBA+ reduction for hitters with a much greater reliability).

Like the thin pitching depth, the hitting depth in Nippon Pro Baseball is not a mine of hidden talent. If we look at the three most recent seasons, weighting those seasons 5-4-3 (with the most weight on the most recent seasons, a la the Marcel projection system), we get this selection of hitters above 120 wOBA+ in the NPB:

Player	wOBA+	PA
Wladimir Balentien	145	1,438
Shinnosuke Abe	140	1,465
Tony Blanco	133	1,183
Takeya Nakamura	129	1,120
Josh Whitesell	126	605
Dae-ho Lee	124	1,099
Yoshio Itoi	124	1,678
Wily Mo Pena	122	507
Hiroyuki Nakajima	121	1,200
Kenta Kurihara	121	595

All these players are above 120 wOBA+, which suggests they could hit at least near league average (100 wRC+) in the majors. But do any of these hitters have enough potential to be an impact player?

We can also see how noteworthy Balentien's success has been. Balentien had a career 72 wRC+ through 559 plate appearances in the majors (though was only 24 years old in his final season). On the other hand, with almost identical numbers in Japan, Fukudome mustered only a 102 wRC+ through 2,276 PA in the majors.

Using our super simple offensive conversion formula from above, we would predict a 125 wRC+ for Balentien. That could place him around the No. 40 hitter in the 2013 season and in the vicinity of Chase Utley and Ryan Zimmerman. But Balentien is playing in the second-most friendly park for right-handed hitters, according to NOM Projection's park factors. A 128 home run factor for righties at Meiji Jingu Stadium no doubt inflates Balentien's NPB numbers and bites into his likely ability for major league success. This makes Balentien's NOM Projection of a .318 wOBA less surprising.

After Balentien, Shinnosuke Abe, a 35-year-old catcher, makes an unlikely major league prospect. The NOM Projections do put the lefty Abe in the .344 wOBA range, best of the current hitter class, but given his advanced age and tender defensive position, his chances for major league opportunities are slim.

Blanco, 32 in the 2014 season, is a journeyman first baseman who had a cup of coffee with the Nationals in 2005. If not for his advanced age, he could possibly challenge for a DH role on a bottom-half AL team. Takeya Nakamura, the 30-year-old corner-infielder and DH, has displayed an effective high-power, moderate-discipline approach when healthy. With his health history, an ample frame and a damning nickname ("another helping," as in: "Pass the plate; I'm still hungry"), Nakamura almost certainly has no major league future outside of designated hitter.

These top four hitters are tough sells. They are all fairly close to a mandatory DH role, and their chances for offensive success are uncertain. Moreover, there is no guarantee any of these players would want to start a new career in the Western Hemisphere, where they would go from superstar to unknown. And even if they did choose to try for a major league career, many are still under contract with their current teams and would thereby be subject to whatever posting system is in place.

Wither Defense?

Yoshio Itoi may rank as the position player closest to certain for posting. A perennial All-Star outfielder, Itoi's statistics in Japan compare favorably to Norichika Aoki's, but Itoi is entering his age-32 season. NOM Projections suggest he could muster a .276/.353/.382 slash line and a .313 wOBA. That wOBA would rank a few ticks under league average in the current run environment (a 98 wRC+ in a neutral offensive park).

With solid defense, or a stronger transition of his power, Itoi could make for a solid bench player or center fielder in a shallow depth chart. But Itoi has primarily played right field since 2012, and his best defensive days are behind him. Norichika Aoki surprised me in 2012 with a 114 wRC+ and 30 steals, so Itoi—who showed a little more gap power than Aoki in Japan—could surpass expectations just as easily. With a favorable transition and good health, Itoi could aspire to be a David DeJesus type outfielder.

And Itoi brings up the bigger missing element of position player analysis: defense. Because of the dearth of advanced statistics available to the public, the pressure is again on scouts to effectively analyze Japanese position players' defensive ability. One assumes the Mariners and Blue Jays saw enough in Munenori Kawasaki to invest a 40-man roster spot in him, and he has rewarded his clubs with possibly three defensive runs through 900 innings ("possibly" because such stats are clearly unstable with so few innings).

Conversely, surprising defensive struggles from Hiroyuki Nakajima have left him awaiting his major league debut. The veteran shortstop, who looked on the brink of joining the Yankees bench in 2012, signed a two-year, $6.5 million dollar deal with the Oakland Athletics as a free agent in 2013. But when his health soured and he struggled defensively in spring training, the A's turned his rehab assignment in Triple-A into a full-season, 40-man-roster-booting assignment. The impressive hitter in Japan (averaging around a 120 wOBA+) did not make an appearance for the Athletics and had an 85 wRC+ through 384 plate appearances in Triple-A.

With Gold Glove defense—and Nakajima was at one time considered among the best defenders in Japan—he might have pressed for playing time in a crowded A's infield. But instead, he became expensive depth for the Athletics.

Takashi Toritani, a 33-year-old infielder from the Hanshin Tigers, is another player whose less-quantifiable defense may make him a legitimate target. Toritani explored the major league market as a free agent in 2012, but tepid interest led him back to the Tigers. A free agent again heading into the 2014 season, and coming off another season in the 115 wOBA+ neighborhood, Toritani may get some consideration for a bench role. Whereas Nakajima may have spoiled the market for many infielders looking for paydays, the low-cost, moderate success of Munenori Kawasaki may have more teams interested in Toritani the second time around.

So where hitters and pitchers appear to be well-gleaned markets, the matter of defenders is much less settled. Because scouts and only scouts can offer opinions about NPB, KBO and CPBL players' defense, there are almost certainly under-appreciated major league talents slipping through the major leagues' talent sieve. Without UZR or Total Zone, rangy, yet awkward players may be getting overlooked. Without PITCHf/x or play-by-play data, the next Jose Molina may be playing in Korea, unnoticed.

This is just another reason why I would like to see some sort of English language service, perhaps something akin to a stripped-down MLB.tv or MiLB.tv, for at least Nippon Pro Baseball. As it stands, non-Japanese speakers have a very difficult time watching NPB games—not just for a lack of finding them, but for a lack of understanding the commentary, the on-screen graphics and online pitch-tracker Yahoo! offers (though its system is a poor proxy for PITCHf/x).

The Future of Japanese Talent

Suffice it to say, there are precious few elite talents in Japan's pro league. But the rate of elite talent appears to be on the rise. A few young position players may be on the horizon.

Entering his age-26 season, Ryosuke Hirata has a 112 wOBA+ (not park-adjusted) over the previous three seasons despite playing in the Chunichi Dragons' pitcher's park. The Chunichi Dragons are not probably ready to shop the young outfielder, but his numbers—and NOM Projections—suggest he could be a season or two away from being a contributor in the major leagues.

And if Tanaka is the must-know name, then the second name to know is Shohei Otani, the two-way phenom. Otani had initially wanted to sign with a major league team out of high school, but when interest from the Rangers, Red Sox, Yankees and Dodgers (possibly among others) proved less aggressive than expected, he entered the NPB draft, where he was sure to reach the top level quickly. Under team control for at least another eight seasons, Otani would need to establish himself as a superior player and be posted by his team, the Nippon Ham Fighters.

But in his brief rookie season, 18-year-old Otani posted a .238/.284/.376 slash with three homers in 204 plate appearances in right field and a 4.23 ERA and 118 FIP- through 61.2 inning pitched, mostly as a starter. Clint Hulsey reports Otani's four-seam fastball averages around 93 mph, with a "baby slider" or hard curve (79 mph) and scintillating sinker (95 mph). Otani initially made waves in Japan and eventually the States when he hit 100 miles per hour on the radar gun during the Spring Kōshien tournament his final year of high school.

While he is a name to keep handy, the Fighters will not consider posting him until his departure can guarantee a franchise-changing income—because, right now, Otani has franchise-changing potential.

Another factor that will determine Otani's major league future—as well as Tanaka's and Itoi's—is a possible change in the NPB-major league posting system. At the time of print, the two leagues had yet to agree on a new system of selling NPB players' contract rights to major league teams. The old system, in place since 1998 (as a reaction to the abrupt Alfonso Soriano and Hideo Nomo transitions), has resulted in undesirable extremes: Exorbitant blind bids for Matsuzaka and Darvish and minimal bids for useful players like Aoki and Iwamura. Future iterations may also add a greater degree of control for the players, who may be able to select which team they prefer among the top three bids.

Japan certainly has at least a few major league prospects capable of successful transition, but it is not alone.

Korea and Taiwan on the Rise

NPB talent is widely considered to occupy a gap between Triple-A and the majors. Korea and Taiwan are a bit less certain. A good estimation puts the Korean league at the High-A to possibly Double-A level. And at least one league source puts Taiwan beneath Rookie-league talent, somewhere in the void of independent league talent.

The sample of player transitions from the Korean Baseball Organization (KBO) to the majors (and vice versa) is smaller than is available in the NPB. And there is more than just a talent difference. The NPB is a larger league—12 teams compared to Korea's nine—though Korea has a 12-team farm system. Meanwhile, Taiwan's Chinese Professional Baseball League (CPBL) has four pro teams with four minor league squads, but the biggest names from Taiwan (Chien-Ming Wang, Hong-Chih Kuo and Wei-Yin Chen) reached the majors either as amateur free agents or via the

NPB. The CPBL has yet to produce a direct transition to a major league franchise, while the KBO has had one player in its history posted to the majors, Hyun-Jin Ryu in 2013.

The disparity in talent levels may be a function of population (South Korea has around 50 million people; Taiwan, about 23 million; Japan has close to 130 million), but the disparity more likely descends from matters of sports culture. My FanGraphs article, "The Determinants of Foreign Talent," explored the relationship between a nation's demographics and its ability to produce major league talent. The most interesting, and I believe most important, relationship between demographics and major league talent comes from the age of baseball in that country, which served as my proxy for estimating the sport's popularity.

Japan has over 140 years of baseball history, and baseball is the undisputed or near-undisputed champion of sports interest. Korea and Taiwan have about 110 years of baseball history each, and soccer (and in Korea, possibly golf) has an edge over baseball. Alternative sports draw athletes from similar talent pools. In a nation like the Dominican Republic or Venezuela, where baseball is a major component of the culture, most talented young athletes will choose to siphon into baseball programs. This results in a sort of plateau of baseball talent.

Like Japan, the KBO limits the number of foreign players on a roster. The Korean teams historically have used their two foreign slots almost exclusively for pitchers. It seems strange that Korea would look for pitching depth in the scraps of the major league's minor leagues, because all but two of Korea's major leaguers (Hee-Seop Choi and Shin-Soo Choo) were pitchers, and even those two Korean hitters were amateurs who developed in the major league minors.

Clint Hulsey has executed a wealth of research on the NPB, KBO and the CPBL. His statistical research suggests that KBO hitters lose about 20 percent of their OPS when converting to the major leagues. In other words, a .900 OPS All-Star in the KBO would become a .720 OPS hitter, good enough for maybe a bench job (and probably a major pay cut).

First-baseman Dae-ho Lee, a 10-year veteran of the KBO Lotte Giants, won his share of Gold Gloves in Korea and has acquitted himself well in his two years in Japan. In his final season in Korea, he had a 136 wOBA+. In his two years in Japan, he has a 124 wOBA+. We might suspect, then, he would hit around league average in the major leagues. He is a popular player and a fixture of the Korean international teams, but his ceiling in the majors would be a James Loney-type career.

On the pitching side, various sources have suggested major league and NPB scouts have been examining Oh Seung-hwan and Yoon Suk-min. What makes these players interesting? Seung-hwan (who in America would likely go by Seung-hwan Oh in the tradition of putting surnames last) has pitched in relief in Korea, earning a silly 1.44 ERA and 41 FIP- from 2011 through 2013. In his 2.2 innings during the 2013 World Baseball Classic, Seung-hwan struck out six and walked no batters. If Oh followed the route of Hyun-Jin Ryu and added 20 or 30 points to his FIP-, he could make for a solid relief ace on most any team (about 65 FIP-). But Oh is entering his age-31 season, and as the hard lesson of Kyuji Fujikawa showed, old relievers are old relievers, regardless of their history of health and success.

Major league scouts have reportedly shown greater interest in Yoon Suk-min, a 27-year-old right-hander. Yoon had a 66 and 75 FIP- in 2011 and 2012 seasons, and looked quite capable (statistically, at least) of following Ryu to America.

But he lost velocity in 2013 and had a stock-damping 96 FIP- in relief. Steve Sypa of Amazin' Avenue described him in 2012 as possessing a mid-90s fastball "with a hard, biting slider and a change-up that major league scouts describe as above average." The change-up-infatuated Rays may like both the repertoire and now the price of Yoon, but his stock has fallen from what he might have hoped for in 2012.

Of the top hitters in Taiwan, there is no one we would expect to hit well in Japan, much less the United States. If we applied a generously low 30-point wOBA+ penalty on Taiwan's best hitter, Lin Zhi-Sheng (or Ngayaw Ake in his native dialect or Chih-Sheng Lin, depending on who's translating), he would still slip beneath a league average bat in the majors. As a middle infielder, he could still be useful around league average, but his defensive talent reportedly would consign him to first base in the majors, and he is entering his age-32 season, well beyond his defensive prime.

And on the pitching side, the top five pitchers of the last three seasons hail from abroad. Ken Ray, the lone, true standout, is a 39-year-old journeyman starter who, in the best of universes, would be a long reliever for the Astros. The only other pitcher remotely close to him is Yu-Gang Fu (69 FIP- in 132.1 innings since 2010). The righty reliever turns 26 in January, and if he continues his dominance, he could push for a career in Japan or Korea. As a reliever averaging 93 mph, standing at around 5-foot-10, it seems unlikely a major league franchise will be the first to send him a letter.

One reason Taiwan appears so relatively bare of talent is that—unlike in Korea and Japan—there appears to be no gentleman's agreement about signing away amateur talent before it reaches the CPBL. Thus players like Chien-Ming Wang (not to be confused with Ching-Ming Wang, above), Hong-Chih Kuo, Chin-hui Tsao and Chin-Feng Chen reached the U.S. minors (and eventually the majors) without stopping by the CPBL.

And there may be more than just the allure of a major league career at play here. The ultra-powerful ownership group and the absence of a CPBL player's union makes a foreign career (in Korea, Japan or the Americas) incredibly enticing for a Taiwanese amateur.

The Future of East Asia

Are the talent levels of east Asia rising? Yes, judging by the raw number of Asians debuting in the majors.

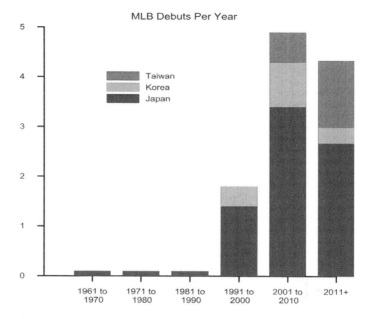

MLB Debuts Per Year

But are the talent levels of east Asian leagues on the rise? This is harder to say. Major league teams have been gleaning the best players from foreign leagues, leaving behind perhaps a similar level of talent as before.

Whenever a player distinguishes himself above the league, the financial incentive for a major league posting for the Japanese or Korean team—not to mention for the player—becomes overwhelming. A team can revitalize its entire roster for years to come with a single posting fee. And the player, even in a part-time role in the majors, can potentially double his income. So, few highly talented players have enough reasons to remain with their native league.

In other words, the talent levels of east Asia may stay the same, but the population of east Asians in the majors will blossom in a corresponding move. So start practicing your konnichi wa, anyong, and ni hao because the more we in the west learn and understand east Asian baseball, the more it will benefit western baseball. Just as major league teams noticed when Nomo showed he belonged in the majors, so it is time for the western hemisphere to notice that east Asia is on the rise.

Resources and Thank Yous

I'd like to send a big thanks to Dan and (@MyKBO) and all the members of the MyKBO.net Facebook group. A hearty thanks to Clint Hulsey's continued assistance and diligent research, as well as Patrick Newman of NPB Tracker, the writers at JapaneseBaseball.com and Brian Cartwright of the Oliver projection system. And thanks to all the Taiwanese, Korean, Japanese and American—North, South and Caribbean—players who braved a new language, culture and league. Without them, we might have four isolated, homogeneous and much less interesting leagues.

History

The Summer of '86

by Joe Posnanski

When I was 19 years old, my Cleveland Indians inexplicably became a pretty good baseball team. It was strange and surreal and comically brief. Their goodness came and went so quickly that nobody in Cleveland seemed entirely sure it had even happened. Was it real? Was it an after-pizza dream? The year was 1986, the height of Reagan, just after the 1985 Bears had shuffled, and it was a pivotal year in my life. That was the year I dropped out of the accounting program in college (dropped out, thrown out, same difference), became an English major and told people I had this crazy idea about becoming a sportswriter. People looked at me like I was crazy. I *felt* crazy. I wonder sometimes if the Indians' sudden and mystifying bit of competence emboldened me and changed my life.

None of us saw the Cleveland rebirth coming, of course. The 1985 version of the team had been the worst of my lifetime, and that's saying something; the Indians had been a consistent joke since I was too young to know. "Don't worry folks," the guide at Cedar Point amusement park said when it seemed like we were being fired upon by gun-toting Native Americans, "Those are Cleveland Indians. And everyone knows, they can't hit anything."

But, as bad as it had been, that 1985 season was something new. In the middle of the 1985 season, the Indians traded their best pitcher, Bert Blyleven, for four players, the most memorable being pitcher Rich Yett, whose name beguiled us as a modern version of "Who's On First."

> *"Who should the Indians start tonight?"*
> *"Not Yett!"*
> *"But you have to make a decision now."*

After the Indians traded Blyleven, their rotation consisted of (in no particular order): Neal Heaton, Don Schulze, Curt Wardle, an ancient Vern Ruhle and—a personal favorite—Jerry Reed. I liked him for the name. There was a country music singer at the time named Jerry Reed who played in all the *Smokey and the Bandit* movies and sang songs like "She Got the Goldmine (I Got The Shaft)" and "With His Pants In His Hand."

For this reason, and this reason alone, I also liked the Cleveland pitcher Jerry Reed and went along with 6,024 others to see him face off against Tom Seaver and the White Sox on a Friday night in July. The game turned out to be Seaver's 296th victory. It was the third of what would be 19 career losses for Jerry Reed.

Oh, those Indians were abominable. They allowed the most runs in baseball. They slugged .385 as a team. They were terrible in close games (14-29 in games decided by one run) and yet they managed the dexterity to get blown out by five or more runs 27 times. The defense might have been their worst trait. They stunk. There's really not much else say about the 1985 Indians.

Well, maybe one thing. That, after all, was the Johnnie Lemaster year. After only one month, the Indians were sort of flopping around but had not yet demonstrated total ineptitude. For one thing, their shortstop—a youngish Julio Franco—hit .400 in April. Because of that, the team was 10-14 on May 7, and that's when someone got the bright idea that Franco needed to be moved from shortstop. I always assumed it was their rather stern-looking manager, Pat Corrales. Reporters who covered Corrales always loved him—he was, apparently, a fantastic story teller—but to a fan he always seemed grumpy and overly concerned about minutia like how Julio Franco is fielding when he's hitting .400. It was true: Franco was not a good shortstop. But on that team, worrying about Julio Franco's defense was like worrying about the paint color of the Hindenburg.

On May 7, the Indians traded two players to San Francisco for shortstop Johnnie Lemaster. At the time, Lemaster was hitting exactly .000. No. Really. He had come to the plate 17 times and not gotten a single hit. It was more or less in character—Lemaster had proven over almost 1,000 big league at-bats that he was utterly incapable of hitting a baseball. His career slugging percentage was .289. Slugging! Managers kept playing him, though, so there was this sense that he must have been a good defensive shortstop. Heck, he had to play a competent shortstop to play in 1,000 big league games with that bat, right?

Anyway, it seems Lemaster was unhappy about not getting more at-bats to waste, and the Giants traded him to Cleveland. Immediately, Corrales moved Franco to second base, a position he had never played, and benched Tony Bernazard, who was actually one of the Indians' best hitters. All for Johnnie Lemaster.

"I don't mean to be rude," Bernazard said at the time, "but who in the hell is Johnnie Lemaster?"

He was about to find out. Lemaster went hitless in his first game. He went hitless the second game. In his third game, he got his first hit...and was promptly caught stealing. In his fourth, Corrales was already so exhausted by Lemaster's lack of bat that he pinch-hit for him in the seventh inning.

Then: Hitless. Hitless. Hitless. But at least he was playing great defense? No. In the middle of the hitlessness, he booted a ground ball that led to a run. That's when Corrales ran out of patience. He benched Lemaster. A couple of days later, he tried Lemaster as a defensive specialist in a game. Lemaster made another error.

Nineteen days after the Indians traded for Johnnie Lemaster, they traded him away to Pittsburgh for a player to be named later. They put Julio Franco back at shortstop. The Indians had gone a tidy 5-12 in those 19 days. Bill James summed it up in the *Baseball Abstract*.

"I spent many years rooting for a terrible team, and I watch this team with a certain sympathy," he wrote. "But I'm sure glad it's not mine."

This was the team I knew going into the 1986 season.

Of course, there was always hope. I had come to think of it as "Rick Waits Hope." Rick Waits was a tall, left-handed pitcher from Atlanta who pitched for Cleveland in the 1970s and early 1980s. He wasn't especially good. But it always seemed like he *could* be good. In 1978, he had what qualifies as a nice year in Cleveland—he went 13-15 with a 3.20 ERA and 4.2 WAR. Perhaps most of all, on the last day of the season he threw nine strong innings against the New York Yankees, beating them and forcing the Bucky "F-----" Dent playoff game. In Cleveland, that was the only sign we needed. From that point on and for the next few years, I would have an annual Rick Waits argument with my father in March. It would go roughly like this:

> Me: This is the year Rick Waits puts it all together.
> Dad: No.
> Me: He will definitely be an All-Star.
> Dad: No.
> Me: I don't know if he can win the Cy Young. Jim Palmer's good. So is Ron Guidry. But I think he has a chance.
> Dad: No.

So, I'm sure I went into 1986 with my usual unfounded Rick Waits hope. The Indians had some young hitting talent—little speedster Brett Butler was coming off a nice season, young third baseman Brook Jacoby* had flashed some power, Tony Bernazard and Julio Franco were back. Joe Carter and Mel Hall seemed promising enough. And the Indians had just drafted a player that scouts were calling baseball's next superstar, a right fielder named Cory Snyder.

*For some reason, around that time I started singing the Terry Cashman "We're Talkin' Base-ball" song using Jacoby's name. I would do this all the time, driving everyone around me insane in the process. I would sing it like so: "We're talkin' baseball, Brook Jacoby-obee; we're talkin' baseball; best player on the globey." I'll bet that it is right about now that Dave and the guys at THT are questioning their questionable decision to let me write this essay.

Snyder might have been the first player I was ever really excited about before he played a single major league game. To me, this part of sports fanhood has changed more than any other the last 25 or 30 years. Our parents didn't care much about the future. Almost nobody followed the draft before our generation. Only the most obsessive followed recruiting. Who cares about players playing high school? Base-ball's minor leagues were just that, *minor* leagues, and while every now and again a minor-league phenom might spark some interest, the general feeling seemed to be: "Eh, I'll wait to see him in the big leagues."

Cory Snyder was a bit different though. He had been on that amazing 1984 Olympic baseball team with Will Clark, Barry Larkin and Mark McGwire. He had this absurdly strong arm, and he had astounding power, and people were calling him baseball's next superstar. We couldn't wait for him to get started.

And so the 1986 season began, and in the beginning the Indians piddled around like usual. Then on April 26, they beat New York at Yankee Stadium, 3-2. The next day, Joe Carter got three hits and the Indians won again. Two days later, Carter moved into the No. 3 slot in the lineup and hit another home run. Cleveland won again.

Then they won again. And again. And again. Ten in a row. It was amazing. It had been four years since the Indians had had a 10-game winning streak, and the last one had come with the season already thoroughly uninteresting. This was *very* interesting. The Indians were in first place. Sure, it was only May 7, but so what?

There was something about this team. All year long, they just kept hitting and hitting and hitting. Joe Carter crushed the ball; he would lead the league in RBI. Cory Snyder was called up on June 13—he hit 24 home runs in 103 games. Tony Bernazard, Julio Franco and Pat Tabler* all hit .300. Brett Butler led the league with 14 triples. Mel Hall cranked 18 home runs in 140 games. The old man, Andre Thornton, one of the great gentlemen of the game, hit 17 home runs in his last full season in the big leagues.

That was actually a year after Tabler got six hits in seven at-bats with the bases loaded, earning him the nickname "Mr. Clutch." In 1986, Mr. Clutch hit just .200 with the bases loaded, but he hit .326 overall.

I realize, by the way, that I'm throwing almost meaningless statistics out there—batting average, RBI, batting average with the bases loaded etc.—but hey, I was 19 years old. I didn't know one stat from another. The point was the Indians were hitting. They led the major leagues with 831 runs, more runs than the dominant 1984 Tigers. And they scored all those runs with exciting young players who were sure to get better.

On July 23—normally a time when Cleveland fans start counting down to mathematical elimination day—the Indians were 10 games over .500 and just five games back in the American League East.

It was nirvana.

The pitching? Yes, well, yes, there were a few issues with the pitching. The Indians, being the Indians, had decided that they would put together a rotation with not one, but *two* knuckleball pitchers. This is perfect Cleveland thinking. Tom Candiotti had a pretty good year (16-11, 3.57 ERA, 4.8 WAR). Forty-seven-year-old Phil Niekro did not (11-11, 4.32 ERA, 0.9 WAR). The rest of the rotation was pretty dreadful, closer Ernie Camacho blew 10 saves, and our favorite name Rich Yett made his Indians debut in a terrible bullpen.

"Is it time for Rich to come into the game?"
"Not Yett!"

The defense? Yes, well, the Indians defense was horrendous. While it's a crude way of measuring such things, the Indians were the only team in baseball to give up more than 100 unearned runs. They led the league in errors, an astonishing *twenty* of them belonging to catcher Andy Allanson, who could not throw and who was the rarest of birds, a 6-foot-5, 220-pound catcher with absolutely no power.

Anyway, those were side notes. The offense was center stage. And it was an amazing offense. That offense kept the Indians sort of, kind of in the race going into August. Then, pitching and defense reared their heads, Cleveland lost 19 of 29 and dropped out. Predictable but disappointing. The Indians even dropped below .500 briefly. But then they went to Milwaukee on Sept. 4 and dazzled us again.

Thursday night, Joe Carter got four hits, Cory Snyder smashed two home runs and the Indians won, 15-4.

Friday night, Cory Snyder hit another homer, so did Brook Jacoby; the Indians mashed 15 total hits and won, 13-5.

Saturday night, Cory Snyder added three more hits, Joe Carter hit two home runs, Brook Jacoby hit another, the Indians cracked 23 hits and won, 17-9.

It was three days unlike any I could remember as an Indians fan. Yes, it was too late for Cleveland to win the pennant. But the Indians were so young. They were so exciting. They scored runs like crazy. In many ways, that was my favorite year as a baseball fan. Everything felt so new, so thrilling. Let's be honest, it had been a bad baseball life up to then—I was willing to grasp for anything good.

But there was something else. The Indians had not only been terrible for years, they had lost the city. My city. I understood. Municipal Stadium, though I loved it, was a dump. It was cavernous and grimy and ancient, like an abandoned place you would see in the Scooby Doo cartoons. Construction beams were Anthony Muñoz good at blocking your view. The infield looked like it had been bombed 10 minutes before game time. The wind howled in from Lake Erie, so you could always tell who was a tourist—they were the ones who did not bring heavy blankets to night games in July. The question wasn't why the Indians were last in attendance. It was: Why would *anyone* go?

And people did not go. It was really that simple. The Indians were so bad, the stadium so depressing, all of it had beaten down one of America's great sports towns. By the early 1980s, Cleveland attendance numbers were the worst in baseball. One of David Letterman's Top 10 lists featured jobs in Hell—ticket scalper in Cleveland was on the list.

Look at the attendance numbers:

- 1983: 9,493 per game (last)
- 1984: 9,063 per game (last).
- 1985: 8,089 per game (last).

Then came 1986. In late April, they Indians drew 9,804 to a series against the Orioles. That's not a game, friends. That was the *whole series*.

But then this team started hitting and hitting, and people got excited about them. You couldn't help it. The Indians drew more than 20,000 for three consecutive games in May—might not sound like much, but it was the first time that had happened since a July 4 series against the Yankees in 1982.

Then they got 48,000 for a Friday night game against the White Sox. More than 43,000 came for the Sunday game of the series. More than 61,000 welcomed them home from a long road trip in late May, and 61,000 more showed up for a Friday game in June against Minnesota. More than 73,000 attended the Fourth of July game against the Royals. Andre Thornton and Cory Snyder homered and the Indians won.

And for a Cleveland boy who had grown up hearing how bad a baseball town Cleveland is, who had grown up hearing ballplayer jokes like, "If your plane has to crash, hope it crashes going *into* Cleveland," who had always believed that there was a baseball spirit in my hometown, it was a beautiful thing. The Indians didn't exactly put up Dodgers attendance numbers, but they drew 1.4 million for the first time since 1959. They had more than doubled their attendance of the year before.

I always said: If you give Cleveland a decent team, just a decent team, they will come out. The 1986 Indians were a decent team. And the fans came out. It was a wonderful year. The future seemed impossibly bright.

In April of the next year, *Sports Illustrated* put the Cleveland Indians on the cover. "Indian Uprising" it said in big letters, and there was a picture of Chief Wahoo with his uncomfortable grin and below were Joe Carter and Cory Snyder smiling the same uncomfortable grin. And then, in smaller letters, it said this:

Believe It! Cleveland Is The Best Team in the American League.

I did believe it. But I was 20 and blind. *Sports Illustrated* should have known better. The Indians lost 101 games. They were, in fact, the worst team in the American League in 1987 by a substantial margin. The grumpy Pat Corrales was fired and replaced by the genial but no more effective Doc Edwards. Cory Snyder struck out 166 times, 15th on the all-time list. He would quietly strike himself out of the game.

Brook Jacoby would become just the second man (Felix Mantilla in 1964 was the first) to hit 30 home runs and drive in fewer than 70 runs. The Indians' utter inability to get on base dropped them to 12th in runs scored. But that wasn't why the Indians were historically bad. The pitching staff was simply a nightmare; it had obviously been put together late one night after a series of drinks. At one point they had 48-year-old Phil Niekro, 42-year-old Steve Carlton and 32-year-old Ken Schrom in the rotation—the three combined for about a 6.00 ERA. The Indians allowed 77 more runs than any other team in baseball. The 957 runs allowed was the most in Indians history. It was the most in baseball since 1939.

So that wasn't good.

That *Sports Illustrated* cover became a symbol of Cleveland sour luck, but maybe that's not the right way to look at it. These days, I like to think of it as a symbol of that crazy 1986 Indians team that had no business being any good but, for some reason, was pretty good. Crazy things happen in baseball.

I especially remember one game in late July against Detroit. The Indians trailed, 7-4, going into the bottom of the eighth.

And: Joe Carter singled. Cory Snyder singled. Pat Tabler singled in a run. Julio Franco singled in two. And then, a personal favorite, Carmelo Castillo, singled in Franco, and the Indians held on for the amazing victory.

Do you know who started the game for Cleveland? Yep: It was Rich Yett. We were so sure it was our time. Turned out, no, it wasn't our time Yett.

Roger Clemens' Place in History

by Craig Wright

I often field calls from reporters wanting to know if a player's career is Hall of Fame caliber. Back before the Mitchell Report came out in December of 2007, none of these calls about Roger Clemens were about whether his career was Hall of Fame worthy, which seemed obvious to anyone. They wanted to know where he ranked among the all-time great pitchers.

I believe there are elements of fine tuning that still could be worked out in calculating Win Shares Above Replacement Value (WSAR—see note at end), but I still find it one of the more helpful measures in answering such questions. Rather than using a straight ranking of career WSAR, though, I do three things with these data before I begin comparing careers.

1. For seasons shorter than 162 games, I prorate the WSAR to the modern schedule.
2. I substitute a reasonable WSAR for any absence due to military service in a time of war. I do this based on calculations from their seasons before and after their tour of duty and with a modicum of adjustment for aging profile. I also downgrade the WSAR for those who played in the 1943-45 seasons when most of the major league talent was in the service.
3. I add bonus "quality" points to the careers.

To understand the logic of this last point, think in terms of how supply and demand affect the building of a winning team. The supply of really good players is very limited. When you can condense a lot of value into a single player, it makes it easier to fill in the other pieces in building a winning team.

That is a different kind of value than what is being captured in Win Shares. I'm not confident in how high to value it, but it is a real factor that should be shaded into these evaluations in some manner.

I assign two levels of bonus points in the Live Ball Era to give a boost to the extra-valuable seasons. If a pitcher has a season with over a dozen WSAR, I increase the portion over a dozen by 50 percent. I also give a Level Two bonus for a season with over 20 WSAR, giving a 100 percent increase for the portion above 20 WSAR. The Level Two bonus is meant to be very rare and in the last 50 years many Hall of Famers never had such a season in their whole careers. In the Dead Ball Era, when it was easy for a pitcher to pile up WSAR in a season because of the willingness to overwork pitchers, the Level One bonus begins at 20 WSAR and there is no Level Two bonus.

If you are Sandy Koufax, this type of bonus is going to increase your career WSAR by about 20 percent. If you are someone who had a long career of good quality but few exceptional seasons, like a Phil Niekro, you will get a boost more like five percent. When I am done massaging career WSAR with my three adjustments, I call it "CC" for "comparative career."

Roger Clemens' "CC" places him among the top three pitchers under the modern rules, behind only Walter Johnson and Grover Alexander.

Top 10 CC (Modern Rules)	
Player	CC
Walter Johnson	393
Grover Alexander	357
Roger Clemens	**336**
Lefty Grove	333
Greg Maddux	308
Christy Mathewson	286
Bob Feller	283
Warren Spahn	265
Tom Seaver	258
Randy Johnson	236

What is interesting about the top 10 list is how rapidly Clemens moved up the list in his later years. His CC through age 33 was very good, but still nowhere near the top of the list. He was eighth and just 11 CCs above No. 10, Jim Palmer, at that age. And Clemens appeared to be slowing down faster than the other pitchers on the list. Only Bob Feller and his ailing shoulder had posted fewer CCs after turning 30.

Top 10 CC (through age 33)		
Player	CC (through age 33)	CC (ages 30-33)
Walter Johnson	322	72.6
Christy Mathewson	286	72.5
Bob Feller	270	23.8
Grover Alexander	249	108.0
Greg Maddux	232	72.3
Lefty Grove	220	137.0
Tom Seaver	200	60.1
Roger Clemens	**196**	**41.4**
Pedro Martinez	191	55.6
Jim Palmer	185	70.7

But Clemens' career had a sudden rejuvenation, and in the coming years he managed to stay ahead of the hard-charging Warren Spahn, who would soon jump on the list in his mid-30s, and Clemens climbed over Tom Seaver, Lefty Grove, Greg Maddux and Feller.

Suddenly, in 1997, at age 34, Clemens set a career high with a 33.2 CC season. In fact, in the long history of the Live Ball Era (1920-present) no other pitcher has ever had such a season after the age of 32. He followed up that remarkable season with a fine season of 21.2 CC. That was the most CCs in consecutive seasons by a pitcher in his mid-30s since Lefty Grove in 1935-36. This was all decidedly odd after his weak transition into his 30s, but it got even weirder as Clemens moved into his 40s.

At age 41, Clemens became the oldest pitcher to win the Cy Young Award. At age 42, he became the oldest pitcher to lead the league in ERA. At age 43, he was a free agent and sat out early in the year as he waited to choose the team he wanted to sign with. Once he chose the Astros, he needed three weeks to get in shape. He did not pitch until Houston's 73rd game of the season, about six weeks prior to his 44th birthday...and then led the league in ERA the rest of the season! It was a surreal feat for someone who was the oldest pitcher in the major leagues.

2006 NL ERA Leaders after 6/21/06		
Player	IP	ERA
Roger Clemens	113.1	2.30
Roy Oswalt	125.2	2.72
Anibal Sanchez	114.1	2.83

Even missing such a large portion of the season at age 43, he still had far more CCs at ages 40-43 than he had had at ages 30-33! Particularly for the ages 41-43, Clemens' performance was off the charts compared to any other pitcher in history at the same ages, including knuckleballers.

Roger Clemens	CC
Ages 30-33	41.4
Ages 40-43	51.3

His edge over the second-best pitcher—Hall of Fame knuckleballer Hoyt Wilhelm—was about the same as the gap between Wilhelm and the sixth-best pitcher, Jack Quinn.

Most CC, Ages 41-43	
Player	CC
Roger Clemens	42.1
Hoyt Wilhelm	31.8
Cy Young	31.6
Phil Niekro	22.6
Nolan Ryan	21.9
Jack Quinn	21.2

The rub in all this is the extreme likelihood that Clemens was using illegal performance-enhancing drugs (PEDs) during this period of his career. Given that Clemens was found not guilty of perjury in his testimony before a Congressional committee, it is worth quickly reviewing the elements that point toward his use of steroids and/or HGH.

His personal trainer, Brian McNamee, testified under oath to several instances when he personally injected Clemens with steroids, and Clemens' DNA was found on materials the trainer said he had saved from times when he injected him with illegal PEDs. McNamee is not the most savory character, but his testimony on such issues has stood up under years of investigation. The other two players whom the trainer testified that he had assisted in their use of illegal PEDs eventually confirmed under oath that that was true.

Clemens' friend and teammate Andy Pettitte used the same trainer and in a sworn deposition Pettitte remembered two conversations in which the trainer had mentioned Clemens' use of PEDs—one in 1999 and the other around 2003. Both conversations predate by many years the trainer's involvement with the FBI, nullifying the claim that the trainer made up such stories under pressure from his plea deal in exchange for his cooperation with the FBI. That point was further established by David Segui's sworn testimony that McNamee had also mentioned Clemens' PED use to him in 2001.

Pettitte also stated in his deposition that he remembered a conversation in 1999 in which Clemens told him directly that he was using HGH. Pettitte also related that in 2005, when the first Congressional hearings on drug use in baseball were going on, that Clemens claimed that Pettitte had misunderstood him and told Andy: "I told you that Debbie [Clemens' wife] used HGH."

Pettitte further stated that shortly after both conversations he had shared with his wife, Laura, the news of both conversations. She confirmed this in a sworn affidavit, including the detail about Clemens' wife.

Neither of the Pettittes was privy to when Debbie Clemens began using HGH. If they had been, they would have realized how ludicrous Clemens was in his claim that he had told Andy in 1999 that Debbie, not Roger, was using HGH. In Roger's own deposition he placed his wife's first use of HGH as coming after the 2003 season—or four years after Andy remembered Clemens telling him of his HGH use.

On the chance that evidence of McNamee injecting him might turn up, Clemens explained to Congressional investigators that McNamee had given him injections, but only of legal stuff, mostly injections of vitamin B12. He also said that it was "fairly common" for ballplayers to get B12 injections, and that it was not unusual to get them from a trainer rather than the team doctor. And yet the three other deposed major league clients of McNamee said that the trainer had never injected them with B12, and none remembered him giving a B12 shot to anyone else, either.

Clemens' deposition mentioned how he recently had run into Dave LaBossiere, who had been the head trainer for the Houston Astros during Clemens' entire tenure there. Clemens said that LaBossiere had reminded him how he had personally given Clemens shots, and without a doctor present. Clemens did not realize the investigators were going to depose LaBossiere, who contradicted Clemens. He told the investigators that in over 20 years as a trainer with the Astros, he had never given a B12 shot to any player and that the team doctors gave nearly all the injections. LaBossiere said he had never injected Clemens with anything.

There were elements in Clemens' deposition/testimony that were at odds with the depositions and affidavits of 15 people: McNamee, the Pettittes, LaBossiere, Dr. Art Pappas, Dr. Ron Taylor, Dr. David Littner, Dr. Alan Gross, Rex Jones, Tommy Craig, Gene Monahan, Scott Shannon, Chuck Knoblauch, C.J. Nitkowski and the Clemenses' nanny, whose name was blacked out in her deposition.

The FBI investigated whether Clemens had committed perjury and advised the District Attorney that he had. After a grand jury had indicted Clemens, Henry Waxman, the chairman of the Congressional committee, acknowledged that he had come to believe that Clemens had lied to the committee.

Bottom line, regardless of the prosecution being unable to prove to a jury that Clemens was guilty beyond a reasonable doubt of perjury in his deposition and testimony before Congress, we have far more reason to conclude that Clemens used illegal PEDs than we have for other players from that era where that charge has been accepted as gospel. And that is without using the context of the unusual aging pattern of Clemens' performance.

Having spent many decades on research on the the aging patterns of major leaguers—21 years of which were working in Major League Baseball in the area of player evaluation—I probably know as much about the subject as anyone. There is an immense abnormality to the way Clemens' performance aged. No other pitcher has ever aged like this. It is reminiscent of the most unprecedented case among hitters—Barry Bonds. And we know Bonds' performance was chemically enhanced. The only thing Bonds denied was having accurate knowledge of what it was he was taking.

When it comes to evaluating Clemens' place among the greatest pitchers in major league history, what exactly do we do with this knowledge—or the assumption of knowledge if you prefer—that Clemens aged unnaturally due to the use of illegal performance-enhancing drugs?

The first step would be to estimate when his use of PEDs first began to abnormally affect the aging of his performance. There is a remarkable line of demarcation in his performance that suggests we should begin with the odd turnaround in his aging pattern in 1997. We know McNamee testified that he first met Clemens in February of 1998, and first injected him with steroids in June of that year. But he also said in his deposition that Clemens already appeared to be taking steroids—at least already had illegal anabolic steroids in his possession—oral steroids that were probably Anavar or Anadrol-50. McNamee testified that the first time he injected Clemens with steroids, it was Clemens who had provided them (Winstrol).

From reading through all the accounts, I think it is most likely that Clemens was taking oral steroids before 1998 and wanted to shift to an injectable steroid, but was queasy about injecting himself. He knew McNamee was experienced with injections from handling the insulin injections of his diabetic son, so Clemens sought him out to help him take this next step. So, let's consider the comparison of Clemens through age 33 (1996) fair game in comparison to other great pitchers, and after age 33 an unfair comparison.

But we do not have to leave it as Clemens being the eighth-best pitcher compared to all other pitchers under the modern rules through that same age of 33. Given that Clemens had been outperformed by every pitcher on that list except Feller over the last four ages (30-33), it is quite possible that a clean Clemens might have slipped back or been passed by Spahn, who had an exceptional aging profile that paid off big in the later years of his career.

As it turns out, while Clemens did not have an exceptional aging profile at that point, it was still better than that of most of the pitchers on the list. Because of differences in how workloads are managed over a career, the average modern pitcher ages better than the average pitcher from those earlier periods. Based on all I have come to understand from studying aging patterns, I would have expected Clemens to age better than Johnson, Mathewson, Grove and Feller.

And because he was a solidly built power pitcher with slightly better-than-average care taken with his workload in his formative years, I also expected him to age better than Seaver, Pedro Martinez and Palmer. Only Grover Alexander and Greg Maddux were expected to age better than Clemens.

Creating a predictive aging profile for Clemens based on his career through age 33, I would have expected him to add 60 CCs to his career total in the coming ages, which is better than many, many Hall of Famers, but is a good chunk less than the 140 CCs the chemically-enhanced Clemens was able to pull off.

With that estimate, Clemens would add more CCs in the coming ages than most of the pitchers who were with him in the top 10 through age 33. He did better than Mathewson (0), Martinez (5), Feller (13), Palmer (22), and Seaver (58). And relative to their prior ability, those 60 CCs have Clemens aging much better than Walter Johnson did, as well. Keep in mind that Johnson—the greatest pitcher of all time—was 81 percent better than Clemens through age 33, and that jumped to 87 percent for the ages 30-33. But Johnson had only 70 CCs after age 33, which is only 17 percent better than my aging estimate for Clemens.

Top 10 CC (Modern Rules) (with estimate of clean Clemens)	
Player	CC
Walter Johnson	393
Grover Alexander	357
Lefty Grove	333
Greg Maddux	308
Christy Mathewson	286
Bob Feller	283
Warren Spahn	265
Tom Seaver	258
Roger Clemens	**256**
Randy Johnson	236

In my estimate of what a clean Clemens would have done past age 33, only Spahn would have passed him in CC. So, there's my answer for where Clemens stands among the greatest pitchers under the modern rules. If you think he didn't use PEDs, his comparative career is the third-best. If you are convinced, as I am, that he used both steroids and HGH in the last eight years of his career, it is fairer to rate him ninth.

A note about Win Shares Above Replacement

The replacement level for WSAR for starting pitchers is 60 percent of the win shares per inning at the league level, projected into the innings of the starting pitcher being studied. This is the same definition used for "Win Shares Above Bench" by Seamheads.com.

I do not believe WSAR is preferable to WAR in all cases, but I do regard WSAR as the superior measure for historical comparisons of starting pitchers.

All systems have weaknesses. For this type of comparison, WSAR produces results that fit better with what makes sense in the whole of our knowledge—our holistic understanding of reality rather than our analytic understanding of reality. I anticipate that when the day comes that it is easier to work with Loss Shares in conjunction with win shares, an even more effective ranking will be possible.

The Most Storied Postseasons

by Dave Studenmund

Poor Hal Smith. If not for Yogi Berra, Mickey Mantle, Harvey Haddix and, finally, Bill Mazeroski, Hal Smith would be a legend in Pittsburgh. Every young Pirates fan would know the story of the backup catcher who smashed the biggest hit in postseason history, the one that gave the Pirates the 1960 World Series championship. For it was Hal Smith, their elders would say, who hit the incredible seventh-game, eighth-inning, three-run home run that capped the Pirates' five-run comeback for their magnificent World Series victory against the juggernaut Yankees.

That would indeed be the story if the Yankees, particularly Berra and Mantle, hadn't delivered their own clutch hits off Haddix in the top of the ninth, tying the game and necessitating a bottom of the ninth...which Mazeroski led off with one of the most famous home runs of all time. So it is Mazeroski's hit we celebrate today; it is the picture of Maz crossing home plate that is so iconic now. Poor Hal Smith.

Still, Smith deserves a special place in history, for his home run is the most important hit in the history of Major League Baseball. Don't believe me? Read on.

Earlier in these pages, Brad Johnson described a statistic called Championships Added (which I'll sometimes call ChampAdded to save space). It is simply the Win Probability Added (WPA) of each play in a game multiplied by the championship value of that game. The math is laid out in Brad's article, and I've also included a couple of web references at the end of this article for further reading.

Let's use Hal Smith as an example. The last game of a World Series is always worth a full championship, because the difference between winning and losing is one and zero championships. In this particular seventh game, the Pirates had just a 30 percent probability of winning before Smith's smash. After the smash, their win probability was over 90 percent. That hit was worth 0.6 Championships all by itself.

To put that in perspective, consider this: The Pirates and Yankees played 154 games during the regular season to win their league pennant and claim 0.5 world championships; the league winner is presumed to have a 50 percent chance of winning the World Series. So Smith accomplished more in one at-bat than the entire Pirates team accomplished in the entire regular season! Time raises the stakes at a rapid pace, until the seventh game of the World Series culminates in the fullest stakes.

Championships Added, like Win Probability Added, is a story stat. It is a wonderful tool for quantifying the most important stories of the postseason. It doesn't really measure value or worth; it certainly doesn't measure potential. It measures the leaps and bounds of each play. Instead of calling these performances the "best" or "greatest," I'm going to call them "the most important" or "the most storied."* This is what we're measuring when we calculate Championships Added.

* *Webster's defines storied as "celebrated in or associated with stories or legends." I think it works.*

My contention is that Smith's hit should be more celebrated, more associated with legend, than Mazeroski's. Think about it. The Pirates were trailing when Smith came to bat; two men were already out. The clock was ticking loudly. Mazeroski's homer, though more memorable because it ended the game, came with none out in a tie game just one inning later. Smith really deserves to be recognized for having stroked the most important hit in the history of baseball.

Don't feel bad for Mazeroski, however. His home run ranks as the fifth-most-important hit of all time.

Two years later, the Yankees were involved in a slightly different thing: The most critical at-bat of all time. Like ChampAdded, criticality is easy to calculate. It's simply the Leverage Index of an at-bat (as measured by the game situation) multiplied by the championship value of the game.

I wrote about the most critical at-bats on the Internet last year. In case you missed it, I've included a link to that article at the end of this one. The most critical at-bat of all time was Willie McCovey's lineout to end the seventh game of the 1962 World Series, with the Giants down by a run and runners on second and third with two outs. Another fun fact you might not have known were it not for ChampAdded.

This is what I intend to do for the next couple of pages: Use ChampAdded to highlight some of the most important plays, games and series in postseason history. In particular, I'm going to tell you who had the second-, third- and fourth-most important hits in history, while I also cover a few other subjects along the way.

Most Storied Games

It is fitting that the most important hit of the postseason occurred in the seventh game of the 1960 World Series, because that game was the most-storied nine-inning postseason game of all time. It was full of lead swings and several late-inning comebacks.

The Pirates had taken a 4-0 lead after the first two innings, with Cy Young Award winner Vern Law on the mound. However, the 1960 Yankees hitters, led by Mantle, Maris and Berra, were not impressed by awards (they had already reached double figures in runs scored in three of the previous six games) and batted back to a 7-4 lead heading into the bottom of the eighth. That's when the Pirates scored five to take a 9-7 lead, only to see the Yankees score two more to tie it in the top of the ninth.

Only to see Bill Mazeroski, who won a Gold Glove in 1960 but was hardly known for his bat, hit a home run.

When you take all the swings in that game, all the tilts of Win Probability from one team to the other, and then when you multiply those swings by a full championship (it being the seventh game of the World Series), you come up with a total of 4.5. So 4.5 championships swung back and forth in that single game. There has never been another nine-inning game like it.

However, there have been three other final games that contained more drama than the 1960 seventh. They just had to go into extra innings to make it.

1924: Giants vs. Senators

6.1 championships were swapped in this 12-inning gutbuster. The game was intriguing from the start.

The Senators' player-manager, Bucky Harris, switched pitchers after the original starter, Curly Ogden, faced just two batters. He brought in the left-handed George Mogridge to face the Giants. By starting a right-hander, Harris got Bill Terry into the lineup, batting fifth, but Terry didn't handle lefties well, so the switcheroo gave the Senators an advantage.

The strategy seemed to work well, as Mogridge took a 1-0 lead (behind a home run by Harris) into the top of the sixth. Unfortunately, the Senators' fielders didn't cooperate, and two errors led to three New York runs in the sixth. The Giants held a 3-1 lead into the bottom of the eighth, but the Senators managed to load the bases with two outs, when Harris stepped up to the plate and hit a grounder to third base. The ball took a bad hop over Freddie Lindstrom's head, and the Senators tied the game.

The Harris hit, which was a single due to the bad hop, was the seventh-most important hit of all time (0.35 ChampAdded). You might also call it the most critical bad hop of all time.

The game remained tied for several innings, until the Senators came to bat in the bottom of the 12th. With one out, Muddy Ruel doubled, Walter Johnson (batting for himself) reached on an error, and the next batter, Earl McNeely, hit a potential groundball double play to third base...where the ball once again took a bad hop over Lindstrom's head and Ruel raced home with the winning run.

1997: Marlins vs. Indians

That great Indians team of the late 1990s made it to the World Series twice, but 1997 was the closest they ever came to winning it all. The seventh game was a low-scoring affair, and the Indians had a 2-0 lead heading into the bottom of the seventh. That's when the Marlins' Bobby Bonilla hit a solo home run to cut the lead to one, where it stayed until the ninth.

The Indians worked mightily to score an insurance run in the ninth, as they placed runners at first and third with one out, but they failed to score. In the bottom of the ninth, Craig Counsell came to bat with runners on first and third and one out and

---

he promptly hit a hard sacrifice "fliner" to right to tie things up. That at-bat was the third-most critical at-bat of all time.

The Marlins threatened to score in the 10th, and then did score in the bottom of the 11th after Counsell (who else?) reached base on a critical error by second baseman Tony Fernandez. The two-out, game-winning single was delivered by Edgar Renteria.

Renteria's hit was the ninth-most important hit of all time. In all, the Marlins and Indians swapped 4.75 championships in this one game. The next year, Wayne Huizenga broke up the Marlins and the Indians have not made it back to the World Series.

1912: Giants vs. Red Sox

You have to go back to 1912 to find the third-most storied final game of all time, the third-most important hit of all time, as well as the fourth-most critical at-bat and the first truly great World Series. It was so great that it included a tie game.

The seven-game series was stretched to eight games due to a tie in the second game, and the eighth, final game was stretched to 10 innings. The Giants took a 2-1 lead with a run in the top of the 10th inning, but they gave the Red Sox a golden opportunity when Fred Snodgrass dropped Clyde Engle's fly ball to start the bottom of the frame.

A couple of batters later, the great Tris Speaker faced the great Christy Mathewson with one out, runners on first and third and the Sox still down by a run. The at-bat ranks as the fourth-most critical at-bat of all time. Speaker singled to right, tying the game and setting up the eventual winning sacrifice fly by Larry Gardner. See, the Red Sox always come through in the clutch.

4.72 championships were swapped in this one game. Speaker's single was worth 0.38 ChampAdded (third-most ever) and in the Series he accounted for 0.45 ChampAdded, the eighth-highest series total of all.

Most Storied Series by a Batter

Thanks to his home run, Hal Smith's performance in the entire 1960 World Series also ranks as the all-time performance in a full Series (0.66 ChampAdded). No other batter accumulated more ChampAdded in a full series than Smith did in 1960. It helps that Smith batted only eight times in the Series, so he didn't have a lot of opportunities to pull his total down.

Extra fun fact about 1960: Mantle's series ChampAdded total ranks as the 11th-largest of all time. It was a storied time.

The second-most storied postseason series batting performance was turned in a little more recently, by one David Freese of the St. Louis Cardinals in 2011. You may remember Game Six of that World Series…you should, because it is the most-storied Game Six of all time.

The Cardinals, who were behind 3-2 in the series, were also down by three runs with two innings to go. They tied it, thanks primarily to Freese's two-out triple in the bottom of the ninth, only to give up two runs to the Rangers in the top of the 10th. They tied it again in the bottom half, thanks primarily to Lance Berkman's two-out single, and then finally won it in the bottom of the 11th on a home run by Mr. Freese.

Overall, that was the 10th most-storied game in postseason history, but it was the highest-ranked game that wasn't a final game. The Cardinals went on to beat the Rangers in the seventh game and take home the World Series trophy. Fittingly, Freese, who amassed 0.6 ChampAdded across all seven games, was named the Series Most Valuable Player.

A Little Sidebar

You may be surprised to learn that two other teams have come closer to winning the World Series than the Rangers did, only to see the other team come back to win it all. Here's a list of the teams that had compiled the highest Championship Expectancy (the probability of winning the championship, which is Win Probability at any point in time during a game times the championship value of the game) without winning it all in the end:

1. 1986 Boston Red Sox

It was the 10th inning of the sixth game of the Series. The Red Sox had just taken a two-run lead (one run off the bat of postseason hero Dave Henderson) in the top of the inning and their closer, Calvin Schiraldi, was on the mound. Two outs, no one on. The Red Sox had a 99.4 percent Championship Expectancy. Three singles, one wild pitch and an error later, they had lost the game, subsequently lost Game Seven the next day and took 18 years to recover.

2. 2002 San Francisco Giants

The Giants had a 5-0 lead over the Angels with one out in bottom of the seventh inning of the sixth game of this Series—a Championship Expectancy of 98.5 percent. Unfortunately for Bay Area fans, Scott Spiezio hit a three-run homer in the bottom of the seventh, Darin Erstad hit a solo shot in the bottom of the eighth, Tim Salmon and Garret Anderson singled and Troy Glaus hit a two-run double to give the Angels a remarkable come-from-behind win after Troy Percival retired the side in order in the top of the ninth.

The Angels went on to win the seventh game, 4-1, and the World Series championship trophy went to Southern California instead.

3. 2011 Texas Rangers

At their peak in that sixth game (bottom of the ninth, one out, up by two), the Rangers had a 98.1 percent Championship Expectancy.

4. 1968 St. Louis Cardinals

The Cardinals, led by Bob Gibson's 1.12 ERA, seemed invincible. When they were leading the Tigers in the World Series by a 3-0 score in the fourth inning of the fifth game (three runs were a whole lot of runs in those days), already up 3-1 in games, they were almost truly invincible, with a 96.7 percent Championship Expectancy.

Eventual World Series MVP Micky Lolich gave up no more runs that game, Mickey Stanley hit a home run and Al Kaline hit a huge two-run single in the seventh and that was the game...and the Series. The Tigers won the sixth game easily (13-1) and Lolich outdueled Gibson by a 4-1 score in the seventh game to win it all for the Tigers.

5. 1960 New York Yankees

The Yankees held a 7-5 lead with two outs in the bottom of the eighth inning and a Championship Expectancy of 93.7 percent. One single and a Hal Smith tater later, and they were goners. This one is notable in that it's the first one on our list to occur in the seventh game.

6. 1985 St. Louis Cardinals

This one hurts most of all. The Cardinals had a 1-0 lead in the in the bottom of the ninth of the sixth game of the Series. Championship Expectancy of 91.8 percent. But umpire Don Denkinger called the first batter, Jorge Orta, safe at first even though replays showed he was clearly out. The Royals went on to score two runs on a Dane Iorg single off Todd Worrell and win the game, 2-1. The Cardinals never had a chance in the seventh game, as they lost 11-0.

7. 1979 Baltimore Orioles

The Orioles held a 3-1 lead in the fifth game of the Series against the Pirates, and they held a 1-0 lead heading into the bottom of the sixth with Cy Young Award winner Mike Flanagan on the mount. Their Championship Expectancy was 91.7 percent.

The Pirates were having none of it. Pittsburgh scored two runs in the bottom of the sixth and cruised to a 7-1 victory over the O's. They proceeded to sweep the final two games from the Orioles in Baltimore and win the Series.

The seventh game of this Series included the second-most-critical at-bat of all time, with Eddie Murray at the plate in the eighth inning, two outs, the Orioles down by two and runners on second and third. Murray flew out to the warning track, the Pirates scored two more in the ninth and that was that.

I love the fact that the two most critical at-bats of all time involved two of the greatest hitters of all time (Murray and Willie McCovey). The fourth-most critical at-bat involved the great Tris Speaker. The third-most critical at-bat involved, well, Craig Counsell.

Back to the Most Storied Series by a Batter

The third-most storied postseason series batting performance was Bucky Harris' 1924 Series (0.57 ChampAdded). We've already talked about that one, but it was so good that it's worth repeating.

Regarding the fourth batter on our list, Chris Jaffe wrote a special piece about the 1972 World Series for the *2010 THT Annual*, in which he said:

> *"The 1972 classic, while a great Series throughout, lacked that one special game. If one made up a list of the 50 greatest games in World Series history, it's possible none would come from 1972."*

Also...

> *"It peaked at the wrong time, with its most impressive highlights occurring in Games Four and Five. Looking at baseball history, it's Games Six and Seven that are best remembered."*

Yet there is one way in which the 1972 Series stands out. The underrated Gene Tenace had a sensational seven games that year, as he went 8-for-23 with four home runs and won the Series Most Valuable Player Award trophy. What's more, Tenace's home runs all came in critical situations: All four of his homers gave the A's a lead (that was in Games One—in which he hit two home runs in his first two at-bats—Three and Five). Overall, he contributed 0.5 ChampAdded in 1972, the fourth-highest total of all time.

The fifth-highest Series total might come as a surprise to you.

The 1925 World Series was a repeat of the 1924 version, with the Senators and Pirates playing each other once again, but it was the Pirates who won the Series this year—this time in just seven games. This series is notorious for Walter Johnson's performance. The Big Train was outstanding in his first two starts, but his final start, in the seventh game, was marred by a steady downpour and poor fielding support.

People talk about Johnson when they talk about the 1925 World Series, but they should also talk about Max Carey. Carey, the Pirates' center fielder, had put up a career year in 1925 after deciding to separate his hands on the bat, a la Ty Cobb. He also had a terrific Series, as he batted .458 and scored six runs. In the deciding seventh game, he doubled three times and stole a base. Altogether, his 0.49 ChampAdded is the fifth-highest total ever.

Other Storied Hits

The second most-important hit of all time occurred in the seventh game of the Diamondbacks/Yankees series in 2001. I know what you're thinking. Luis Gonzalez's single off Mariano Rivera to win it all for the Diamondbacks must be it, right? After all, it capped a two-run bottom of the ninth that resulted in a tremendously dramatic 3-2 Game Seven win against the greatest closer of all time, right?

Wrong. The second-most important hit occurred two batters earlier, when Tony Womack smacked a double down the right-field line with one out and runners on first and second. That hit tied the game and was worth half a championship (literally 0.50 ChampAdded). Gonzalez's single was worth "only" 0.16 championships; after all, the bases were loaded with just one out. Even if Gonzalez had hit into a double play, the game would have gone into extra innings. If Womack had hit into a double play, the Series would have been over.

In fact, Womack's at-bat ranks as the fifth-most critical of all time. That swing of possible events—from a home run to a double play—gave it a level of criticality rarely seen in postseason history. And Womack delivered.

I hope you remember that the third-most important hit was Tris Speaker's single in the 1912 World Series. It was worth 0.38 ChampAdded.

The fourth-most important hit didn't come in the seventh game of a World Series. In fact, it wasn't hit in a World Series at all. The fourth most-important hit ever was Atlanta's Francisco Cabrera's single to left in the 1992 National League Championship Series against the Pirates.

The Braves were losing, 2-0, heading into the bottom of the ninth inning of the final game of that NLCS. But they scored a run on a Ron Gant sacrifice fly, then loaded the bases for Cabrera with two outs. Cabrera's single scored David Justice, and a sliding Sid Bream beat Barry Bonds' throw to give the Braves the pennant.

Before Cabrera's hit, the Braves had just a 26 percent probability of winning the series. After the hit, they had won it all. 100 percent. Cabrera's single had such a huge impact that it breaks through the list of World Series hits to take over the fourth spot all-time, at 0.37 ChampAdded.

And then there was the fifth, Mazeroski (also 0.37 ChampAdded).

I know that I've wandered around a little bit here, so let me conclude this section with two tables of the biggest single hits and the biggest series of all time, as measured by ChampAdded totals.

Single Hit Leaders	Total
Hal Smith	0.636
Tony Womack	0.498
Tris Speaker	0.382
Francisco Cabrera	0.368
Bill Mazeroski	0.367

Series Leaders	Series	Total
Hal Smith	1960	0.656
David Freese	2011	0.602
Bucky Harris	1924	0.573
Gene Tenace	1972	0.504
Max Carey	1925	0.494

The Most Storied Postseason Careers

Career totals for ChampAdded can be misleading, because it's easy to have a big impact with just one hit. Hal Smith, for instance, with just eight postseason at-bats, has the fifth-highest total ever.

The 10 highest career ChampAdded totals are…

Batter	Total
Mickey Mantle	0.856
David Freese	0.836
Pete Rose	0.814
Lance Berkman	0.745
Hal Smith	0.656
Lou Gehrig	0.636
Dwight Evans	0.599
Tris Speaker	0.560
Reggie Jackson	0.550
Yogi Berra	0.547

Mickey Mantle batted .257/.374/.535 in the postseason, in 273 plate appearances, all in the World Series. His biggest Series were 1960, 1952, 1964 and 1953. He never really had a bad Series. His home run in the seventh game of the 1952 Series, which gave the Yankees the lead for good, was his second-biggest hit (after his single in 1960) and biggest home run.

I compiled this list before the 2013 postseason, which is why David Freese ranks second. If you add in the 2013 results, Freese drops out of the top ten careers and David Ortiz is sixth, just ahead of Dwight Evans, which proves that postseason fame is truly fickle.

Pete Rose had a long career and played with many teams that made the postseason. His best Series was in 1975, the fabled Carlton Fisk/Bernie Carbo series against the Red Sox. Rose's biggest hit was a seventh-inning single that tied the seventh game.

Lance Berkman's 2011 World Series was the seventh-highest ChampAdded series of all time, thanks mostly to his two big hits in the sixth game. Like Mantle, he was a steady postseason performer and batted .317/.417/.532 overall.

Hal Smith.

Talk about postseason performers. Lou Gehrig batted .361/.477/.731 in the postseason and certainly suffers in ChampAdded because his teams were rarely challenged, even in the World Series. From a ChampAdded perspective, his most notable Series was in 1928, when the Yankees swept the Cardinals. Gehrig batted .545/.706/1.727. (1.727. That was his slugging percentage.) In his next postseason, in 1932, he hit .529/.600/1.118.

As I said earlier, ChampAdded doesn't measure value.

I'll finish extemporizing on the career ChampAdded list with Dwight Evans. Evans appeared in the postseason only four times, in the World Series only twice, and he batted just .239/.333/.425 in those appearances. But he made his hits count.

This is a list of what Evans did in the three most critical at-bats of his postseason career (listed in descending order of criticality):

- Doubled to score two runs and pull the Red Sox within one run of the Mets in the eighth inning of the final game of the 1986 Series.
- Walked with the bases loaded in the third inning of the final game of the 1975 Series against the Reds.
- Walked to lead off the bottom of the eighth inning with the seventh game tied against the Reds in the 1975 Series.

Evans might be the anti-Gehrig. His basic stats don't look particularly good, but he had opportunities to do the right thing in the right situation, and he often did.

And Finally...

Ron Gant appeared in the postseason in six different years, with the Braves, Reds and A's. In 210 plate appearances, he batted .228/.292/.402. What's more, in the 10 most critical at-bats of his postseason career, in descending order, he...

- Lined out
- Struck out looking
- Grounded out
- Flew out
- Grounded out
- Grounded out
- Hit a line drive into a double play
- Grounded into a double play
- Lined out
- Fouled out

His -0.82 ChampAdded is the worst career total ever.

References

- Dave Studenmund, "The One About Win Probability," The Hardball Times, *hardballtimes.com/main/article/the-one-about-win-probability*
- Dave Studenmund, "The most critical at-bat of all time," The Hardball Times, *hardballtimes.com/main/article/the-most-critical-at-bat-of-all-time*
- Dave Studenmund, "Tensest Series of all time," Baseball Prospectus, *baseballprospectus.com/article.php?articleid=16359*

Crossword Puzzle

by Shane Tourtellotte

2013 marks a milestone, the 100th anniversary of the invention of the crossword puzzle. From what was expected to be a one-off diversion in the Dec. 21, 1913 edition of the *New York World*, the crossword has grown into a shared obsession, an indispensable part of Americans' leisure time. A lot like baseball, actually.

To honor the centennial, we present our own anniversary crossword puzzle with a baseball flavor, and 1913 baseball at that. There are plenty of baseball-themed answers, as there should be for this book, but nothing that should baffle our usual readers (for a couple of the more esoteric acronyms, you can always consult the glossary).

We hope you enjoy this change of pace from THT, even if it is just a one-off diversion. Of course, we've heard that before…

ACROSS

1. Boston has a Big one
5. Most famous Moneyball stat
8. Rays
13. '30s pitcher Hildebrand
14. An equal
16. Ice house
17. *Baseball headline of 1913: Part 1*
20. '90s Phillie Relaford
21. Precursor to "Humbug!"
22. W.S. winner, all but twice
23. T, in Morse
25. Maris, informally
28. *Part 2 of headline*
36. 7.08(a)(1), e.g.
37. Guilty or not guilty
38. Car, or French city
40. '89 Series Game 1 matchup: Giants___
41. Resp. to a ques.
42. The root of poi
43. "… ___ pass Go, …"
45. Molina's glove
47. Dickie, drilled in '84
48. *Part 3 of headline*
51. A rocky (not Rockie) hill
52. Little friend of Pooh
53. One minus BABIP, almost
56. Terrific Met in '69

58. Hack's 191
62. *Conclusion of headline*
68. Robinson's favorite watercraft?
69. Stealer's edge
70. *This type*: Abbr.
71. What Sandman does and Mariano did
72. Defensive metric: Abbr.
73. '60s Yankee Dale

DOWN

1. Captive from battle
2. Yankees' unlucky 13
3. Trim
4. Woes
5. 5-Across plus 67-Down
6. Boston National, 1936-40
7. Part of MPH
8. "Camera Eye" Max and family
9. The Chicken's first home?
10. Matty or Moises
11. Berg and Drabowsky
12. He had 66 in'98
15. 'Spare' bone
18. 2013 DBack Gregorius
19. Baltimore nobility (RIP, 2013)
24. What's the Matterhorn?
25. 2001 M's pitcher John
27. Scene for stickball, maybe

28. Old-fashioned: Abbr.
29. "It's ___ here!"
30. City just north of Dallas
31. Ump's possible shout
32. Jean material
33. Negro Leaguer Luke
34. Harmon's home state
35. The Hammer
39. Zero
44. Browns pitcher Bill, or harness racehorse
46. Chinese general who was chicken?
49. 1913 Giant and Red Heinie
50. Spelling, not Hunter

53. Twelve, to Clemente
54. Non-desperate Longoria
55. '90s "La Boheme" remake
57. Parnell or Allen
59. Get the water out
60. "___ the Woods"
61. "The Man" (RIP, 2013)
63. '50s Preacher in blue
64. It's 'new' to a German
65. '67 Triple Crown winner
66. East Germany: Abbr.
67. TB/AB

1	2	3	4		5	6	7			8	9	10	11	12
13					14			15		16				
17				18					19					
	20						21					22		
			23	24	25			26		27				
28	29	30	31				32	33				34	35	
36					37				38					39
40					41					42				
43			44		45			46		47				
	48			49					50					
		51				52								
53	54	55		56		57			58	59	60	61		
62			63			64	65	66					67	
68					69					70				
71						72				73				

You can find the answers on pg. 303.

Birthday Bonanzas

by Chris Jaffe

On June 8, 1977, veteran Red Sox pitcher Rick Wise stood on the mound to start the third inning and saw what would normally be a pleasant sight for any pitcher. There at the plate stood longtime Orioles shortstop Mark Belanger.

Though a respected player, Belanger had kept his slot in Baltimore's starting lineup for the past decade solely because of his glove, not because of his bat. In his 18-year career, Belanger would hit a measly .228 with no power. And so far, 1977 was proving to be a brutally bad batting season for Belanger, even by his standards; he came to the plate with a futile .187 average.

By all reason, Belanger should have been doomed against Wise. But not this day, not on June 8. Mark Belanger owned this day. You see, June 8 was his birthday.

In his career, Belanger would go 11-for-24 with a pair of doubles and six walks on June 8, quite a bit better than his normal performance. Sure enough, Wise lost his third-inning battle to Belanger, who rapped a clean single against him. Next time up, Belanger drew a walk. Happy birthday to Mr. Belanger.

Does it make sense that players could perform better on their birthdays? My first study for The Hardball Times showed that when a longtime player for a team returned to his old park for the first time as a visitor, he typically performed better than expected. There could be a similar phenomenon going on here.

Or it could just be random happenstance and Mark Belanger could be an outlier. Find enough players and you can find someone who did really well on his birthday, even if there is no overall trend. Bill James studied how players did on their birthdays in some of his early Abstracts. He looked at 1980 and 1982, and noted that players hit better overall on their birthdays, but when he continued the study for 1983 and 1984, the pattern no longer held up.

Studying it: An Overview

Looking it up, it turns out that players don't do better than normal on their birthdays. I found 213 hitters who played in 10 or more games on their birthdays from 1916-2012. By OPS, most actually did worse on their birthdays. Among the group, 117 underperformed their normal OPS, 95 did better, and one player, Hall of Famer Harry Heilmann, perfectly matched his lifetime OPS on his birthday: .930.

In all, these guys played 2,612 birthday games—quite a nice sample size. That's pretty equal to the career of Lou Brock or Derek Jeter. In those games, they hit .280 with a .784 OPS. That's not bad, but then again, to last long enough to play 10 or more birthday games, you have to be a pretty good player. Overall, these players hit .282 with a .791 OPS in their careers—nearly identical to their birthday numbers.

Per 162 birthday games, here is their aggregate batting line:

G	PA	AB	R	H	2B	3B	HR	RBI	BB	K	SB
162	644	566	83	158	28	4	15	78	65	69	11

Best Birthday Performers

Okay, so most hitters don't improve their performance on their birthdays. But even if guys like Belanger are outliers, who are the biggest outliers of all? Which hitters have the biggest improvement over their regular performance on their birthdays? Here are the top 10, as determined by birthday OPS divided by career OPS:

Player	G	Bday OPS	OPS	Improvement
Mark Belanger	10	1.108	.580	91.1%
Ray Boone	10	1.265	.789	60.3%
Rabbit Wartsler	10	.903	.587	53.8%
Randy Winn	12	1.106	.759	45.7%
Greg Gross	10	1.036	.723	43.3%
Chipper Jones	13	1.325	.930	42.5%
Tony Phillips	10	1.082	.763	41.8%
Duke Snider	12	1.293	.919	40.7%
Doug Rader	13	1.016	.725	41.2%
Joe Judge	13	1.113	.798	39.5%

Boy, Mark Belanger is an outlier of outliers! He batted .458 on his birthday, more than twice his normal average.

Any day Belanger contributed with his bat was a bonus for his employers in Baltimore. He was there for his glove. In fact, according to Wins Above Replacement, Belanger anchored the best fielding team of all-time, the 1973 Orioles, at 13.6 defensive WAR. Belanger was their star glove man, at 4.0 fielding WAR. In fact, the second-best fielding team ever is the 1969 Orioles (11.5 fielding WAR—which shows just how great the 1973 team was), and Belanger was that club's starting shortstop as well. In 1969, Belanger went 2-for-3 on his birthday, and in 1973 he was 0-for-1 with a walk.

This is a fun list because it's so arbitrary. If you were to see a list of the 10 best birthday OPS performers, it would be a much more traditional roll call of great hitters. Duke Snider, Chipper Jones, Ray Boone and Joe Judge would still be on it, joined by Lou Gehrig, Frank Thomas, Todd Helton, Jim Thome, Alex Rodriguez and Derrek Lee. A lot a Hall of Fame and star quality players there. The lesson would be that even in a list of best players on one given day, the best players in history will still typically dominate.

Here on the birthday-improvement list, though, you get guys from all sorts of eras, born in every month from April to September, from all types of positions, and of varying levels of quality. One of these hitters was playing in every season from 1916-2012, excepting the World War II years.

The furthest-back player on the list is Judge, so if you went back in time, at one point he'd be No. 1 on the list above. Judge manned first base for 20 years, from 1915-34, mostly with the Washington Senators. For 18 years he teamed with Hall of Fame outfielder Sam Rice; the duo set a record that still stands for most career games played alongside each other.

Judge is easy to overlook. Despite a lengthy career, he virtually never led the league in anything. He topped the American League in games played in 1918; that's it. His most notable feature was that he hit a ton of triples: 159. Sure, players hit a lot more triples back then, but Judge retired ranked 34th all-time. Fittingly, Judge is the all-time (well, since 1916 anyway) record holder for most birthday triples, with four. He legged out two on his 30th birthday on May 25, 1924. That's the only two-triple game I came across.

A career .298 hitter, Judge improved notably on his birthday, batting .392. He had a 10-game birthday hitting streak, which ties Earl Averill and John Olerud for longest birthday batting streak I found. Had he never played another birthday after that, Judge would have ranked second on the list above, by going 19-for-41 with all his extra-base hits. As an old man, he was 1-for-10 with a single on his birthday.

If Judge had been No. 1 on the above list through the mid-1930s, the man who would have passed him was Rabbit Warstler, who played shortstop from 1930-40. Essentially, Warstler was a poor man's Mark Belanger. Like Belanger, Warstler made it to the majors on the strength of his glove, not his bat. However, he wasn't the all-time great defender Belanger was. Warstler was just a good glove man.

Incredibly, he wasn't even as good at the plate as was Belanger. Though Warstler had a better career batting average, .229 to .228, he also played in a higher-average era. Warstler's career OPS+ is 59, well under Belanger's 68. Warstler's memorable nickname was a reference to the best defensive shortstop of the early 20th century, Hall of Famer Rabbit Maranville. In fact, the two Rabbits played together in 1935, Maranville's last big league season.

Warstler makes this list rather cheaply. Not only did he appear in the bare minimum 10 games, but he had zero or one plate appearances in four of them. He batted .375 with a few walks and a triple, which was enough to really stand out against his overall batting average.

Warstler's unlikely place atop any kind of all-time hitter leader board ended with Boone. The patriarch of one of baseball's three-generation families (son Bob was at one point the all-time leader in games caught, and grandsons Aaron and Bret made their marks), Ray Boone was a slugger. While playing for the Indians and Tigers, he finished in the top 10 in homers three times and twice drove in 100 runs, leading the league with 116 RBI in 1955.

Boone was also a great birthday slugger, posting a .828 slugging percentage on July 27. He never played on his birthday until he turned 27, but the next year smashed two homers on his birthday. The following year he hit a triple. When he turned 31 in 1954, he went 4-for-7 with another triple during a doubleheader. In 1957, he hit a three-run homer.

Boone's .828 birthday slugging percentage is the second higher of anyone, behind only Snider, who smacked balls around at a .848 clip. It's very impressive that Snider made the list above. While batters like Warstler and Belanger could benefit from comparing their birthday performance with a very poor regular performance, Snider is a Hall of Famer—the only Hall of Famer listed above (though Jones should join him in Cooperstown soon). Twice, Snider enjoyed a two-homer game on his birthday—he's the only person who did that.

Worst Birthday Performers

Enough of the happy talk of best birthday performers—who gave themselves unhappy birthdays? Here are the worst birthday underachievers in terms of comparing birthday OPS to overall OPS.

Player	G	Bday OPS	OPS	Decline
Vinny Castilla	14	.486	.797	61.0%
Ken Griffey Sr.	10	.474	.790	60.0%
Mark Grudzielanek	11	.405	.725	55.8%
Rick Dempsey	10	.358	.666	53.7%
Paul Waner	12	.466	.878	53.1%
Vada Pinson	14	.408	.769	53.0%
Dan Dreissen	13	.399	.767	52.0%
Phil Cavaretta	10	.383	.788	48.7%
Jim Bottomley	11	.422	.869	48.6%
Manny Ramirez	13	.455	.996	45.6%

One of the biggest names here is Hall of Famer Paul Waner. Though he had more than 3,000 career hits, he was just 6-for-39 on April 16. He did walk nine times, but that was about all he had going for him. All of Waner's hits were singles. Only one person accumulated more birthday trips to the plate without an extra base hit: Roy McMillan. Random fact: the first time Waner appeared in the starting lineup came on his 23rd birthday.

Waner was known as quite the drinking man. Supposedly, his approach to batting while inebriated was to aim at the middle of the three balls he saw. While he had a great run, his ways likely cost him the back portion of his career. In his first dozen seasons he averaged more than 200 hits a year. Only Ichiro Suzuki can top him there.

Waner also averaged over 40 doubles a year, with 481 in his first 12 seasons, behind only Albert Pujols and Joe Medwick.

But then Waner got really old, really fast. After hitting .348 in his prime, Waner batted just .288 the rest of the way. Sure, baseball averages were down as a whole, but that was a steep drop. A man historically prolific at getting hits got 679 in his last 757 games. You have to wonder if clean living would have helped him.

This relates to his birthday performances, too. Sure the numbers above for Waner could just be a fluke and mean nothing. Then again, given his penchant for carousing, was Waner out celebrating his birthday in the first hours after midnight?

That makes me wonder about another player on the list: Phil Cavaretta. The longtime Cubs first baseman never had a reputation as a carouser, but he did play nearly his entire career for the Cubs, whose home games were always played in the daytime because Wrigley Field lacked lights. Perhaps that's overthinking it, though. After all, if it were really that simple, there would be a ton of players of 1916-1930s here, when no teams had lights.

There is one Hall of Famer on the list besides Waner: Sunny Jim Bottomley. The National League first baseman from the Great Depression is most famous for driving in 12 runs in one game. While he made Cooperstown, he's generally regarded as one of the mistaken picks, a guy selected because he was a friend and former teammate of longtime Veterans Committee leader Frankie Frisch.

While Bottomley doesn't belong in Cooperstown, he really was something in his prime. In 1925, as the Cardinals first baseman, he led the league in hits and doubles. The next year, he topped the NL in doubles, RBI and total bases. In 1928, he finished first in homers, triples, total bases and RBI. In his prime, he was a quality hitter with plenty of power and his share of walks. But on his birthday, he never did much of anything, going 6-for-43 with three doubles.

While Waner is the most prestigious player on the list, he isn't the greatest natural hitter. That would be Manny Ramirez. Manny wasn't being Manny on the field on May 30. He went just 6-for-44 with three extra base hits—all doubles. He was at his worst early in his career. Through 2003, he had just two singles in 24 at-bats.

Maybe the most interesting name of the list is Rick Dempsey. Just as it was difficult for Snider or Jones to make the earlier list, because they had to greatly outperform their normally fantastic performances, Dempsey had to do far worse than his typically underwhelming performance. And underwhelm he did, going 3-for-19 with a walk (like Warstler, Dempsey was often a part-time player on his birthday).

Dempsey had the longest career of anyone here—24 seasons—but he lasted because of his defense. He wasn't a terrible hitter, but he had a .666 career OPS. Dempsey spent time as a backup backstop with the Twins and Yankees before finally catching on in his late 20s with the Orioles. He was a teammate of clutch birthday god Belanger for the better part of a decade.

Dempsey moved on to several other teams in the late 1980s and early 1990s. His most memorable moment may have come with the Dodgers, when he hit a solo homer in the top of the 22nd inning for the only run in a 1-0 LA triumph. Dempsey eventually returned to Baltimore in 1992, and the team called on him to catch the final inning of the final game ever played at old Memorial Stadium (the pitcher was fellow returning longtime Oriole Mike Flanagan). That ended Dempsey's career.

An honorable mention needs to be made for Aug. 1 baby Milt May. A longtime catcher, May played on his birthday seven times, and never once got a hit. Nor did he ever draw a walk. In 24 birthday plate appearances, his lone moment of glory came on his 29th birthday in 1979—when he got hit by a pitch.

For the record, the hitter with the most birthday games is Carl Yastrzemski. He appeared in 20 games, nosing out Al Lopez and Cal Ripken Jr. with 19. Interestingly, the three have birthdays within a week of each other.

Best and Worst Birthday Pitchers

That's hitters—now what about pitchers? By their nature, these are a lot more random. Position players are out there every day, but pitchers only occasionally. So it's possible for a pitcher to have a nice long career and never appear on his birthday.

Among starting pitchers, the April-to-September births with the most impressive careers who never appeared on their birthday are Vida Blue and Curt Simmons. The most overall appearances for someone who never saw action on his in-season birthday was Jeff Brantley: 615 games, but none on his Sept. 5 birthday.

The man with the most birthday mound appearances is long-ago AL 200-game winner Sad Sam Jones, who pitched at least 10 times on his birthday (the data goes back only to 1916, and his career goes back to 1914). Jones had two birthday shutouts, but those were nearly his only wins.

Sad Sam is the counting stat king on birthdays, with the most games (10), starts (nine), innings pitched (69.1), hits allowed (70), runs allowed (32), earned runs allowed (25), walks (25), and batters faced (294). He's also the all-time birthday loss leader, with a record of 3-6.

Jones was a pretty good journeyman pitcher from 1914-35. A more recent comparable for him might be Kenny Rogers. Both were 200-game winners who were never elite pitchers but lasted two decades pitching for multiple teams. Rogers had a better win-loss record, but also had more help from his hitters.

Jones had more extremes in his career arc. Rogers was well-traveled, but Jones played for almost every pre-expansion AL team. He got his start with the Indians, breaking ground as one of the game's early relief pitchers. He set a major league record when he appeared out of the bullpen 39 times in 1915. After that, the Indians made Jones part of an explosive trade. He, another player, and a giant bag of cash went to Boston in exchange for center fielder Tris Speaker, one of the standout stars in baseball.

For Jones, Boston would be the best of times and the worst of times. He won a World Series title with the team in 1918, which also served as his breakout season—he led the AL with a .762 winning percentage after going 16-5. One of the few losses came on his 26th birthday on July 26, when he gave up seven runs in four innings.

However, the next year something went wrong with Jones' arm, and he went 12-20 with an ERA well worse than league average (and his second straight birthday loss). Then the team began selling off its best players, most infamously sending Babe Ruth to the Yankees. Jones' arm recovered, and he even went 23-16 for the second-division Red Sox in 1921.

That strong season made Jones a tradeable commodity, and the Red Sox sent Jones where they'd already put many of his teammates, to the Yankees. His high point came in 1923, when he won 21 games and helped the Yankees claim their first World Series title. In fact, Jones was the man on the mound when New York recorded the last out to clinch the championship.

Things again went haywire for Jones' arm and in 1925 he had a season in hell, leading the league with 21 losses and helping the Yankees to their only losing season between 1919 and 1965. From that point, Jones was never a star, but he was never a disaster. He sojourned from the Browns to the Senators and finally to the White Sox, where he ended his career. He never made it to the Tigers or A's, having to settle for playing for "only" three-fourths of the then-existing AL squads.

He pitched on his birthday for every team but Cleveland. The highlight may have been his final birthday game. On July 26, 1934, the White Sox put Jones on the mound on his 42nd birthday, and he gave them a very special present—a complete game, six-hit shutout. It wasn't the best of his birthday starts—he threw a three-hit shutout with the Red Sox in 1920—but it has the advantage of being the last of Jones' 36 career shutouts. Jones is easily the oldest pitcher to have a birthday shutout.

Only one pitcher even comes close to Jones: rubber-armed AL journeyman Bobo Newsom. He's constantly a tad under Jones in birthday stats, with eight starts, nine appearances, 59.2 innings pitched, 58 hits, and 20 walks, all good for second place. Newsom is first place in just two categories. One is complete games, with five. The more notable is wins; Newsom posted a 5-1 mark on his birthday.

That's quantity—what about quality? Let's start with Jim Rooker. He was a late bloomer in the 1970s who didn't really catch on with a club until he was 26 years old. He had a decent run as a mid-rotation starter for the Pirates in the mid-1970s.

With Pittsburgh, Rooker twice started on his birthday, and in those games made a notable achievement: most career birthday innings pitched without allowing a run. He celebrated his 32nd birthday by throwing nine shutout innings for the Pirates on Sept. 23, 1974. He didn't get the complete game shutout, but did pick up the win as Pittsburgh scored the game's only run in the top of the 10th. Three years later he threw seven shutout innings against the Cubs, giving him 16 career innings on his birthday, and no runs allowed. He did this despite fanning just four batters in those 16 innings.

Another all-time great birthday pitcher is Jerry Reuss. In four birthday starts he came away with four wins. This wasn't an offense-aided 4-0 record, either; he posted a 1.69 ERA. He threw one shutout, and all of his efforts were quality starts. As it happens, Reuss and Rooker were teammates for a few years in Pittsburgh. It's a shame for the Pirates that they couldn't have had pitcher birthdays happen all the time. They would've dominated.

Reuss' career resembled Jones'. Like Jones, Reuss was a 200-game winner who lasted a long time without ever necessarily being an ace. Reuss pitched for even more teams—eight—but then again there were 26 franchises during his career. Like Jones, Reuss lasted exactly 22 seasons. Reuss actually was a four-decade player, as he lasted from 1969-90. He's the most borderline four-decade player of all-time, with less than 15 innings pitched outside of the 1970s and 1980s. He appeared in one game in 1969 and lasted seven innings. In 1990, he threw 7.2 innings.

Another all-time great birthday winner is Gaylord Perry. In four starts, he went 3-0 with three complete games, two shutouts, and a 1.57 ERA in 34.1 innings. Perry is arguably the best birthday pitcher of them all, and at the very least he's the best Hall of Fame birthday pitcher.

Perry is often overlooked in favor of his contemporaries, Tom Seaver and Steve Carlton, and is most remembered for his favorite pitch: the spitball. But Perry came close to being the most revered pitcher of his generation. Just a simple fluke of fate prevented him from gaining that reputation. For nearly a decade, Perry worked in the Giants' starting rotation alongside another well-known Hall of Fame hurler: Juan Marichal.

Though they worked for the same team at the same time and had the same hitters bat for them, Perry and Marichal had very different offensive support levels. From 1964-71, Perry started 272 games for the Giants, and in that time the team gave him league average offensive support. When you adjust for the park, it was a tad under league average. But when Marichal took the mound—276 times from 1964-71—his run support was fantastic. The hitters who made an average lineup for Perry were world-beaters for Marichal. Adjusted for park, Marichal's run support was 20 percent above league average. If Perry had started on Marichal's days and vice versa, Perry would have had maybe 20 more wins—and become the winningest pitcher of his generation. Marichal probably would have missed Cooperstown.

Another potential effect is that the Giants might never have traded Perry away. But trade him they did, sending him and Frank Duffy to the Indians for fastballer Sudden Sam McDowell, who was past his prime. (Adding further insult, the Giants had gained Duffy by trading a young George Foster to the Reds for him. Thus in two trades they turned Foster and Perry into a broken-down McDowell. Ouch.) Perry played another dozen seasons, won two Cy Young Awards, and ultimately became the first pitcher in 20 years to win 300 games.

As for his birthday performance, Perry can also claim a nice achievement that no one else I came across accomplished: He once celebrated his birthday by posting his 20th win of the season. When Perry turned 36 years old on Sept. 15, 1974, he led the Indians to a 1-0 win over the Orioles, giving him a 20-10 record on the season. Also, that was Perry's second straight birthday shutout, part of a stretch of 22 consecutive scoreless birthday innings, an achievement even more impressive than Jim Rooker's lifetime 16 scoreless birthday innings. Jones was the only older pitcher to toss a birthday shutout.

One of the least successful birthday pitchers is Big Daddy Rick Reuschel. He had plenty of quantity with a lack of quality on his birthday. In five starts, he went 1-4 (only Jones had more losses). His 5.12 ERA is bad enough, but he also had unearned runs in most of his starts; he gave up 6.25 runs per nine innings. In just 31.2 innings, he allowed nine doubles (more than any other pitcher), two triples and four homers. As a rule, you don't want to approach an extra base hit every other inning.

Win Probability Added (WPA) really hates Reuschel's birthdays, giving him a career birthday mark of -1.173, the worst of any pitcher. Given that WPA is the story stat that tries to quantify how the game feels, it could not have been much fun to be Reuschel during his baseball birthdays. More than any other pitcher, he kept giving up the big hits that cost his teams games.

It's a shame, because Reuschel is one of the most underrated pitchers of recent decades. WAR positively adores Reuschel, crediting him with 68.2 wins above replacement level, which tops pitchers like Jim Palmer, Bob Feller and Carl Hubbell.

How did Reuschel score that high? Simple—his teammates gave him really lousy support. Let's look at defense. According to WAR, the worst fielding team in baseball history was the 1974 Cubs: -14.4 fielding WAR. Reuschel started 38 games for that team (and had three relief appearances). The Cubs had a negative defensive WAR every year he pitched in Chicago—and that's where he spent his prime.

It's not just fielding, either. In 1977, Reuschel won 20 games for the Cubs despite terrible run support. In his 37 starts, they scored 131 runs, which works out to 3.54 runs per start. That doesn't sound too bad, but 1) Wrigley Field was an extreme hitters park that year—only twice in stadium history did it have a higher park factor than in 1977—and 2) 1977 was one of baseball's occasional Silly Ball seasons, with the league scoring 4.40 runs per game. Adjusted for park and league, Reuschel's run support was just 73 percent of league average, which is the worst run support for any 20-game winner in the last 100 years.

Reuschel had a great, and easy to overlook, prime in the 1970s. He had arm trouble in the early 1980s, but recovered nicely. At age 36 in 1985, he went 14-8 with a 2.27 ERA. Three years later, he won 19 games for the Giants. At age 40, he started the All-Star game and helped pitch the Giants to their first pennant in decades.

Reuschel may not have been the equal to Jim Palmer or Carl Hubbell. I'm not saying that WAR doesn't overrate him. But he was a legitimately great pitcher—except when it was his birthday.

Conclusion

Some studies are intended to be deeply meaningful. This isn't one of them. After all, players generally do about the same on their birthday as they do normally. But a study can still be fun and interesting, and some of these results qualify.

Analysis

Shifty Business, or the War Against Hitters

by Jeff Zimmerman

Over the years, players have shifted around from different positions on the field depending on the game situation. A team expecting a bunt will bring in its infielders. When a power hitter is up, it will move the outfielders back. If a double play is needed, the second baseman and shortstop will move closer to second base. And, in extreme situations, a team will even move all the infielders to one side of the field against decided pull hitters.

Indians manager Lou Boudreau made the infield shift famous when he used it against Ted Williams in the second game of a doubleheader on July 14, 1946. He moved all four infielders to the right side of second base after Williams had doubled down the first-base line in his first at-bat of the game (and homered three times in the first game of the doubleheader).*

*This inspired White Sox manager Ted Lyons to claim that he had found the flaw in Boudreau's shift: "Boudreau doesn't put anyone in the right-field bleachers."

This was a more extreme version of the shift employed against Cy Williams in the late 1920s, when the shortstop would move to the right of second base and the third baseman would play a little to the left of second. On the other hand, the typical Cy Williams shift included moving the left fielder to center field—leaving the left field area completely uncovered.

Williams (Ted, that is) famously never altered his batting approach against the shift, causing Ty Cobb to exclaim, "The way those clubs shift against Ted Williams, I can't understand how he can be so stupid not to accept the challenge to him and hit to left field." Later in his career, Williams learned to adjust to the slider by hitting more to left (as he admitted in an interview with Leigh Montville), but it was the pitch that made him change his approach, not the shift.

These days, with the astounding wealth of batted ball and defensive data, teams are using the shift more often and in more extreme ways. The impact on baseball has not been negligible.

When a team shifts, it can position its players many different ways. The data I will be using are from InsideEdge, which tracked 24 different types of shifts and field positioning during the 2013 season. Following is a list of some of the types of shifts and positions, the number of times they were employed, the Batting Average on Balls in Play (BABIP, which doesn't include home runs) and the percentage of hits that were double and triples (XBH%) against each type of shift.

Note: For all the data, all pitcher plate appearances have been removed. Also, the data acknowledge a shift only when there is a ball in play. If a shift was on during a strikeout, walk, etc., no data were collected.

Shift Description	Number	BABIP	XBH%
No shift	105,880	.300	7.3%
Three successive players on one side of infield	2,620	.267	6.8%
Three successive players almost on one side of infield, but SS or 2B still barely on their side of bag	3,675	.296	6.2%
Three non-successive players on one side of the infield (i.e. 3B in RF, but SS on left side)	125	.200	5.6%
Catch-all category used for other odd shifts by multiple players	110	.336	7.3%
Infield up: all four infielders playing on the grass (half way doesn't count).	891	.418	6.7%
No doubles defense: both corners guarding lines; OF deep	127	.394	5.5%
Corner(s) playing WAY in on grass; expecting bunt	867	.265	4.5%

There were apparently no true Ted Williams shifts last year; no one placed all four infielders on the right side of second base. But some form of the shift (three players on one side, or almost three on one side) was used nearly 6,000 times when the ball was struck into play. That's a whole lot of shifting.

As you can see, BABIP was only .267 when the strong shift was employed, but .296 when the weak shift was employed. It's hard to make sense of these numbers unless you remember that a very strong bias is at play here: Shifts are applied only against certain types of players, so comparing one set of shift data directly against another doesn't quite work.

It is interesting that doubles do decrease when teams play the "no doubles" defense, but BABIP goes up. And when corners play in, expecting the bunt, they evidently get the bunt; as witnessed by the .265 BABIP result.

For the rest of this article, I am going to focus on the major infield shift…the one in which only one fielder is truly left on one side of the infield (the second, third and fourth categories listed above). Unless noted, all the statistical values will be the combined value of the infield shifts.

To get the best sense of how well the shift works, let's look at specific players. Here are the 20 batters who saw the shift most often when they put the ball in play, and their stats both with the shift in play and without it.

Name	Bats	Batted Balls into Shift	BABIP: Shift	BABIP: No Shift	Diff	XBH%: Shift	XBH%: No Shift	Diff
David Ortiz	L	266	0.312	0.330	-0.018	8.7%	14.7%	-6.0%
Adam Dunn	L	200	0.255	0.288	-0.033	4.5%	7.5%	-3.0%
Chris Davis	L	199	0.302	0.425	-0.123	10.1%	17.0%	-6.9%
Adam LaRoche	L	160	0.288	0.272	0.016	5.0%	6.6%	-1.6%
Josh Hamilton	L	150	0.273	0.330	-0.057	6.0%	12.0%	-6.0%
Ryan Howard	L	149	0.309	0.500	-0.191	10.7%	20.0%	-9.3%
Carlos Pena	L	140	0.293	0.250	0.043	8.6%	3.1%	5.4%
Pedro Alvarez	L	122	0.303	0.279	0.025	6.6%	7.6%	-1.0%
Jay Bruce	L	116	0.233	0.363	-0.130	9.5%	11.5%	-2.1%
Travis Hafner	L	115	0.244	0.290	-0.046	5.2%	5.3%	0.0%
Brian McCann	L	105	0.171	0.260	-0.088	0.0%	7.1%	-7.1%
Prince Fielder	L	103	0.291	0.302	-0.011	3.9%	8.4%	-4.6%
Justin Smoak	B	102	0.304	0.288	0.016	6.9%	6.0%	0.9%
Anthony Rizzo	L	101	0.238	0.269	-0.031	5.9%	10.8%	-4.8%
Kendrys Morales	B	100	0.280	0.282	-0.002	3.0%	7.5%	-4.5%
Brandon Moss	L	96	0.292	0.321	-0.030	9.4%	9.5%	-0.1%
Raul Ibanez	L	93	0.204	0.279	-0.074	3.2%	8.9%	-5.6%
Carlos Santana	B	91	0.253	0.342	-0.089	8.8%	11.0%	-2.2%
Ja. Saltalamacchia	B	90	0.300	0.416	-0.116	14.4%	15.5%	-1.1%
Robinson Cano	L	85	0.318	0.324	-0.006	8.2%	7.2%	1.1%

Summing up the numbers, these 20 players accounted for 2,583 (or about 40 percent) of the recorded shifts last year. BABIP decreased for 16 of the 20 and their BABIP collectively fell 37 points—from .314 when hitting with no shift on to .277 when hitting with the shift on. In other words, the shifts worked.

You probably noticed that there isn't a right-handed batter on the top 20 list. Switch-hitting and left-handed hitters are more likely to see shifts. Shifts run to the pull side of the hitter, and when a right-handed hitter gets shifted, the first baseman needs to field the entire right side of the infield, and either he or the pitcher will need to make the play at first base. It takes a fairly athletic first baseman to pull that off.

Here is a breakdown of how often each type of shift was used against left-handed or right-handed batters. You can rest assured that virtually all the shifts against switch-hitters occurred with a right-hander on the mound.

Bats	Full Shift	Partial Shift	Other Shifts	Total
Left	1,858	2,196	182	4,236
Both	351	557	33	941
Right	411	922	14	1,347

Besides the difference in total number of shifts, the difference in full and partial shifts for right-handed hitters and left-handed hitters is also substantial. Right-handed hitters are much more likely to see a partial shift than a full shift.

There is something else these batters have in common: they are slow; they can not, will not or do not bunt; and they pull the ball a lot on ground balls and line drives. To show you what I mean, here are the Bill James Speed values and Pull% for line drives and ground balls for the top 10 most-shifted players.

Name	Speed Score	GB Pull%	LD Pull%
David Ortiz	3.5	82%	60%
Adam Dunn	1.1	80%	66%
Chris Davis	3.1	86%	67%
Adam LaRoche	4.0	83%	65%
Josh Hamilton	4.5	70%	64%
Ryan Howard	2.7	82%	74%
Carlos Pena	2.9	75%	59%
Pedro Alvarez	3.1	83%	57%
Jay Bruce	3.6	73%	58%
Travis Hafner	3.8	84%	48%
Average	**3.2**	**80%**	**62%**

Note: Pull data are for the entire half of the field. The Pull% values from baseballheatmaps.com

For comparison, the league-average hitter pulls ground balls about 72 percent of the time and pulls line drives about 50 percent of the time. These hitters, on the other hand, are likely to have a speed score of four or less, pull ground balls 80 percent of the time and pull line drives 62 percent of the time. This is the prototype of the shiftable batter.

One player on whom the shift had a huge impact was Chris Davis. Over the first four months of the season, he hit into an average of 29 shifts per month, and was able to maintain a .304 batting average and .359 BABIP. Over the last two months of the season, teams shifted more often against him...41 times per month. Consequently, his batting average was .250 and his BABIP was .293.

The shift was killing him. Without a shift employed, Davis hit for a .425 BABIP, with a extra base hit percentage of 17 percent, over the course of the 2013 season. When the shift was set, his BABIP dropped to .302 and XBH% to 10 percent.

Which raises the question: Why not bunt against the shift? Players bunted a ball in play against the shift just 48 times last season. They reached base 58 percent of the time. It is ridiculous that players don't bunt more often against the shift. The other team is dropping your BABIP nearly 50 points and you won't give up a little pride to get on base at a greater than 50 percent rate?

Some players do use the bunt. Last season, these seven players successfully bunted a ball in play against the shift more than once:

- Carlos Gonzalez (reached base on four of five bunts)
- Luke Scott (three of four)
- Curtis Granderson (one of four)
- Lance Berkman (two of four)
- Carlos Pena (two of four)
- Matt Joyce (three of three)
- Carlos Santana (one of two)

Of the 26 times these seven players bunted, they reached base 16 times. Again, I will stress that the bunt is a completely underused tactic.

One player who did improve his approach against the shift was Adam Dunn. According to CSN Chicago...

> *Disgusted that he felt good at the plate but had only poor results to show for it, the White Sox slugger dramatically switched his approach in early June. A veteran pull-hitter known for his long-ball prowess, Dunn has worked to become more of a straightaway hitter in his 13th season in the majors....His well-rounded attack hasn't just made Dunn a more complete hitter—it has forced teams to take notice...."Ever since I started getting shifted, it was like, 'This is ridiculous,'" Dunn said. "You do everything right and you hit a ball as hard as you can in short right field, where maybe it's even a double, and it's an out. But the thing I've done for the most part all year is just have been more consistent hitting...This is the best it's been since I've been here." (Source: http://www.csnchicago.com/white-sox/shift-against-sox-slugger-all-dunn)*

In June, teams shifted against Dunn more than any other month, but his BABIP saw an almost 200 point jump from May, and stayed high for the rest of the year.

Dunn	Apr	May	June	July	Aug	Sept
BABIP	.139	.135	.326	.371	.286	.286
Shifts	36	37	43	35	28	21

As Dunn experienced success against the shift, teams began to shift against him less frequently. Fun trend to watch in 2014: see if Dunn maintains his new batting approach against the shift, and if teams continue to shift against him less frequently.

Switching perspectives, let's ask which teams used the shift most often. New baseball strategies, such as (going way back) the intentional walk or (more recently) the bullpen specialist are typically adopted slowly over time. You often see a wide difference in use of the strategy on a team-by-team basis.

As to the infield shift, the Orioles used it most often, 470 times, and the Nationals employed it the fewest times, 41. The Brewers shifted a lot, but they preferred the partial shift to the full shift.

For your information, here is the entire list:

Team	Total	Full shift	Partial Shift	Other shifts	Team	Total	Full shift	Partial Shift	Other shifts
Orioles	470	253	175	42	Blue Jays	177	59	104	14
Rays	466	253	196	17	Mets	154	83	66	5
Brewers	425	119	303	3	D-backs	152	54	93	5
Pirates	422	169	246	7	Tigers	143	67	74	2
Astros	407	183	210	14	Giants	136	49	86	1
Red Sox	364	218	123	23	Marlins	122	36	84	2
Cubs	343	107	221	15	Rockies	119	40	77	2
Yankees	326	111	206	9	Braves	108	19	84	5
Athletics	306	154	143	9	Padres	88	31	54	3
Royals	275	94	176	5	White Sox	83	11	72	0
Indians	252	155	95	2	Cardinals	66	1	62	3
Rangers	249	124	122	3	Twins	65	20	25	20
Mariners	230	56	172	2	Dodgers	50	16	34	0
Reds	221	35	182	4	Phillies	48	11	32	5
Angels	216	80	132	4	Nationals	41	12	26	3

American League teams shifted 60 percent more often than National League teams. The key reason is the lack of a designated hitter in the NL. Not having the DH limits shifting for two reasons. First, a slow, good hitter is more likely to be a DH. The most shifted-against player, David Oritz, was primarily a DH in 2013. Second, teams don't really have enough hitting information against the opposing pitcher to justify a shift.

It may seem that, with the success teams are seeing with the shift, they would use it more often, but that didn't happen during 2013. In fact, the use of the shift actually declined as the year progressed.

- March/April: 1,415 shifts
- May: 1,389
- June: 1,042
- July: 844
- August: 927
- September: 907

Did teams stop believing in the shift as some players, like Dunn, started to beat the strategy? Not quite. The main cause for the drop in shifts was that some of the top shifted-against players got hurt or were given less playing time as the season progressed. Here is a list of some of the main contributors to the drop and the number of plate appearances they had per month.

Name	Mar-May	June-July	Aug-Sep
Ryan Howard	198	119	0
Carlos Pena	207	118	3
Travis Hafner	157	136	6
Carlos Gonzalez	235	196	5
Albert Pujols	236	207	0
Jose Bautista	216	233	79
Lance Berkman	199	83	12
Luke Scott	94	161	17
Total PA	1,542	1,253	122
Total Shifts Seen	434	266	16

I added the number of total shifts seen by these batters in the last row. If you do the quick math, you see that these players actually did experience a lower rate of shifts used against them. Is this a trend that will continue into next year? Have teams already started to pull back from using the shift?

Well, some players got the shift more often as the season progressed.

Name	Shifts - 1st Half	Shifts - 2nd Half	1st half BABIP	2nd half BABIP
Pedro Alvarez	49	73	.301	.251
Matt Adams	22	39	.368	.308
Kyle Seager	6	28	.319	.245

These three players saw teams shift against them significantly more as the season moved forward. If you hadn't known about the shifting, you might have thought that the three just struggled in the second half of the season. They did, but it was due to the opposition's strategy. Expect this threesome to get shifted on more often in 2014.

So the trends aren't clear, but the effectiveness of the shift, and its uneven use, leads me to believe that it will be employed more often next year.

It's a funny thing. Over the last five years, a wave of new and precise research has made its way to baseball teams. Batted ball and defensive positioning data are one example; another is the wealth of data available from tracking technologies such as PITCHf/x and Trackman. I think you can make the point that these new technologies are helping pitching and defense more than offense.

Rays manager Joe Maddon thinks so too, and said so to MLB.com:

"A pitcher pretty much knows a tendency of a hitter that holds true...And the defense pretty much knows a tendency that's going to hold true. All this stuff, all this new stuff that everybody is utilizing definitely weighs more heavily in favor of the pitching and defense. The hitter's not really picking up any really good nuggets compared to what the pitching and defense is."

For another example, see Jon Roegele's article in this *Annual* about the growing strike zone, the likely role of PITCHf/x and its impact on run scoring.

It seems that this is a trend that will only continue. Shifts will be used not only more often, but more creatively. As teams uncover the relationships between hitting tendencies, pitcher strengths and fielding reactions, their strategies will become more complex and, well, interesting. Hitters, like Adam Dunn, will have to adjust.

Watch the game within the game. It will never end.

Voting Patterns for the MVP and Cy Young Awards

by Shane Tourtellotte

Last year, the American League produced one of the most contentious races for the Most Valuable Player Award in recent memory. This isn't to say that it was one of the closest races we've seen: Miguel Cabrera of the Detroit Tigers easily outpaced the Los Angeles Angels of Anaheim's Mike Trout, 22 first-place votes to six. That wide spread, if anything, merely inflamed the unyielding convictions and harsh sniping between both sides of the debate.

Trout partisans tended toward the sabermetric side of the ledger, though with side appeals to more old-fashioned viewpoints. WAR metrics put Trout head and shoulders above Cabrera, by 10.0 to 6.9 according to FanGraphs' numbers, and 10.9 to 7.3 according to Baseball-Reference. Trout supporters praised his all-around excellence, not only batting for both average and power, but playing a great center field and using his speed for both steals and taking the extra base with high success. Compared to Cabrera's subpar play at third base and uninspiring speed, this left the Tiger looking one-dimensional to Trout's fans. Throw in that Trout's season was the best ever seen from an age-20 player, and his supporters concluded it was only natural that a historic season be capped with the MVP Award.

Cabrera boosters cited history for their side, as well. Cabrera's .330 batting average, 44 home runs, and 139 runs batted in won him the Triple Crown, a feat not seen since Carl Yastrzemski's amazing 1967 season made his Boston Red Sox's Impossible Dream season come true. A Triple Crown winner not getting the MVP was unthinkable in their eyes. (It wasn't unthinkable to the voters. Out of nine Triple Crown winners from 1933 to Yaz in '67, only five won the MVP Award. Chuck Klein lost in 1933 to Carl Hubbell. Ted Williams got stiffed twice, by Joe Gordon in '42 and Joe DiMaggio in '47. Lou Gehrig in 1934 finished an astonishing fifth, behind three Tigers and his own teammate, Lefty Gomez.) Also, Cabrera turned up his play when it counted, setting a blistering pace in the second half of the season, while Trout cooled off in August and September.

Cabrera's excellence provided the V in MVP, as Detroit won its division while Trout's Angels couldn't even scrape into the wild-card game (LA might have won one more game than Detroit—in a tougher division—but it didn't get the Angels a 163rd game). As for defense, Cabrera willingly switched to a position he hadn't played in several years, to fill a hole left by Victor Martinez's season-long injury. Didn't such flexibility, such sacrifice, provide value to Detroit, his fans argued. And so what about a great rookie season? Rookies have their own award. It shouldn't affect

MVP consideration, or it should actually penalize them: Trout will have plenty more opportunities to win the MVP than Cabrera in his late prime did.

Our readers certainly have their own opinions in the debate, and may be able to guess mine, as well. While that is the jumping-off point for this article, it isn't the focus. All the various claims to have the key to a correct MVP vote made me wonder what factors actually do persuade the awards voters, separate from whether they really should. To do this, I looked at recent voting for not only the MVP, but the Cy Young Award. What I discovered was sometimes predictable, and sometimes quite surprising.

Criteria and Method

For my study, I examined the years 1996 through 2012, all the baseball seasons since the last strike ended. My reason for cutting things off at that date was that one of my lines of inquiry concerned month-to-month performance, which would have been skewed by the shortened 1994 and 1995 seasons. This produced sets of 34 votes each for the MVP and Cy Young.

I took data for the top three finishers in each vote, in a broad range of metrics both simple and advanced. Some of the metrics (e.g., wRC+ for MVP and xFIP for Cy) are so new that FanGraphs breaks them out by month only back to 2002, but I kept them for the sake of thoroughness, and to help determine whether monthly changes in the new and complex stuff was making any impression on voters. I will note throughout the piece when a metric has this limited coverage.

My intent to compare batters to batters forced two alterations in the MVP votes, in years when pitchers finished in the top three. In each case (Justin Verlander winning the MVP in 2011 and Pedro Martinez finishing second in 1999), I removed the pitcher from the results and promoted the position players behind him one slot apiece. This is a rough solution, but one that makes sense in that I mean to observe players' relations to each other in the stratosphere of MVP voting, not merely to the ordinal numbers of first, second, and third. Pedro's 1999 season provides an added hiccup, as Roberto Alomar and Manny Ramirez finished tied for third in MVP voting. They both get promoted to a tie for second.

I considered, but rejected, a similar combing out of relievers from starters for the Cy Young Award. One can fairly argue that relievers, especially closers, are a different animal from starting pitchers, judged by different criteria. But there's no good place to stop once traveling down that road. Catchers are plausibly in a different category from other position players; middle infielders have defensive demands that corner outfielders don't face. Starters and relievers have the same goal of preventing runs. They are judged by ERA and strikeouts and walks and OPS-against, by criteria that overlap almost completely and allow for direct comparison. Eric Gagne's place in the Cy Young voting, and Mariano Rivera's several places, are secure.

For each award year, I recorded which of the top-three finishers—I will borrow the podium from the Olympic Games and henceforth call them "medalists"—had the best result in each of the statistical categories I covered (others in the league may have beaten them, but I am focusing only on those with strong award consideration). I tabulated the results in two ways. The first begins with a simple count of how often the award winner led the medalists in that category. I convert that to a percentage figure, with 33.3 percent being what one would expect from random chance.

The second was a touch more complex. I counted how often the stat leader was the first, second, or third-place finisher. I assigned a positive point for each time it was the award winner and a negative point each time it was the third-place finisher, then divided by the number of awards. This produces a number somewhere between +1 and -1, depending on how often the stat leader got gold or bronze. The scale deliberately resembles that used to measure positive and negative correlation, and I will call it that in this article, though it isn't quite the same thing.

To give an example: In the NL MVP races, the first-place finisher had the highest unadjusted OPS of the three medalists 10 times, second place had it four times, and third place three. $10/17 = 59$ percent for the first measure is easy enough, and $(10-3)/17 = +0.41$ for the second isn't that tough, either. Both metrics show a pretty strong correlation.

These tabulations are intended to measure the correlation between various stats and the voting, but a common statistician's caution is in order: correlation is not causation. Sometimes voters will be basing their decisions on a particular stat; sometimes it'll be a spillover from something else, maybe one of the components going into a more advanced stat. The results will not be fully explanatory, though they may well be predictive. Future years will help decide that.

Down the Stretch They Come

A leading argument of Cabrera's supporters was that he played better than Trout in the final months of the season, when the games mean more (it is, in fact, this assertion that set me on the course of researching this article). We can set aside the argument over whether a game in September actually does mean more than one in May, or only appears to. We're searching not for the objective, but for the subjective: whether the voters follow this line of thinking.

Using data from FanGraphs, with some supplemental numbers from Baseball-Reference, I tracked five metrics month-to-month for the MVP medalists, and four metrics for the Cy Young medalists. For the MVP, the metrics were OPS, OPS+, isolated power, weighted on-base average (wOBA), and weighted runs created (wRC+). I used both raw OPS and OPS+ because voters could well be swayed by numbers unadjusted for their offensive context, aka Coors Field Syndrome, or PETCO Syndrome in the reverse case (monthly breakouts for wOBA and wRC+ were both truncated at 2002).

The Cy Young metrics were strikeouts, strikeouts per nine innings, opponents' OPS+, and opponents' wOBA (truncated to owOBA). I used two strikeout metrics to give weight to both the accumulation that favors starters, and the rate production that gives relievers their chance to make an impression. Also, for both awards these were the most relevant statistics with easily gathered monthly breakdowns. I did not care to throw away scarce data.

To include the whole season in the monthly divisions, games played in March count under April, and regular-season contests in October count under September. This standard grouping method produces a marvelous little illusion in one individual case. Rivera finished third in Cy Young voting in 2004, with 66 strikeouts in 78.2 innings. Broken down by month, 11 of them came in April, 11 in May, and so on to 11 in September. It is a string of uncanny consistency—broken up only by the bothersome facts that two of his "April" strikeouts came in March, and one "September" K fell in October (that last one is forgivable—he did his best work in October).

The breakdowns by month for the MVP categories are in the tables below. The first table shows the percentage of times the award winner led the league in that specific stat. The second table is the "correlation" between voting order and stat order. Numbers in parentheses show how many awards are included in the sample for the monthly metrics. For full-season stats, they are 34 apiece, 170 for the full set. Random chance would produce 33 percent and 0.00 in each case.

Award Winners/Category Lead Percentages						
Metric (yrs)	OPS (34)	Iso (34)	wOBA (22)	wRC+ (22)	OPS+ (34)	All (146)
March/April	35%	44%	36%	36%	35%	38%
May	32%	29%	36%	32%	32%	32%
June	44%	44%	45%	45%	41%	44%
July	41%	21%	45%	45%	38%	37%
August	59%	50%	59%	64%	59%	58%
Sept./Oct.	53%	41%	55%	55%	53%	51%
Full Season	47%	46%	50%	50%	44%	55%

Correlation						
Metric (yrs)	OPS (34)	Iso (34)	wOBA (22)	wRC+ (22)	OPS+ (34)	All (146)
March/April	.06	.22	.09	.09	.04	.10
May	.06	-.03	.09	.05	.04	.04
June	.09	.19	.14	.18	.07	.13
July	.21	-.04	.27	.27	.16	.16
August	.44	.28	.36	.45	.46	.40
Sept./Oct.	.28	.16	.27	.27	.31	.26
Full Season	.25	.25	.31	.32	.28	.28

The evidence for the greater importance of later months is overwhelming. For only one metric do any of the first-half months show a stronger correlation than any of the second-half months: isolated power, with its anomalous July. The final two months of the year are obviously influential in swaying voters' minds, though with the strongest effect counter-intuitively coming in August. Were this result less robust—August leads all months both in firsts and correlation across all five metrics, and beats the full-season marks to boot—I might chalk it up to random variation and say that it's the last two months together that really matter.

It's too strong for that, though. The numbers tell us that MVP voters make up their minds in large part based on August performance. If an MVP-caliber player has a hot August, or especially a hot August and September, he is in the catbird seat. That is precisely what happened with Cabrera in 2012.

After an almost suspiciously strong result with the MVP voting, one can be relieved, after a fashion, that the Cy Young results are more muddled. This time, all full-season stats have the same number of awards in the sample as the monthly breakdowns. The 33 percent and 0.00 baseline remains in place.

Award Winners/Category Lead Percentages					
Metric (yrs)	K (34)	K/9 (34)	oOPS+ (34)	owOBA (22)	All (124)
March/April	53%	44%	41%	30%	43%
May	50%	59%	32%	23%	43%
June	62%	56%	38%	41%	50%
July	60%	62%	38%	45%	52%
August	54%	53%	44%	45%	49%
Sept./Oct.	56%	47%	37%	64%	50%
Full Season	71%	59%	41%	45%	55%

Correlation					
Metric (yrs)	K (34)	K/9 (34)	oOPS+ (34)	owOBA (22)	All (124)
March/April	.31	.24	.26	.05	.23
May	.29	.44	-.09	-.18	.15
June	.47	.32	.03	.09	.24
July	.46	.50	.25	.32	.39
August	.32	.41	.18	.23	.29
Sept./Oct.	.24	.21	-.02	.55	.21
Full Season	.56	.35	.15	.30	.34

Once again, second-half performance corresponds more closely than first-half results with how the award medalists shake out, but without the same down-the-line clarity. Both of the advanced metrics show negative correlations in at least one month, one of them in September. The strikeout metrics hold up much better, with no correlation below 0.2—though again, September is curiously weak, the weakest of all months. Possibly this is due to down-ballot pitchers catching fire in September and boosting themselves to a third-place showing, but that is speculation.

If there's a single month when pitchers make their Cy Young cases, it is July. The tracking with the votes is nearly as strong as for August and the MVP, but Cy July is not as far ahead of the pack as MVP August was, so it stands out less as an indicator. The full-season metrics correspond roughly as well as July's, also. September surprisingly has one of the weakest relationships to the award, under-performed only by May.

Why would voters care less about the final month for pitchers? I speculated it could be because they're being played less, either to set them up for the playoffs or shut them down to save their arms. Cy Young winners led the other medalists in season innings pitched 19 times out of 34, but for September innings pitched had the lead only 15 times. That's moving in the right direction, but it isn't convincing. The question will remained unanswered for now.

Sharper-eyed readers will have noticed how strong the correspondences for the strikeout-based metrics are. I will have more to say about that later.

Are Award Winners Anointed With Champagne?

Looking over the months April through September got us some useful answers, but there are more to be found in a month that's not even supposed to count for these regular-season awards: October.

Cabrera's Tigers were three games behind the Chicago White Sox as late as Sept. 18, but roared back (I know, sorry) in the final two weeks to finish three games clear and win the AL Central. The Angels had a calamitous April before Trout was even called up, and despite making up some ground in the campaign's final month, finished four games out of the Wild Card hunt. Many commentators considered the teams' finishes to be germane to the MVP voting. An excellent season for a team that narrowly wins its division would have to be more valuable than one for a team that misses the postseason entirely, since it helped its team reap the value of a playoff berth.

Those with long memories may recall the related controversy surrounding Andre Dawson's MVP-winning season in 1987. Dawson claimed the award for playing on a Chicago Cubs squad that finished last in the NL East, beating out Ozzie Smith of the division-winning Cardinals. This drew howls of indignation from people who observed—to borrow Branch Rickey's formulation against Ralph Kiner—that the Cubs could have finished last without Dawson, but that the Cards might not have finished first without Ozzie. The controversy did not fade after one year, as that award buttressed Dawson's case for his eventual Hall of Fame election, which again many people—though not necessarily the same ones—thought was a mistake. Luckily, it did nothing to retard Smith's induction.

The debate comes down to a matter of semantics. Those on the Cabrera/Smith side contend that the word "valuable" in Most Valuable Player has a specific, intended meaning that favors players on successful teams. If the founders of the award had wanted voters choosing the best player separate from team performance, they say, they would have named it the Most Outstanding Player Award, or something else that didn't imply a connection. The Trout/Dawson side scorns this as hair-splitting, and calls for evaluating a player's performance in isolation, ignoring the ancillary matter of how well his 24 teammates played.

Does the Cabrera/Smith argument persuade the voters? The best way to decide this is to compare how the voting pool acts toward the MVP Award with how those voters act regarding an award with no implied connection to team success. The Cy Young Award suits the case admirably.

Looking at how many of the medalists for each award were on playoff teams, there is no great difference. Exactly half of the medalists for both the MVP and Cy Young, 51 out of 102 apiece, played on teams that won their division. An added 17 MVP medalists copped Wild Card berths, while 11 Cy Young medalists made October by the side door. It looks like there's only random variation between the two, until you look at the award winners themselves.

MVP	Div.	WC	Out
First	23	4	7
Second	11	6	17
Third	17	7	10

Cy Young	Div.	WC	Out
First	14	2	18
Second	19	3	12
Third	18	6	10

Two-thirds of MVP winners were also division champs, and just one-fifth missed the playoffs altogether. For the Cy Young, more than half of all the winners started their offseason regimens earlier than they had hoped. This is precisely what we'd expect to see if MVP voters were favoring playoff-bound players and Cy Young voters were not, or much less so.

Comparing the medalists emphasizes the pattern. For the MVP, silver and bronze were both likelier than gold to miss the postseason, or to just squeak in as Wild Cards. The gap is especially wide between first and second place, strongly suggesting that it is often a deciding factor in choosing between them.

The reverse is true for the Cy Young: second and third place are likelier than first to win the division or draw a wild card. It might be that superb pitching work stands out more on mediocre teams than for powerhouses who presumably have several players producing at high levels. Recent anecdotal cases come easily to mind: Zack Greinke, Felix Hernandez, R.A. Dickey. Regardless of reason, Cy Young winners are not collecting their hardware on the backs of their teammates.

So here we have a clear-cut confirmation. MVP voting is substantially influenced by the playoff fortunes of candidates' teams, especially compared to the Cy Young. This doesn't speak to whether the voters should be doing so. The voting guidelines given out by the Baseball Writers' Association of America (BBWAA) deliberately finesse the issue:

> *"There is no clear-cut definition of what Most Valuable means. It is up to the individual voter to decide who was the Most Valuable Player in each league to his team. The MVP need not come from a division winner or other playoff qualifier."*

The voters get to decide the criteria, and some of them are using their prerogative to give playoff qualifiers added weight. They're breaking no rules; they're not defying the BBWAA in any way. It may be a problem, depending on your point of view, but it isn't a scandal or a crisis, not unless and until the Association changes its policy.

The Jewels in the Crown

Winning the AL Triple Crown was an epochal achievement for Cabrera, something that around half of all baseball fans had never seen in their lifetimes and that some pundits thought we would never see again. It made a compelling case that Cabrera was the league MVP, even if, as I have already noted, such cases have not always compelled the voters. Underpinning the case is that Cabrera led the league in three offensive categories that have, for a very long time, been thought highly indicative of overall excellence: batting average, runs batted in and home runs.

The leading edge of sabermetrics has, for some time, considered those first two statistics to be overrated, for reasons I won't reiterate here (home runs are still rated as pretty awesome). Award voters are, shall we say, not uniformly supportive of leading-edge sabermetrics, though more inroads are being made each year. Since there's only one Triple Crown winner in my study range, it makes more sense to look at the components of the Triple Crown—and some other related "simple" metrics—to see how strongly the voters are leaning on the more established numbers to guide their decisions.

I'll examine the counting stats first. Along with RBI and home runs, I will throw in runs scored, the natural complement to RBI. Historically, table-setters who pile up runs scored have fared poorly in MVP voting compared to the players who drove in those runs. At least, that is the common impression, one that may have to change.

Home Runs	41%	+.22
RBI	26%	-.06
Runs Scored	35%	+.15

For runs scored and RBI, the second-place medalists led the most times, and they missed with homers by the width of a shared lead, 14 to 13.5. Runs batted in shockingly ended up with a negative correlation, and runs scored were not far behind the glamor statistic of long balls. With 34 races studied, there are the familiar risks that small samples bring, but it's intriguing to note that none of these counting stats match the correlation of the worst of the advanced MVP stats observed in the "Down the Stretch" section.

The "triple-slash" numbers—batting average, on-base percentage and slugging percentage—are better at tracking with MVP winners, though with one serious difference.

AVG	56%	+.37
OBP	38%	+.22
SLG	59%	+.40

MVP voters still like batting average, even if they like slugging a little bit more. More galling to sabermetricians, they aren't that taken with on-base percentage, the original darling of analytics and still widely lauded as the best simple measure of a player's offensive worth. On the grounds for condemning award voters as Luddites, valuing on-base percentage well behind batting average would probably come high on the list. At least, if one were spoiling to make that fight even more intense than it is now.

There is one interesting influence on the triple-slash relationships: the wide difference between the leagues in how OBP corresponds with the MVP voting. I will look at this later.

Pitchers have their own version of the Triple Crown: leading the league in wins, strikeouts and ERA. It isn't as exclusive as the batters' version, being achieved more than twice as often, but it's an even surer route to award voters' hearts. No Triple Crown pitcher has failed to win the Cy Young since the award was inaugurated in 1956. That certainly suggests that voters want to see success in those categories, and the numbers bear this out.

Wins	47%	+.24
Strikeouts	71%	+.56
ERA	47%	+.21

The correspondences for wins and ERA are only moderate, certainly not eye-popping. The strikeout link, however, is eye-popping. One related category that beats the other two is total innings pitched, coming in with a +.29 correlation. There's an obvious if indirect link between innings pitched and excellence: only very good, and healthy, pitchers are likely to be sent out every fifth day and allowed to pitch consistently deep into games. History has seen poor teams send their best pitchers out constantly to cover for their sub-par moundsmen, but such sacrificial workhorses seldom win glory.

Leading Indicators

I examined a wide swath of statistics for correspondence to MVP voting, but so far I have shown only certain related groups of them. It's time to pull the camera back and show the broader picture. I covered 13 offensive categories, along with the monthly breakdowns for five of them. I'll now be looking at them all together.

Instead of choosing either the percentage or the correlation score by which to rank the categories, I opted for a combination of both. I converted the percentage of firsts over to the -1 to +1 scale, for balance. In a hypothetical block of 30 award seasons, 10 firsts would mean a score of 0, 20 firsts would produce a +0.5 (halfway from random to perfect correspondence), five firsts would make a -0.5 (halfway from random to pure negative correlation), and so on. I then averaged the two scores together to rank them. If this strikes you as a bit forced, rest assured that it doesn't really matter very much. Ranking the stats by either of our two measures would result in virtually the same order.

Monthly breakdowns for August are included with the year-long statistics, and are marked as such. All statistics cover 34 MVP Award votes, except for those marked with an asterisk(*), which have records only for 22 award votes. Here they are, in order of correspondence to the voting.

Metric	Corr.	Metric	Corr.
Aug. wRC+*	.45	wOBA	.28
Aug. OPS+	.41	Aug. ISO	.26
Aug. OPS	.41	OPS	.23
SLG	.39	OPS+	.22
Aug. wOBA*	.38	ISO	.22
bWAR	.36	HR	.17
AVG	.35	OBP	.15
fWAR	.33	Runs	.09
wRC+	.29	RBI	-.13

The strength of the August stats shows itself clearly here: four of the top five slots go to them. Runs, RBI and homers are stuck in the basement, along with on-base percentage, a surprisingly bad correspondence for these traditional measures. We may think of some MVP voters as hidebound devotees of the old counting stats, but at least in the wider sense that simply is not the case, not any longer.

Of the more modern metrics, WAR comes out best, as measured either by Base-ball-Reference (bWAR) or by FanGraphs (fWAR). I will have more to say about this after the Cy Young table. OPS, adjusted or not, turns out rather middling. It's an equal combination of the high-rating slugging percentage and the low-rating on-base percentage, but falls two-thirds of the way toward the lower end of that range. Given that the spread in slugging numbers is wider than for on-base percentage, and that MVP candidates are likely to be pushing the upper bounds of those spreads, the rela-tive dominance of OBP in the combination is counter-intuitive.

The statistics for pitchers merit the same treatment. I covered 15 categories, listed below. I am not including the best of the monthly breakdowns this time, as they are not as dominant as Augusts were for the MVP races (you can look back to check them if you like). The best of the July figures would rise only to fifth place on the table below. The rankings are done as before; the asterisks mean the same thing.

Metric	Corr.	Metric	Corr.
K	.56	owOBA*	.24
bWAR	.53	Wins	.22
FIP-*	.47	ERA	.21
xFIP-*	.47	ERA-	.20
fWAR	.43	oOPS+	.13
FIP	.37	BB/9	.08
K/9	.37	HR/9	-.04
IP	.32		

The fielding-independent pitching (FIP) measures are rather new, but correspond well to Cy Young Awards, especially with normalization for park effects in the FIP-metrics. One strongly suspects the voters aren't tracking FIP, but are reacting to the components of FIP: strikeouts, walks and homers. The xFIP variant trims out home runs, substituting the league-wide home run rate on fly balls that the pitcher gives up. This doesn't change the ranking, confirming that voters don't care much about the long balls pitchers give up. Observe the bottom of the table, and you'll see that they don't worry about walks, either.

That leaves one component carrying the burden, strikeouts, and it turns out you would do better counting them alone. Of all the relationships I uncovered in the survey, the one between raw strikeout numbers and Cy Young voting is the strongest. Lead the top award contenders in strikeouts, and it will genuinely be a surprise if you do not take home the honor. I have been careful about asserting one-way causation in these correspondences, but here I feel confident: voters want to see you punch out opposing batters, and everything else comes second.

Again, WAR measures produce strong correspondences, with the Baseball-Refer-ence version ahead of the FanGraphs number. The two organizations calculate WAR somewhat differently. B-R uses Defensive Runs Saved (DRS) on defense, while FG uses Ultimate Zone Rating (UZR). For pitchers, B-R rates them on Run Average, which ends up crediting batting average on balls in play (BABIP) to the pitcher, while FanGraphs uses FIP numbers, which exclude BABIP and presumably the good or bad effect of the defense behind him. There are a few more technical divergences.

It would be a mistake to conclude from these numbers alone that bWAR is a better gauge of player excellence than fWAR. It's a better gauge of how the voters will move, and that is a different if related thing. The bWAR advantage more likely means that voters are crediting results on balls in play to pitchers rather than filtering them out. Less work, but probably less accurate as well, if the Three True Outcomes school has it right.

It's interesting that wins and ERA, the traditional measures of a pitcher's excellence, don't track that well with the voting. Once again, there is an area where the writers aren't leaning on the traditional numbers the way that skeptics of their expertise would think. Overall, the Cy Young voters seem to be ahead of their counterparts in embracing the most modern wisdom, but the MVP voters are getting there too.

Leagues Apart

Throughout this article, I have combined the votes for NL and AL awards into a whole. This seemed wise, as the voters for both are drawn from the same pool, the membership of the BBWAA. There ought to be little organizational difference in how voters for the different leagues apply their standards and criteria. In practice, however, a number of differences did stand out. These may possibly be artifacts of the whims of chance, but I will lay the matter out for readers to decide.

The widest divergence in results between the leagues was for the correspondence of on-base percentage to MVP voting. In 10 out of 17 NL races, the OBP leader among the medalists took the award; in the AL, it was just three out of 17. The low overall OBP-MVP correlation is due to those AL races, for which the numbers are in outright negative territory.

There is one partial explanation for the NL numbers being higher, and his name is Barry Bonds. During the 2001-04 streak when he won four consecutive MVP awards, he led the league—indeed, all of baseball—in OBP all four years (he led in slugging the same four years, but took only one home run crown, and no RBI titles). Voters were probably not honoring Bonds for all the walks he took, except as a side effect of the massive power threat he posed.

This example does raise a salient point. The best sluggers often run up top-drawer on-base numbers due to pitchers working around them, meaning that, at the heights of performance that tend to merit MVP Awards, OBP and SLG are more coupled together than they seem at first glance. It follows that some of the positive correspondence between OBP and MVP is piggy-backing on power hitting that, by itself, would be enough to earn the awards. On-base percentage's link to MVP Awards thus could be even weaker than the numbers show. On-base percentage evangelists may have more work ahead than they know.

Another league divergence comes in whether MVP medalists played on post-season teams. National League voters liked to see MVP contenders be on October contenders, but AL voters *really* liked to see it. I will re-cast one of my earlier tables, showing the specific breakdown.

NL MVP	Div.	WC	Out	AL MVP	Div.	WC	Out
First	10	2	5	First	13	2	2
Second	7	2	8	Second	4	4	9
Third	8	2	7	Third	9	5	3

For gold and bronze, the stronger relationship in the AL is clear: a combined 12 missed the playoffs in the NL voting, but only five in the AL. Note also the preponderance of AL MVP winners playing on division title winners. The results do flatten out at second place. Could it be that, when choosing between two top contenders, AL voters relegated the player whose team didn't take its division to second?

The pattern did not recur strongly with Cy Young voting. Here, NL voters were more likely to fill their ballots with division champs, but this asserted itself in second and third place, not with the award winners.

The final discrepancy is a much broader one. In MVP voting, NL ballots were more likely to correspond with the statistical measures I examined than were AL ballots. There is a reverse trend for the Cy Young, the AL showing the closer correspondence, but that difference is a much thinner one, one-half to one-fifth as large. I will concentrate on the MVP gap.

I first noticed the divergence in monthly breakdown numbers, but found that they also applied to the full-season statistics, and I will stick with the latter here. In the 13 offensive categories I studied, NL voters had MVP winners leading the medalists in their categories 111 out of 221 times; the AL, 91.5 out of 221 (if you want that in percentage terms, it's 50 to 41). Correlation numbers for the NL were +0.326, while just +0.174 for the AL. Roughly a third of these differences can be accounted for by the OBP numbers I've already cited in this section, but with so much more to explain, it's less that on-base is driving this difference than that it is just an extreme example of it.

If AL voters don't follow the numbers that closely, what do they follow? Luckily, I provided an answer a few paragraphs back: they fill the gap with playoff appearances. These two pieces of the puzzle fit. Moreover, they fit in mirror image for the Cy Young voting. National League Cy voters care a little less about the individual statistics, and a little more about making the postseason, both to a lesser degree than with the AL and MVP Award.

As I said before, there's no obvious structural reason for one group of baseball writers to vote in a certain pattern, and another group to vote in a reverse pattern, just because of the leagues for which they happen to be voting. Still, they do it, with a substantial effect on MVP voting in the AL. Perhaps there are other factors that come into play. American League voters might be giving added weight to defensive performance, which I did not include in this study (aside from the part it plays in WAR). The example of 2012 argues against it.

The Years Ahead

By the time you read these words, the winners of the 2013 MVP and Cy Young Awards will have been revealed. As this article was written before the votes were revealed, due to the necessities of publishing, I do not know as I write what you know as you read. I considered using the correspondences I've mapped out to predict the winners, for you to immediately judge me a success or failure, but decided against it, at least in these pages. I may have done so at The Hardball Times website, waiting there for you to check out, but nothing stops you from running over the numbers yourself to see how the categories lined up with the winners this year.

While there's value in showing how the numbers correlated with the votes over the years, the greater value will come with future seasons as the patterns strengthen, or weaken. The truly robust linkages will hold up, and gain in their abilities to predict what choices the voters will make. Those strong links, and the weak ones, will provide a widening window into the minds of the BBWAA voters as they make their decisions, and possibly show us how their collective thinking develops over the years. Sabermetricans would applaud a spate of MVP Awards for leaders in on-base percentage, though I strongly doubt it will begin soon enough for Joey Votto this year (I know I said I wouldn't predict, but that one doesn't require me to be Nostradamus).

Perhaps the one thing to take away from this study is that there are patterns to the voting, that it isn't an incomprehensible Brownian motion. They may not be the patterns we would like; they may not be the patterns that align with the best measures of player value, as we judge them. It's other people's judgment we're measuring, and there are a few keys to it—or a few Ks, in the case of the Cy Young. If we want to argue for a preferred result in some future ballot—and we surely will—perhaps there will be a lever here and there to push.

The award we save could be Mike Trout's.

The Strike Zone During the PITCHf/x Era

by Jon Roegele

When you think of baseball, you think of a game that never changes, right? The rules are the same as they were over 100 years ago, right? The bases still 90 feet apart? Well, one of the most important parts of baseball has changed significantly in the past five years, and the good news is that we have the technology to spot it.

In 2007, new technology created and maintained by SportVision called PITCHf/x gifted public baseball analysts with a wealth of new data to explore. Using a system of cameras mounted in Major League Baseball stadiums to track the position of each pitch delivered over the course of the season, a number of pitch characteristics are derived and stored. These include pitch velocity, pitch movement and the location where the pitch crosses the front of home plate.

Since that time, a number of studies have expanded our understanding of pitchers, hitters and umpires. Algorithms have been developed to classify pitches as curveballs or sliders, or any other pitch type based on the characteristics of the pitch. We can determine how often pitchers throw within the strike zone. We can calculate how often hitters chase pitches out of the strike zone. We can compare the called strike zones among umpires and see how much these vary in a given season or over several seasons.

It's the strike zone that I'd like to examine more closely. I pulled PITCHf/x data and split the plane at the front of home plate into a 1x1 inch grid pattern to examine the effect of different game conditions on the called strike zone. For each cell of the grid, I calculated the percentage of called pitches that crossed the plate within it. I deemed the cell as part of the strike zone if more than half of those were called strikes. Aside from giving a nice visual of the called strike zone, this methodology makes it easy to calculate the area of the strike zone in square inches, simply by summing the number of cells included in the zone.

I should point out that some inaccuracies do exist in the PITCHf/x data upon which this analysis is based. Noted PITCHf/x analyst Mike Fast attempted to calculate the average pitch location error by ballpark over the first several seasons that PITCHf/x data was available. His results showed that the typical error is less than one inch in both horizontal and vertical locations, in particular starting in the first full season of data in 2008. For the purposes of this study, given that I will be averaging data across all ballparks, such minor error effects should be insignificant.

So what's changed? The strike zone has changed. In fact, the strike zone is more than five percent bigger than it was five years ago, growing from 436 square inches in 2008 to 459 square inches this past year.

Year	Avg. Size of Called Strike Zone (sq. inches)
2008	436
2009	435
2010	436
2011	448
2012	456
2013	459

Breaking things down a little, there has been a very clear expansion of the called strike zone down around the knees. In 2008, no square inch below 1.75 feet above the ground was in the strike zone (as I've calculated it). Now, there are 30 square inches in that area in which pitches are called strikes more often than not.

Year	Avg. Size of Called Strike Zone Size Under 1.75 Feet from Ground (sq. inches)
2008	0
2009	0
2010	6
2011	11
2012	19
2013	30

I want to examine in more detail how the strike zone has changed since these data have been publicly available and investigate the effects on the game such changes may have made.

Called Strike Zone

An effective method to visually demonstrate the changing strike zone is to look at a map of the area around the strike zone showing the difference between the ways the zone is being called now and in the early days of PITCHf/x availability. Since a full season of PITCHf/x data was not collected in 2007, for the purposes of all comparisons in this study, I will compare 2013 data with 2008 data. This ensures that I am comparing full season data. The maps presented below are split into two, one for left-handed hitters and one for right-handed hitters. Images are shown from the home plate umpire's perspective.

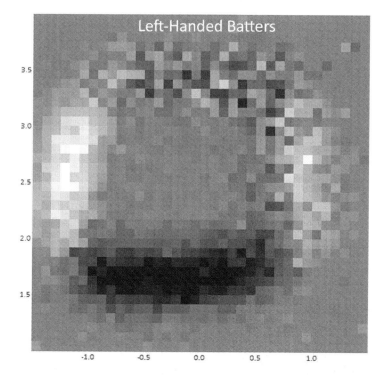

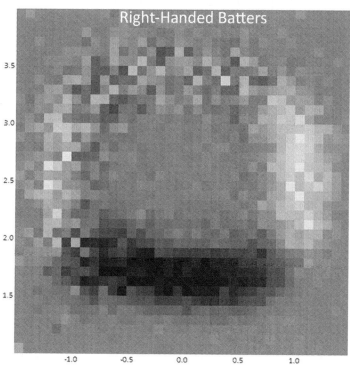

In these images, the grey background highlights areas with a relatively static called strike zone between the two seasons. Darker squares indicate a higher percentage of called strikes in 2013, while lighter squares imply that more balls were called in 2013.

Several themes are immediately apparent from this visualization. The first is that there is no doubt the low strike was called more often this past season than just five years before. Note how everything two feet off the ground and below is trending toward more strikes being called. The second observation is that for both left-handed and right-handed hitters, the outside strike was called less often in 2013 than in 2008. These regions are both light in the images above.

The final observation, admittedly a little less obvious, is that on the inside corner for all hitters, there appears to be a trend toward calling more pitches over the edge of the plate strikes, while pitches just inside are tending to be called balls more frequently. This is one of the presumed benefits of such a tracking system, in that it appears that umpires are improving on their success rate on the inside corner as it pertains to following the rulebook strike zone.

The three areas I will investigate in some detail in this study are:

- The outside corner for left-handed hitters (between -1.0 feet and -1.5 feet from the center of home plate, more than two feet from the ground)
- The outside corner for right-handed hitters (between 0.75 feet and 1.25 feet from the center of home plate, more than two feet from the ground), and
- The bottom of the strike zone (between 1.5 feet and two feet off the ground).

Note that the outside areas measured are not symmetric about the center of home plate, because the strike zone for left-handed hitters has traditionally been called in a manner that sees the zone shifted away from the hitter by two to three inches.

Outside Edges and Bottom of the Zone

With the most prominent areas of interest identified, I can now check how much change has occurred at the outside edges and the bottom of the strike zone.

Called strike percentage by region, by year			
Year	Outside Left-handed	Outside Right-handed	Bottom
2008	29.0%	40.8%	29.6%
2009	29.0%	34.8%	30.1%
2010	27.7%	36.0%	33.2%
2011	25.2%	33.5%	35.7%
2012	24.9%	33.3%	40.6%
2013	18.5%	34.0%	43.8%

The decline is evident across the board on the outside edge strike. We can only assume that these changes have been sanctioned by MLB, perhaps as a result of the PITCHf/x data.

The zone for left-handed hitters has been pulling in bit by bit, until this past season when a significant reduction occurred. However, the called zone on the outside edge for right-handed hitters shows a different history. The largest single correction in this regard came in the 2009 season, when the zone contracted notably. Since that time, this segment has been treated roughly the same, with the largest improvements being in the pitches the most off the plate.

There is no mistaking the trend across the league toward calling more strikes on pitches in the lowest potential area of the strike zone. In particular, the called strike rate for all pitches in the band between 1.5 feet and 1.75 feet off the ground has skyrocketed, more than doubling since the first season where PITCHf/x data was available, from 14.6 percent originally to 32.2 percent this past season.

Pitcher Adjustments

With the called strike zone changing as it has over the past several years, it is interesting to consider how pitchers have adjusted with respect to pitch location. After all, teams are certainly monitoring strike zone changes closely as well. You'd think that as pitchers became less likely to get called strikes on the outside edge and more likely to satisfy umpires at the bottom of the zone, there would be a shift in pitch location to reflect these facts.

And it's true. Pitchers have been keeping the ball down more frequently. Pitches have been taken from above 2.5 feet off the ground, in particular from the outside edge and beyond, and moved below 2.5 feet from the ground. This trend can be observed through the following table.

Percentage of pitches thrown under 2.5 feet off the ground, by year	
Year	Pitch % < 2.5 feet
2008	54.5%
2009	54.4%
2010	55.9%
2011	56.1%
2012	58.5%
2013	59.0%

On average, five out of every 100 pitches have been moved from above 2.5 feet to below this line since the introduction of the PITCHf/x data set. This means the high/low balance has shifted from 46/54 in 2007-2009 to 41/59 in 2013. This is quite a dramatic drop in pitch height.

The following tables illustrate the magnitude of this shift in pitch location over time in the areas of interest for this study.

Percentage of pitches thrown by region, by year			
Year	Outside Left-handed	Outside Right-handed	Bottom
2008	10.2%	9.7%	16.9%
2009	10.5%	8.9%	16.8%
2010	10.1%	9.0%	17.4%
2011	10.0%	8.8%	17.3%
2012	9.6%	8.5%	18.1%
2013	9.4%	8.5%	18.2%

It is notable to me that this transformation appears much milder in comparison to the rate of change of called strikes in these regions. To put things simply, it would appear that pitchers have taken about 1.3 percent of all pitches thrown and moved them from the outside edge to the bottom of the zone since the strike zone changes became most visible. The called strike zone data would suggest that, in particular, pitchers may not be taking full advantage of the area over home plate between 1.5 feet and 1.75 feet off the ground that we identified earlier as the fastest growing area for called strike percentage. Pitches to this area have risen from 7.4 percent of all pitches in the first three seasons of PITCHf/x data to only 8.2 percent of all pitches in 2013, despite more than twice the likelihood of being a called strike.

The tables above are merely observations. There is nothing to prove how much, if any, the expansion of the called strike zone has to do with these changes in pitch locations. While I suspect this is part of the impetus, there is also perhaps a growing appreciation of pitchers generating ground balls, which involves a more focused approach to keeping the ball down. Differing pitching coach philosophies and different ballparks with their own park effects or even individual pitcher strengths may also be significant contributing factors.

Doug Fister and Jered Weaver present an interesting contrast. These are the two right-handed starters with the most significant changes in pitch frequency in the growing lower area of the strike zone, but they've been moving in opposite directions. Consider their pitch location histories in these areas of interest during the period in which the most prominent strike zone changes have been observed.

Doug Fister, percentage of pitches thrown by region, by year				
Year	Outside Left-handed	Outside Right-handed	Bottom	Avg. Fastball Velocity
2010	9.7%	8.7%	13.1%	88.3
2011	11.2%	7.5%	14.2%	89.6
2012	10.7%	5.6%	18.1%	89.1
2013	10.0%	5.2%	20.7%	88.6

Jered Weaver, percentage of pitches thrown by region, by year				
Year	Outside Left-handed	Outside Right-handed	Bottom	Avg. Fastball Velocity
2010	12.0%	6.9%	18.1%	90.1
2011	12.6%	8.3%	16.5%	89.2
2012	15.6%	8.3%	17.0%	88.0
2013	17.3%	10.4%	14.9%	86.8

Fister's rise to success has been partly fueled by his growing attention to the lower part of the strike zone. This rise is most notable since his time in Detroit, where all Tigers starters have pitched more frequently than average to the bottom area of the zone. Despite his falling numbers to the outside regions of study, Bill Petti and Jeff Zimmerman's Edge% statistic—which represents pitch frequency to the edges of the plate—indicates that Fister has been at an elite level in recent seasons. Apparently, he is still throwing near the edges a lot, but is targeting the less dynamically changing inside corner more consistently and not pitching far enough outside as to be as affected by the strike zone tightening.

As Weaver has seen his fastball velocity decline significantly, it seems that he has adjusted by targeting the outer edge of the plate more often. This is a common approach for pitchers as they age. Unfortunately for him, he has done so at precisely the time when the strike zone is squeezing in at the sides and showing the most pronounced addition at the bottom.

All things considered, hitting the edges of the plate is not a bad practice at all. It just happens that a pitcher can expect, on average, fewer called strikes in these areas than just a few seasons ago. Of course these observations of strike zone differences are averages, and individual circumstances such as having a catcher who excels at pitch receiving (such as Hank Conger) and a pitcher with exceptional pitch movement (such as Weaver) may be more important considerations.

It appears clear to me that pitching success does not hinge on one's ability to adapt to these strike zone changes with great efficiency. There are several examples of Cy Young Award-quality pitchers who have attacked the growing low strike area at well below the league average in recent seasons. It merely seems to me that pitchers would benefit by taking advantage of this newest addition to the called strike zone where possible, while recognizing that outer areas that have traditionally been called strikes are contracting.

Batter Adjustments

As the called strike zone has changed and pitchers have started keeping the ball down more often, it is worthwhile asking whether hitters have adjusted their swing tendencies. We might expect fewer swings off the outside corner, but more swings in the newly called low-strike region.

On the whole, these changes are not as clearly evident as the others, but we do see them. This aligns with the shift in the called strike zone and coincides with movements in pitch location by pitchers around the league.

The following table shows the magnitude of the swing differences.

Percentage of pitches for which batter swings by region, by year			
Year	Outside Left-handed	Outside Right-handed	Bottom
2008	28.3%	38.6%	45.6%
2009	29.0%	37.3%	45.0%
2010	28.7%	36.9%	45.4%
2011	29.4%	37.0%	46.9%
2012	29.5%	37.0%	47.5%
2013	27.1%	37.4%	48.3%

For both outside edges, it is hard to point to a consistent trend in batter swing tendencies. While in general we can say that in 2013 the swing rates were lower compared to early PITCHf/x seasons, the decline has not been close to monotonic nor has it been very significant in nature. Perhaps the most obvious decline here has been realized by left-handed hitters off the outside corner in the most recent season, coincident with the largest single-year drop in called strike rate in this area over the years of study.

Swing rates on lower pitches have been on the rise since 2010, matching closely with the timing of the expansion of the strike zone in this low area, as shown earlier. The area between 1.5 feet and 1.75 feet off the ground is again the fastest changing region, with swing rates climbing from 42 percent in the early years of PITCHf/x data to 45.4 percent in 2013.

It appears that batters have adjusted more consistently to changes occurring at the bottom of the strike zone than at the outer edges of the plate.

Effects on the Game

While I find the above observations of umpire, pitcher and batter behavior in the PITCHf/x era intriguing, the real question is what impact, if any, these changes have made on the game. We can measure a few specific impacts.

Strikeout and Walk Effects

Much has been written about the rising strikeout rate across the league over the past several seasons. Given that the strike zone has been changing most notably in our areas of interest, the net change in called strikeouts and walks for all plate appearances ending with a pitch to one of these areas can provide a measure of the impact of the zone change on league strikeout rate.

The net effect of the changing strike zone has been an increase in called strikeouts and a decrease in walks. Here are two tables that show the results of called final pitches in strikeouts and walks, when those pitches cross home plate in the particular zones about which we have been talking.

Called strikeouts ending on pitch to region, by region, by year				
Year	Outside Left-handed	Outside Right-handed	Bottom	Total
2008	596	913	1,406	2,915
2013	345	730	2,338	3,413
Net Change	-251	-132	932	498

Unintentional walks ending on pitch to region, by region, by year				
Year	Outside Left-handed	Outside Right-handed	Bottom	Total
2008	1,112	855	2,507	4,474
2013	1,156	782	1,851	3,789
Net Change	44	-73	-656	-685

As you can see, the changes in the strike zone resulted in a net effect of 498 more called strikeouts and 685 fewer unintentional walks—based only on the impact of the final pitch.

These effects are indisputable in that they are pitches in these regions that directly caused actual game occurrences. In my opinion, these differences are also almost completely caused by the set of changes we've discussed. Of course any effects of the heightened focus on catcher framing that has spawned from this same PITCHf/x data are inherently captured by the methodology used by this study.

Another set of events that we can measure and compare are swinging strikeouts in the same regions, based only on the location of the final pitch in the strikeout.

Swinging strikeouts ending on pitch to region, by region, by year				
Year	Outside Left-handed	Outside Right-handed	Bottom	Total
2008	712	1,253	4,526	6,491
2013	812	1,147	5,008	6,967
Net Change	100	-106	482	476

Once again, strikeouts are on the rise and are primarily being driven by occasions in which a hitter swings through a pitch in the lower region of interest for this study. Relatively speaking, pitchers threw roughly 8 percent more pitches to the area in 2013 than 2008 and hitters struck out about 11 percent more often on these pitches.

In this case, I would expect that the changes in strike zone are not the only things making an impact on the swinging strikeout rate. Gradually climbing velocity rates are an example of a confounding factor that makes this particular increase a less direct effect of the changing strike zone.

Nevertheless, in total these regions of study have witnessed an increase of 974 strikeouts and a decrease of 685 walks between 2013 and 2008. To put those numbers in perspective, in 2008 the league strikeout rate was 17.5 percent and the unintentional walk rate was 8 percent. If the 2008 strikeout and walk totals were adjusted by the effects that we've documented here, the strikeout rate would rise to 18 percent and the unintentional walk rate would drop to 7.6 percent. The actual 2013 average strikeout rate was 19.9 percent and the unintentional walk rate was 7.4 per cent.

In other words, the changing strike zone has made an impact, but it's only part of a bigger story.

Run Environment Effects

It is also no secret that run scoring has been down in recent seasons. Teams scored close to half a run less per game on average in 2013 than they did in 2008.

To calculate the potential impact of the changing strike zone on run scoring, I looked at the effect that taken pitches in our regions of interest had on the count in the two seasons. For example, having a 1-1 pitch that was called a ball in 2008 suddenly get called a strike in 2013 changes the batting environment; the success rate of hitters is much lower when facing 1-2 counts than on 2-1 counts. Less success leads to fewer runs scored.

To estimate the effect at this level, for each possible count in a plate appearance, I calculated the expected run difference between having the next pitch called a strike versus having it called a ball. To do so, I calculated the weighted on base percentage (wOBA) for all plate appearances in a season in which a particular count was reached at any point, then divided the change in wOBA when the next pitch was a ball or strike by the yearly wOBA constant to arrive at an expected run difference in each of these cases.

The values that I calculated for each season are shown in the table below. These align closely with run values published by John Walsh based on 2007 data.

Expected run difference for next pitch strike vs. next pitch ball, by count, by year				
Count	2008 ball	2008 strike	2013 ball	2013 strike
0-0	0.034	-0.039	0.034	-0.038
1-0	0.058	-0.047	0.050	-0.043
0-1	0.026	-0.053	0.029	-0.051
2-0	0.105	-0.058	0.099	-0.049
1-1	0.046	-0.059	0.045	-0.058
0-2	0.021	-0.178	0.022	-0.155
3-0	0.118	-0.064	0.112	-0.058
2-1	0.099	-0.065	0.090	-0.067
1-2	0.040	-0.198	0.035	-0.178
3-1	0.182	-0.072	0.170	-0.073
2-2	0.092	-0.239	0.085	-0.213
3-2	0.254	-0.330	0.243	-0.298

If you think about this for a moment, it should be clear that a full-count pitch that is ruled a strike rather than a ball is producing a strikeout instead of a walk, so is actually changing the final outcome of a plate appearance. On the other hand, the first pitch of a plate appearance puts a hitter at 0-1 instead of 1-0, which is far from an insurmountable hole. It should be no surprise, then, that the former case produces a much higher expected run difference than the latter.

With the expected run differences in hand, I counted the total number of called balls and strikes per count for each of our three study areas in 2008 and 2013. Then I calculated the total expected runs for the three areas based on the above table and the actual balls and strikes thrown. The following totals show the results.

Results of called pitches in three regions of interest, by year			
Year	Number of balls	Number of called strikes	Expected runs
2008	91,727	37,866	2,606
2013	85,556	42,456	1,892

The expected run totals that I calculated were 2,606 runs in 2008 and 1,892 runs in 2013. This means the estimated cumulative effect of altered counts caused by calling the strike zone on the outside edge and lower limits as was done this past season compared to 2008 is that 714 fewer runs were scored. Of course this is just an estimate based on league average performances in each season, but it gives us an estimate of the kind of impact the called strike zone changes may have had on the game, aside from just more strikeouts and less walks.

To put some context to that number, if we subtract this number of runs from the 2008 season total, the average number of runs per team per game drops from 4.65

to 4.50. In 2013 the average number of runs scored by a team in each game was 4.17. So you could say that one-third of the offensive decrease over the last five years has been due to the growing strike zone.

The strike zone has been changing since the possibility arose of grading umpires with newly installed pitch-tracking technology. Presumably, MLB has backed these changes, as it has the tools to direct umpires to call the strike zone differently.

In the PITCHf/x era, the bottom of the strike zone has been expanding at a higher rate than the edges have been contracting, leading to a larger strike zone. This imbalance has paved the way for higher strikeout totals and lower walk totals. The changes have altered more pitch counts in favor of the pitcher, leading in total to a larger number of less successful plate appearances from batters and fewer runs scored.

The beauty of the situation is that all teams have access to all of this information, plus much more that is not available for public consumption. As in any other business, teams that are able to recognize trends quickly and adapt accordingly will put themselves at an advantage in this wonderful, hotly contested game.

References and Resources

- Jon Roegele, "The Living Strike Zone," Baseball Prospectus, *baseballprospectus.com/article.php?articleid=21262*
- Mike Fast, "Spinning Yarn: How Accurate is PitchTrax?," Baseball Prospectus, *baseballprospectus.com/article.php?articleid=13109*
- Phil Birnbaum, "The Run Value of a Ball and Strike," By the Numbers Newsletter, *philbirnbaum.com/btn2000-02.pdf*
- John Walsh, "Searching for the game's best pitch," The Hardball Times, *hardballtimes.com/main/article/searching-for-the-games-best-pitch*
- Bill Petti, "The Difference Pitching on the Edges Makes," FanGraphs, *fangraphs.com/blogs/the-difference-pitching-on-the-edge-makes*
- wOBA Constants, Fangraphs, *fangraphs.com/guts.aspx?type=cn*
- PITCHf/x Database, Baseball Heat Maps, *baseballheatmaps.com/pitch-fx-download*

Loss in Movement as the Game Progresses

by Noah Woodward

The story is among the classics in baseball history. The major players were Pedro Martinez, Grady Little and some numbers. It was the seventh game of the 2003 American League Championship Series, and Martinez was about to make his third trip through the Yankees lineup even though he had thrown 115 pitches. When Little asked, Martinez insisted he was fine. The situation suggested he wasn't.

Martinez had a great 2003 season. He came in third in American League Cy Young Award voting after he posted a 2.22 ERA (the lowest in the majors) and a 1.04 walks plus hits per inning pitched, or WHIP (second-lowest). Martinez actually managed to strike out more hitters in fewer innings than his competitor in the Cy Young race, Roy Halladay.

On the other hand, Halladay posted a 22-7 record that year, and it's probably that simple fact that propelled him to the top of the Cy Young voting. Martinez's 14-4 record surely cost him, though it understated his contributions to the Red Sox that season.

The accumulation of wins is a fickle pursuit, but one thing a pitcher can do to maximize his chances of picking up a win is simply to stick around. Good pitchers who are able to pitch deep into the later innings of games are more likely to receive run support, at the same time keeping the ball out of the hands of less-skilled middle relievers. Halladay, for instance, was a horse in 2003. He averaged about seven and a third innings per start, and completed nine games all by himself.

Martinez, on the other hand, averaged somewhere around six and a third innings per start, and threw just three complete games. Martinez pitched no more than seven innings in all but five of his 29 starts. You can think of him as a decade-old version of Stephen Strasburg, but with a perfectly healthy elbow and a little more attitude.

So why exactly was Martinez so limited in his usage? The most convincing evidence comes in a troubling pattern that he exhibited that season. Martinez was untouchable from pitches one through 25 in his 2003 starts, with a ridiculous 9.33 strikeout-to-walk (K/BB) ratio, allowing just two home runs in 181 plate appearances. From the next pitch on, however, everything seemed to go downhill. If we look at opponent on-base plus slugging percentage (OPS) in terms of 25-five pitch intervals, here is what we see from him:

- Pitches 1-25: .498
- Pitches 26-50: .589
- Pitches 51-75: .588
- Pitches 76-100: .644
- Pitches 101+: .706

Most pitchers' performances decline during a game, just like Pedro Martinez's. This past season in the majors, batters had a .700 OPS against starting pitchers the first time through the lineup; this statistic jumped to .730 the second time through. How about the third? .760. Strikeout rates, walk rates, and extra-base hit rates appear to correlate pretty well with times through the order, too. Roster limitations aside, we understand that the ideal workload for most pitchers is fewer than a dozen batters per game.

Familiarity is probably one reason for the within-game decline. As batters become more familiar with the pitcher's stuff and approach, they adjust during the game, learn to lay off certain pitches and better time their swings.

But how much within-game performance loss is due to familiarity, and how much is in fact due to fatigue? This is nearly impossible to answer, because you can't have within-game familiarity without fatigue. That is, you can't have a hitter face a pitcher multiple times in a game without that pitcher first tiring himself out by facing other hitters along the way. Because of the way the game is played, a pitcher usually throws at least 30 pitches before facing the same hitter twice.

For this reason, traditional and sabermetric measures of success, dependent on pitch count, are influenced by both familiarity and fatigue. Runs allowed, strikeouts per nine innings, and even swinging-strike rates are influenced by the quality of the pitch thrown, and the knowledge that a hitter gains from previous at-bats in the same game.

If we want to try to isolate the impact that fatigue has on effectiveness, then we have to focus solely on pitch quality. For the purposes of this study, I will define pitch quality, or "stuff," as the combination of speed and movement of a fastball. A starter who possesses a fastball with both of these qualities misses more bats than the average starter, and also prevents more runs with the pitch.

Let's not take this assertion as fact. In order to evaluate the connection between positive performance, velocity and movement, we need data on each of these three things. Fortunately, we have PITCHf/x for that.

We're entering an era in which all major league ballparks are going to have cameras pointed at anything that moves on the field. In fact, this era already has begun. Sportvision's PITCHf/x system has allowed us to (roughly) classify pitch types, speeds, locations, etc. The technology isn't perfect, but it has given us something to get excited about over the past few years. One useful bit of information that PITCHf/x provides is pitch spin deflection values, which help us estimate pitch movement. In this article, I'm going to consider how these vary with production and fatigue.

Before I go any further, I want to bring up concerns that others have regarding the use of spin deflection estimates provided by PITCHf/x. One thing I should make clear is that spin deflection is measured as the horizontal and vertical deviation from a straight-line path, and *not* actual pitch movement. Spin deflection values also do not incorporate outside forces like gravity and drag. While spin deflection is not exactly the same thing as movement, it does act as a valuable proxy for it.

Look at the charts below. The data behind these graphs include over 1.5 million fastballs thrown by starting pitchers from 2010-2013. FanGraphs calculates the run value of every pitch by looking at one of two things:

- If the ball is put in play, the run value of the outcome.
- If the ball isn't put into play, the run value of the change in count.

Run values are expressed as "linear weights," in which the average run value is set at zero. In 2003, for instance, the average run value of a single was 0.45 runs, while the average run value of a strike on a 1-1 count was -0.08 runs (that's a negative number). Any difference in the pitcher's favor is a negative, while any difference in the batter's favor is positive.

The process for assigning run value to a ball or strike was pioneered by Hardball Times writers Josh Kalk and John Walsh (as well as FanGraphs' Dave Allen) several years ago. It is determined by analyzing the difference, in our example, of the final outcome of all plate appearances that have a 1-1 count and the final outcome of all plate appearances that have a 1-2 count. The difference is the run value of the ball.

You'll find a similar approach elsewhere in this *Annual* in Jon Roegele's article about the strike zone.

Anyway, each graph depicts the relative effectiveness (in terms of runs allowed or prevented per pitch thrown) of the pitch characteristics that I described above. In the first, we see that velocity is strongly related to run prevention. As the velocity of a fastball increases, the run values go down—meaning that the pitch results in fewer runs scored.

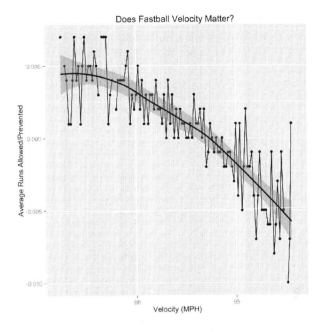

We see similar trends in the next two graphs, which depict vertical and horizontal spin deflection. As the graphs show, the more deflection on a pitch, the fewer runs allowed, on average.

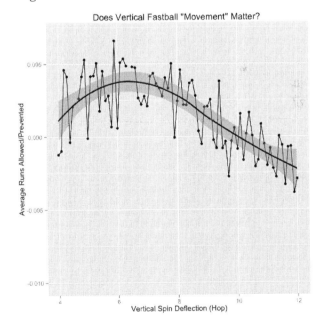

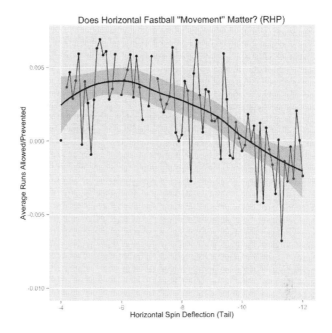
Does Horizontal Fastball "Movement" Matter? (RHP)

With one caveat, pitchers allow fewer runs on pitches with more spin deflection. In fact, a two-inch increase in horizontal (or vertical) spin appears to have roughly the same effect on results as a two-mile-per-hour increase in velocity. True, we can't look at these results in a vacuum—but it is clear that spin deflection matters.

What is our one caveat? Both types of spin interact with each other and with velocity, and this interaction explains the peaks we see in the spin graphs above. Adding more vertical spin deflection to pitches that already have three to six inches of it appears to produce worse outcomes for pitchers, but remember that these pitches often have larger horizontal spin components (think two-seam fastballs and sinkers).

Now that I have examined the relevance of velocity and spin deflection, I want to look at how these fastball characteristics are affected by fatigue.

Fastball velocity, as it relates to fatigue, has been fairly well researched. In 2011, Jeremy Greenhouse of Baseball Prospectus came out with a study suggesting that velocity peaks around pitch 20 and steadily declines throughout the rest of a start. That's why it makes sense that flamethrowers like Aroldis Chapman often face pitch count limits of 20-30 pitches in an outing, because this type of reliever relies heavily on velocity and (not much else) to be successful.

While Greenhouse looked at only a pitcher's fastest 25 percent of all fastballs thrown, my sample of all fastballs thrown suggested that fastball velocity peaks a little earlier than 20 pitches. I also found that velocity then declines from this peak for about 10 to 15 additional pitches before flattening out for the rest of a start. It is worth noting, however, that while fatigue clearly drives velocity downward, some pitchers also demonstrate the ability to increase velocity in tough situations. You can read more on that finding by checking out Roegele's recent work for Beyond the Box Score.

While the average major league pitcher loses velocity as the game progresses, almost one in four gains at least a little bit of velocity while throwing more pitches. Who are these pitchers, and what makes them so special? Justin Verlander throws hard, and it turns out he gains more velocity per pitch than any other starter in the game. I'll have more on him later. The rest of these pitchers aren't exactly soft-tossers, either. Derek Holland, Max Scherzer and Edwin Jackson all have league-leading fastballs in terms of velocity, and all three post at least modest gains as they pitch in a game.

However, the majors' three hardest throwers, Matt Harvey, Stephen Strasburg and Jose Fernandez, all are in-game velocity losers. By and large, the sweet spot for those who gain velocity is a baseline fastball in the 90-93 mph range.

So what about the other component that helps make up "stuff," movement? I'm not sure how anyone—commentators, pitching coaches or even scouts—can determine when a pitcher has lost an inch or two of movement. It definitely makes sense that fastballs flatten out as a pitcher fatigues, but really, how do we actually know that this happens?

In attempting to answer this question, I examined the relationship between spin deflection values and pitch count, which serves as a measurable indicator of fatigue. This technique required grouping and averaging of thousands of fastball spin deflection values according to pitch count level and creating unique regression "slopes" (or trend lines) for each pitcher in my sample. Positive slopes indicate that a pitcher gains fastball movement throughout a start, and negative slopes indicate the opposite. Composite slopes combine horizontal and vertical components.

The chart below depicts the number of starting pitchers who experience horizontal, vertical and composite movement gains and losses as a result of fatigue. So, for example, 74 starting pitchers lose horizontal movement as they throw more pitches. The information presented provides mixed support for what I'm sure most of us thought to be true: Most starting pitchers lose fastball "hop" as they fatigue, and most also lose overall spin deflection. However, the same cannot be said for horizontal spin.

Component	Losers	Gainers	% Losers
Horizontal Spin	74	71	51.0%
Vertical Spin	115	30	79.3%
Composite Spin	111	34	76.5%
Velocity	109	36	75.2%

This table isn't enough to help us conclude that fatigue weakens movement. We need to keep in mind that a pitcher who loses spin deflection in one dimension might be gaining it in another, and this exchange might actually benefit that pitcher.

For example, spin deflection readings for starters who throw two-seam fastballs are tricky to interpret. It makes sense that pitchers would gain horizontal movement at the expense of vertical movement, so a loss in vertical movement can be associated with better results for this type of pitch. These pitchers should not be confused with another more concerning group—the composite spin deflection losers. These pitchers lose both horizontal and vertical movement as a result of fatigue.

Below, I'll discuss a few pitchers who lose in terms of spin deflection and velocity. I'll make connections between these trends on overall performance when possible, and then do the same for those who notably resist the effects of fatigue on fastball effectiveness.

The Losers

Jake Westbrook

This 36-year-old starter suffers from major fatigue issues. It isn't tough to spot the impact that his lack of fastball endurance has on his performance. Westbrook is not a bad starter for the first few innings of a game, but he is an awful one in the middle and late innings as his pitch count rises. His K/BB ratio plummets from around 1.18 to .40 after his 75th pitch, while his OPS-against jumps from .734 to .912. Westbrook's fastball velocity declines about 2.3 mph per 100 pitches, and the horizontal spin deflection he gets on it declines by about an inch per hundred. For a pitcher who relies on sinker-type movement, these trends are troubling.

Jason Marquis

Marquis loses 1.6 inches of horizontal movement and 2.1 mph off his sinker per one hundred pitches. For Marquis, the raw results don't reflect the decline he sees in sinker effectiveness. This may be because he cuts his sinker usage from about 64 percent at the start of a game down to about 51 percent by the 50th pitch. Marquis knows that his sinker is not a plus offering by the fifth inning of a start, and he began to rely heavily on his slider last year to compensate.

Roy Halladay

Remember him? It has been 10 years since he won that Cy Young in 2003. We can only speculate as to the impact of wear and tear on Halladay's in-game endurance, but it is clear that he now becomes less effective as he throws more pitches. Halladay loses horizontal movement on his sinker and on his cutter at a rate that is greater than all other qualified starters except Marquis. He also lost, on average, .76 miles per hour per start over that span. Halladay's declining within-game fastball usage mirrored its change in quality pretty well over the past two years, and his off-speed pitches kept him afloat until he broke down in 2013.

Travis Wood

Last year, high pitch counts really were a problem for the Chicago left-handed starter. While he performed much better than the league-average pitcher his first two trips through a lineup, he tended to collapse if Cubs manager Dale Sveum leaned on him for any more than that. From pitches 1-75 in 2013, Wood's OPS-against was .586. From pitch 76 on, his OPS-against rose by 231 points to .816. Wood was essentially this past year's Pedro Martinez.

Wood throws three different types of fastballs. On the whole, he loses about 1.2" of horizontal fastball deflection for each 100 pitches thrown, while also losing 1.2 mph per fastball over that same span. These amounts may not seem large, but they both rank in the top 25 percent of all starting pitchers. Finally, Wood's vertical spin deflection decreases ever so slightly as he fatigues. Because Wood loses in terms of composite movement and in terms of velocity, we can argue with confidence that he loses "stuff" as his pitch count rises.

The Gainers

Justin Verlander

We all know that basic human limitations don't really apply when it comes to Verlander. Detroit's ace gained an average of 1.96 mph per 100 pitches thrown from 2012-2013, and he leads in this category by a large margin.

He struck out almost 27 percent of all batters he faced last year after the 100-pitch mark, and he allowed a total of seven extra-base hits in 109 plate appearances. The righty is able to gain a modest 0.28 inches of horizontal movement per 100 pitches on his fastball, and he does this without sacrificing any vertical hop.

Chris Tillman

Tillman's strikeout rate and walk rate improved as he made his trips through opposing lineups last year. In doing so, he won over Orioles fans while establishing himself as the team's most dependable starter. Tillman is a velocity gainer, adding about 0.8 mph per 100 pitches to a plus offering. But Tillman is also unique in that he doesn't lose horizontal movement while steadily gaining velocity throughout the course of a start.

Jorge De La Rosa

In 2013, left-hander De La Rosa gained an average of 0.91 inches in horizontal spin deflection per 100 pitches, arguably the highest in-game lateral spin increase for any qualified starter throwing a sinking fastball. He is a surprising leader in this category, but the results back up his constantly improving fastball quality.

Unlike many other horizontal-spin gainers, De La Rosa doesn't lose velocity. In fact, he gains almost a full mile per hour per 100 pitches thrown. His strikeout numbers also remain stable as his pitch counts mount. In pitches one through 50, De La Rosa struck out around 14 percent of all batters he faced. His strikeout rate for any pitch after that point was about 13 percent. Tommy John surgery looks to have created the perfect example of anti-fatigue in De La Rosa.

Other Tommy John Survivors

De La Rosa's strong recovery and resistance to fatigue motivated me to take a closer look at other starters who pitched in 2012 or 2013 with fresh ulnar collateral ligaments in their elbows. Westbrook, Strasburg, John Lackey and Adam Wainwright are some of the most recent pitchers to go through this process and live to pitch in either 2012 or 2013. We already know that Westbrook doesn't handle fatigue well, but let's see if the others held up better.

They didn't. All three saw moderate-to-severe declining fastball velocities by pitch count in 2012-2013. Lackey leads all starters with almost three mph lost from his first pitch to his 100th. Wainwright and Strasburg lost 1.3 and 0.73 mph per 100 pitches, respectively. Lackey was able to gain in terms of horizontal spin, but all were losers in every other category. These five pitchers obviously don't tell all in terms of Tommy John surgery as it relates to pitcher fatigue, but this group warrants its own study.

Conclusions

I've attempted to prove two things. First, fastballs with less hop, tail, bite, or hair (if you're a Dennis Eckersley fan) are less effective than other fastballs. Second, for a majority of starting pitchers, fatigue does have an adverse effect on spin deflection. While we don't have PITCHf/x data on Pedro Martinez in 2003, the data that we do have today suggest that fatigue has a clear effect on overall fastball effectiveness.

Now that we have explored the general trends that professional pitchers exhibit, more work needs to be done on the basis of the individual pitcher level. Each pitcher is unique, and as we have just seen, all react differently to the rhythm of the game and to the burden of throwing 100 pitches in a start.

For some, the data provide useful bits of information that may or may not have practical implications. For example, Jon Lester's fastball is at its best the first time he throws it, and the next 10 or so he throws after that also have exceptional movement and velocity. However, he also experiences a constant dramatic decline in fastball "stuff" until he throws his 30th pitch or so.

Pitch count data will allow us to examine fatigue in a way that has never been done before. The opportunity to relate patterns in pitch effectiveness and pitcher release point to fatigue already allows teams to make effective usage decisions that minimize arm injury risk. The height of a pitcher's elbow at release is commonly associated with fatigue, and may also be linked to ligament tears. Soon enough, the fan will be able to monitor these critical points of fatigue from home.

References

- Jeremy Greenhouse, "Spitballing: Fourth Time's the Harm," Baseball Prospectus, *baseballprospectus.com/article.php?articleid=13117*
- Jon Roegele, "How and When Does Velocity Change During a Start?," Beyond the Box Score, *beyondtheboxscore.com/2013/5/16/4334912/how-when-does-velocity-change-during-start-game-pitchfx-sabermetrics*

Uncovering the Mysteries of the Knuckleball

by Alan M. Nathan

The knuckleball is perhaps the most mysterious of baseball pitches. It is thrown slower than normal pitches, it is barely spinning, and it appears to float to home plate. Its motion seems to be very unpredictable by anyone: the batter, the catcher, and even the pitcher himself. Moreover, there is a common perception that a knuckleball does not follow a smooth path to home plate, but instead "dances," "flutters" or "zigs and zags," with seemingly abrupt changes of direction. It's no wonder that it is so difficult both for the batter to hit and for the pitcher to command. Indeed, very few pitchers in the history of Major League Baseball have had much success mastering the knuckleball. That makes the recent success of R.A. Dickey, winner of the 2012 National League Cy Young Award, all the more impressive.

As a result of Dickey's success in the past few years, there has been renewed interest in knuckleballs in the baseball world. Indeed, many recent articles have been written in both the mainstream media and the blogosphere attempting to answer the question: What makes an effective knuckleball? Moreover, Dickey's success also has driven new efforts to train knuckleball pitchers early in their careers. One such effort is the International Knuckleball Academy, a training ground based in Vero Beach, Fla., where young pitchers can learn to master the craft of knuckleball pitching. The ultimate goal is to bring knuckleball pitching into the mainstream of baseball.

It is perhaps a very fortunate accident of nature that Dickey's success with the knuckleball has occurred during an era in which pitch-tracking technologies have revolutionized our ability to analyze pitching. These technologies, PITCHf/x and TrackMan, allow an analysis of the trajectories of all pitches, whether knuckleball or otherwise, with unprecedented precision. As a result, we are now able to quantify both the magnitude and the direction of knuckleball movement, to compare it to that of ordinary pitches, and to investigate its erratic behavior. These technologies also allow us to investigate more detailed aspects of the trajectory, allowing us to quantify the extent to which the common "zig-zag" perception is supported by the data. A parallel development has been wind-tunnel experiments to investigate the aerodynamic forces on a knuckleball and how they depend on the seam orientation. Taken together, the trajectories and the forces are leading to a better understanding of how a knuckleball behaves and why it does what it does.

In this article, I will discuss the recent developments, starting with a brief review of the new technologies. Then I will focus on how those technologies have been used to gain new insights into the character of knuckleball trajectories, including its movement. I will then attempt to reconcile those trajectories with what we know about the forces on knuckleballs from wind tunnel experiments. I will conclude with a detailed case study that shows great promise in uncovering the mysteries of the knuckleball.

Review of Pitch-Tracking Technologies

What we know about knuckleball trajectories comes from two relatively new technologies that are utilized in major league ballparks these days. One of these is PITCHf/x, a video-based tracking system that is permanently installed in every major league ballpark and has been used since the start of the 2007 season to track every pitch in every MLB game. The system consists of two cameras mounted high above the playing field that determine the location of the pitched baseball over most of the region between release and home plate at 1/60-second intervals. Those positions constitute the "raw trajectory," which then is fitted to a smooth function using a constant-acceleration model, so that nine parameters (9P) determine the trajectory: an initial position, an initial velocity, and an average acceleration for each of three coordinates. From the 9P description, all of the relevant parameters for baseball analysis can be determined, including the release velocity, the location at home plate, and the movement. All the 9P information for each pitch is freely available to the public.

The other new technology is TrackMan, a phased-array Doppler radar system that is installed in several major league ballparks. It determines the full pitched-ball trajectory from release to home plate in 1/250-second intervals. Much like PITCHf/x, all of the relevant parameters for baseball analysis are determined by fitting the raw trajectory data to a smooth function, which is proprietary but probably not very dissimilar to the 9P fit used in PITCHf/x. TrackMan data are not publicly available, due to their business relationships with more than half of the major league clubs.

The Character of Knuckleball Trajectories

To study the character of knuckleball trajectories, it is necessary to have access to the raw trajectory data rather than the 9P or similar smooth-function fit to the data. Such a fit is entirely appropriate for studying ordinary pitches based on what we know about the aerodynamic forces that govern the motion of those pitches. What we know is that these forces are nearly constant over a typical trajectory, so the 9P model is an excellent approximation of the actual trajectory. An even better approximation would be to let the aerodynamic forces be proportional to the square of the velocity. I call this the 9P* model and will discuss it further below.

On the other hand, we know far less about the forces responsible for the knuckleball, so we really do not know how well it is described by the 9P or 9P* models. Indeed, those are precisely the issues we want to investigate, and that requires access to the raw tracking data. Accordingly, I obtained raw PITCHf/x data from four high-quality starts by either Tim Wakefield or R. A. Dickey during the 2011 season:

- May 1, 2011, 266 total pitches (70 knuckleballs by Wakefield)
- June 19, 2011, 278 total pitches (96 knuckleballs by Wakefield)
- Aug. 29, 2011, 201 total pitches (77 knuckleballs by Dickey)
- Sept. 17, 2011, 235 total pitches (87 knuckleballs by Dickey)

Each pitch was tracked over the approximate region of seven-to-45 feet from home plate, resulting in about 20 sequential points on the trajectory, a few more or less depending on the release speed and precise tracking region. The 9P* model was used to fit each trajectory to a smooth curve.

One way to characterize the smoothness of the trajectory is to compare the fitted smooth curve to the actual data. The distribution of root-mean-square (rms) deviations of the data from the smooth function, in units of inches, is shown in the following box plots for each of the four games, where the white and grey boxes are for ordinary and knuckleball pitches, respectively.

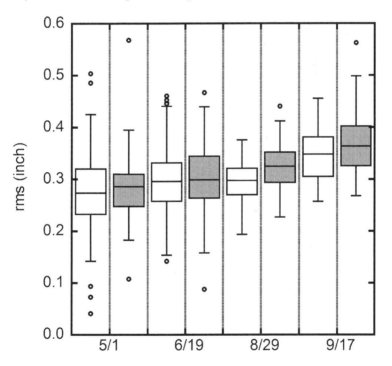

For ordinary pitches, which are expected to be very accurately described by the 9P* curve, the non-zero rms values are almost certainly due to random noise that is inherent in any measurement system. Taking median values as our estimate, that noise is approximately 0.3 inches per point on the trajectory, a very small value. Indeed, one would be very hard pressed to obtain tracking data more precise than these. There are small differences from one game to another that probably can be attributed to differences in camera placement and/or calibration.

But the truly remarkable thing about these plots is that they show quite clearly that the rms distributions for knuckleballs are not very different from those of ordinary pitches. Relative to ordinary pitches, the knuckleballs have a slightly higher median value (the horizontal line in each box) and a very similar interquartile distance (shown by the height of the box). We end up with the unavoidable conclusion that within the overall precision of the tracking system (~0.3 inches), knuckleball and non-knuckleball trajectories follow a 9P* curve nearly equally well. A similar conclusion is reached if a constant acceleration (9P) model is used.

To demonstrate this point more vividly, I now show a bird's-eye view of four different trajectories from the Aug. 29 game.

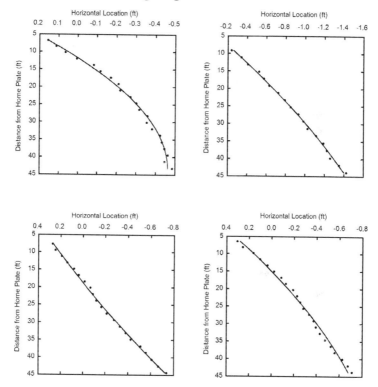

The upper two are ordinary pitches, the lower two are knuckleballs. The left side shows a trajectory with rms close to the median; the right side shows a trajectory with the largest rms value for that game. Note that the release point is near the bottom of each plot, home plate near the top. The first thing to note is that, on average, the curve follows the general trend of the data, with maximum deviations no more than half an inch. This goes a long way toward justifying the use of the 9P or 9P* fit for baseball analysis. More on this below. However, while the curve describes the average trend of the data, a closer inspection shows an interesting feature for the lower-right plot, the knuckleball with the largest rms value. Despite not deviating from the curve by more than half an inch, the data do not randomly fluctuate but rather appear to oscillate about the curve, making one full oscillation over a distance of about 25 ft. This behavior suggests that the pitch undergoes several distinct changes of direction, none of them very large. Despite ending up in the heart of the strike zone, this particular pitch was taken for a called strike, apparently fooling the batter completely. I will return to an analysis of a similar pitch below. Despite the unusual behavior of this pitch, I emphasize that it is definitely the exception rather than the rule, with the vast majority of pitches from these games following the smooth curve very closely.

The Movement of a Knuckleball

Next, I want to investigate the movement of a knuckleball, where "movement" is defined as the deviation of a pitch from a straight line with the effect of gravity removed. To appreciate why a knuckleball is so different, it is helpful to place it in context by discussing what is normal. All pitches, whether normal or otherwise, slow down due to air resistance, losing about eight percent of their initial speed by the time they cross home plate. They also deviate from a straight-line path due to the combined effects of gravity, which pulls everything down, and the other "aerodynamic forces."

For normal pitches, which are spinning rapidly, the aerodynamic force causing the movement is called the Magnus force. The strength of the Magnus force increases as the spin rate increases. The direction of the Magnus force is such as to deflect the ball in the direction that the front edge of the ball is turning, as seen by the batter. Thus, balls thrown with backspin deflect upwards, those thrown with topspin deflect downward, and those thrown with sidespin deflect left or right. And, of course, anything in between is possible, depending on how the spin axis is oriented. For example, a two-seam fastball thrown by a right-handed pitcher will deflect up and to the catcher's left.

Now let's take a look at the movement of a subset of Dickey's pitches thrown during the 2012 season. They are shown on a polar plot, where the distance from the center is the release speed at 55 ft., and the angle is the direction of movement, as seen by the catcher.

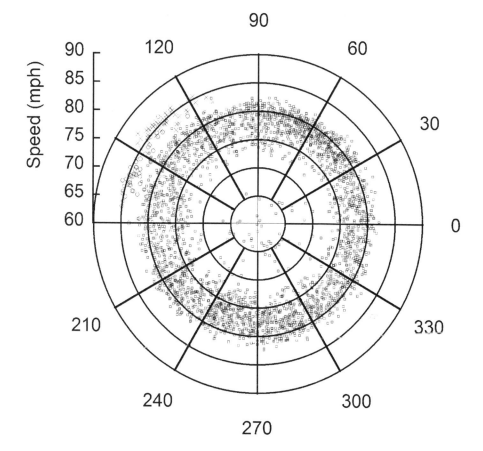

The ordinary pitches fall into two categories: four-seam fastballs denoted by the x's and two-seam fastballs (or sinkers) denoted by the o's, both of which are thrown at mid-80s speed. Relative to the four-seam, which has mainly upward and a little arm-side (or tailing) movement, the two-seam has less upward and more tailing movement. These features are all rather standard fare for anyone who has ever done this type of analysis. The important feature of these pitches is the clustering behavior of the movement. That is, the angular range for the movement of a given pitch type is limited in extent and, therefore, rather predictable. This predictability conforms with what we know about how pitchers pitch. Namely, for a given pitch type, a pitcher tries to release the ball with a consistent axis of rotation. Our understanding of the Magnus force tells us that if the axis of rotation is consistent, then the direction of movement also will be consistent.

Now take a look at the knuckleballs, denoted by the squares. In contrast to the ordinary pitches, there is no clustering of the knuckleball movement. The knuckleball seems to be erratic in the sense that the direction of movement is entirely random from one pitch to another and, therefore, unpredictable. Another way to say the same thing is that whatever aerodynamic force is acting on the knuckleball to cause the movement seems to have a random direction from one pitch to another. This is one feature of knuckleballs that we will try to understand in the context of the wind tunnel experiments.

Let me now summarize what we have learned from analysis of trajectories:

- To within our ability to measure with the tracking systems, knuckleball trajectories mainly follow a trajectory as smooth as that of ordinary pitches. There are exceptions, but they constitute a relatively small percentage of knuckleball pitches.
- The movement of knuckleballs is erratic and unpredictable.

I next turn to a discussion of wind tunnel experiments to see the extent to which they can explain what we observe from trajectory analysis.

Reconciling Wind Tunnel and Trajectory Data

Wind tunnel experiments are used to measure the aerodynamic forces on a baseball (or any other sports ball) as a function of wind speed, spin, etc. Much of what we know about air resistance and the Magnus force on sports balls comes from such experiments. For the knuckleball, the classic experiment was done nearly 40 years ago by Robert Watts and Eric Sawyer (*http://baseball.physics.illinois.edu/WattsSawyerAJP.pdf*). They investigated how the aerodynamic forces on a non-spinning baseball depend on seam orientation. A simplified version of their findings is shown on the plot, where positive/negative forces corresponds to up/down on the diagram of the ball, which also shows how the angle is defined.

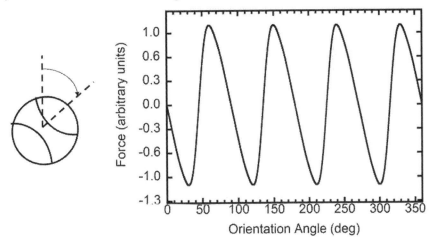

The wind blows from right to left, and as the orientation of the ball is changed, the seam pattern maps out the four-seam configuration. What we learn from this is that the size and direction of the force is strongly dependent on the seam orientation. Indeed, aerodynamicists tell us that when the on-coming air encounters a seam, the character of the air flow is altered in such a way as to deflect the ball one way or another, depending on the orientation of the seam relative to the air flow. The result is a sine-wave-like pattern that is repeated four times in one revolution, exactly what one would expect for the four-seam configuration. More recent data taken in the past year confirm this finding. Moreover, the more recent data also investigated the two-seam configuration. Strangely, that pattern is much more complicated and not yet fully understood. Therefore, pending a better understanding of that pattern, I will confine my investigations to the four-seam configuration. Note that the force scale is shown in arbitrary units. However, recent data confirm that the size of the knuckleball force at its peak is comparable to the Magnus force on a four-seam fastball.

Armed with a force-vs-orientation profile, it now is possible to do mathematical simulations of knuckleball trajectories to see how they compare with actual data. Some results are presented in the plots, which show a bird's-eye view similar to that shown of the actual data but with the horizontal scale in inches.

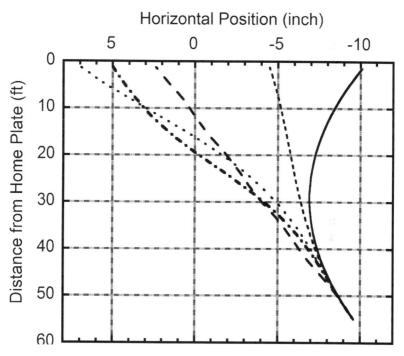

All pitches are thrown with the same release point, speed (75 mph), direction, and initial seam orientation (78°). However, they are thrown with different rotation rates, given as the angle through which the ball turns between release and home plate: solid line 0°; short dashes 18°; dots 72°; dash-dot 99°; long dashes 360°. Therefore, all five trajectories start out at the same point and are heading in the same direction. However, their eventual fate differs greatly. At one extreme is the pitch corresponding to 0° (no rotation). In that case, the force is constant both in magnitude and direction,

---

much like that of ordinary pitches, resulting in the largest amount of movement. The other extreme is the one corresponding to 360° (one full revolution), so that the force profile undergoes four complete oscillations. In that case, the force is changing in direction so rapidly that the ball cannot keep up with it, so the ball ends up going more or less straight, i.e., no movement, just as shown in the plot. That confirms the well-known fact about knuckleballs that too high a rotation rate results in a considerable loss of movement. Between these two extremes, the simulations show that the character of the trajectories is a very strong function of the rotation rate, with small changes in the rate leading to large changes in where the ball crosses home plate. Although no plots are shown, the trajectory is also sensitive to small changes in the initial orientation of the seams. This sensitivity to small changes in the initial conditions is an example of chaotic dynamics and almost surely goes a long way toward explaining why the movement of the knuckleball is unpredictable.

Now take a closer look at the dash-dot trajectory, for which the force undergoes a bit more than one complete oscillation. The net effect is quite evident in the trajectory, as the ball initially breaks to the left, then breaks to the right about 20 ft. from home plate. The net movement is not great, only about 2.5 in. (compare with the long dashes), but this pitch is quite likely to fool both the batter and the catcher. Of course, it is only a simulation. Moreover, it utilizes only the four-seam data, whereas most knuckleballs these days are thrown in the two-seam orientation. Nevertheless, pending a more complete understanding of the two-seam force profile, it is encouraging that some of the same features observed in actual tracking data also show up in the simulation. To emphasize that point further, I will now turn to a detailed analysis of an actual pitch.

Anatomy of a Really Nasty Pitch

On June 13, 2012, Dickey pitched a one-hitter against the Tampa Bay Rays at Tropicana Field. In the bottom of the third, he struck out Will Rhymes with a truly nasty pitch. Modern technology has given us two different tools for analyzing this pitch. First, a high-speed video allows us to see the motion of the ball, including its rotation, in great detail. Second, the TrackMan system is set up in Tropicana Field, allowing a rather precise measurement of the entire trajectory of the pitch from release to glove. So let's take a look at how those two compare with each other and see if we can understand the trajectory based on what we know about the knuckleball forces.

First take a look at the animated gif of the high-speed video at *http://baseball.physics.illinois.edu/KBall/dickey-rhymes-hd.gif*, if you can. Being careful not to be fooled by the upward movement of the camera or the movement of the catcher, see if you can notice that the pitch undergoes two distinct changes of direction. Shortly after release, it appears to swerve to Dickey's right; later it swerves back to the left. Poor Will never had a chance. In fact, even the catcher has a lot of trouble with the pitch, as we can see from the movements of his head and glove. There seems to be no question that this pitch gets very high marks on the nasty scale.

The other interesting thing to note on the video is the spin, which is easy to follow by watching the progress of the MLB logo on the ball. Dickey has said that he tries to throw the ball in the two-seam orientation with about 0.5 revolutions of topspin. This pitch is nothing like that. Instead it undergoes about 1.5 revolutions between release and catch with nearly pure gyrospin; that is, the rotation axis is about the direction of motion, much like a spiral pass in football or a bullet fired from a rifle. If nothing else, this demonstrates the difficulty for even a skilled pitcher like Dickey in reproducing the initial conditions.

Now let's take a look at the TrackMan data, shown as the circles in the plot.

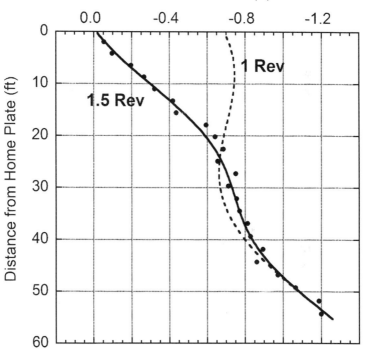

One can clearly see the same features that are observed in the video, namely, an initial break to the right followed by a second break to the left. Given that the ball is thrown with gyrospin and given the symmetry of the ball, the force that causes the movement must be constant in magnitude. Moreover, the direction of the force must rotate along with the ball about the direction of motion, initially pointing in the upward direction, then rotating clockwise as seen by the pitcher (counterclockwise as seen by the catcher). That makes it very easy to simulate this pitch with three unknown quantities that are adjusted to fit the data: the rotation rate, the initial direction, and the magnitude of the force. The result is shown as the solid curve, which does a remarkably good job at accounting for the tracking data.

Now we come to the key point: Given a complete mathematical model that describes this pitch (the solid curve), we now can investigate what would happen with slightly different release conditions. So, for example, the dashed curve shows the trajectory expected if everything were exactly the same except the rotation rate, making 1.0 rather than 1.5 revolutions. The difference between the two curves is stark, with the actual trajectory going right over the middle of home plate, whereas the alternate trajectory hitting the outside corner, a difference of over eight inches. Indeed, judging from the movement of the catcher, the alternate trajectory was expected, whereas the actual trajectory seemed to break toward the middle of the plate at the last moment. By the way, there are comparable multiple breaks in the vertical direction that I am not showing, since they are masked by the much larger effect of gravity.

There is no question that this pitch is extremely effective at fooling the batter. Was it thrown this way intentionally by Dickey? Has he discovered a new "gyroball knuckleball?" Should he try to throw this pitch more often? Suffice it to say that I would love to know the answers to these questions.

Summary and Outlook

With the combination of precise tracking data, wind tunnel experiments, and high-speed video, we are slowly but surely uncovering the mysteries of the knuckleball. We now have a working hypothesis for the erratic nature of knuckleball movement, having to do with small changes in the release conditions. We understand that knuckleball pitches with multiple changes of direction are the exception rather than the rule, at least to within the precision of the tracking data. We further understand that the amount of movement is not necessarily indicative of the nastiness of the pitch, since a pitch thrown with multiple changes of direction—one guaranteed to fool the batter—necessarily has a net movement that is small. We understand why too high a rotation rate has the opposite effect, not fooling the batter at all, given that such a pitch travels pretty much in a straight line. And we have started to make progress reconciling these features of the actual tracking data with wind tunnel experiments.

There still are many things we would like to understand better, particularly the force profile in the two-seam orientation. Indeed, we really would like to understand the forces with the ball oriented in an arbitrary configuration. So there is still plenty of work to do. Nevertheless, the progress made thus far is very pleasing.

It is a pleasure to thank Sportvision and TrackMan for supplying me with raw tracking data. I also acknowledge many fruitful discussions with Professors Rod Cross, Robert Watts, and John Borg.

Noteworthy 2013 Leaderboards of Note

by Carson Cistulli

Humility was among the virtues mostly highly prized by the Ancient Romans. So thoroughly was this the case that a general, passing through the streets upon his return from a military victory—and surrounded by the sort of riches one would have secured by means of sacking a foreign city—would arrange for a servant to accompany him and provide a constant reminder of his own (i.e. the general's own) mortality, lest he be carried away by the praise of an adoring public. "Memento mori," the servant would whisper—a phrase that, translated roughly into English, means "moment of death."

The effect is less morbid than one might assume immediately. As both French philosopher Michel de Montaigne and American recording artist 50 Cent have probably stated at some point, one is only capable of living authentically when one has acknowledged that he or she will someday die. That fact established, life becomes a many-splendored thing, whereas maybe it was a lesser-splendored thing previously.

One is able, in the modern era, to achieve nearly this same effect without having to bother with the hassle and expense of hiring a servant to that end—namely, by means of the baseball leaderboard. "A year has passed," announces the leaderboard. "You've gotten older," it implies by so announcing. "Live your life to the fullest," it whispers—but only metaphorically, because leaderboards lack the power of speech.

Below, The Hardball Times presents a series of four leaderboards—which, in addition to serving as a reminder of the *memento mori*, are each some combination of informative and amusing.

Best Pitches

There probably are multiple ways to identify what the league's "best" pitches are—and, of course, the effectiveness of one offering in a pitcher's repertoire depends on the quality of all the others, too.

One way of evaluating the quality of a pitch, using a methodology developed by Dave Allen, is to see what it's been worth in terms of linear-weight runs. What follows are the top 10 pitches by linear-weight runs (relative to league average) for every 100 thrown—with a minimum of 250 thrown for each pitch. In the chart below, FA means four-seam fastball, FT means two-seam fastball, FC means cut fastball, FS means splitter, SL means slider, CU means curveball and CH means changeup.

Name	Team	Type	IP	%	R/100
Koji Uehara	Red Sox	FS	74.1	48.2%	3.72
Craig Kimbrel	Braves	SL	67.0	28.2%	3.62
Glen Perkins	Twins	FT	62.2	39.1%	3.43
Cole Hamels	Phillies	CH	220.0	25.0%	3.40
Sonny Gray	Athletics	CU	64.0	26.3%	3.33
Clay Buchholz	Red Sox	FC	108.1	24.9%	3.22
Tyson Ross	Padres	SL	125.0	32.2%	3.19
Hyun-Jin Ryu	Dodgers	CH	192.0	22.4%	3.07
Jim Johnson	Orioles	FA	70.1	24.6%	3.02
Greg Holland	Royals	SL	67.0	39.6%	2.99

Notes

- Despite having prooduced park-adjusted xFIPs about 40 percent better than league average between 2010 and '12 while working in relief for the Baltimore Orioles and Texas Rangers, right-hander Koji Uehara received attention commensurate with his talents only this past season with the Boston Red Sox. Perhaps it's because his run-prevention figures were even better than usual; perhaps it's because he played in one of the league's most vibrant sporting markets; or perhaps it's because he did most of his work in 2013 as an Official Closer. Whatever the case, his splitter was the league's best pitch per 100 thrown.

- A huge disappointment for Craig Kimbrel, this: On last year's edition of the best-pitches leaderboard, two of his offerings—the slider and fastball—appeared among the league's top 10. In 2013, however, his fastball prevented only 1.6 runs above average per every 100 thrown. One can only assume that retirement is imminent for the Atlanta Braves closer.

- Philadelphia Phillies left-hander Cole Hamels' changeup is the highest-ranked pitch among starters by the methodology used here—and Hamels himself is the only starter among those here to have recorded 200-plus innings. Despite an April that saw him post a walk rate (10.6 percent) nearly double his career average, Hamels was basically himself again for the remainder of the season. For the third time in six years, his changeup was worth greater than 20 runs above average, according to PITCHf/x data.

Minor League kwERA Leaders

Work by Russell Carleton demonstrates that while pitcher strikeout and walk rates tend to stabilize rather quickly (at about 70 and 170 batters faced, respectively), home-run rates require a considerably larger sample. As such, FIP numbers (which include home-run rate) distort what might be called a pitcher's "true-talent ERA." An alternative to FIP is kwERA, an ERA estimator developed by Tom Tango that accounts only for a pitcher's strikeout and walk rates. Below are the top-10 minor-league starters by kwERA, all with a minimum of 170 batters faced so as to allow a reliable sample size for both of the relevant inputs. In addition, only those pitchers who made starts above Rookie ball have been considered.

Name	Org	Level	Age	G	GS	IP	K%	BB%	kwERA
Danny Salazar	CLE	AA, AAA	23	21	20	93.0	35.5%	6.6%	1.93
Shane Dawson	TOR	R, A-	19	11	7	46.0	33.9%	5.6%	2.00
Austin Voth	WAS	R, A-, A	21	11	11	46.1	31.6%	3.4%	2.02
Cole Sulser	CLE	A-	23	15	9	54.0	29.3%	4.4%	2.41
Ryan Doran	ARI	R, A-	22	13	12	77.0	27.4%	2.9%	2.46
C.J. Edwards	---	A, A+	21	24	24	116.1	33.1%	8.8%	2.48
Julio Urias	LAD	A	16	18	18	54.1	31.8%	7.6%	2.50
Anthony Bucciferro	CHW	R, A	23	16	15	90.2	25.7%	1.6%	2.51
Luis Severino	NYY	R, A	19	10	8	44.0	29.6%	5.6%	2.52
Severino Gonzalez	PHI	A, A+, AA	20	25	14	103.2	29.3%	5.4%	2.53

Notes

• The Cleveland Indians' Danny Salazar began the 2013 season as a half-prospect with 34 innings above High-A and a Tommy John procedure in his recent past. He finished it as Cleveland's starter in the Wild Card play-in game against the Tampa Bay Rays. While that particular appearance was less than ideal, his season was entirely impressive, as the young right-hander parlayed his mid-90s fastball and terrifying split-changeup into success at Double-A and then Triple-A before a major-league stint saw him strike out nearly a third of the 211 batters he ultimately faced.

• As noted above, Shane Dawson of the Toronto Blue Jays organization produced some of the most impressive defense-independent marks of any minor-league starter in 2013. That he did it while pitching as a 19-year-old at entirely age-appropriate levels is also very encouraging. What's surprising, given the results, is Dawson's pedigree. The left-hander was only a 17th-round pick in the 2012 draft out of Lethbridge Community College in Alberta, Canada. Alberta hasn't produced as much talent as British Columbia or Ontario, for example. In fact, a brief inspection of the data reveals that the longest tenured major-leaguer from the province is likely right-hander Mike Johnson, who recorded -1.7 WAR while tossing 217 innings in the majors for the Orioles and Montreal Expos from 1997 to 2001.

- The age listed for Julio Urias is not a misprint: He was just 16 years old for the majority of last season. Signed by the Los Angeles Dodgers out of the Mexican League in August of 2012, the left-handed Urias made his debut professional debut in late May of 2013—and did so in the Class-A Midwest League, becoming the youngest player in that league by nearly two years. By all accounts, Urias has command of three pitches (a fastball, curveball, and changeup), although there's probably cause for somewhat muted optimism: At just 5-foot-11, Urias has little room for the sort of physical projection one might otherwise expect from such a young prospect.

Reckless Power (RECK) Leaders

While patience and power are two different skills or tools, it's also generally the case that batters who hit for power are likely to draw more walks, simply because pitchers are afraid of conceding the home run.

Certain players, however, seem to have little interest in taking the walks their power has earned for them. Reckless power is what we might say they have. RECK is a toy metric designed to identify the players who displayed the most reckless power. It's calculated by dividing Isolated Power by Isolated Patience, or, stated differently, (SLG – AVG) / (OBP – AVG). The results appear to approximate the Richter Scale, such that less than 2.0 is barely felt, 5.0 is considerable, and 9.0 and up happens less than every 10 years and is totally destructive.

Name	Team	PA	AVG	OBP	SLG	RECK
Adam Jones	Orioles	689	.285	.318	.493	6.3
A.J. Pierzynski	Rangers	529	.272	.297	.425	6.1
Torii Hunter	Tigers	652	.304	.334	.465	5.4
Alfonso Soriano	- - -	626	.255	.302	.489	5.0
Will Venable	Padres	515	.268	.312	.484	4.9
Marlon Byrd	- - -	579	.291	.336	.511	4.9
Manny Machado	Orioles	710	.283	.314	.432	4.8
Salvador Perez	Royals	526	.292	.323	.433	4.5
Carlos Beltran	Cardinals	600	.296	.339	.491	4.5
Nate Schierholtz	Cubs	503	.251	.301	.470	4.4

Notes

- Baltimore's Adam Jones is one of only two players to have appeared on the RECK leaderboard from last year's edition of the *THT Annual*, as well. It's not entirely shocking, this: Jones' physical talent is clear, as is his proclivity for swinging. Among all qualified hitters, Jones recorded both the second-highest percentage of swings outside the strike zone (44.8 percent) and also total swings (58.1 percent), according to PITCHf/x.

- Finishing first in both of the aforementioned categories—at 47.6 percent and 60.2 percent, respectively—was Texas catcher A.J. Pierzynski, the only other batter here to have also appeared among 2012's RECK leaders, as well. To what degree Pierzynski is "reckless" or not can be debated—and one hopes that it will be some day, preferably by Ivy Leaguers wearing crested blazers. That Pierzynski has demonstrated above-average power in recent years can't be debated, however— nor can the notion that he's somewhat indiscriminate about which pitches he offers at.

- Quite unlike Jones and Pierzynski, St. Louis Cardinals outfielder Carlos Beltran is a player who's been known for some time as one of the league's more patient hitters. Between 2003 and '13, he recorded only two seasons with a walk rate below 10 percent (league average is generally around eight percent). One of those was 2005, his disappointing debut season with the New York Mets; the other one was 2013 itself. Despite the slight decline in plate discipline, the 36-year-old Puerto Rican native still managed to accumulate 24 home runs in 600 plate appearances while making half of those appearances at the pitcher-friendly Busch Stadium.

Baserunning (BsR) Leaders

Players can produce runs on the basepaths by two means, either by (a) stealing bases frequently and at an efficient rate or (b) taking extra bases (and not getting thrown out while so doing) when a batted ball has been put into play.

FanGraphs measures the former of these using Weighted Stolen Base Runs (wSB); the latter, by way of Ultimate Base Running (UBR). wSB estimates the number of runs a player contributes to his team by stealing bases, as compared to the average player. UBR accounts for the value a player adds to his team via base running during different baseball events. Adding together wSB and UBR produces the baserunning (BsR) component for WAR at FanGraphs.

Below are top-five baserunners from 2013, among non-pitchers, according to BsR.

#	Name	Team	PA	SB	CS	wSB	UBR	BsR
1	Jacoby Ellsbury	Red Sox	636	52	4	8.3	3.2	11.4
2	Rajai Davis	Blue Jays	360	45	6	6.4	3.8	10.2
3	Elvis Andrus	Rangers	698	42	8	4.6	5.3	9.9
4	Eric Young	- - -	598	46	11	4.5	5.5	9.9
5	Mike Trout	Angels	716	33	7	3.1	5.0	8.1

And since we don't want to let only the best players earn notierity, below are the bottom-five players according to BsR, as well.

#	Name	Team	PA	SB	CS	wSB	UBR	BsR
633	Jonathan Lucroy	Brewers	580	9	1	0.9	-6.5	-5.6
634	Alberto Callaspo	- - -	516	0	2	-1.3	-4.4	-5.6
635	Allen Craig	Cardinals	563	2	0	-0.2	-5.8	-5.9
636	Victor Martinez	Tigers	668	0	2	-1.4	-6.8	-8.2
637	Paul Konerko	White Sox	520	0	0	-0.5	-7.9	-8.4

Notes

- Toronto outfielder Rajai Davis more or less represents the best-case scenario for what a player can provide with top-flight speed and instincts. With a 10.2 BsR, Davis recorded about one win exactly from baserunning alone—this from a player who produced a 1.2 WAR overall in 2013. Phrased differently: Nearly all of his value in 108 games and 360 plate appearances came by way of runs produced on the bases.

- Mike Trout's base-stealing record in 2013, while fine, was less impressive than in his rookie season. He stole fewer bases (33 vs. 49) and was caught more often (seven vs. five). Accordingly, he was unable to match the league-leading 7.0 wSB he recorded in 2012. That said, he produced precisely the same number of runs via other baserunning events, leading to a still very much above-average 8.1 BsR.

- By all accounts, White Sox first baseman/designated hitter Paul Konerko is beloved by the residents of Chicago's South Side. By one account—specifically, the nerdy baseball stat BsR—he's been one of the league's worst baserunners for a while now. Some recent finishes for Konerko by that same metric: 637th (out of 637) in 2013, 628th (out of 632) in 2012, 640th (out of 641) in 2011. The last time Konerko recorded a positive BsR figure was 2001.

Game Theory Modeling the Batter-Pitcher Confrontation

by Dave Allen & Kevin Tenenbaum

Put yourself in Aaron Crow's shoes on Aug. 17 of this year. In a tie game with no outs in the bottom of the ninth inning, Crow decides to throw a fastball low and away to Miguel Cabrera. Cabrera places it into the right field seats for a walk-off home run. We wonder what is going through both Crow's and Cabrera's heads during this at-bat.

Crow may think that it's best to throw his fastball, but he is uncertain where to locate it. He knows that his fastball is most effective when it is thrown low and away. Then, he realizes that Cabrera knows his fastball is good when thrown low and away, and will probably be looking there for the pitch. Knowing this, Crow decides to throw his second-best pitch and tries to make the hitter chase a high fastball. Crow wonders whether Cabrera might be expecting this strategy. After deliberating on this for several seconds, he chooses the fastball low and away and throws the pitch.

Cabrera then must decide whether he should swing at Crow's fastball. He knows the pitch is likely to be a strike, and what the average outcome will be if he chooses to swing at the pitch. He also has some information about the pitch: He observes the first approximately 270 milliseconds of its trajectory before he has to make his almost unconscious decision.

Introduction

This process can go on forever with no obvious solution for either player. The only way to truly uncover each player's best option is to use a sub-field of economics called Game Theory. Game Theory is the study of strategic decision-making. More specifically, it is a way to figure out which of a set of strategies a player should employ in a game against others.

This field has many applications for baseball, which researchers have only begun to explore. Here are three notable articles which have done that:

- Mitchel Lichtman's chapter in *The Book: Playing the Percentages in Baseball (2007)*: "Bluffing in Baseball"
- "When a Pitcher Meets a Hitter," by David Gassko (2010) at HardballTimes.com
- Matt Swartz's five-part 2012 series on Game Theory at HardballTimes.com

"Bluffing in Baseball," a chapter from *The Book*, discusses many aspects of how Game Theory can be applied to baseball strategy. Lichtman discusses the sacrifice bunt, stolen bases and pitchouts, and pitch selection in this chapter. As far as pitch selection goes, Lichtman does not solve for an optimal (or Nash Equilibrium) solution to the question of how often pitchers should throw each pitch. Rather, he embarks upon a more qualitative explanation of how Game Theory should be applied to baseball and presents a few approximate solutions.

Gassko presents a method for determining how often pitchers should throw certain pitches. He assigns a value to each of the two pitches examined, which vary with the hitter's expectations for the upcoming pitch. He then solves for the equilibrium solution for how often the pitcher should throw each of the two pitches.

As far as we can tell, this was the first attempt to apply Game Theory quantitatively to pitch selection in the public sphere. This is a great article, which serves as a fantastic reference about Game Theory and pitch selection, but it also left room for future research. Gassko chose the relative payoff values for each pitch type rather than using empirical data to determine these values. Also, he assumed that the hitter is expecting a certain pitch at all times.

In part two of his five-part series on Game Theory and baseball, Swartz examines the Game Theory of pitch selection using a method that builds off what Gassko did two years earlier. In this implementation, however, Swartz has the hitter's strategic choices as "swing" or "no swing" rather than the expected pitch. This is more realistic because this is the actual choice a hitter must make.

While Swartz's game theoretic analysis of pitch selection is groundbreaking work, there are a few places where more can be done. Here we introduce four improvements that make the game-theory model of the batter-pitcher confrontation more realistic:

1. We use empirically measured run values, from the PITCHf/x database, rather than choosing values for each pitch.

2. The pitcher and catcher choose where to aim the pitch (presumably the catcher's target). In this article, we assume the pitcher is going to throw a fastball and find the optimal locations for this fastball. Thus, the pitcher's strategy set is continuous (a location in 2D space).

3. The pitcher's outcome is stochastic, or somewhat random; the pitch does not end up exactly where he aimed it.

4. Finally, the batter has some information about the location of the pitch before he decides to swing. In previous Game Theory applications this was not the case.

These additions make it much harder to analytically derive the optimal solution for both parties. Instead, we simulate the game (the at-bat) to find the run value of hypothetical pitcher and batter strategies, and then use a genetic algorithm to search for optimal solutions. These two steps, the at-bat simulation and genetic algorithm search for optimal solutions, are described below.

This method is very flexible and allows us to examine the optimal solution for specific situations. The strategy for the batter is going to change if he is in a 3-0 count versus a 0-2 count. And the strategy for the pitcher is going to change if he is up against an extreme groundball hitter or an extreme flyball hitter. We explore some of these specific situations in our analysis. To simplify the analysis we look only at at-bats between right-handed pitchers and right-handed batters.

Methods

The at-bat model

This model takes pitcher and batter strategies as inputs and outputs the run value of an at-bat between these strategies. The model, shown below, proceeds in a number of steps.

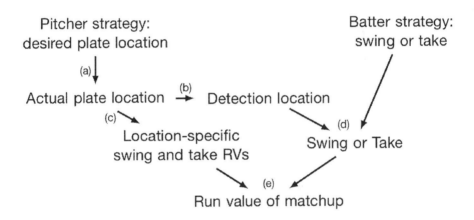

a. The pitcher's strategy is a location to which he wishes to pitch, the catcher's target. This step models the randomness of pitch locations (the pitcher does not necessarily pitch to his desired location). The actual location is a random one chosen from a distribution centered at the desired spot.

b. The batter gets partial information about the pitch before he decides whether to swing. At the time when the batter has to decide whether to swing the pitch is in the "decision plane." To find its location in this plane we find all fastballs in the PITCHf/x database that end up at this pitch's plate location. We then find all their locations in the decision plane, and give this pitch a random location centered at the mean of those decision locations.

c. Looking at all fastballs from RHPs to RHBs in the PITCHf/x database (or just those in the specific situation we are interested in examining; e.g., just 3-0 fastballs) we calculate the average location-specific run value for both taken and swung-at pitches. That is the expected run value of a taken fastball at a specific location, and the expected run value of a swung-at fastball at a specific location.

d. The batter strategy is a shape in the decision plane. If the pitch is inside this shape, he swings at it. If not, he takes it.

e. Based on the location-specific run value and whether the batter swings or takes, we calculate the run value of the at-bat.

Finding the optimal solution using a genetic algorithm

Now we want to know what the optimal solution is for both the batter and pitcher. Because the model is relatively complicated we were not able to optimize analytically, as you would find the Nash Equilibrium in a simple game. So instead we used a genetic algorithm approach. This is an often-used optimization technique that takes its inspiration from biological evolution by natural selection.

We start with a "population" of 1,000 randomly generated pitcher strategies (places to aim) and a population of 1,000 randomly generated batter strategies (parameters describing the shape in the decision plane to swing at). The diagram below shows how we proceed.

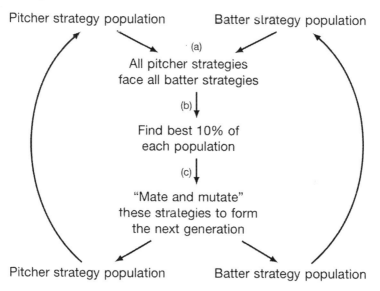

1. Each one of the pitcher strategies faces off against each one of the batter strategies in an at-bat, as described in the model above. For each strategy, we sum its run values against all opposing strategies.

2. The 10 percent of the pitcher strategies with the lowest total run values and 10 percent of batter strategies with highest total run values are selected.

3. The pitcher strategies randomly "mutate and mate" to form the next generation. This involves randomly pairing them and averaging their values, and

---

then with some chance perturbing some values a small amount. The same is done for the batter population. These strategies form the next generation, progeny of the most "fit" strategies from the previous one. Then the process starts again.

The algorithm is run for 500 generations, by which point both batter and pitcher data stabilize to consistent strategies, the optimal strategies.

Results

Using the method outlined above, we are able to determine the best fastball location strategy in varying counts. The model outputs are in the form of a graph. The labeled point is the location the pitcher should aim for, and the ellipses emerging from that show the random spread of where the pitch actually ends up. The dotted ellipse represents the batter's strategy: Inside that shape he should swing at least 95 percent of the time. His actual strategy is an ellipse is the "decision plane," and we have "pulled it forward" to the plate. The graphs are from the catcher's perspective so the batter stands to the left of the graph.

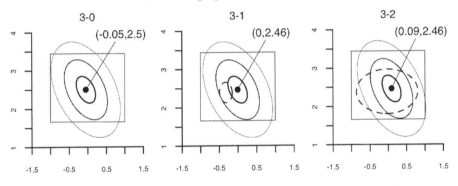

As you can see in the above graphs, the optimal location for fastballs in three-ball counts indicates that the pitcher's strategy should change slightly based on the number of strikes on the hitter. While the pitcher's strategy does not change drastically as the count varies, the model does recommend that the pitcher shift his intended location away a little less than an inch for each additional strike on the hitter.

There is virtually no trend in the optimal vertical location for pitchers in three-ball counts. This lack of a trend is most likely a result of the pitcher's need to throw a strike in these situations. The optimal vertical location of about 2.5 feet probably maximizes that probability of throwing within the vertical boundaries of the strike zone.

The model does not think there is any location in which the batter should swing at least 95 percent of the time. This does not mean that the hitter should never swing at a fastball in a 3-0 count. Rather, it means he must have more information indicating he should swing besides simply location.

It is also important to remember that these results are for the average hitter, so we may find that certain hitters with a lot of power (see Cabrera, Miguel or Davis, Chris) should swing at fastballs down the middle in these counts much more often than a hitter with little power (see Pierre, Juan).

In the 3-1 count, hitters should swing at few pitches more than 95 percent of the time. These pitches fall into what would be considered the hitter's wheelhouse. This is also known as the area that is about belt high and slightly on the inner half of the plate. These pitches make home runs that are fun to watch because they tend to be towering shots that make you feel as if your stomach has dropped down to your feet.

When the hitter has two strikes, however, the situation changes drastically. At this point, he must protect the plate, as any strike that he does not swing at will result in a strikeout. Therefore, he must be much more aggressive than in the first two counts. As you can see, the hitter's optimal strategy is to swing at the pitches that are definitely strikes greater than 95 percent of the time.

Now that we have discussed the match-up between the average major league hitter and pitcher, we can start looking at how the results change for different types of hitters and pitchers. First, we will look at how the average pitcher should throw to hitters with varying groundball tendencies averaged over all counts. Remember, we are looking only at fastballs from right-handed pitchers to right-handed batters.

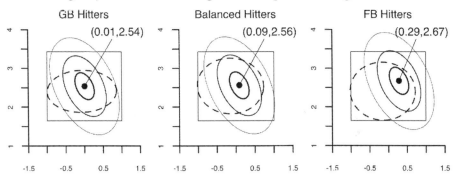

Looking first at hitters with a high groundball percentage (top 50 groundball percentage over 2010-2012 with at least 500 balls in play), we see that it is best to aim down the center of the plate and miss either high or low. This is because most hitters who have a tendency to hit ground balls are unlikely to hit for power. Therefore, you want them to put the ball in play early in the count and get their single out of the way or get ahead in the count.

As we shift to the next graph, we see the optimal location pitchers should use against the 50 batters closest to league average in groundball percentage. The optimal location strategy against these balanced hitters is to throw slightly to the outer portion of the plate while essentially maintaining the vertical location from groundball hitters.

When facing intense flyball hitters, pitchers should throw mostly high and outside. We believe that the vertical increase is the result of a sampling bias present in the data. Hitters with a higher tendency to hit fly balls are actually taller than those who hit ground balls more often. Therefore, the center of the strike zone for flyball hitters is slightly higher than it is for groundball hitters. This bias is most likely the cause for the increase in optimal vertical location for flyball hitters.

The corresponding horizontal shift toward the outer part of the plate is most likely because flyball hitters tend to hit for more power, particularly pull power. Therefore, it is in the pitcher's best interest to throw fastballs away from the hitter so that he cannot turn on the pitch for an extra-base hit.

Finally, we will look at the results for pitchers with high- and low-velocity fastballs. In these figures, we are looking at the fastest 10 percent of fastballs, the 10 percent right in the middle, and the slowest 10 percent. These are taken for all counts, and again just for right-handed pitchers to right-handed batters.

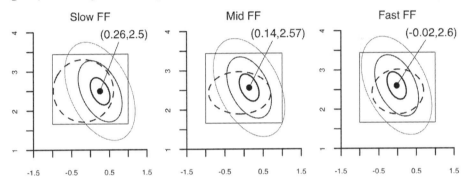

As you can see, pitchers should throw more toward the outer portion of the plate as their velocity declines. This result makes sense logically; a Bronson Arroyo, with his 87 mph fastball, should probably try to paint the corners more than Stephen Strasburg with his 95 mph fastball. This is intuitive, because it is much more difficult to hit a 100 mph pitch than an 85 mph pitch when they are both down the middle of the plate.

However, you can make up for the lack of velocity with good command of the pitch (i.e., throwing to the outside part of the plate). Additionally, faster pitches should be located closer to the top of the strike zone. This result is also intuitive, because it is much harder to get on top of a faster pitch than it is a slower pitch when it is in the top part of the strike zone. These high fastballs can be dangerous if you miss your spot; the hitter is likely to hit the ball very hard. However, the added fastball velocity makes it more difficult for the hitter to hit these pitches hard, making it more worthwhile for pitchers who have high fastball velocities to throw to the top of the strike zone more often than pitchers with low fastball velocities.

Conclusions

All models make simplifications and assumptions. As these simplifications and assumptions are removed, the model becomes more complicated. Here we examine a game in which the pitcher has a continuous, stochastic strategy and the batter gets partial information about the pitcher strategy. These make the game a more realistic model of real at-bats, but mean that we had to simulate—rather than analytically solve—the game to find a solution. But this added flexibility also allowed us to examine specific situations and find how batters and pitchers should behave in them—a powerful tool. These results add support for common baseball knowledge, but also allow us to quantify aspects of this knowledge; e.g., how much further outside should you pitch to a power hitter than a contact hitter?

Still, there are simplifications and assumptions in our model. We look at a single pitch type, have a simplified version of the information a batter gets about a pitch, and assume the location-specific run values do not change (if a pitcher really did pitch to the same location over and over, the batter would adjust and the run value of that location would go up). These provide places for future researchers to build on our work.

Revisiting *The Book's* "Mano a Mano" Chapter

by Steve Staude

In chapter three of Tom Tango, Mitchel Lichtman and Andrew Dolphin's ground-breaking *The Book*, the authors explore the topic of batter/pitcher confrontations. They begin by finding batters who "owned," or were owned by particular pitchers. Ultimately, they conclude that having owned a pitcher in the past is very far from a guarantee of owning him in the future. The batter's performance against the rest of the league over the time period is a better predictor of how he'll perform against a given pitcher than is his history against that pitcher, generally speaking. It's a matter of sample size; a batter typically doesn't face a specific pitcher nearly often enough to make the role of randomness in the results a minor one.

The authors move on to analyzing batters' results against groups of comparable pitchers, or "famiglias," as they put it. By looking at each batter's results against types of pitchers rather than individual pitchers, they of course manage to have larger plate appearance samples to work with, but they still conclude that the samples are too small; there is "too much noise masking the truth under those numbers," they write. Having given up on finding anything useful in their pitcher family studies, they proceed to analyze general traits for the rest of the chapter—flyball hitters versus groundball pitchers in general, for example—and find some pretty convincing results on those fronts. But I was left wondering if taking a different path in the pitcher family study might have avoided a dead end.

One thing *The Book*'s authors mentioned in the chapter was "if other pieces of data were more widely available, like percentage of curve balls thrown, average speed of fastball, arm angle, or release point, whether they tend to pitch up or down in the zone, or in or out, we would have used those as well." I think if all of these traits had been taken into account, along with the ones already in use (handedness, and strike-out and walk frequencies, and groundball tendencies), then batter plate appearances would have been spread out far too thin across too many pitcher families. Then we'd be back to the same sample size issue as before, only worse. But I did think that look-ing at fastball speeds and curveball frequencies were particularly interesting ways to approach this subject. Incidentally, FanGraphs, where I happen to be on the payroll, provides exactly that information.

For this study, I'll be looking at three factors: handedness (which *The Book* points out is pretty important), fastball velocity, and—rather than percentage of curveballs thrown—the total breaking ball percentage. I chose only these three factors because I wanted to try to avoid running into the same sample size issue *The Book*'s authors did. I was interested in what effects the combination of a rocket fastball and an apparently strong arsenal of breaking pitches might have on some hitters. As an aside, I'd assume that if a pitcher throws a high proportion of breaking pitches despite having an outstanding fastball, his breaking stuff also must be very good.

Specifically, fastball velocity will be represented by vFA (pfx), which is a pitcher's average four-seam fastball velocity, as measured by PITCHf/x. Breaking Ball%, meanwhile, is the sum of PITCHf/x's accounting of the sliders, curves, knuckle-curves, slurves, and knuckleballs thrown, as a percentage of total pitches (SL%, CU%, KC%, SC%, and KN%, respectively, added together). Now, PITCHf/x classifications have their issues, but for the simple purpose of lumping pitchers into low, mid and high groups of fastball velocity and breaking ball percentage, I feel reasonably confident that PITCHf/x errors won't be a major problem.

The pitcher families are composed of all major league pitchers from 2007 through 2012 with at least 10 innings pitched. Why such a low innings requirement? Well, unlike stats such as ERA or strikeouts per inning, these factors are measuring what the pitcher actually threw, not what became of the pitches after he threw them. A pitcher who posted a .100 batting average-against on balls in play over 10 innings wasn't necessarily pitching well, but you can't chalk up a 99 mph vFA over 10 innings to luck—you can take it at face value that the pitcher was legitimately throwing a very fast fastball.

The pitchers were divided evenly by the following boundaries:

Group	Velocity (mph)	Breaking Ball %
Low (1)	under 90.1	Under 21.7%
Mid (2)	90.1 to 92.3	21.7% to 29.3%
High (3)	over 92.3	over 29.3%

Combined with handedness, this yielded 18 distinct families of pitchers, for which I chose a representative as the head of each:

		Velocity			
		Low	Mid	High	
Breaking Ball %	Low	Mark Buehrle	Cliff Lee	David Price	LHP
	Mid	Barry Zito	C.J. Wilson	CC Sabathia	
	High	Wandy Rodriguez	Francisco Liriano	Clayton Kershaw	
	Low	Jon Garland	Dan Haren	Max Scherzer	RHP
	Mid	Jered Weaver	James Shields	Justin Verlander	
	High	Bronson Arroyo	Adam Wainwright	A.J. Burnett	

You'll see me use shorthand to describe the groups at times in the article. "L" is for lefty, "R" is for righty, "1" is for low, "2" is for mid and "3" is for high. The codes have three characters, indicating handedness, velocity and breaking ball percentage, in order. For example, lefties with high velocity and low breaking ball percentage will be denoted as L31 (David Price's group).

Now, here's where I hope I don't lose you: Whereas *The Book* used wOBA as the basis for its comparisons, I wanted to use something simpler and less subject to the effects of statistical noise and park differences. I also wanted to use something that would lend itself to statistical significance testing more easily than wOBA does.

I'll be using the binomial test, which is an exact test for statistical significance, unlike chi-square tests, which are just approximations that can break down with small sample sizes. In binomial tests, you're looking for a "yes" or "no" answer—did they strike out or did they not? It deals with probabilities, in other words. wOBA itself doesn't directly reflect any particular probability; it's a jumble of several probabilities, weighted with the goal of valuing a player's contribution to run-scoring. The appendix of *The Book* contains a section called "Random Variation in Multinomials" that explains the proper method to deal with wOBA in this way (applicable in a multinomial test of significance), but using it would add too much complexity to the calculations for me to handle, for now.

What I chose to study was therefore K%, or strikeouts per plate appearance. I'd have used wOBA if it were possible, as it of course tells us something more important than K% about offensive production. Still, I hope you'll agree with me that strikeouts are a good, simple way to get a fair and objective idea as to whether a hitter is particularly good or bad at handling a family of pitchers.

The overall K% for each family were:

		Velocity			
		Low	Mid	High	
Breaking Ball %	Low	15.5%	18.7%	23.2%	LHP
	Mid	15.4%	19.7%	22.0%	
	High	18.6%	22.0%	23.5%	
	Low	16.0%	17.0%	19.7%	RHP
	Mid	15.4%	17.9%	20.0%	
	High	16.3%	18.8%	21.2%	

Here, we see that the overall trend is for high-velocity pitchers, high-breaking ball% pitchers and lefties in general to have higher K%. But that's not really the point of this study. What we'll be looking for is whether individual batters do significantly better or worse against these families than expected.

How do we determine what to expect when a batter matches up against one of these families? For one, you have to consider the batter's typical strikeout rate. If none of the three factors we're grouping the pitchers by directly matter to a batter, you'd expect the batters with higher K% to have higher K% against all these pitchers, across the board (other than due to random effects). I think we know that's not going to happen—a lefty batter who strikes out 25 percent overall is probably going to strike out less often than that against righty pitchers and more against lefties. But we'll see about that.

More specifically, the method I'll be using to come up with expected K% for each batter against each family is called the odds ratio method, which also has been called the log5 method. Besides the overall K% of each family, and of each batter, it considers the league average K%, which was 18.23 percent over the sample period. If you assume each group of pitchers overall has faced a representative sample of the major leagues as a whole (probably not a 100 percent accurate assumption, by the way, but close enough, I think), that means you'd expect a hypothetical batter who happened to strike out 18.23 percent of the time overall to strike out at the average rates against each individual family that you see in the last table. Again, that's based on the assumption that the pitcher handedness, velocity and breaking ball percentage make no special difference to the batters, beyond the overall K% of each pitcher group; this is our null hypothesis in the test.

Tango and Lichtman were actually two of the people who brought the odds ratio method to my attention during my ongoing research into batter-pitcher match-ups at FanGraphs. In a two-part series there, I wrote about observed and expected match-up strikeout rates, based on the pitcher's historical K% against the handedness of the batter in question, and vice versa. I was also able to use the odds ratio method there to good results.

The odds ratio formula for the probability of a strikeout when batter with "B" K% faces pitcher with "P" K% where league average is "L" K%:

$$\frac{B \times P \div L}{B \times P \div L + (1-B) \times (1-P) \div (1-L)}$$

It actually gets a little more complicated than that—you have to isolate the batter, pitcher and league stats from each other. So, if I was looking for the expected K% for when Ichiro Suzuki faced the Verlander family, I factored out:

- All the plate appearances where Ichiro actually faced a Verlander-type from his K%.
- The PAs where the Verlander family faced Ichiro from their K%.
- Both Ichiro's and all the Verlander family's PAs from the league K% (adding the intersection of Ichiro and the Verlander's back in, so that those PAs only get removed once).

The reason this has to be done is that it would be improper to let what actually happened influence our expectation of what theoretically should have happened. The implication of this is that if you were projecting Ichiro's K% vs. all lefties, you'd exclude his actual K% against lefties from consideration, and base the projection entirely on how he did against righties. This might sound crazy to you, but it fits perfectly with the goal of the study: What we'd be looking for there is whether Ichiro's K% against lefties is significantly different from his K% against righties.

I won't leave you hanging—here's Ichiro's lefty/righty breakdown:

Vs.	K	PA	K%	Expected K%	p-Value
LHP	126	1,335	9.4%	10.4%	13.5%
RHP	302	2,937	10.3%	9.4%	5.9%

The p-values you see indicate the likelihood that the difference between the expected and actual K% is due to chance, according to a one-tailed binomial test. So, there's a 13.5 percent chance that Ichiro's K% against lefties would, by a fluke, show up as 9.4 percent or less, despite his "true" K% against them (i.e., what the number he would converge toward if you could replay his seasons an infinite number of times) being 10.4 percent. As you can see, a higher number of PAs in a sample will make differences more convincing—the 5.9 percent p-value for him vs. righties PAs gives us quite a bit more confidence that he truly strikes out less against lefties. Still, I'll be going with the conventional (though arbitrary) 95 percent confidence level standard, meaning 5.9 percent uncertainty doesn't quite make the cut (100 percent - 5.9 percent = 94.1 percent confidence).

Plenty of other batters do easily make the 95 percent confidence level cut, however. Out of the top 300 batters in terms of total PAs (best sample size), 159 have p-values under five percent vs. lefties, while 213 make the cut vs. righties. Again, the trend is more apparent vs. righties because of the larger sample sizes. You'd expect five percent of the 300 batters—15 batters—to make the cut purely by chance, so clearly there's a very real effect going on here. In fact, I'll put a p-value on that: A decimal followed by 201 zeroes, then a one. So, basically, it's almost impossible that there's no difference in how frequently these hitters strike out against lefties and righties.

Here are the batters who most certainly differ in striking out vs. lefties and righties, according to p-values:

Player	Versus LHP		Versus RHP	
	PA	K%	PA	K%
David Wright	990	12.8%	2,856	21.6%
Nick Swisher	1,213	15.5%	2,529	24.0%
Ryan Howard	1,257	33.7%	2,324	25.2%
Andre Ethier	1,026	21.9%	2,507	15.0%

That doesn't mean these are the largest lefty vs. righty discrepancies out there, just the most significant (considering sample sizes). The p-values say there's practically no chance that the differences aren't legitimate.

I'll do the same thing, this time only separating pitchers by velocity: Out of the same most prolific 300 batters, 88 strike out against high-velocity pitchers at significantly different rates than expected. Not nearly as convincing as the lefty-righty differences, but there's still practically no chance that what we're seeing is a complete fluke (p = $2.4 \times 10\text{-}42$). Against low- and mid-velocity pitchers, the number of batters different from expected at the 95 percent confidence level were 78 and 71, respectively (still leading to extremely small p-values).

Here are the biggest standouts (for better or worse) against high-velocity pitchers (xK% is expected K%, based on odds ratio):

Player	Overall K%	Vs. High-Velocity Pitchers				
		K%	xK%	Diff	PA	p-value
(Overall MLB)	18.2%	20.6%	-	-	330,132	-
Carlos Peña	27.2%	26.3%	32.3%	-6.0%	1,205	.00%
Jeff Mathis	27.2%	24.5%	33.4%	-8.9%	519	.00%
Nelson Cruz	22.1%	28.0%	22.6%	5.4%	893	.01%
Bobby Abreu	17.9%	17.6%	21.6%	-4.1%	1,206	.03%
Hunter Pence	18.5%	24.3%	19.8%	4.5%	985	.03%
Clint Barmes	18.7%	24.7%	19.5%	5.2%	718	.04%
Delmon Young	17.5%	22.0%	18.3%	3.7%	1,160	.08%
Corey Hart	20.3%	26.1%	21.6%	4.4%	933	.08%
Miguel Montero	19.3%	25.0%	20.2%	4.8%	728	.09%
Jamey Carroll	14.0%	18.7%	14.6%	4.1%	731	.13%

By the way, the p-values you're seeing are from one-tailed tests, but the direction of that tail is being determined by whether the observed value is higher or lower than expected.

Carlos Peña and Jeff Mathis may strike out a lot, but they do convincingly buck major league players' general trend of striking out at a higher rate against high-velocity pitchers. Nelson Cruz, on the other hand, shows himself to be more vulnerable against hard throwers than his overall numbers might suggest.

By now, you might be thinking, "wait a second... you're talking a lot about expected K%, but how do I know your expectations are good ones?" Well, here's a bit of evidence to show the expectations are on the right track:

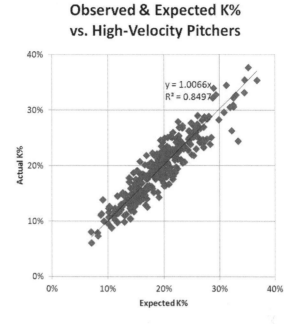

**Observed & Expected K%
vs. High-Velocity Pitchers**

The chart looks at the usual 300 batters, by the way. The results are pretty great, I'd say. They could be better, I'm sure, as there are some confounding factors making their way into this. For a hint at one, look at the plate appearances in the overall sample, split by family:

		Velocity			
		Low	**Mid**	**High**	
Breaking Ball %	**Low**	65,213	55,117	17,867	**LHP**
	Mid	51,335	31,181	20,984	
	High	45,639	15,319	8,958	
	Low	57,342	79,077	94,412	**RHP**
	Mid	80,541	133,450	97,919	
	High	77,211	93,555	89,992	

Lefties are hugely skewed toward being soft-tossers, when compared to righty pitchers. What this means is you should expect lefty batters to have an advantage over righty batters in facing high-velocity pitchers in general, as such pitchers are overwhelmingly right-handed. That's why we'll continue to break things down into categories, although the three factors we're looking at obviously won't be able to explain everything.

But first, let's look at the results for just breaking ball percentage. Of 300 batters, 65 were outliers against high breaking ball percentage pitchers, as were 65 vs. low and 53 against mid-breaking ball percentage pitchers. Considering we expected 15 outliers, these results are still highly statistically significant, though not as much as the velocity findings, and not even close to as high as the handedness findings. Here are the biggest outliers against high-breaking ball% pitchers, in terms of significance.

Player	Overall K%	Vs. High Breaking % Pitchers				
		K%	xK%	Diff	PA	p-value
(Overall MLB)	18.2%	19.1%	-	-	330,674	-
Josh Hamilton	19.7%	15.8%	22.5%	-6.8%	849	.00%
Ryan Howard	28.1%	33.3%	27.3%	6.1%	1,116	.00%
J.J. Hardy	15.0%	12.9%	17.0%	-4.1%	978	.02%
Erick Aybar	11.8%	15.7%	11.4%	4.4%	694	.03%
Brandon Inge	25.2%	29.9%	24.8%	5.1%	793	.06%
Austin Jackson	24.7%	21.5%	27.6%	-6.1%	531	.07%
Miguel Olivo	27.4%	24.8%	30.1%	-5.4%	691	.10%
Shane Victorino	11.4%	13.9%	11.0%	2.9%	1,156	.11%
Jason Giambi	21.8%	19.0%	24.4%	-5.4%	500	.24%
David Wright	19.3%	22.4%	19.2%	3.2%	1,180	.32%

So, while the overall trend is for high breaking ball percentage pitchers to have higher K%, Josh Hamilton actually has done quite a bit better against them than against the other types. Meanwhile, Ryan Howard, though he strikes out a lot in general, is especially vulnerable against breaking ball pitchers.

Admittedly, the breaking ball percentage factor is the shakiest variable I'm using in the study. First, not all breaking balls are created equal. Second, just because a pitcher throws a lot of breaking balls in general doesn't mean he'll throw a lot against a particular batter (or class of batter, e.g. lefties or righties). With velocity, that's not much of a concern—a pitcher might try to crank up his velocity a little against a big-time batter, but that's probably not going to make a big difference, in general. And, unless there are any switch-pitchers out there that I'm unaware of, I don't think pitcher handedness will change by the batter they're facing.

Now, breaking things down a step further, let's look at pitchers split only by handedness and velocity. The number of "hits"—batters significantly different (with 95 percent confidence) from their expectations—were as follows (out of 300):

L1*	L2*	L3*	R1*	R2*	R3*
114	72	63	62	84	83

Here, L1* signifies left-handed pitchers with low velocity, and any breaking ball percentage (the asterisk signifies "any"). Again, this is out of 300 batters, so the results are highly significant. Here's a sampling of just the p-values of the players with the most total plate appearances (this time, they're unidirectional, with a low p-value indicating the batter hit better than expected against the family, and a high p-value indicating he hit worse than expected):

Player	L1*	L2*	L3*	R1*	R2*	R3*
Ichiro Suzuki	20%	17%	43%	85%	64%	43%
Adrian Gonzalez	12%	78%	100%	4%	12%	71%
Prince Fielder	100%	88%	88%	1%	20%	4%
Derek Jeter	27%	1%	15%	49%	79%	85%
Miguel Cabrera	44%	50%	55%	9%	61%	82%
Robinson Cano	95%	86%	96%	2%	15%	5%
Michael Young	0%	97%	5%	75%	100%	2%
Albert Pujols	1%	58%	32%	75%	100%	30%
Nick Markakis	69%	40%	73%	87%	17%	16%
Dan Uggla	30%	43%	65%	7%	100%	46%

Two things you may notice are: 1) a lot of randomness; and 2) a player's p-values are generally more influenced by the handedness of the pitcher than they are the velocity, it would appear. I mean, if a batter has a high p-value against family L1*, you can count on him having high values against the other lefty families more than you can count on him having a high value against R1*, the righty counterparts of L1*. To shed some light on that, here's a correlation table for batters' differences between actual and expected K% vs. each family:

	L1*	L2*	L3*	R1*	R2*	R3*
L1*	1					
L2*	0.35	1				
L3*	0.45	0.34	1			
R1*	-0.38	-0.39	-0.42	1		
R2*	-0.48	-0.38	-0.40	0.09	1	
R3*	-0.51	-0.38	-0.30	-0.03	-0.02	1

Notice, for example, how the correlation between batters' K% discrepancies (actual vs. expected) against R1* and L1* pitchers is -0.38? That's a moderately strong indication that if a batter hits better than expected against soft-tossing lefties, he'll tend to hit worse than expected against soft-tossing righties, and vice versa. Remember, the expectation presumes handedness doesn't matter, whereas these results strongly suggest it does, outweighing whatever effect velocity might be having. Their results against L1* pitchers, relative to expectations, have a lot more in common with those vs. L2*, with a 0.35 (positive) correlation.

You have to look a lot more carefully to see the effect velocity might be having in the mix: There's a slight tendency for results against same-speed group pitchers to be more positively correlated (or less negatively correlated).

Now let's look at the data from another angle, taking only handedness and breaking ball percentage into account. Here are the counts of batters (out of 300) with statistically significant differences:

L*1	L*2	L*3	R*1	R*2	R*3
85	94	86	72	78	73

"L*1" here refers to lefty pitchers with any velocity level, who throw few breaking balls. These numbers are less dramatic than those in the previous example, but still significant.

The patterns once again have a lot of randomness to them, so let's go straight to the overall trends, according to a correlation table on the observed—expected K% discrepancies:

	L*1	L*2	L*3	R*1	R*2	R*3
L*1	1					
L*2	0.34	1				
L*3	0.34	0.34	1			
R*1	-0.36	-0.39	-0.42	1		
R*2	-0.53	-0.38	-0.40	0.09	1	
R*3	-0.40	-0.38	-0.30	-0.03	-0.02	1

So, once again, the handedness factor hugely drowns out the other one.

Moving on to taking only velocity and breaking ball percentage into consideration, here are the 95 percent confidence outlier counts in each group:

*11	*12	*13	*21	*22	*23	*31	*32	*33
52	50	48	52	50	54	51	46	46

Highly significant, once again, yet much less so than the others. I ran a correlation table on these too:

	*11	*12	*13	*21	*22	*23	*31	*32	*33
*11	1								
*12	0.01	1							
*13	0	-0.02	1						
*21	-0.05	-0.18	-0.07	1					
*22	-0.25	-0.17	-0.16	0.03	1				
*23	-0.07	-0.14	-0.11	-0.09	-0.05	1			
*31	-0.16	-0.19	-0.26	-0.09	-0.13	-0.17	1		
*32	-0.19	-0.15	-0.17	-0.16	-0.16	-0.18	0.03	1	
*33	-0.18	-0.15	-0.17	-0.18	-0.09	0.04	-0.12	0.03	1

Hmm, just a bunch of pretty weak correlations, really. Results against opposite types of pitchers (e.g. *33 vs. *11) do tend to be at least a little bit negatively correlated, so that's better than nothing.

I should also note that the R-squared stats between expected and observed K% seriously break down at this level. Remember how it was about 0.85 in the scatter plot earlier, for just high-velocity pitchers? Well, for the individual families, most righty families are still very respectable—in the 0.6 and 0.7 area—but for the hard-throwing lefties, they're pathetic, being in the 0.1 and 0.2 area. Given the plate appearance sample size discrepancies, that makes some sense.

Well, there's only one thing left to do—show you the results for the families. Listed from top to bottom in each family's box are:

1. The number of batters significantly different from their expected K%.
2. The p-value for the above number of significantly different batters, in terms of percentage (i.e, the chance of seeing at least that many significantly different batters by pure coincidence).
3. The number of plate appearances against this family by the 300 batters being studied.

		Velocity			
		Low	Mid	High	
	Low	51	43	28	LHP
		0.00%	0.00%	0.13%	
		44,068	37,456	12,530	
	Mid	45	38	40	
		0.00%	0.00%	0.00%	
		35,356	21,331	14,340	
Breaking Ball %	High	59	21	27	
		0.00%	7.76%	0.26%	
		31,049	10,200	5,954	
	Low	34	29	52	RHP
		0.00%	0.06%	0.00%	
		38,310	54,151	65,503	
	Mid	38	39	42	
		0.00%	0.00%	0.00%	
		54,751	92,611	67,874	
	High	39	43	37	
		0.00%	0.00%	0.00%	
		52,788	63,044	61,092	

Here, we finally see sample-size problems making themselves clearly felt, as a lot of batters weren't able to face certain families of lefties often enough to make their results statistically significant. For Family L23 (the Liriano family) in particular, we can't say with 95 percent confidence that there are a significant number of batters differing from expectations.

The correlation table I prepared for the families is too big to display here, but suffice to say, it was pretty unimpressive. Correlations were fairly weak across the board (topping out at 0.38), with a lot of randomness to them. The only clear trend was that batters' numbers against lefty and righty pitchers were once again anticorrelated (negative correlation). But the apparent importance of the velocity and breaking ball factors has now been obscured at this level.

Before I throw my hands into the air in surrender, I thought I'd show you a case study. I present to you Carlos Peña, whom I pointed out as being the most significantly better-than-expected at not striking out against high-velocity pitchers. Here are his breakdowns, with his p-value listed in each box. Like a previous table, these p-values are unidirectional, with a low p-value indicating that Pena hit better than expected against the family, and a high p-value indicating he hit worse than expected:

		Velocity			
		Low	Mid	High	
Breaking Ball %	Low	86.39%	42.00%	25.37%	LHP
	Mid	99.90%	57.08%	99.49%	
	High	98.19%	74.34%	33.47%	
	Low	94.27%	98.99%	0.82%	RHP
	Mid	88.60%	16.74%	0.01%	
	High	15.59%	8.51%	18.62%	

While he's fairly consistent in doing relatively well against high-velocity pitchers, his performance against Family L32 (Sabathia family) really stands out against that trend. The p-value for that family indicates with very high confidence that he strikes out a lot more than expected against this particular bunch of high-velocity pitchers. Now, Peña bats lefty, so you'd expect him to do worse against the high-velocity lefties than righties. Still, clearly you can't rely on him to be "clutch" against all flame-throwing pitchers.

Peña had 78 plate appearances against the Sabathia family over this span. Of those, 31 happened to be against Sabathia himself, who torched him for 18 strikeouts. Sabathia doesn't strike out batters at a higher rate than the rest of his family, but he is 6-foot-8, which is unusual. Perhaps Peña's problem is with very tall pitchers. Or the combination of a very high release point and a bad batter's eye up high in a certain stadium. We could probably think of a hundred different factors that could play some role, if we thought about it hard enough. Maybe it was just a fluke? Or maybe considering just these three factors isn't enough. Who can say for sure?

So, what did we learn from all this? First, that some batters do show particular strengths and weaknesses against certain types of pitchers, above and beyond what you'd expect given the overall numbers of those involved. Second, we learned that the handedness effect is more important than the velocity and breaking ball percentage factors, by a long way. Third, that the authors of *The Book* were smart not to waste too much time trying to figure out something as elusive as what I aimed for in this study.

Moving forward, I think the best approach is probably to move away from the idea of using pitcher families in match-up analyses. The expected match-up strikeout rates in the present study are derived from the strikeout rates of entire groups of pitchers. This may work fine when analyzing a batter's results against a large group of pitchers, but when looking at his match-ups against smaller families of pitchers, it's more likely that he'd have faced some samples of pitchers that aren't entirely representative of their families as a whole. That is, the batter might have a disproportionate number of plate appearances against pitchers who have a higher K% than their family average, for example. Or there could be other idiosyncrasies to some of these match-ups that show through more.

The point is, perhaps the individual pitchers involved need to be taken directly into account, with some regression to deal with sample size issues. I think a better starting point for studying the effects of factors like velocity and breaking ball percentage might be to use the lefty-righty K% splits for both the pitcher and batter involved. This is the direction I started off in for my FanGraphs study, but as you can see, this is a complex area, and there's a long way to go.

Et Cetera

Glossary

BABIP: Batting Average on Balls in Play. This is a measure of the number of batted balls that safely fall in for hits (not including home runs). The exact formula we use is (H-HR)/(AB-K-HR+SF).

Batted ball statistics: When a batter hits a ball, he hits either a ground ball, fly ball or line drive. The resulting ground ball, fly ball and line drive percentages make up a player's mix of statistics, with infield fly balls, or pop-ups, being tracked as a percentage of a player's total number of fly balls.

BB%: Walk rate measures how often a position player walks—or how often a pitcher walks a batter—per plate appearance. It is measured in percentage form.

BB/9: Walks allowed per nine innings

BsR: UBR+wSB. UBR, or Ultimate Base Running, accounts for the value a player adds to his team via baserunning. It is determined using linear weights, with each baserunning event receiving a specific run value. wSB, or Weighted Stolen Base runs, estimates the number of runs a player contributes by stealing bases, as compared to the average player.

ChampAdded: The proportion of a world championship contributed by a player or team, based on the impact of a play on a team's winning a game, and the value of that game within the context of winning the world championship. Please refer to "The One About the 2013 Postseason," for more information.

Defensive Efficiency: The percentage of balls in play converted into outs. It can be approximated by 1-BABIP.

DRS: Defensive Runs Saved. DRS rates players as above or below average based on "runs," with data from Baseball Info Solutions used as an input. It tracks a number of different aspects of defensive play, including stolen bases, doube plays, outfield arms, robbing home runs and range.

ERA: A pitcher's total number of earned runs allowed divided by his total number of innings pitched, multiplied by nine.

ERA-: A pitching version of OPS+ and wRC+: 100 represents a league-average ERA, and a smaller ERA- is better.

ERA+: ERA measured against the league average and adjusted for ballpark factors. An ERA+ over 100 is better than average, less than 100 is below average.

FIP: Fielding Independent Pitching, a measure of all things for which a pitcher is specifically responsible. The formula is (HR*13+(BB+HBP)*3-K*2)/IP, plus a league-specific factor (usually around 3.2) to round out the number to an equivalent ERA number. FIP helps you understand how well a pitcher pitched, regardless of how well his fielders fielded.

FIP-: A pitching version of OPS+ and wRC+: 100 represents a league-average FIP, and a smaller FIP- is better.

ISO: Isolated power. This is a measure of a hitter's raw power, or how good they are at hitting for extra bases. Most simply, the formula is SLG-AVG, but you can also calculate it as such: ((2B)+(2*3B)+(3*HR))/AB.

K%: Strikeout rate measures how often a position player strikes out—or how often a pitcher strikes out a batter—per plate appearance.

K/9: Strikeouts per nine innings

kwERA: An ERA estimator that works similar to FIP, but takes home runs out of the equation. The formula is: 5.40-12*(K-BB)/PA.

LI: Leverage Index. LI measures the criticality of a play or plate appearance. It is based on the range of potential WPA outcomes of a play, compared to all other plays. 1.0 is an average Index.

Linear Weights: The historical average runs scored for each event in a baseball game.

OBP: On-base percentage, an essential tool, measures how frequently a batter reaches base safely. The formula is: (hits+walks+hit-by-pitch) divided by (at-bats+walks+hit-by-pitch+sacrifice flys).

OPS: On Base plus Slugging Percentage, a crude but quick measure of a batter's true contribution to his team's offense. See wOBA for a better approach.

OPS+: A normalized version of OPS that adjusts for small variables such as park effects and puts OPS on a scale where 100 is league average, and each point above or below is one percent above or below league average.

PITCHf/x: Sportvision's pitch tracking system that has been installed in every major league stadium since at least the start of the 2007 season. It tracks several aspects of every pitch thrown in a major league game, including velocity, movement, release point, spin and pitch location.

Pythagorean Formula: A formula for converting a team's Run Differential into a projected win-loss record. The formula is RS^2/(RS^2+RA^2). Teams' actual win-loss records tend to mirror their Pythagorean records, and variances usually can be attributed to luck.

You can improve the accuracy of the Pythagorean formula by using a different exponent (the 2 in the formula). The best exponent can be calculated this way: (RS/G+RA/G)^.285, where RS/G is Runs Scored per Game and RA/G is Runs Allowed per Game. This is called the PythagoPat formula.

SIERA: Skill-Interactive Earned Run Average estimates ERA through walk rate, strikeout rate and ground ball rate, eliminating the effects of park, defense and luck.

Slash Line: At times, writers may refer to a batter's "slash line," or "triple-slash line." They mean something like this: .287/.345/.443. The numbers between those slashes are the batter's batting average, on-base percentage and slugging percentage.

Total Zone: The lone defensive stat calculated exclusively from Retrosheet play-by-play data. It is the defensive stat used in both WAR calculations for games played prior to the UZR era (2002-present).

UZR: A fielding system similar to Defensive Runs Saved. Both systems calculate a fielder's range by comparing his plays made in various "vectors" across the baseball diamond to the major league average rate of plays made in those vectors. Both systems also look at other factors such as the effectiveness of outfield throwing, handling bunts and turning double plays.

WAR: Wins Above Replacement. A "win stat" that calculates the number of wins a player contributed to his team above a certain replacement level. WAR is calculated at FanGraphs and Baseball Reference. Though the two implementations vary a bit, they share a common framework that includes a linear weights approach to runs created, advanced fielding metrics, leverage for relievers and replacement levels that vary by position. In addition, beginning in 2013, both versions unified their definition of replacement level, making the two versions more directly comparable.

Win Shares: An all-encompassing look at a player's value. Each team win is made up of three win shares, though the calculation for deriving each player's Win Shares is complex and based on the defensive position they play, among other things.

wOBA: A linear weights offensive rating system that is similar to OPS, except that it's set to the scale of on-base percentage.

wOBA+: A linear-weights based hitting statistic indexed against a yearly league average. A 100 wOBA+ represents a league-average hitter. A 110 wOBA+ hitter is 10% above league average. Unlike wRC+, wOBA+ does not use park factors, and presented here ("Finding the Translation: Quantifying Asian Players") does not use linear weights of the native league, but rather 2012 MLB linear weights.

WPA: Win Probability Added is a system in which each player is given credit toward helping his team win, based on play-by-play data and the impact each specific play has on the team's probability of winning.

wRC+: Like OPS+ and ERA+, wRC+ is scaled so that 100 is average and a higher number is positive. The "RC" stands for Runs Created, but it's not Bill James' Runs Created. It's a "linear weights" version derived from wOBA.

xFIP: Expected Fielding Independent Pitching. This is an experimental stat that adjusts FIP and "normalizes" the home run component according to the number of fly balls a pitcher allowed.

For more information on these and other statistics, visit: *hardballtimes.com/main/statpages/glossary* or *fangraphs.com/library*.

Who Was That?

Dave Allen teaches biology at Middlebury College. In his spare time, which is becoming increasingly limited, he likes to think and write about baseball. He is particularly interested in using pitch-tracking data (PITCHf/x) to answer questions about the game.

John Beamer is a baseball nut living in a soccer-mad country. That means MLB. TV is his best friend, and fortunately the term 'blackout restriction' is meaningless. When not indulging his baseball passion, John most enjoys spending time with his wife and three sons. He thinks the middle one has the best shot of making the bigs—expect his debut around 2032!

Craig Calcaterra is the lead writer for HardballTalk at NBCSports.com. He lives with his daughter Mookie, and his son Carlo, in a fortified compound on the outskirts of Columbus, Ohio.

Dave Cameron is the managing editor of FanGraphs, and he also contributes regularly to ESPN and the *Wall Street Journal*. More importantly, he's a leukemia survivor, and will take any opportunity given to shamelessly suggest that you donate both blood and platelets. He's happy to still be writing about trivial things like baseball.

Carson Cistulli has been hurting FanGraphs' credibility, in one way or another, since 2009.

Karl de Vries is a writer and journalist who lives in Montclair, N.J. His work has appeared in the Official 2008 Major League Baseball All-Star Game program, as well as The Star-Ledger, Newsday and FoxNews.com. A long-suffering Mets fan, Karl longs for the day that his team returns to the company of competitive baseball, and he still maintains that "Ken Griffey Jr. Presents Major League Baseball" is the best baseball video game ever made.

Joe Distelheim, The Hardball Times' chief copy editor, is a lifelong Cubs fan and a lifelong newspaperman. Despite overwhelming evidence that both institutions are in decline, he continues to believe in them.

Larry Granillo is a weekly contributor at Baseball Nation and the author of the Tater Trot Tracker. His secret wish is for Minute Maid Park to put the flag pole above the wall and move the train out to center field.

History instructor by day, baseball nerd by night, **Chris Jaffe** leads the most exciting double life imaginable—with the exception of every other double life you can imagine. Still, it keeps THT's resident Cubs fan happy. He is also the author of *Evaluating Baseball's Managers*, a book that won The Sporting News-SABR Award for outstanding baseball research.

Bill James vigorously denies any and all rumors about him.

Brad Johnson is a baseball addict and a statistics junkie who currently resides in Atlanta, Ga. He played four seasons of injury-plagued baseball at Macalester College from 2006-2009, and has since made the transition to a purely off-the-field existence. You can find his work on The Hardball Times and FanGraphs.

Jeff Moore is the founder of MLB Prospect Watch and is a writer for The Hardball Times and Baseball Prospectus. A former college baseball player and college coach, he still holds three NCAA records from his playing days. He currently resides in Delray Beach, Fla.

Blake Murphy is a news editor at The Score and freelancer writing about four sports—think Bo Jackson, but without the being really good at every sport part. He plans to be in the best shape of his life for spring training this year.

Alan Nathan is Professor Emeritus of Physics at the University of Illinois at Urbana-Champaign. After a long career as an experimentalist doing subatomic collisions, he now spends his time studying the baseball-bat collision, among other topics in the physics of baseball.

Rob Neyer's first love was a girl named Tracy, and his second was the Kansas City Royals; both went unrequited, and today he toils as SB Nation's National Baseball Editor while trying to recover from those childhood traumas.

John Perrotto lives in Beaver Falls, Pa., and has covered Major League Baseball for 26 seasons and was a Pittsburgh Pirates' beat reporter for 22. Among the outlets he covers baseball for are USA TODAY, Sports On Earth, Baseball America, The Sports Xchange, the Beaver County Times and the Uniontown Herald-Standard.

Mike Petriello lives in New York City and contributes regularly to ESPN and FanGraphs, and serves as an editorial producer for Sports on Earth. He also writes about the Dodgers daily at the unfortunately-named Mike Scioscia's Tragic Illness, for some reason.

Mike Podhorzer produces player projections using his own forecasting system and is the author of the eBook *Projecting X: How to Forecast Baseball Player Performance*. His projections helped him win the inaugural 2013 Tout Wars mixed draft fantasy league, cementing his status as champion nerd.

Joe Posnanski is the national columnist for NBC Sports. He has written three books, including the Casey Award winning *Soul of Baseball* and has won more than his share of awards, but he is most proud of the authentic Duane Kuiper hat he keeps by his desk. Sadly, the hat does not fit—his head is too big.

Jon Roegele is a baseball researcher and writer for The Hardball Times and Beyond the Box Score. He has devoted the bulk of his research endeavors to those involving PITCHf/x data.

Eno Sarris enjoys beers, brats and baseball, in a different order every day. This year, he spent his time asking ballplayers about stats for FanGraphs as a member of the Baseball Writers Association of America. He's still in one piece.

Greg Simons has been writing about baseball in various formats since the last millennium. He's been a part of The Hardball Times crew since 2010, serving as a double-threat editor-writer, though this is his first time writing for the *Annual*. When not writing, editing and reading about baseball (along with eating and breathing it), he plays it, too, participating in vintage base ball games around the Midwest.

Steve Staudenmayer (**"Staude"** for short) is firmly in the running for the unofficial title of "Nerdiest Writer on FanGraphs." He is a fairly recent MBA graduate who enjoys working with spreadsheets and statistics a little too much.

For more than 10 years, **Dave Studenmund** has been writing about baseball, managing baseball websites, producing baseball books and helping other baseball nuts with their work. He does it for the glory.

Paul Swydan once yelled to Brian Daubach in the on-deck circle at Fenway Park that he should tuck in his back pocket. Daubach did, in fact, tuck in said pocket.

Jeff Sullivan lives in the good Portland and writes a lot at FanGraphs and likes both of those things. In his free time, all of those descriptions still apply, along with other ones. He doesn't have a cat, but he can see one from his apartment sometimes.

Kevin Tenenbaum is a junior Math Major at Middlebury College. This past summer, he interned for the Baltimore Orioles. He is the co-founder of the Middlebury Baseball Analysis Club, and he spends his free time playing intramural sports and log rolling.

Shane Tourtellotte is a refugee from the Northeast living in Asheville, N.C., still resisting the Braves' charms for old flames in Pennsylvania and the South Bronx. He's published a few hundred thousand words of science fiction, but this didn't strike other people as bizarre enough, so he has branched out into baseball. He still thinks the moon would be a cool place to play a game.

Steve Treder has been a writer for The Hardball Times since its founding in 2004. He's also been a frequent contributor/presenter in other forums, such as the SABR national convention, the NINE Spring Training Conference and the Cooperstown Symposium. He is currently working on a biography of Horace Stoneham. He roots for the Giants from his home in Santa Clara, Calif.

Jack Weiland is a fiercely proud Midwesterner who paradoxically lives in Boston with his wonderful wife, Bianca, and their many animals. He just finished his rookie season at THT, where he writes about fantasy baseball. He's honored to be part of the crew.

Bradley Woodrum is a freelance writer in Florida with a master's degrees in economics. His writing credits include FanGraphs, ESPN.com, DRaysBay, Cubs Stats and the bathroom stalls at Jacksonville University.

Noah Woodward writes for The Hardball Times. He is a senior economics major at Davidson College and he is excitedly searching for his first position in Major League Baseball.

Craig Wright worked 21 years in Major League Baseball in scouting and player evaluation. He is a noted baseball historian and his latest book, *Pages from Baseball's Past*, is now in bookstores.

Jeff Zimmerman currently writes for FanGraphs and RoyalsReview.com, and his own website that he hosts with his brother Darrell, BaseballHeatMaps.com. He was amazed this past year to find out someone actually read and appreciated his work by awarding Bill Petti and him the SABR Analytics Research Award for Contemporary Analysis. He still resides near Wichita, Kan., with his baseball-tolerant family, wife Kristen and kids, Ruby and Cole.

Crossword Puzzle Answer

(it's on pg. 196, in case you missed it)

P	A	P	I		O	B	P			B	E	A	M	S
O	R	A	L		P	E	E	R		I	G	L	O	O
W	O	R	L	D	S	E	R	I	E	S	G	O	E	S
	D	E	S	I				B	A	H		U	S	A
			D	A	H		R	O	G					
T	O	P	H	I	L	A	D	E	L	P	H	I	A	
R	U	L	E		P	L	E	A		S	E	D	A	N
A	T	A	S		A	N	S			T	A	R	O	
D	O	N	O	T		M	I	T	T		T	H	O	N
	F	O	U	R	G	A	M	E	S	T	O	O	N	E
		T	O	R			R	O	O					
D	E	R		T	O	M				R	B	I	S	
O	V	E	R	T	H	E	N	Y	G	I	A	N	T	S
C	A	N	O	E		L	E	A	D		I	T	A	L
E	N	T	E	R			U	Z	R		L	O	N	G

29879847R10172

Made in the USA
Lexington, KY
10 February 2014